Descartes' Philosophy Interpreted
According to the Order

Volume II

The Soul and

MARTIAL GUEROULT

Descartes' Philosophy Interpreted According to the Order of Reasons

Volume II

The Soul and the Body

Translated by
Roger Ariew

With the Assistance of
Robert Ariew *and* Alan Donagan

University of Minnesota Press, Minneapolis

This work was supported by a grant from the Translations Program of the National Endowment for the Humanities, an independent federal agency, which supports the study of such fields as history, philosophy, literature and languages.

English translation © 1985 by Roger Ariew (based on 2nd ed.).
Originally published as
Descartes selon l'ordre des raisons, vol. II, *L'âme et le corps,*
1st ed. Copyright © 1952 by Editions Montaigne.
2nd ed. Copyright © 1968 by Editions Montaigne.
Published by the University of Minnesota Press,
2037 University Avenue Southeast, Minneapolis, MN 55414
Printed in the United States of America.

Library of Congress Cataloging in Publication Data

Guéroult, Martial.
  Descartes' philosophy interpreted according to the
  order of reasons
  Translation of: Descartes selon l'ordre des raisons.
  Contents: v. 2. The Soul and the Body
  1. Descartes, René, 1596-1650. I. Title.
B1875.G813 1985 194 83-21771
ISBN 0-8166-1257-9 (hc.)   ISBN 0-8166-1259-5 (hc., 2-vol. set)
ISBN 0-8166-1258-7 (pkb.)   ISBN 0-8166-1260-9 (pbk., 2-vol. set)

Contents of
Volumes I and II

Contents
Volume II
The Soul and the Body
(The Sixth Meditation)

Descartes' Philosophy Interpreted
According to the Order of Reasons

Volume II

The Soul and the Body

CHAPTER IX

Concerning the Existence of Material Things. The *Nexus rationum* of *Meditation VI*

1. First Perspective *(x):* Problems Concerning the Existence of Bodies and the Foundation of Sciences; a Glimpse at Three Proofs Concerning Bodies

Meditation VI completes the unfolding of the chain of reasons. It also presents the maximum of complexity; this is something natural for a final reason, which is necessarily the most composite and most difficult of all the reasons.

We must first consider, as the title of the *Meditation* indicates, that the *Meditation* intends to prove the existence of material things and thus to accomplish the task that Cartesianism gives itself with respect to three kinds of fundamental existences—to establish necessarily the existence of my mind (in *Meditation II*), the existence of God (in *Meditation III*), and the existence of bodidies (in *Meditation IV*).

In conformity with the rule of the division of the difficulty and in conformity with the order, the problem of the existence of material things is resolved in two steps: *Meditation V* proved the reality of their essence; *Meditation VI* will prove the reality of their existence.

The demonstration of this second step is conducted methodically: on the basis of the previously demonstrated reality of the essence of material things, that is, on the understanding, it first concludes that their existence is possible;[1] then on the basis of the presence of imagination in the self, it concludes that it is probable;[2] and finally on the basis of the presence of sensation in the self, it concludes that it is certain.[3]

We must then recognize—and the title of the *Meditation* also indicates this—that the *Meditation* intends to prove the real distinction of body and soul by the objective validity that divine veracity confers on the clear and distinct notions of thinking and extended substance, which have the necessary property of excluding each other reciprocally.[4] This is even, as Descartes tells

3

us, his "principal aim."[5] In fact, this doctrine, by assuring the destruction of substantial forms, establishes mathematical physics on the wreckage of Scholastic physics.[6]

We must finally recognize—even though the title does not mention this—that the *Meditation* intends to establish the substantial union of soul and body by means of the presence in us of imagination and sensation: "In this very *Meditation VI,* in which I have discussed the distinction between mind and body, I have also shown that the mind is substantially united with the body; and in order to prove this I have used reasons that are stronger or more convincing than I can remember having seen any elsewhere."[7] Nevertheless, the substantial union is not mentioned in the title, and Descartes specifically states that it is treated in a subsidiary fashion here because it does not belong to his "principal aim": "There are two facts about the human soul on which depend all the things we can know of its nature. The first is that it thinks; the second is that it is united to the body and can act and be acted upon along with it. About the second, I have said hardly anything; I have only tried to make the first well understood. For my principal aim was to prove the distinction between soul and body, and to this end only the first was useful, while the second might have been harmful."[8]

This latter text indicates that the conception of the union of soul and body is not developed here for its own sake. In fact, it will require a separate work: *The Treatise on Passions.* However this does not prevent the *Meditations* from giving an incontestable proof of it—as we are assured by the *Replies to Objections IV.* Moreover, nowhere else will this proof be presented with the same strength, because nowhere else is the proof attached to the entire order of reasons.

The text also indicates that the two aims, to prove the real distinction of body and soul, and to prove their substantial union, are contrary aims. In fact, since the substantial union is "experienced every day . . . it is the cause of our not discovering easily without deep meditation the real distinction between body and soul,"[9] such that, even after having provided the most solid logical demonstration, it is difficult to remain persuaded: "I had almost the same experience as the astronomers, who, after many proofs had convinced them that the sun was many times larger than the earth, could not avoid judging that it was smaller than the earth when they viewed it with their eyes."[10] That is why "those who never philosophize" and who remain strangers to metaphysical meditation, "making use only of their senses, conceive this union without difficulty,"without being able to conceive the distinction, while those who are used to philosophizing and who are detached from the senses, moving in the sphere of pure understanding, can no longer conceive the union that contradicts the rational evidence of the necessary distinction between the two substances: "It does not seem to me that the human mind is capable of conceiving very distinctly, at the same time, the distinction and the union between soul and body, because it is necessary for this to conceive them as a single thing and at the same time to conceive them as two—which is contradictory."[11]

From this we can see that knowledge of the distinction and knowledge of the union are referred to two different kinds of knowledge, the former to reason, and the latter to sensation. In order to have access to the former, we must "shut our eyes, plug our ears," in brief, "we must turn aside all our senses";[12] in order to have access to the latter, we must, in some way, shut ourselves from pure understanding, "put aside clear and distinct ideas, and particularly the reasons that have proven the distinction of substances," in order to abandon ourselves completely to the experience of sensation.[13] But in order *to prove* the reality of the union and at the same time to discover *what it is,* meaning a substantial union of two distinct substances, it is necessary to address ourselves to the understanding, and to establish preliminarily both that body is really distinct from soul, and that body exists. In the end, it is the understanding that will validate the competency of sensation and will trace its limits.

The proof of the union and the proof of the existence of bodies will not present, in spite of their necessary certainty, the same degree of evidence and certainty as the proof of the real distinction of body and soul, to the extent that these proofs could not rest exclusively on the ideas of the understanding and must appeal to sensation. Since it rests on the intuition of the clear and distinct ideas of thinking and extended substance, the proof of the distinction is as certain as a mathematical truth, and is of the same nature as the knowledge of my nature in the Cogito, or of necessary existence in the idea of the perfect—it is the knowledge of the necessary property of an essence. On the other hand, the proof of the union and the proof of the existence of bodies do not rest on the intuition of an idea, but on the certainty guaranteed by God of an inclination and of sensations. Thus, I know in all certainty that body exists without having the vision of this existence, which remains unknown in itself. "In considering these arguments more closely [the reasons to conclude that material things exist—M. G.], we come to know that they are not as firm nor as evident as those that lead us to the knowledge of God and of our soul."[14] However, we shall see that this lesser degree of firmness and evidence does not move them out of the domain of the truly certain, into the domain of the likely and probable, the domain of "moral" certainty. Otherwise, physics would be merely probable or possible, while it is certain.[15] Descartes remarks, on the contrary, that the proofs by sensation are certain, in opposition to the argument drawn from imagination, which is only probable. If that forms would be verified as impossible, and the mathematical character of physics would remain assured, but this physics would be reduced to the consideration of a certain group of intelligible relations determined by the play of our sensation, from among all the possible geometrical relations. From the fact that our sensible world could not be attributed to the causality of external bodies, we would obtain a physics similar to a Malebranchian physics, in which we could even definitively exclude the existence of matter, as in Berkeley's physics. Thus Descartes has no "need"to prove the existence of bodies in order to establish against Scholastic physics the geometrical character of the new physics, unless, contrary to the order, the proof of the real separation is in fact conditioned by the proof of existence, as has been suggested by a commentator, and "Descartes needed an external world in order to prove the real distinction of soul and body."[21] But that is, as we shall see in due time, an unacceptable thesis. The real distinction of soul and body not only makes no appeal to the existence of the external world, and has no need to make any, but this existence could not be proved unless we had already been able to establish solidly, in a manner completely independent of what follows, that body is really distinct from soul.

3. Second Perspective *(y)*:Critical Problems (Objective Validity of Sensible Ideas); Intersections of the Various Lines of Inquiry; the Three Goals of the Investigation

As impressive as this set of results is, it constitutes only one part, the most external and most immediately visible part: the part concerning the positing of material existences, the foundation of the various sciences, the nature of their truth, their respective methods, and the determination of the roles that reason and sensation play. But other less visible and deeper results can be discerned, results on which the first bundle depends, and which follow directly from the effective principles of the demonstration and the proceedings governing it. They are the results that follow from the psychological and metaphysical investigations of *Meditations III* and *IV.*

We have seen how the complete disappearance of the hypothesis of universal deception before the inverse principle of divine veracity, which is, in fact, the principle of universal veracity, substituted for the resolution to doubt, the inverse resolution to destroy all doubts. If God is absolutely veracious, since God is the author of my self and all things, it is absolutely impossible that *anything* deceives us and that *we* are mistaken.

Confronted with the obscure and confused ideas of the senses, divine veracity necessarily maintains the same universal requirement. As little objective reality as these ideas possess, God is its author. This reality therefore could not be deceptive.

We will then come upon two ways of conceiving the question:

1) From the first point of view, we will attempt simply to restore and safeguard *some intrinsic truth of the senses,* which leads us to consider the problem of sensible error as a function of this truth and to attribute to this error a cause foreign to the senses themselves—namely our freedom, our judgment.

2) From the second point of view, we will discover *a certain intrinsic falsity in the senses themselves* which leads us to consider the problem of sensible error as a function of this falsity and to attribute a cause to it, or an occasion, located in the senses themselves

1) *By situating ourselves in the first point of view,* we will discover two problems:

A. The problem of establishing effectively that sensible ideas have their own truth and, consequently, to discover a certain indubitable objective validity in them and to determine the limits of this validity in order to specify *to what extent* these ideas are not deceptive.

B. Once this problem is resolved, we will have to attend to a second problem: how is it that we can be mistaken with respect to these *true ideas,* or with respect to what is true in them?

A. The first problem follows from the problem of *Meditation III.* There we were concerned with investigating the objective validity of our various ideas—if, to what extent, and how they enable me to go outside myself. This problem was resolved affirmatively for clear and distinct ideas, whose objective validity is now firmly established. It seemed resolved also for obscure and confused ideas, but negatively: the material falsity of these ideas appeared as indubitable as the indubitability of the material truth of clear and distinct ideas. But divine veracity constrained us to reconsider the question—to admit that obscure and confused ideas were barren of any objective validity would be to admit that God deceives us and would contradict the principle that everything that has an objective reality (as little as it is) has an objective validity, a truth (as little as that is). We would therefore have to take up again, with respect to sensible ideas, the laborious task that *Meditation III* had assumed, which had terminated in the establishment of clear and distinct ideas only. We will have to investigate whether I have what is needed to discover the means of determining in all certainty a foundation for the objective validity of my sensible ideas. And we will see reappear an inquiry symmetrical to that of *Meditation III,* in which we attempted to discover the thing outside of me that corresponds with my idea, by means of the principle of at least an equal quantity of formal reality in the cause as objective reality in the effect.[22] As in *Meditation III,* this inquiry will present a dual aspect: on the one hand, we will demonstrate an existence; on the other hand, we will resolve a critical problem of knowledge by establishing the objective validity of an idea. In *Meditation III,* the existence to be proven was that of God, and the objective validity to be established was that of our ideas in general, a validity finally recognized for clear and distinct ideas through the intermediary of the idea of God. In *Meditation VI,* the existence to be proven is that of material things; the objective validity to be established is that of our sensible ideas.

But why is the problem posed again for sensible ideas, and why does it require an extra effort? Cannot the demonstration of the veracious God, which was accomplished in *Meditation III,* suffice to invest them with their truth, in the same way that it invested clear and distinct ideas with their truth? Not at all. For clear and distinct ideas were not in themselves, for our finite understanding, the object of any natural doubt; on the contrary, the nature of our minds leads us to recognize spontaneously their incontestable truth. The only doubt that reached them was the doubt of the evil genius. Once the evil genius disappeared, this doubt vanished, and divine veracity, by its presence alone, automatically reinstated complete veracity to these ideas. Here, on the other hand, we are concerned with sensible ideas, obscure and confused ideas. The destruction of the metaphysical doubt by divine veracity does not destroy ipso facto the whole layer of hyperbolic doubts of natural origin, upon which the metaphysical doubt was merely added: doubts issuing from the errors of the senses, from the illusions of dreams, from hallucinations or deliriums of madmen, from the illusions of amputees, from the false sensorial information due to pathological problems, etc. This set of errors and reasons for doubt remains and, in fact, resists the principle of divine veracity, which must be satisfied, in the face of these errors, to proclaim only a rule against which the fact seems to be opposed. This is an aggravating circumstance; the objective reality of sensible ideas is so weak that a minima of truth corresponds to their minima of reality, and our mind, which is of finite capacity, seems incapable of discriminating between being and nothingness in this infinity of smallness, of capturing within this obscure content the portion of truth that could be enclosed in it. In this sphere, an antagonism is produced between divine veracity and the doubts adhering to the nature of ideas, an antagonism that was completely absent in the sphere of clear and distinct ideas. Divine veracity does take on the inverse aspect of the resolution to doubt that governed in the first three *Meditations* because of the fact of the evil genius. It enters into battle with the set of hyperbolic doubts of natural origin, exactly in the same fashion as had the principle of universal deception with respect to the natural certainty of my understanding. But although, in the first case, the battle ended with the total defeat of the negative principle, it ends here with the total triumph of the positive principle. The principle of divine veracity, as the reductive principle of natural doubts, therefore will have to play in *Meditation VI* an infinitely more active role than in *Meditation IV* or *V*. To a greater extent than in *Meditation IV*, it will assume both a normative and heuristic role, comparable, in certain respects, to the role of the idea of the perfect in *Meditation III*.[23]

B. The second problem follows from the problems of *Meditation IV*. It will also have a dual aspect: we will have to explain how, in fact, in spite of the truth of the senses, errors are produced with respect to them, and we will have to discover how, metaphysically, this error is conceivable, meaning compatible with divine veracity. The explanation of the fact therefore will have to be such that God appears as not being anything directly with respect to it. The principle of this dual solution is furnished immediately by *Meditation IV* itself—namely, the misuse of our freedom. However, the other elements of the solution cannot subsist as such and must be at least adapted to the region in which the problem is posed in this case, the region of the senses. In the sphere of the understanding, error arose out of the limitation of our understanding, an occasion for my infinite will to hurl my mind into the confusion of clear and distinct ideas with obscure and confused ideas, by affirming obscure and confused ideas as if they came from the realm of the clear and and distinct. But here we are concerned with the truth of an obscure and confused idea itself. If, in this respect, error can be considered still as arising from the limitation of our understanding, it is on the condition that we conceive that this limitation entails, in a symmetrical fashion, an adulteration of obscure and confused ideas through their assimilation with clear and distinct ideas. In brief, the limitation of the understanding is considered, in the first case, insofar as it brings forth a corruption of the idea of the understanding by sensible ideas; here it is considered insofar as it brings forth a corruption of the sensible idea, a perversion of "my nature" (in the strict sense) by the understanding.[24]

2) *By situating ourselves in the second point of view,* we would admit or we would realize that the senses deceive us directly by themselves and admit of an intrinsic falsity.

At first the problem seems simplified. We no longer have to ask ourselves how it happens that we are mistaken when the idea is true, since it is intrinsically false. However, the simplification is merely apparent, for although we no longer have to resolve the problem of formal error, we do have to resolve the problem of intrinsic falsity. And there we still have to find a dual solution: we will have to explain by what mechanism this intrinsic falsity can be produced, in fact, and we will have to discover through this explanation that God is not directly implicated with respect

to it. With respect to the first point, the explanation will no longer be
psychological, but psychophysical. With respect to the second point, the
problem will be much more difficult than in *Meditation IV* precisely because
of the falsity of the senses that adhere to it.[25] Since it comes from God
as the creator of the senses, which, in us, are independent of us, it could
not be thrown back on us, insofar as we would be its authors, that is,
thrown back on our freedom. In order to release God from the responsibility
we will therefore have to discover an original solution here, a solution
whose elements are not given to us in *Meditation IV,* except for some
references to a theodicy.

In this perspective, the inquiry as a whole, thus characterized under
this triple aspect (1A and B, and 2),[26] is once again illuminated. It appears
no longer as having simply an end directed toward the sciences and their
objects—to establish the existence of material things, to discover the principle
and the methods of the various sciences, to adapt the method with respect
to the differences of objects, and to discover the appropriateness of such
and such of our faculties with respect to the knowledge of these objects—
but as pursuing a critical internal end of psychology and theodicy. Critical
end: to determine the objective validity of certain ideas, to complete the
determination of the validity of our different items of knowledge, and to
resolve the problem of the limits of our faculties; psychological end: to
explain sensible error; metaphysical and theological end: to justify God.

4. *Nexus Rationum:* The Joining of the Two Perspectives, the Combining of the Six Themes and Its Double Development, in Descending Orders, in Three Degrees. The Counterpoint of *Meditation VI*

Meditation VI ought not be characterized according to one of these two
perspectives alone *(x* or *y),* but according to both at the same time. It
is at the same time a demonstration that is turned outwardly toward external
things (to prove the existence of bodies, their real distinction with my soul,
the substantial union of my soul and my body, and to establish the various
sciences) and a critical investigation that is turned inwardly (toward the
objective validity of my sensible knowledge, the human problem of sensible
error, and the problem of a justificatory theodicy). These ends are all
indissolubly associated: thus, the objective validity of sensible ideas within
their domain is only proven by the demonstration of the existence of bodies
and the union of my soul to a body; similarly, in *Meditation III,* the problem
of the objective validity of ideas in general was resolved by the proof of
the existence of God outside my idea. The proof of the real distinction
is indispensable for determining the limits of the sensible faculty, as well
as the nature and principal occasion of formal error in this domain. Finally,

divine veracity is the indispensable principle without which the proofs of existence could not be achieved, whereas the demonstration of the effective objective validity of sensible ideas in their domain and the discovery of the psychophysical mechanism of sensible errors are indispensable for establishing that nothing, in fact, contradicts God's goodness and veracity.

If we considered the second perspective *(y)* itself, and the two points of view that we have discovered in it—1) the problem of the intrinsic truth of the senses and the extrinsic character of formal error, and 2) the problem of the intrinsic falsity of the senses—we would perceive that *Meditation VI* simultaneously considers two points of view. On the one hand (1A), it establishes the intrinsic truth of the senses; on the other hand (2), it must recognize, in some cases, an intrinsic falsity in the senses. As a result, it is required to treat the problem of error in equal degree according to two separate aspects: the problem of formal sensible error, relative to the falsity of judgment stemming from our freedom (1B), and the problem of the intrinsic falsity of sensible information, falsity in which our freedom does not intervene as a factor (2). But, as we have seen, the two problems relative to error, the problem of formal error and the problem of material falsity, also involve a double inquiry for each, since this inquiry must be a psychological or psychophysical inquiry, which attempts to explain a fact of consciousness, and a metaphysical investigation or theodicy, which attempts to exculpate God.

And we know that the second perspective *(y)* intersects with the first *(x)*. Consequently, the problem of the intrinsic truth of the senses, insofar as it may be confused with the problem of its objective validity, itself has two aspects, being on the one hand a true critique of knowledge (inquiry into validity) and on the other, the proof of an existence (the existence of body, in this case).

Therefore a close intertwining of six large problems is produced: 1) the problem of the existence of bodies (of the union of soul and body); 2) the problem of the objective validity of sensation and of the limits of that validity; 3) the problem of the psychological explanation of formal error with respect to the senses; 4) the problem of the theological justification of this error; 5) the problem of the psychophysical explanation of the intrinsic falsity of the senses; 6) the problem of the theological justification of this falsity. *Meditation VI* will develop according to these six different and, at the same time, convergent lines.

Finally, these six problems will be treated and resolved *at the same time.* Until now, they have been treated separately. The problem of the objective validity of ideas, or the problem of their truth, was treated separately in *Meditation III,* and the problem of (formal) error was treated separately in *Meditation IV.* Here they must be resolved together, since they overlap each other. In *Meditation IV,* the problem of error benefited from the solution that *Meditation III* had furnished to the problem of the intrinsic truth of ideas (of their objective validity): since clear and distinct ideas were scientifically reinstituted as intrinsically true, there remained for us to seek only how we were mistaken with respect to them—the only problem was therefore the problem of formal error. Here, on the contrary, the problem of the intrinsic truth of sensible ideas is not yet resolved, since it is posed only when we place into question the falsity of the senses. As a result, the double problem of error, both metaphysical and psychological—how could God have rendered error possible, and what, in fact, is the mechanism of this error—is intertwined with the problem of objective validity. There are thus three hypotheses to consider: either sensation is intrinsically false, and we must explain how God could have placed in us an intrinsically false idea and how, being veracious, he had the right to do so; or else the intrinsic falsity is only apparent, God does not deceive us, formal error comes from us alone, but then sensible ideas are intrinsically true and we must effectively determine *what is the objective validity of that idea*—we must *prove its truth* by showing in an indubitable fashion to which reality outside of us it refers; or else the two hypotheses may be joined together by limiting each other reciprocally—the senses can have intrinsic truth in some respect and intrinsic falsity in some other respects.

The combination of these six problems does not exhaust the complexity of *Meditation VI,* which has a complexity suited to the natural complication of a final reason. Moreover, the investigation is developed according to the rational order of the various faculties of knowledge, by descending from the mode of knowledge expressing the essence of the soul—*understanding* (which certifies the *possibility* of the body)—to the mode of the soul that is most foreign to it[27]—*sensation* (which certifies the *certainty* of its existence)[28]—by passing through *imagination,* an intermediate faculty (which certifies its *probability*).[29]

Once we have attained the zone of demonstration by sensation in which we see clearly the implications of the six problems we have distinguished, the division of the difficulty leads once again, according to the order, to the separate and successive examination of the various elements of the final proof (the proof of the substantial union), according to their hierarchical subordination, by descending toward the less clear and distinct elements: the proof of the real distinction of soul and body, which is a truth of pure understanding,[30] the proof of the existence of bodies resting on constraint, having made abstraction of the qualitative element of sensation,[31] and the proof of the union resting on quality, meaning on what there is in sensation that is most properly obscure and confused.[32] A combination of six closely interwoven themes, and the double development in three degrees, of their descending hierarchy, all of which is strictly governed by the order—such is the general economy of *Meditation VI,* which truly appears as a remarkable sample of a philosophical counterpoint.

The Realm of the Understanding: The Possibility of the Existence of Material Things. The General Theory of Possibility

1. Demonstration of the Possibility of Material Things

The demonstration of the existence of material things, which consists of seeking whether it is possible to discover a reason allowing us to conclude necessarily that there are ideas in me referring to a material thing outside of me, is part of a general framework into which, as we have said, was already inscribed *Meditation III,* which sought whether there is some idea in us that necessarily possesses objective validity—that is, that requires me to posit an outside cause for it as its model and archetype.

A similarity of aims governs a similarity of proceedings. Consequently, the only method here would be an "internal examination" and an orderly consideration of the various categories of ideas and faculties: innate, artificial, and adventitious ideas; the understanding, imagination, and sensation. But the order is inverted: instead of climbing the ascending series of ideas by degrees in order to culminate with the clearest and most distinct of all ideas (the idea of God), the foundation of all certainty and of all essential and existential objective validity, as in *Meditation III,* we will climb down from the highest faculty, the understanding, and from ideas that are most clear and certain (the clear and distinct ideas of bodies), whose certainty is complete, toward the lower faculties: imagination and sensation. That is because we are concerned here with establishing the existence of the most humble thing—the body—and not that of the highest thing—God.

First I discover the clear and distinct ideas of material things in my understanding. Because of divine veracity, these ideas are true: they are natures or essences that entail the possibility of existence. Therefore material things are *possible.*[1]

This conclusion results necessarily from *Meditation III.* There we examined ideas in order to discover whether there is one among them that necessarily possesses objective validity—meaning whether there is one that refers necessarily to something outside of me—and we discovered that this privilege can only be granted to the idea that encloses an infinite objective reality. Thus only the idea of God could have been immediately invested with a double objective validity, both essential and existential. However, since we perceive from the first inspection, without the slightest doubt, that clear and distinct ideas other than that of God enclose a finite quantity of objective reality, my understanding judges them as necessarily true: that is what constitutes their evidence. Because of the indubitable presence in them of an objective reality, clear and distinct ideas indubitably have God as their author, and my mind could not be deceived when considering them as true—meaning as expressing an intelligible reality to which God could, if he wishes to, make an existential reality correspond. That is why they possess an essential objective reality, since they are intrinsically true, even when I perceive them in dreams. Thus, doubt cannot reach them, aside from the metaphysical doubt that vanishes once the necessary existence of the veracious God appears to me. Since they are real, and since God is the supreme reality, they are true; since they are evident, and God is the supreme veracity, again they are true. They are evident because they are real, as God is veracious because he is real. The three-fold equality of their reality with God's reality, of their evidence with his veracity, and of their reality with truth, guarantees their truth.[2]

On the other hand, obscure and confused ideas remain deprived of this essential objective validity because, since they possess only an infinitely small objective reality, my understanding can never know whether this reality is or is not; that is why the understanding, perceiving them obscurely and confusedly, judges false, or at least doubtful. Clear and distinct ideas of material things therefore attest in all certainty, because of their essential truth, to the very possibility of these things.

But they cannot attest to anything more than that. The finiteness of their objective reality excludes necessary existence from them, because only an infinite essence, which consequently has infinite power, possesses existence necessarily in virtue of the very superabundance of its power; it alone entails certain existence. Finite essences, because of the limitation of their being and power, contain in themselves only possible and contingent existence.[3] Since their truth is only intrinsic, meaning indifferent to the real existence of corresponding things, they cannot furnish us any assurance with respect to this subject. On the other hand, although I only know through them that these things are possible, I know this possibility indubitably, "for there is no doubt that God has the power to produce everything that I am able to conceive with distinctness, and I have never supposed that it was impossible for him to do anything, except when I found a contradiction in being able to conceive it well."[4]

In *Meditation I,* the regressive analysis that led to the Cogito had already posited mathematical ideas as ultimate constitutive and unbreakable elements, as the conditions of possibility of all my representations of sensible things. They now appear as conditions of possibility of the things themselves, and no longer merely as conditions of possibility of our representations of things.[5] By conferring upon them the objective validity that they lacked, by means of the demonstration of the veracious God, my science has transformed the truths of the understanding into truths of things.

2. Conditions of the Possibility of the Representation of Things and Conditions of the Possibility of Things; Confrontation with Malebranche's Thesis

We can easily discern what is specific to the Cartesian thesis by contrasting it with Malebranche's thesis. Malebranche also bases the objective validity of clear and distinct ideas on the coincidence between the conditions of possibility of my representation and the conditions of possibility of things: on the one hand, ideas are, for me, conditions of possibility of my representation of sensible things; on the other hand, they are, in God, as the archetypes of creation, conditions of possibility of the very existence of these things. Thus the correspondence between my idea and the fundamental reality of the thing outside of me is assured. If one holds to that, one can say that this correspondence [of ideas] is based on the identity of the two orders of conditions, in the same way as in Descartes' philosophy.

But the foundation of this identity is completely different through and through. For Malebranche, if an idea, the condition of my representation of things, is at the same time the archetype of these things in God, that is because of the substantial identity of these conditions within universal Reason, which is my light, and the rule of creation, which is something that even God cannot avoid. For Descartes, this foundation disappears, and freedom is substituted for the necessity of Reason in God. There is thus the possibility of total dissociation between the rule of my representation and the rule of creation. And this total dissociation is in fact avoided only because of divine veracity, which allows it, in some way, to subsist as a rule. Since the identity of the two orders is not consubstantial with God's Reason, but issues from his freedom, it is conditioned by the latter. The agreement of the two orders is therefore purely extrinsic.

As a result, the possibility of things for God cannot be reduced for Descartes, as it can be for Malebranche, to the possibility conceived by my understanding—that is, to the possibility of things for myself. According to Malebranche, God cannot create anything free from the conditions posited by the idea, meaning outside what our reason (which is the same as God's) conceives as possible. For Descartes, on the contrary, although we are certain that God can create everything that we conceive as possible, we cannot be assured that he cannot create what we conceive as impossible: "I hold as certain and I believe firmly that God can make an infinity of things that we are not capable of understanding or of conceiving."[6] Thus he can unite substantially, by his omnipotence, substances that I conceive as incompatible in themselves, or give independent existence to modes that I conceive as inseparable in themselves from their substances.[7] In fact, God has an infinite power that nothing can limit, and we know that, far from being subordinate to order, truth, and good, he has, on the contrary, instituted them freely.

3. The General Theory of Possibility; God's Omnipotence and Absolute Impossibilities, the Order of Uncreated Truths

Is that to say that the word "impossible" has no meaning *either with respect to God or with respect to things?* Clearly not, for if nothing is impossible in itself, everything would be possible; the possible would no longer be opposed to the impossible and the possible would have no meaning either. It would then be useless to state that material things are possible. We must therefore clarify the correlative notions of possible and impossible.

First, God's omnipotence, which by definition entails that nothing is impossible for it, establishes at the same time a higher order of impossibility, namely, that which cannot exist except by the negation of this very omnipotence. Therefore, in spite of everything there is something impossible for God—that which would limit his omnipotence or his being (being and power are identical). In brief, God excludes nothingness. As a result, everything that entails nothingness is an *absolute impossibility*. Thus, it is absolutely impossible that God does not exist;[8] that he is a deceiver; that he can make it be that what is, or was, is no longer; that he can detract from the principle of causality; that he can create independent beings (from which results the necessity of continuous creation); that he cannot create what we conceive as possible; that he can tolerate atoms; that he can create a void. In fact, God cannot not be, since he is defined as the being who is all powerful[9]—to the extent that he has less being, he has less power.[10] He cannot be a deceiver, for to deceive is to lean toward negation; it is to wish for nothingness, to limit one's being and power.[11] He cannot make the past not to have been, for that would be to transform truth into falsehood, being into nothingness.[12] He cannot detract from the principle of causality, for that would entail being creating nothingness, or nothingness creating being.[13] He cannot create independent beings, for he would thus demonstrate that his power is finite.[14] He cannot create a void, for void is a nothingness and has no properties.[15] He cannot not make what we conceive as possible, for that would testify to his powerlessness. Therefore he cannot tolerate atoms, for his power would be limited if it were deprived of the ability to divide a portion of extension which, however small, is clearly and distinctly conceived in itself as still divisible.[16]

The infinity of omnipotence therefore creates for God a set of absolute impossibilities, in the same way that the infinity of being entails the impossibility of nonbeing, since being alone is, and nonbeing is not. Descartes merely takes up here the Platonic-Augustinian tradition of Saint Anselm. "But how art thou omnipotent," writes Saint Anselm, "if thou are not capable of all things? Or if thou canst be corrupted, and canst not lie, nor make what is true, false—as, for example, if thou shouldst make what has been done not to have been done, and the like—how art thou capable of all things? Or else to be capable of these things is not power, but impotence . . . . Therefore, O Lord, the more truly thou are omnipotent, since thou art capable of nothing through impotence."[17]

To these absolute impossibilities are attached the principles that *nothingness has no properties,* and *in order to think one must exist* (for to think is a property, and nothingness has no properties)[18] and consequently the Cogito itself, which is inconceivable without consciousness of the principle *in order to think one must exist.* From these impossibilities is also derived the principle of the immutability of divine will,[19] which establishes outside our understanding, and for God himself, a new absolute impossibility: the impossibility to change the truths that he has freely instituted, for a will that corrects itself is an inconstant will, a will that is affected by a defect *(defectus),* and consequently an imperfect and limited will. This impossibility to change the truths, once they have been instituted, will be a necessary element of the demonstration of the real distinction between soul and body, for if God can decide from all eternity to change in existence the rules of eternal possibility that he has instituted for our finite understanding, given that he is not himself bound to these rules, he cannot make these rules cease from being valid as such. That is why he could truly unite, in fact, two substances that are repugnant to each other, into one existing composite substance, but he cannot make of them a single and same thing in essence, which would be to abolish intrinsically the eternal truth that made of them two really different substances.[20]

Far from arising from the principle of contradiction, this Parmenidean principle of the impossibility of nothingness and the necessity of being must, on the contrary, be considered as its foundation. The principle of contradiction is only a "maxim" derived from our idea of the infinity of God's being, which reveals to us, with the absolute negation of nothingness by being, all the principles that are immediately implied in it (the principle of causality, the principle that nothingness has no properties, that in order to think one must exist, etc.). Because of its emptiness and sterility, the principle of contradiction, which is a purely formal principle, contrasts with the full and fruitful principles, which are both material and formal, of the Cogito and God.[21] Thus, Descartes has already resolved for himself a post-Kantian problem: to discover a principle both material and formal, and the foundation of the formal principle of contradiction, which, uniting in itself the necessity of this logical principle with the fruitfulness of a real principle, would be the very principle of reality *(Realität).*

4. The Original Certainty of Uncreated Truths. Opposition between Descartes and Malebranche

All these truths that flow necessarily from God's omnipotence, and to which God himself cannot subtract himself, are first truths that are situated to some extent *above the eternal truths instituted by divine free will.* Closely intertwined with the being of the Omnipotent Being, they cannot not be. Therefore they cannot have been freely created; they are *uncreated.*

We can understand that, given his tendencies, Malebranche was led by this to substitute for the principle "in order to think one must exist," the principle "nothingness has no properties," or "nothingness is neither visible nor intelligible," in such a way as to deduce the Cogito itself from his principle, and thus to take his point of departure directly from the vision of the Divine Being. This initial deviation can appear insignificant. However, it radically changes all the perspectives.[22] No doubt, in Descartes' philosophy, the Cogito is conditioned by the principle *in order to think one must exist,* and this principle itself is reducible, in the end, to the principle *nothingness has no properties,* whose foundation is the idea of being; no doubt the notions that are subtracted from metaphysical doubt, such as causality, God's immutability, etc., are all precisely of the order of uncreated truths. However, that does not prevent doubt, and not the certainty—and even less the vision—of God, from remaining the point of departure of Descartes' philosophy. In fact, the principles that are invulnerable to metaphysical doubt do not owe their invulnerability to their uncreated character, meaning to their absolute necessity in God; since God is unknown, or at least assumed unknown initially, this necessity for God cannot be known to us in the least, at first. That is why certain truths of this order (some of the most important ones, such as the existence of

God's veracity) are denied by the hypothesis of the evil genius. That God exists and is not a deceiver is, in fact, an absolute necessity, an uncreated truth. We must have, or pretend to have, an obscure and confused knowledge of God in order not to perceive this. Moreover, to believe that God deceives me is the same as to believe that he does not exist; since deception is [part of] nothingness, to prove that God exists is, ipso facto, to prove that he is veracious. The hypothesis of the evil genius, which is itself an absurd hypothesis, is therefore possible only when one lacks the knowledge of God that testifies to this absurdity. Hence, since the point of departure is the fiction of the evil genius, it cannot be found in the knowledge of God, upon which depends, however, the very truth of the principle without which the Cogito would be impossible. From this we see that the certainty of these propositions, which are invulnerable to metaphysical doubt, is discovered originally as a fact in myself, and not as flowing from their necessary foundation in God.

It remains for me to know how I can, when I have an obscure and confused knowledge of God, doubt his veracity, in the name of the evil genius, whereas the principles that are closely intertwined with God (causality, in order to think one must exist, nothingness has no properties, etc.) remain at the same time invulnerable to the malevolent doubt. The only conceivable response is that, even when the knowledge of God is obscure and confused in me, I have sufficiently clear and distinct knowledge of these principles in order to remain incapable of doubting them metaphysically. In other words, the divine absolute necessity of these principles is immediately perceived in them as a necessity, without my having as yet knowledge of its divine origin, without my knowing that it is in itself based in God's absolute being. Thus I can doubt God metaphysically without being able to doubt them. On the other hand, their certainty is as inexplicable as it is indubitable. It is a certainty of fact, as is the certainty of the Cogito. In any case, their privilege cannot arise from the fact that they are uncreated truths, since this privilege is lacking to some of them. Both eternal created and uncreated truths are subject to the same charge, and cannot be established as a rule except by means of clear and distinct knowledge of the existence of God. The only difference is that divine veracity is required in order to guarantee the former, while it does not have to intervene in order to impose the latter. The privilege of the primitively indubitable principles arises, as Descartes has told us, from the fact that they do not entail any affirmation of existence, and the evil genius strikes at all existences, except mine.

5. Impossibilities for Our Understanding. Absolute and Relative Contradiction. Possible and Impossible Labyrinth of the Continuous. Absolute Certainty of Human Science and God's Absolute Omnipotence

Aside from the *impossible in itself and for God,* there is the impossible for our understanding: that is what implies a contradiction with the truths and the necessities that were freely instituted in my mind by God's infinite omnipotence. By definition, these necessary truths could not contradict or limit this omnipotence. As a result, the impossibility for our understanding is not an impossibility for God, nor, in principle, an impossibility for things in themselves, outside the understanding, "because, from the very fact that a thing is outside my understanding, it is evident that it is not contradictory, but possible."[23] These truths form the set of our clear and distinct ideas, and of mathematical essences in particular. They do not express the totality of God's omnipotence, but only one of its possibilities; they are simply *of the being,* but not *the whole being.* That is why God, who could never create the false, which is nothingness, could have created other *truths,* for in this way he would have created other beings, and not nothingness.

But the question remains about whether the principle of contradiction belongs to the order of uncreated truths and defines absolute possibility and impossibility, or whether it belongs to the order of created truths, and defines possibility and impossibility relative to our understanding. To the extent that it derives immediately, as a general principle, from the infinite reality of God and from the necessities implied by it, it clearly belongs to the sphere of uncreated truths; it is closely intertwined with divine omnipotence, governs things necessarily, and can never be placed into doubt. But, on the other hand, we see Descartes oppose at every occasion God's omnipotence with what our understanding conceives as impossible from the fact that our understanding conceives it as contradictory.[24] From this we must conclude that there are two orders of contradiction:[25] One refers to divine omnipotence, and belongs to its very definition; it is absolute, valid for God himself, and determines the sphere of divine impossibilities. The other refers to the capacities of our understanding and to its principles; it derives from God's freedom along with the understanding itself and determines impossibilities only with respect to man.[26] These two principles are easily distinguished, for the former expresses the *incompatibility between being and nonbeing,* whereas the *latter decrees the reciprocal incompatibility of some ideas or some beings.* And it is evident that God is above this latter incompatibility, since he has freely created all these various beings, and if he has decided to have us conceive them as incompatible in order for us to conceive them as separate, meaning as truly different, he can, by means of his omnipotence, unite them or separate them as he wishes.[27] Moreover, it is clear that God, by means of his omnipotence, could have created an order of things such that what appears to us as incompatible, impossible, and contradictory, is not so and does not appear to be so. He could have made a "mountain without a valley" and established that 1 and 2 do not add up to 3.[28] For he could have created, in this way, some other truth (and not something false) and some other being (and not some nothingness). The only thing that he cannot do is to create something false and some nothingness.

What is impossible for our understanding is therefore in no way, by hypothesis, something impossible for God, if we conceive that God can create what we do not understand. However, it does not follow that the rules of possibility that God has instituted for our understanding as eternal truths lose all objective validity, and that, in things such as God has created them, what is conceived as impossible by our thought can be possible in themselves. This hypothesis can be conceived only in *Meditation I* and *II,* where in the order of reasons divine veracity was not yet established. Lacking a particular revelation, either by means of natural sensation or the Scriptures, we ought to consider as necessarily excluded from the world of which God is the author all that we conceive as impossible. In fact, since God is veracious, he has instituted the truths of our understanding as having to be objectively valid—he has given our thought a clear and distinct knowledge of the true conditions of possibility that he has really established for this world. Moreover, he has instituted these conditions as having to be valid eternally, since his will is immutable. Thus the impossibility for our understanding *is ipso facto the impossibility for things,* even though it is not, in any way, *an impossibility for God's omnipotence.*[29] We can say that the impossibility occurs here, not because God *cannot do it,* but because God *does not wish to do it.* Although the absolute impossibility in God is like the negative testimony of the unlimitedness of his omnipotence—which cannot not be omnipotence—the impossibility for our understanding, insofar as it is also an impossibility in things, is the positive manifestation of an omnipotent will, which is the creator of these things, to the extent that this will is immutable and veracious. It is therefore impossible to find shelter in God's omnipotence in order to deny the validity of all human science and reasoning, and to affirm that God could have effectively placed in our universe things that are conceived as impossible for our understanding.

However, for reasons that escape us, but that arise from the impenetrable aims of divinity, and that are justified as a rule by the principle of the best, God could have placed in our universe, in fact, by means of his omnipotence, things that clearly are repugnant to the possibilities conceived by our mind—for example, he could have instituted the union of body and soul in a composite substance (and also other mysteries of union and separation that are above nature, such as incarnation and transubstantiation).[30] But then God, who is veracious, teaches them to us indubitably. We can therefore admit nothing as being real in things that contradict the rules of possibility for my understanding, as long as my understanding does not discover, in the unimpeachable testimony that God himself brings to us, *a necessary and sufficient reason to admit it.* Thus we could never accept that God had, by means of his omnipotence, united substantially my soul to a body, in opposition to the positive impossibility that our reason sees in this, unless God taught it to us specifically, by a sensation whose nature and conditions are such that our understanding itself, in the name of divine veracity, commands us to consider it as indubitable. This teaching confirms for our understanding the care taken by the author of our origin that we are never deceived by the faculties that he has placed in us. It therefore confirms divine veracity. Our understanding would be deceiving us, in fact, if it were not warned by sensation about the exceptions that God has created in his laws. The understanding, to which is reserved the privilege of knowing God's necessary veracity, is constrained, in virtue of this very veracity, to agree that God does not deceive us by giving us sensible ideas and also that he enables us to avoid error in this way. It will have to endorse the teaching of the senses, a teaching that it repudiates naturally because of the obscurity, confusion, and deception that the senses bring to their own necessities. But the understanding must recognize at the same time that, since it is thus instructed about an exception to the general laws of rational possibility whose objectivity is guaranteed by God's veracity, the latter shelters it against a fundamental error relative to my own composite nature. Finally, the necessity of essences remains what it is, even when God's omnipotence detracts from it. That is the case with the union of soul and body, which contradicts their respective natures, but cannot modify them; that is why we must always conceive them as separable.[31]

The impossible and the possible appear to my understanding in two different ways. In the first way, the understanding conceives clearly and distinctly that the thing is positively possible or impossible. For example, it conceives clearly and distinctly and most positively the impossibility for God's infinity to have limits. It is then constrained to bring forth a judgment of impossibility on the thing. In the second way, the understanding does not conceive how the thing is possible or impossible, and it is not able to conceive that it is positively one or the other. For example, it does not understand that the division to infinity can be completed, nor that there can be a number of all the numbers; nevertheless, it does not see that this completion or that this number of all the numbers is positively impossible. In this case, it is not constrained by any clear and distinct idea. Therefore it remains free to affirm or not to affirm the impossibility or the possibility. But, since the understanding ought never proceed to an *affirmation* without sufficient reason, it is required to suspend its judgment and to remain undecided between the possible and the impossible, unless some sufficient reason coming from elsewhere imposes a decision. From this arises the distinction between the infinite and the indefinite: in the former case, I perceive clearly and distinctly that there can be no end in it; in the latter case, I do not conceive clearly and distinctly how there could be an end in it without, in addition, conceiving clearly and distinctly that it is necessary that there is no end in it: "In order to say that something is infinite, we must have some reason that allows us to know it as such, which we cannot have except for God alone; but in order to say that it is indefinite, it is sufficient to have no reason to prove that it has limits. . . . Therefore having no reason and even not being able to conceive that the world has limits, I call it indefinite. But I cannot deny that there may be some reasons known to God, though they are incomprehensible to me; that is why I do not say absolutely that it is infinite."[32]

The negative impossibility arising from the incapacity of our mind, that is, from its finiteness, allows me to admit that the infinite omnipotence of God could have accomplished what I do not understand as possible—for example, that he could have completed the division of matter. But, on the other hand, the very infinity of God constrains me to admit as effectively possible what I conceive as merely negatively possible, that is, the thing whose impossibility I do not perceive positively. Thus, not conceiving in any way that it is impossible to divide extension indefinitely, I do not see how God would not divide it to infinity; for otherwise, I would limit arbitrarily his omnipotence by refusing him the power to accomplish what I do not judge as impossible. That is why I ought to conclude positively that there are no atoms: "There is a contradiction in saying that there are atoms that we conceive as extended and as indivisible at the same time, because, even though God might make them such that they could not be certainly divided by any creature, we cannot comprehend that he is able to deprive himself of the faculty of dividing them himself. . . . The case is different with the divisibility of matter; for although I cannot count all the parts into which it is divisible, and consequently say that the number is indefinite, I cannot be certain that God could never complete their division, because I know that God can do more than I could ever comprehend."[33]

Thus the double principle, God *can do more* than I can comprehend, but *he cannot do less* than I can comprehend, allows me to resolve one of the aspects of the Leibnizian problem of the *labyrinth of the continuum* or the Kantian problem of the *Second Antinomy of Pure Reason*.[34] But although the first argument, God can do more than I can comprehend, is a simply negative argument that cannot prove by itself the complete division of matter (we will need a sufficient reason drawn from physics),[35] the second argument, God cannot do less than I can comprehend, constitutes a sufficient reason upon which arguments from the physical order will be added. By itself it is sufficient to establish the rejection of atoms. The antinomy is therefore resolved by the equal affirmation of two propositions, one positive and the other negative: the completion of infinite division and the rejection of atoms, because of the simply negative conception of the impossible and the possible, such as it results from the relations of God's omnipotence with our finite understanding.

We are again confronted with two cases with respect to the positive impossibility. Either this impossibility concerns God himself, as when I perceive that the idea of infinity positively excludes the possibility of any limit. In this case, my understanding must conceive this impossibility as absolute. Or else it concerns created things, for example, when I conceive very positively that it is impossible that two substances do not exclude each other, or that two modes of a substance exist separated from the substance, or that 2 times 1 is 3. In this case, I must necessarily conceive this impossibility in the things themselves, since the veracious God did not make things other than I conceive them. However, given that his omnipotence is never limited by the necessities that it has put forth, I must conceive as possible that he has effectively created something that contradicts them (for example, a union of soul and body). But then, since God is veracious, he must enable me to know this indubitably (in this case, by means of sensation).

In brief, because of his omnipotence, God can do everything in principle— even that which we judge as positively impossible—on the condition that this is not repugnant to his omnipotence, meaning that it does not concern absolute impossibility. But since he has instituted as eternal truths everything that our understanding perceives as positive impossibilities, and since he is immutable and veracious, God could not do anything in this universe that we judge excluded by the latter. However, if it happens that he does accomplish any of these, he will warn us indubitably. Moreover, he can still accomplish what we do not understand the possibility of, as in the case when we do not have sufficient reason to judge the thing necessarily as positively impossible; further, nothing prevents him from accomplishing what our understanding conceives as possible.

This doctrine of the possible and impossible, is, as we can see, completely original and extremely different from all the conceptions [of possible and impossible] in the philosophy of the great Cartesians: Malebranche, Spinoza, and Leibniz. It contains more than just a seed—although in an extremely particular form—of the distinction, which was taken up by Leibniz, between *absolute necessity* and necessity *ex hypothesi.*

CHAPTER XI

The Realm of the Imagination:
The Probability of the Existence
of Material Things

1. On the Examination of the Imagination

Divine veracity has given much weight to the possibility of material things, such as it is verified by the presence of the essence of things in our understanding. We are certain that they can exist within the framework of this universe whose necessary conditions have been instituted by the veracious God's free, but immutable, will for all eternity. However, these essences cannot teach us anything more about this. We must therefore go down one degree in the chain of reasons and turn toward the category of ideas immediately below: that of imaginative ideas.

The conclusion relative to the possibility of the existence of material things that was derived from their essences was merely a recall of the results acquired from *Meditations III* and *V*—Descartes remarks that "at least I already know it [that they can exist]."[1]

The examination of imagination, which will now persuade us that the existence of things is at least probable, will bring forth a new element.

2. The Various Kinds of Mental and Corporeal Imagination

Descartes understands two different things by imagination: imagination as mental faculty, which is the soul exercising an action on the brain, and corporeal imagination, which consists of the capacity of the body to preserve the traces of actions exercised on it, either from within or from without.[2] This capacity resides in the pineal gland, but also in each organ of the body, and finally in the body as a whole. Since, on the other hand, mental imagination can be intellectual or sensible, there are in reality four kinds of imagination, as there are four kinds of memory: intellectual and sensible memory, not residing in the body; corporeal memory inscribed on the brain, and corporeal memory extending into our organs and our muscles (for example, the memory of the fingers of a lute player[3]). In addition to these four forms of reproductive

29

imagination, there is a creative imagination, which forms new ideas.

But it is clear that we would not be dealing here with any other question than with the mental faculty, since we do not know whether body exists, and since we are attempting to go from our soul and what we find in it, precisely to prove that body exists. If there is a corporeal imagination, we should attempt to discover it through mental imagination.

Located between the understanding and sensation, mental imagination exhibits the characteristics of an intermediary faculty. Since it can be supported by ideas of the understanding and sensible ideas, it is divisible into two: a higher imagination, by which the soul can represent to itself imaginatively innate ideas (*ideae intellectae*)—that is, the imagination of geometrical things; and a lower imagination, by which it can represent to itself imaginatively adventitious ideas (*ideae sensu perceptae*[4])—that is, the imagination of sensible qualities.

The kinds of imagination that Descartes considers here are only reproductive and not creative imagination. The faculty of factitious ideas, meaning the one that forms new images by combining arbitrarily remembered images, is set aside.[5] In fact, it is clearly evident that this faculty, insofar as it entails something created by me, could not allow me to conclude the existence of a body independent of me.

Descartes will attempt to base the affirmation of an external body by considering the higher and lower imagination, one after the other.

3. Proof of the Probability of the Existence of Material Things in Virtue of the Hypothesis That Explains the Fact of the Imagination of Geometrical Ideas

My consciousness has allowed me to know clearly and distinctly, from *Meditation II* on, that imagination is *different from pure intellect* and does not belong to the essence of my mind, which can subsist without it. With respect to how imagination differs from the essence of my mind, it seems that one can conclude that it depends *on something that differs from my mind,* since mind cannot produce from itself what is not included in its pure essence. Thus, the difference in me between my intellectual faculty and my nonintellectual faculty would be related to the difference between the essence of material things and their existence outside me.

It remains for us to know whether this thing that is different from my mind is in fact the body. This conclusion appears likely if we consider the difference of the behavior of my soul with respect to imagination and with respect to the understanding: in the former case, we notice that it requires a *mental effort* that is foreign to intellectual processes. Thus, when I wish to materialize a geometrical essence in an image, I need "a particular application of mind." The more complex the notion is, the more strenuous is this effort; the harder the imaginative actualization, the more it becomes confused, until our capacity is completely surpassed—as in the case in which I try to imagine polygons with greater and greater numbers of sides.[6] Imagination therefore reaches its limits extremely fast, and it is thus to be contrasted with the understanding, which, conceiving with equal ease an infinite multitude of notions, appears to have "almost"no bounds with respect to it.[7] Moreover, the effort required by imagination seems to entail that the mind is applying itself to something foreign to it that resists it— in brief, that could only be the body. I could therefore conclude from this that *body exists.* But since the soul can apply itself to this body as it wishes in order to materialize its concepts, it seems that one can also conclude that the body is *closely linked and joined to the soul;* we would be conceiving then, that in pure intellection, the soul turns to itself in order to consider the ideas that are contained in it, while in imagination, it turns toward its body (the brain) in order to contemplate the idea which it etches there and which it derives from its intellect.[8] The imagination therefore testifies to the fact that body exists and that my soul is united to a body.

We must first note that such a conclusion is extremely limited, for it allows me to posit only the existence of *my body,* and not that of material things in general. Moreover, although I am led to conceive that there is a difference between my body and my soul, I do not learn, in this way, of what this difference consists. Since the difference between imagination and the understanding is only modal, it cannot by itself allow the inference that the reason that explains it is something really and substantially different from my mind. This drawback is serious because, to the extent that body is given to me only in its close union with soul, nothing can lead me to think that it differs substantially from soul. On the contrary, we know that the immediate consciousness of the union of body and mind negates the knowledge of their distinction. But nothing else can allow me to know certainly that this union is substantial, for, although the body is given to me as continuously and closely associated with my soul, the body is not given to me as intimately intertwined with my soul, but as opposing it and resisting its effort.

Second, as plausible as is the conclusion that I have a body, it is not certain. It is valid only if we admit a hypothesis invoked in order to explain a phenomenon ascertained in my soul. But this hypothesis itself does not have any necessity: I judge it probable, lacking a better one.[9] We must remember that any hypothesis that bases its legitimacy solely on its ability to explain a fact remains a simple supposition, which can, from one moment to another, be replaced by a better one *(aequipollentia hypothesium).* It can allow me to have only *moral* certainty. That is why it can never be more than merely probable. That is the case of the hypothesis that verifies a successful decoding, or of the physical hypothesis applied simply on the phenomena it accounts for, and not deduced from certain a priori principles.[10]

In order to render the hypothesis certain in this case, we would have to prove that it is the only possible hypothesis as a rule. Such a proof is lacking here, and other hypotheses remain conceivable. In *Meditation III,* I noted that the objective reality of ideas other than the ideas of the understanding was so weak that my soul had in itself a formal reality that was more than sufficient in order to account for it. Moreover, the sensation of effort does not imply necessarily that what resists my mind is external to it, since I experience inclinations in me that resist my will.[11] In addition, this sensation contains above all the consciousness of my own activity. It unfolds in the absence of external things, "as if with all windows closed."[12] It depends on the arbitrariness of our will. There are as many characteristics that relate it to me as to non-me. Is not the mark of what is imposed from the outside, on the contrary, the characteristic of being outside one's consent? Does not Descartes have to address the *constraint* of sensation, which the *effort* of imagination could not establish incontestably, in order to prove the existence of these material things? Normally, in order to raise myself to the idea of an action of which I would not be the author and, consequently, to arrive at an external reality (God, body, etc.), I would have to begin with a passion that I experience. And imagination is an action.[13]

This hypothesis with respect to the imaginative process, which allows it to succeed over the others because it is a more convenient and satisfying explanation, would be certain only if we could prove what is in question, namely, the existence of bodies.[14] From this we ought to conclude in addition that if ever we would be able to administer this proof, the theory of imagination we conjecture about here will become ipso facto absolutely certain.

4. Unfruitful Appeal to the Imagination of Sensible Ideas

Can the imagination of sensible qualities, of colors, sounds, tastes, pains, etc., bring to us what the imagination of geometrical ideas could not furnish?[15] The imagination of sensible qualities is not conceived as an effort to materialize the ideas of my understanding in my body, but as an effort to apply to ideas that have been received previously—in reality to traces already etched on my brain, meaning conserved in corporeal memory— the action of my soul, in order to arouse the mental images tied to these traces. But this activity is not essentially different from the one by which the soul itself etches ideas of the understanding onto the brain, except for a small difference. The difference resides in that the things to which it is applied could not have reached my mind except through the agency of the senses.

The imagination of sensible qualities therefore cannot bring us anything more than what the imagination of geometrical ideas brought us, in this case. On the one hand, its images are much less distinct than the images of mathematical objects,[16] for they are not permanently supported by clear and distinct ideas that are innate to our understanding, as the latter are. On the other hand, its images do not have the distinction special to sensations, that sensible qualities are more expressive and lively,[17] and that, thus, they appear in their way more distinct than the ideas of the understanding and the evocations of memory.[18]

Therefore we have to consider directly, and not through imagination, this characteristic mode of thinking that I call *sensing* or *sensation (sensus)* in order to see whether we could derive from it the certainty that bodies exist.[19] As for imagination itself, since it is an action under all its forms, it is definitely useless for this kind of undertaking.

CHAPTER XII

The Realm of the Senses: The Certainty of the Existence of Material Things

1. The Real Orientation of the Inquiry: The Appeal to the Immediate Given of the Senses

With sensation or the senses, which are, among all the faculties of my soul, the farthest from that which constitutes its essence, namely pure understanding, the existence of material things ceases to be merely possible or only probable and becomes rigorously certain.

Reflection on sensation necessarily involves two aspects: 1) enumeration of sensations and attention to the manner in which they appear to consciousness; 2) information about judgments of objective validity that at first appear to be indissolubly and originally tied to them.

We will attempt to find the bedrock or clay of authentic sensation under the heap of prejudices that alter or hide it. From this arises the importance of the critique of judgments that will take up the greater part of this inquiry, except when we will have to examine the problem of the intrinsic defects of the senses, at the end of the analysis.

In fact, it is always the understanding that knows. The senses do not know. They offer to the understanding a content by which the understanding, with the help of judgment, can know. As has been established by *Meditation III*, the only element in us that can involve error is judgment. And all the other contents of my consciousness, and consequently sensation considered in itself, are beyond formal falsity, which can arise only from judgment. The critique of the senses, with a view toward discovering a remainder of substantial truth in it, will therefore be, in fact, a critique of judgment applied to the senses.

What we understand by senses is, in reality, a complex of three elements: 1) modifications caused in the corporeal organism by external objects; 2) everything that results immediately from this for the mind, namely, the various raw sensations, both internal and external; 3) judgments that we bring on them from our childhood, which can suppose reasoning—they depend on the understanding alone. But this intervention of the understanding escapes our attention by habit, and we attribute to the senses themselves what actually comes from the intellect. It is only when we rectify our false reasonings and we correct our false habitual judgments that, struck by the novelty of the judgments that intervene, we become aware of the intervention of the understanding. We then say that it has *redressed* the senses. But in reality, what it has redressed is not the senses, but the prior ill use it had made of itself.[1]

The work of *Meditation VI* will therefore consist in accomplishing for sensation the work that the preceeding *Meditations* had accomplished for the idea of the understanding: it will consist in lifting sensation's covering in order to consider it bare, in the same way we were concerned, with respect to a clear and distinct idea (the idea of any body whatsoever, wax, for example) to "lift its covering in order to consider it bare."[2] But the covering that hid the clear and distinct idea of the wax from us was woven from sensible qualities arising from imagination and the senses, whereas the covering that hides the authentic reality of sensation from us is woven from ideas coming from the understanding. Moreover, our judgment is equally culpable in both cases—it is always judgment that manufactures deception. Here as elsewhere, we need to return to *the immediate givens of consciousness.*

As we know, to discover the immediate givens of consciousness behind the fictions that hide them from us will be a task pursued by many philosophers, including Henri Bergson.[3] But, of the two goals that Descartes proposes, to discover the immediate given of understanding, and to discover the immediate given of sensation, Bergson retains only the latter—he is only concerned with finding the qualitative element that has been adulterated and hidden by concepts arising from the intellect. That is because Bergson, in opposition to Descartes, sees in the concepts of the understanding only fictions and not immediate givens. No doubt he distinguishes authentic intelligence (the intelligence of *homo sapiens*) from pseudointelligence (the intelligence of *homo loquax*), but this opposition does not restore to the concept the character of basic original given that it has in Cartesian philosophy. Finally, for Descartes, what the analysis discovers as the irreducible authentic given at the base of consciousness, after uncovering the purely rational idea or the sensation, the (mathematical) essence or the (sensible) quality, is never something fluid and moving, as it is for Bergson, but a fixed, hard, and solid nature—the bedrock or clay upon which he plans to build the unshakeable and definitive monument of modern science.[4]

2. The Four Principal Parts of the Inquiry

Since attempting to discover whether sensation can supply us in all certainty with the proof that material things exist amounts to asking oneself whether it has an objective validity or not, and to what extent it does, it is evident that the only goal of the investigation is to discover whether the sensation which is immediately present to my consciousness offers one or several characteristics that *require me* to recognize in all certainty the legitimacy of the objective validity that judgment attributes to it formally. We rediscover here the formulation of the problem posed in *Meditation III*.

Thus four parts of the inquiry can be determined:

1) The recall of various judgments of objectivity tied to various sensations: "I shall recall in my memory what are the things that I formerly held to be true because I had received them through the senses."

2) The examination of the "foundations on which my belief was based."

3) The examination of "the reasons that since then have required me to consider them doubtful."

4) The definitive determination of the nature, degree, and limits of the objective validity of sensation: "Finally I shall consider what I ought now to believe about them."[5]

The first three points take up succinctly the results of methodical doubt, such as it was exercised in *Meditation I*, and the exposition and refutation of reasons in favor of the objective validity of sensible ideas—already treated in *Meditation III*. The fourth point utilizes, in one part, the metaphysical results of *Meditation III, IV*, and the beginning of *V*.

1) *I judge by means of sensible ideas that I sense myself united to a body and that material things exist.*

The internal senses teach me that I am united to a body, which I consider as part or all of me, placed within a world of bodies receiving from them certain advantages linked with pleasure, and certain disadvantages linked with pain; they also teach me that I experience corporeal appetites (hunger, thirst) and passions of the soul (joy, sorrow), which bring me corporeal inclinations. The external senses lead me to believe that I perceive in bodies extension, shape, and movement, and all sensible qualities—tactile (hardness, heat, etc.), visual, olfactory, gustatory, and auditory—and that I can distinguish bodies from one another by means of them.[6]

2) *These judgments appear founded.*

With respect to external sensations and the affirmation of external bodies, even though in fact I only truly sense qualities in my thought, it is not without reason that I believe that I sense things entirely different from me, namely, the bodies from which they proceed. These reasons, ranked in order of increasing strength, are four in number:

A. These qualities present themselves to me *without my consent.* My will cannot subtract itself from them when they occur, nor can it provoke them at its leisure when they do not impose themselves on me. I therefore appear to myself as constrained *to experience them or not to experience them,* according to whether the corresponding external things are present or absent.[7]

This reason also justifies the judgments brought upon the union of soul and body from internal sensations. This justification remains limited, however, because it allows judgment to conclude for a union without being able to specify in what this union consists. Judgment can posit it only insofar as the constraint requires the soul to conceive that a thing external to it must concur with it in order to produce sensations that it relates to itself; it therefore judges that these sensations do not stem from it alone. In brief, the union is posited here only because of *the externality of the body* with which I am united, by virtue of a judgment that posits that an external cause must concur with the internal cause: "We ought also conclude that a certain body is more closely united to our soul than any other in the world, because we perceive clearly that pain and other sensations occur to us without our foreseeing them, and that the soul, by knowledge that is natural to it, judges that *these sensations do not arise from itself* insofar as it is a thing that thinks, but insofar as it is united to another extended thing that is moved by the disposition of its organs, and that we call the human body."[8]

The *constraint,* as a general reason to found the existence of material things, was already alleged in *Meditation III.*[9]

B. Ideas arising from the senses are infinitely livelier and more expressive than those I have from my mind, either from the understanding or from imagination and memory. It is therefore natural to judge that they stem from something other than my mind.[10]

The above reason appears here for the first time.

C. Having no knowledge of material things outside of what comes to me from sensible ideas, it is natural that I judge them similar to these ideas.[11]

Until now the above reason had been invoked only in passing in *Meditation III:* "I see nothing that appears more reasonable to me than to judge that this alien entity sends to me and impresses on me its likeness rather than anything else."[12]

D. My experience proves to me that I use the ideas arising from the senses more often than those arising from my reason; that most of the ideas I form by myself are composed of ideas arising from the senses, and that they are less true and expressive than the latter. It is natural that I conclude from this, with the Scholastics, Epicureans, and other empiricists, that "I have no idea in my mind that I have not previously acquired through my senses."[13]

This reason had not yet been alleged.

With respect to the internal sensation of appetites, passions, inclinations, etc., and the affirmation of my union with body, four reasons also give objective validity to my judgment.

A. I cannot be separated from my body as from other bodies.[14]

B. I experience in it, and for it, all my appetites and all my affections.[15]

C. I experience my pleasure and my pain in its parts and not in those of other bodies. These three reasons are mentioned here for the first time.[16]

D. I notice that the link established between the sensation of pain and pleasure and the sadness and joy of my soul, between the emotion of the stomach I call hunger, the dryness of the throat I call thirst, and the corresponding appetites of drinking and eating, is in itself not rational and is taught to me by "nature," meaning by an instinct alien to pure understanding. Similarly, it is "nature" that has taught me "everything that I judge about the objects of the senses, since I notice that these judgments predate all the reasons that could constrain me with respect to them."[17]

In this category, the fourth reason is the most important, since it has a general validity and it concerns both external and internal senses. It had already been invoked by *Meditation III*, with respect to sensations, as *the first reason* to believe in the existence of material things outside me.[18] The constraint was invoked there only secondarily. The inclination or natural propensity that leads me to believe in this existence refers expressly to nature, because of this constraint.[19]

The most important foundations (because they are the most general) of objective validity brought upon the sensorial given are therefore *constraint* and *nature*. Both intervene together in the sphere of external sensations, where they establish the judgment brought upon the reality of external things, and in the sphere of internal sensations, where they establish the judgment brought upon the union of my soul with a body. Moreover, even though they are distinct from one another, since nature is the instinct or inclination that leads me almost invincibly, because of sensation, to bring this or that judgment of objective validity, and since constraint is one of these sensations upon which my inclination to judgment rests, they belong both to the same sphere because they are *sensed*, meaning *experienced*. In this respect, they are both opposed to will, since inclination or nature enters into conflict with it as does constraint.[20] Furthermore, that is why we can attempt to ruin the objective meaning of constraint by reducing it to the constraint that inclination exercises on will: it is sufficient to conceive that the sensation of constraint can arise in us from an unconscious power to produce sensible ideas, capable of opposing themselves to my will in the same way as inclination.[21]

Since it is the argument of choice in favor of the externality of material things to myself, constraint can be invoked alone in order to attest to the existence of bodies—that is the case, for example, in the *Principles,* or in the letter to Hyperaspistes of August 1641.[22] Constraint is, in this case, a perfectly sufficient criterion that provides, in some way, its content for the quasi-invincible inclination that is referred to it, meaning to nature; inclination (or nature) is, in fact, merely the irresistible tendency to subscribe to that which constraint imposes on us. With respect to proving the substantial union of soul and body, constraint, as we have seen, is an insufficient criterion. It simply certifies that something identified with myself, like pain, for example, must not be explained only by myself, but also by the action on me of something that is foreign to me. Thus it is incapable of testifying to the substantiality of this union. This substantiality can only be taught to me by "nature."

Therefore, we understand that Descartes, in spite of the generality of the two criteria, favors constraint among the criteria of the existence of material things, and nature among the criteria of the substantial union of soul and body.

3) *However, these judgments can be rejected.*[23]

In fact, we were able to invoke positive reasons for doubt against them, and also to establish the insufficiency of the positive reasons that argue for them.

The positive reasons to place them into doubt are of two orders: a specific order resting on the errors of the senses relative to things (errors with respect to the magnitude, form, and distance of objects, etc.), as well as on myself (illusions of amputees, deliriums, pathological problems, etc.),[24] and a general order leading to the most hyperbolic doubts, one founded on the illusion of dreams and another on the hypothesis of the evil genius.[25]

The positive reasons to accept them seem insufficient. Descartes limits himself to criticizing the two main ones: nature and constraint;[26] he goes more quickly over them than he did in *Meditation III.* We note that nature leads us to many things from which reason rightly deters us. In fact, we have observed in *Meditation III* that nature leads us to the bad as well as to the good; it can therefore lead us to the false as to the true. It has no relation with the natural light that teaches us the truth. As for the constraint exercised on us by sensible ideas, this proves nothing more than that they are caused by external things, since an unknown faculty in me could just as well be producing them.[27] This is an objection that *Meditation III* upheld by means of two arguments: i) the inclinations that come from me are often in disagreement with my will; ii) sensible ideas seem to be imposed on me in dream, and yet they come from me.[28]

The refutation of the three first reasons supporting the judgments about the union of soul and body is virtually contained in the refutation of the reason derived from nature.

Descartes does not bother to refute the second reason, dealing with judgments about the existence of external bodies (vivacity and expressive character of sensation). No doubt he believes that the objective appearance of dreams implicitly contains this refutation. He neglects to relate, with respect to the third reason (the reason to affirm the similarity of our ideas with things), the critique that he had constructed in *Meditation III,* that established the dissimilarity between the two ideas we have of the sun as sensible sun and as astronomical sun.[29]

4) *Definitive determination of the nature, degree, and limits of the objective validity of sensation.*

Descartes announces that, because of his possession of the two fundamental truths that he has now acquired, namely knowledge of his soul and of the veracious God, author of his origin, he will be able to resolve the problem of the objective validity of the senses by *a reciprocal limitation* of the affirmations ventured by our primitive judgments and the generalized doubt that later struck at them radically: "I do not think in truth that I ought rashly *to admit everything* that the senses seem to teach us, but on the other hand, I do not think that I should *doubt them in general.*"[30]

3. The Primary Importance of the Fourth Part: The Determination of the Nature, Degree, and Limits of the Objective Validity of Sensation. The Three Stages of This Determination: Proof of the Distinction of Soul and Body, Proof of the Existence of Bodies, Proof of the Union of Soul and Body. The Dissociation of the Characteristics of Sensation and the Distinction between the Two Proofs. The Role of Divine Veracity

The purpose of the first three points was to recall and to reunite the givens of the problem. The fourth brings forth its solution. It constitutes the core of *Meditation VI.*

The Cartesian demonstration is very strict and rigorously follows the order of reasons. It has three stages.

The first stage is devoted entirely to the demonstration of the real separation of the substances, soul and body. It uses the results of *Meditation II:* the science of the nature of my soul as pure thought, of the nature of my body as pure extension, and of the distinction between substances and between modes and substances. The core of the demonstration consists in validating as a necessary truth of things what until *Meditation II* was only a necessary truth for my understanding. Divine veracity constitutes, in this case, the *nervus probandi,* as the immediate guarantee of the essential objective validity of clear and distinct ideas.

The second is devoted to the demonstration of the existence of material things. It presupposes the preceding proof, because it is not possible to prove that bodies exist outside me if we are not first certain that bodies have a nature alien to my soul, and that consequently they are able to act as an external cause capable of accounting for constraints on me. This second proof, which is intended to establish the objective validity of sensible ideas, unfolds within a framework similar to that of *Meditation III,* which also sought to discover some idea such that we were necessarily required to recognize its objective validity. However, the criterion of this necessity will not here be the quantity of objective reality in the idea (even though the presence of such a reality in the idea would allow the affirmation of the existence of a formal reality as cause), but the two characteristics proper to sensible perception—the sensible constraint and the invincible inclination tied to it, which leads us to recognize body as its cause. The former testifies to the action of an external but indeterminate cause; the latter allows its determination by assigning it to an existing body, to the exclusion of all other things: it thus specifies the meaning of the objective validity that accrues to sensible idea. Divine veracity also intervenes here as *nervus probandi.* But it does not merely guarantee the elements of the proof that arise from clear and distinct ideas; it also guarantees the criteria drawn from the two characteristics of sensation (constraint and inclination). Yet the intervention of divine veracity, in this case, is not gratuitous, but *necessary.* Indeed, divine veracity immediately guarantees the truth that our pure mind necessarily gives to clear and distinct ideas because of its nature. And since our intelligence holds obscure and confused ideas as false, divine veracity must guarantee that intelligence is right when recognizing them as false. However, divine veracity is universal and everything that is real is true. Since obscure and confused ideas (sensations) are real, as little reality as they may have, they must be true to the extent that they are real, and divine veracity *must* guarantee their truth. Thus divine veracity must concurrently guarantee the falsity that intelligence attributes to obscure and confused ideas, and the truth that sensation ("nature") recognizes in them. The problem cannot be resolved unless the truth guaranteed to intelligence and to sensation are two different *truths,* each true in their own domain, insofar as intelligence and sensation constitute two different *realities.* As a result, it will be necessarily true that, at least in this respect, what is false in the domain of intelligence (essences) could be true in the domain of sensation (existences), what is true for intelligence could be false if it is referred to the things of sensation, and that, if what is obscure and confused can trouble the exercise of intelligence, the understanding can also trouble sensation—"nature"—by perverting it. Divine veracity guarantees to each of these two kinds of ideas a truth appropriate to its nature and its sphere, at the same time that it denounces and testifies in some way to the falsity that results for each from their reciprocal usurpations. It is entitled to enter into a duel against the general doubt that hovers about the senses in virtue of the undeniable errors of which it is the cause; and it receives the confirmation due to it from the very fact that it succeeds in having us discover in sensation, by guaranteeing it, the objective validity appropriate for its sphere and proper to the quantity of objective reality of its content; this validity is its ability to allow us to know the existence of bodies.

The prior proof concerning the distinction of soul and body had as result the rejection of sensation as outside any valid knowledge concerning the real properties of bodies. It thus founded the purely mathematical character of physics, but it was negative with respect to sensible knowledge, which was simply condemned as improper. The proof of the existence of bodies is not satisfied with this negative conclusion. Considering sensation in itself, it discovers that it has a positive function, that of procuring the knowledge of existing material bodies. Thus it can give to experience a role in physics, insofar as physics does not reduce to the study of body in general, as does speculative geometry, but is defined by the study of particular existing bodies.

The third stage is devoted to the proof of the substantial union of soul and body.

In opposition to what has occurred until now, the problem of the existence of external bodies and that of the union of soul and body will be treated as distinctly separate as the problem of the distinction of soul and body was from that of the existence of body. In the first part of *Meditation VI,* at the moment when, by means of the examination of imagination, we were able to posit the probability of the existence of bodies, external body was given to me only as united to my soul. In the enumeration of reasons that establish the natural judgments with respect to the senses, the distinction between the reasons for affirming the existence of body and the reasons for affirming its union with my soul was doubtless almost accomplished, but as yet only approximately. During this third stage, on the contrary, Descartes dissociates in sensation the element referred properly to the externality of body from the one referring to the union of soul and body, and he is led to isolate the question of the substantial union from the question of the existence of body, in the same way that he isolated the latter from the question of the real distinction between mind and extension. In this way the complete dissociation of the proof of union and the proof of distinction is accomplished. And this dissociation is indispensable, because without it, one runs the risk of hiding the distinction, since the union, conceived without the prior knowledge of the distinction, is incapable of revealing its dual character of substantial and composite. And this dissociation is itself possible only through a strict discernment of the respective criteria that found these various proofs.

We have already introduced the consideration of internal sensations to this problem of union. They testify immediately to such a union by teaching us something that is in some way self-sufficient: affective constraint, the character that they possess in common with external sensations, simply attests to the externality of that which I sense I am united to. But the problem is considered, in this case, with an amplitude that much surpasses the simple preoccupation with determining the degree of objective validity it is suitable to recognize with respect to the teaching of internal sensation. In fact, it is posited from the general character that renders specific all sensible ideas in contrast to the ideas of the understanding, namely the qualitative—in brief, the obscurity, confusion, and the set of errors that flow from it. That is why it is expressly linked to the conclusions of the second proof and governed by them. This conclusion is that sensation, which is capable of certifying the existence of bodies, and the varieties of existing bodies because of their qualitative variations, deceives us with respect to their nature because of its intrinsic obscurity and confusion. And in some respects, this conclusion contradicts God's own veracity.[31] How could a veracious God have put into sensation, in addition to the constraint and natural inclination that are indispensable for allowing us to know the truth relative to the existence of material things, the quality of obscurity and confusion, meaning the quality that would be valuable only for deceiving us about the true nature of these things? In opposition to what has been discussed until now, divine veracity is not simply called on to guarantee what truth there can be in the objective reality—however small it is—of an idea, but it intervenes directly in order to govern an inquiry intended to allow God's vindication; toward this end it discovers a certain utility for an element which is not an objective reality, but which is the seemingly purely aberrant aspect of an idea capable of possessing some objective validity by another means. The aspect that is added onto the small content of the idea is the *qualitative* aspect.

This third proof will no longer unfold in the manner of the preceding proof according to the plan of *Meditation III,* which was simply intended to discover the objective validity of ideas, but according to the plan of *Meditation IV,* which was devoted to the solution of the problem of error, governed entirely by the universal requirement of the truth flowing from God's veracity. Consequently, we will have to explain the origin of this qualitative aspect—that is, of obscurity and confusion as such—and to explain it in such a way that neither God's veracity nor his goodness is compromised, nor is his responsibility directly involved in the errors at issue. We will have to justify quality—at least a certain part of it—in its intrinsic truth, as belonging to the truth that accrues necessarily to everything real in this world, by discovering in quality some useful function that will be a substitute for objective validity. The substantial union will bring forth the complete solution of this problem: first it will allow the explanation of the nature of this qualitative aspect, since obscurity and confusion are the immediate results of this union; then it will allow one to found the truth of the qualitative aspect by revealing its dual function, which is to teach us about this union, and to bring us information necessary for the maintenance of its integrity.

Obscurity and confusion are therefore false—meaning entirely devoid of objective validity—only under a certain relation, that is, relative to the essential nature of things, which only clear and distinct ideas lead us to know. They are completely true under another aspect, that is, with respect to what, among existing bodies, is useful or harmful to our own body and consequently to our composite nature. As in *Meditation IV,* the scientific explanation of the phenomenon will satisfy the metaphysical requirements of God's veracity. God has not deceived us by putting the obscurity and confusion of the qualitative into us; this obscurity and confusion in itself is not deceptive, and in its proper domain, it fulfills a useful informative function for which alone it is qualified.

Here, what receives a guarantee of truth from divine veracity is simply "nature" alone, as an instinct immediately linking the sensed quality with an objective significance of biological value relative to my body. Thus the proof could not be accomplished without the complete elucidation of the concept of "nature." At the same time we see that the role of divine veracity as *nervus probandi* grows in importance as we go from the first to the third proof.

The result of the two latter proofs will be to fix precisely the limits of the objective validity of sensation and to distinguish each of the two kinds of objective validity that accrues separately to each of its two fundamental characteristics: constraint, on the one hand, and obscurity and confusion, on the other. First, the general objective validity of sensation will be strictly limited to the realm of *my composite nature.* Then, within this realm, its validity will appear as twofold: i) by its degree of objective reality and by the constraint that sensation refers to the existence of bodies; ii) by the qualitative—the obscure and confused—that it refers to the whole of my composite nature and to the relations of advantage and disadvantage between this whole and external bodies. Finally the three proofs link up with one another according to the analytic order of reasons: the proof of distinction is a condition of the proof of existence, and the proof of existence is a condition of the proof of union, without any reciprocity or entanglement. To change the order of the proofs is to mix up the order of reasons and to prevent oneself from grasping the force of their demonstration.

CHAPTER XIII

Proof of the Real Distinction between Soul and Body

1. The First Part of the Proof

Meditation VI involves, in one and the same demonstration, the three proofs about body. That is because they all have the same goal: to establish and determine the objective validity of sensible ideas. We have seen Descartes trace in advance the framework of the solution: to limit the doubts against sensation while limiting the claims of the judgments that give rise to doubt. The proofs of the existence of material things and of the union of my soul with a body will reduce doubts by conferring a measure of validity to sensation. The proof of the real distinction between soul and body, although it is the indispensable condition for the two other proofs, will reduce the claims of judgment about the senses, by limiting its validity to an extremely narrow sphere.

This latter proof, which is the first in the order of reasons, has two parts. First it establishes the real distinction between the two substances,[1] and then it establishes the real distinction between the set of modes belonging respectively to the one and the other.[2] The demonstration rests exclusively upon clear and distinct ideas.

Knowing, in virtue of *Meditation III* (which has proven God and his veracity) that what is valid necessarily for my understanding—for my science—is valid necessarily for things, and knowing clearly and distinctly, in virtue of *Meditation II,* that the essence of the soul—thought—is necessarily conceived as complete, meaning as substance, and consequently independent of body, and that the essence of body—extension—is also conceived as substance and consequently independent of everything that is mind, I conclude necessarily that body and soul are in themselves completely and truly—meaning *really*—two separate substances. Consequently, whatever the vicissitudes of their existence and even if, in existence, they are presented to me as united, I know that this union could not change the real irreducibility and independence of their essences, and that God, who could have effectively united them in existence by means of his omnipotence, could also separate them by means of the same omnipotence and allow them to exist separately without anything in their nature being altered by this.[3]

We could not object that soul and body are united by nature, given that they are united naturally, in fact, by the ordinary power of God, although their separation would not be natural, requiring the extraordinary power of God. In fact, we would be giving the word *natural* the sense of *ordinary* or *habitual,* which is not the sense of *essential;* and moreover, we ought to note that the omnipotence that has united them can be divine or not, and if it is divine, it can be ordinary or extraordinary, without anything being changed in this way for the respective natures of the two substances. They are not rendered in this way either more or less independent in themselves, whatever is their union or separation in existence. Thus "no matter what power produces this separation, we are compelled to judge them different."[4] Since soul and body are by their essences two really separate substances they are also necessarily separable in fact and in existence: any power whatsoever can separate them, if they are united in fact, as long as we conceive it to be sufficient, meaning that it is at least equal to the power that has united them. Consequently, God's omnipotence can be sufficient, whether it is ordinary or extraordinary; and it would not matter to the question if this omnipotence were not God's omnipotence.

In order to understand this proof fully, it would be useful to present it from another perspective. If we consider our experience, soul and body appear to us as united naturally, in fact; that is why a man taken by the life of the senses is without fail led to think that they are but one and the same noncomposite nature, and that their real separation is impossible.[5] But it would be truly impossible only if we conceive them clearly and distinctly as being one and the same noncomposite substance. And, on the contrary, our understanding conceives them as two substances excluding themselves in an absolute manner. Therefore, in opposition to the facts, we ought to consider that the two substances are really distinct. And since they are essentially distinct, we ought to conceive that, in fact, they remain, within the existence in which they are united, in spite of this union, irreducible in their nature, and that they could easily be separated and exist one without the other. It would even be contradictory for them to be inseparable.[6] Since this possibility of separation belongs to the (eternal) truths of our under-standing, it could not be excluded unless it were contradictory with God's omnipotence. But we are assured that God can always do what we conceive clearly and distinctly—to deny this proposition would be to limit his omnipotence arbitrarily. Therefore, although they are united in fact, body and soul could be separated in fact, and could in fact exist separately from one another. Thus, having established as an eternal truth the real separation of the substances soul and body, we can establish, by means of God's omnipotence, that the fact of their substantial union in existence does not prove anything against their real separation, since God could, in fact, create them as separate existences.[7]

Thus we see that the proof of the real distinction, established solely by means of clear and distinct ideas, can only be established *against sensation,* that is, against an existing fact certified by the senses. That is why Descartes presents the conclusion of his proof in opposition with the certainty of the union: "And although perhaps (or rather certainly, as I will soon show) I have a body with which I am very closely united, nevertheless, it is certain that I, that is, my soul . . . is completely and truly distinct from my body, and that it can exist without my body."[8]

2. The Necessity to Establish the Proof in Spite of the Fact of Union; a Consequence of This for the Structure of the Proof. Appeal to God's Omnipotence

It is necessary for the proof of distinction to be established against the fact of union, for this determines its structure (meaning the appeal to God's omnipotence). If sensation did not first reveal to us the fact of the union of soul and body, this appeal would be useless in persuading us of their separability, for nothing would contradict the natural necessities of my understanding. But the contradiction of this fact with these necessities requires me, in order to do justice to them, to refer to God's omnipotence, which we know to be capable of undoing what it has done, when what has been thus done is in opposition with these necessities. Let us take, in contrast, the case of an evident proposition of the understanding that is never contradicted by experience, for example, that the sum of the angles of a triangle is equal to two right angles; it is sufficient that we perceive it clearly and distinctly for the objective validity of this property with respect to all possible existence to be posited immediately in all certainty. Since geometry does not have to validate this proposition in spite of an experience that appears to be contrary to it, it does not need to invoke divine omnipotence for it. Moreover, no one would be able to invoke divine omnipotence against it in order to contest that the truths it demonstrates are, in all certainty, applicable a priori to experience, under the pretext that God could, by means of his omnipotence, create existing triangles in the world that would violate these truths for "we do not take it as a mark of impotency when someone cannot do what we do not comprehend to be impossible, but only when he cannot do something we conceive clearly to be possible."[9] There would not therefore be sufficient reason for the hypothesis, even though we know that God's omnipotence, which has created eternal truths, is not tied by their necessity. But there is a reason that speaks against it. Since God's will is immutable and God is veracious, we are certain, in fact, that existing things cannot not always verify eternal truths. If God had decided to make an exception, as in the case of the union of soul and body, he would have given us, from all time, an irreducible evidence that would have constituted a sufficient reason to accept it. Finally, we ought to note that if God, by means of his omnipotence, can create in existence some fact that is repugnant to eternal truths, he cannot, in this way, abolish them, because his will would then be intrinsically contradictory, and would cease to be immutable and perfect. These truths therefore preserve their validity eternally in spite of this fact. Thus, God can easily unite in existence two substances that are eternally repugnant to this union, so as to make a composite nature, but he could not make of them a single thing in essence, without any composition.[10]

This reasoning, which appeals to the original conception that Descartes constructs about possibility, can be better understood if we evoke the inverse case as contrast to the proof of the distinction of soul and body: the proof of the union. In this proof we will be concerned to establish in existence the reality of a fact emanating from God's omnipotence, which contradicts what my understanding judges necessarily to be the only possible thing in existence. For, since the distinction between soul and body is an eternal truth, soul and body ought effectively to be separated in existence. Ought I deny the fact of their substantial union in virtue of its incomprehensibility by having recourse to the *principle of common measure,* which excludes all relation, and a fortiori all fusion, between two radically disparate realities (as do Gassendi, Spinoza, Malebranche, Leibniz, Berkeley, etc.)? Not if the fact is truly indubitable; for I know that divine omnipotence is not limited to the necessities of my finite understanding. Moreover, even though this belies an eternal truth, in fact, God does not deceive us, since he has taken care to place our understanding, from all time, before an absolutely indubitable evidence of this union, under the form of a sensation, and since he has given to our understanding the means to be assured of the veridical nature of this evidence. God's omnipotence can be legitimately invoked here against the requirements of eternal truth, since God has given us sufficient reason for this recourse by putting sensation in us, and by conferring on my understanding the capacity to recognize that in this case, this sensation states the truth.

Thus in the two cases, whether we invoke God's omnipotence in order to confirm the eternal truth before a fact belying it, or whether we invoke it in order to accept against this eternal truth the reality of a fact that violates it, we have a sufficient reason that justifies this recourse—from which it derives its efficacy. In the former case, the sufficient reason is the imprescriptible character of eternal truth, such as natural light reveals it to our understanding; because of this character, we are assured that God is always capable of realizing what our understanding conceives as possible, in spite of the fact that the contrary can exist in fact. In the latter case, the sufficient reason is a certain evidence (no doubt extra-rational) but whose validity is capable of being recognized by our very reason; in this way we are warned in all certainty that God has used his omnipotence in order to realize in fact, in things, an exception with respect to these necessities that our understanding judges inviolable. And the mysteries essential to religion enter in this latter case.[11] But God's omnipotence does not allow us to invoke it in order to contest without reason and at our whim the rules of possibility inscribed from all eternity in our understanding. Thus, God's veracity, joined to his immutability—which is itself founded in his omnipotence—prevents this omnipotence from introducing any degree of anarchy within the world without the rational rule being able to impose a limit to this omnipotence, in some small degree, in return. Thus is explained that omnipotence can, without contradiction, serve in two contrary ways, in the proof of distinction and in the proof of union: i) it serves to maintain the truth of essence against the truth of existence, the rule as against the fact, relative to what the understanding conceives as necessary and alone possible in fact; ii) it serves to confirm a fact and a truth of existence, against the rule and the truth of essence, relative to what sensation reveals to us as real. In addition, since divine veracity, which guarantees the indubitability of the ideas of the understanding and of the senses within their respective sphere, is known solely by reason, and since it belongs to reason alone to recognize the claims and divine origin of sensation, reason still remains the supreme authority. Thus God puts us in the presence of two revelations differing in nature—that of the understanding and that of the senses—without having the sovereignty of natural light, which is partially belied by the senses, ever threatened by this.

The fact that the proof of distinction cannot be accomplished except against the evidence of the senses allows us to perceive that the proof would limit the claims of the senses. But we can also foresee that the senses, bringing forth the certainty of a fact that contradicts the immediate necessities of the understanding, will have to constrain the understanding to limit its prerogatives relative to the zone reserved for the prerogatives of the senses.[12]

3. Independence of This Proof from the Proof That Follows. Refutation of the First Part of a "Paradox" Attributed to Descartes

We also see that the proof of the real distinction of soul and body is completely accomplished without having the least recourse to the demonstration of the existence of bodies. If it were not thus, and if the proof of existence implied the proof of the union of my soul to a body, we would have to conclude that Descartes is actually basing his proof of distinction on the proof of union. There would thus be interdependence and confusion between the three proofs. That is what Gilson has called the "Cartesian paradox."[13] But it seems to us that this paradox, which in truth would be a most devastating paralogism, is completely foreign to Descartes.

We must first note that the principle of this interpretation rests on the identification of *real* and *existing*.[14] And the word *real* is not used by Descartes, in this case, in the sense of *existing*. What Descartes is concerned about is the reality of substances—whether existing or not— and the reality of their distinction, and it is sufficient to prove that body and soul are substances in order that their real distinction be established ipso facto. "Substances that can exist one without the other are really distinct by definition X," writes Descartes in the Geometrical Summary. "And mind and body are substances . . . ; therefore mind and body are really distinct."[15] Thus, it is perfectly useless, in order to prove that substances are really separate, to prove that they exist; but it is necessary and sufficient to prove that they are substances (that is, that we can think of one without the other), and to establish the existence of a veracious God, to be assured of the objective validity of what we think. Finally, in the presence of the fact of the union of substances, we will have to maintain their rigorous separation of nature, which is in no way altered by their contingent composition in existence, since God's omnipotence could, at any instant, put an end to the latter, in conformity with the imprescriptible and always objectively valid necessities of the ideas of our understanding.

If Descartes defers the proof of the real distinction of body and soul until *Meditation VI,* that is not because it could not be completed without establishing the existence of bodies, but only because all the elements necessary to the proof (namely, God's veracity and omnipotence, and the objective validity of clear and distinct ideas) are gathered only after *Meditation V.*[16] We have seen that Descartes expressly formulates the conclusion that the soul and body are really separate before attempting the proof for the existence of bodies. Moreover, once the latter is accomplished, we never see him state (neither in the *Meditations* nor in the other works) that now that the existence of bodies is proven, their real separation with the soul will finally be demonstrated.[17]

We should note (and this is the ultimate argument for Gilson's thesis) that the real distinction between substances does not allow one to base the real distinction between *existing* substances unless these substances exist. If body did not exist, it would not differ from soul in existence. The proof of the existence of body is therefore necessary in order to complete the proof of the distinction of soul and body, which otherwise would remain only possible without ever becoming real in the sense of *existing*. Gilson notes that "[God's—M. G.] veracity supposes in fact that the real distinction of things does not depend on the fact that they are separated or united in experience, but only that, as a rule, their ideas are distinctly separable or not. Whether or not there is a body, or whether or not my soul is united to my body, it remains that the essence of soul is really distinct from the essence of body."[18] One cannot state this better. But Gilson adds: "Therefore, the distinction as rule is complete, and the distinction of fact is possible." In Gilson's mind, this means that the latter proposition is doubtful. But this conclusion is illegitimate. For Descartes, the distinction is completely established as a rule, which means that it could not be placed into doubt *as a fact* by any fact whatsoever. Therefore, if we could not establish that body exists, this existence would remain doubtful, of course, but the real distinction between soul and body would not become doubtful, and would not remain merely *possible,* but *necessary and certain:* existing souls would not remain any less separated *in fact* from everything belonging to body, whether body exists or not. "We attain only a possible creator in God himself," adds Gilson, "and the real distinction of soul and body remains in some way merely possible."[19] That is an obvious remark; but we cannot conclude from it that, if the existence of body could not be proven, the real distinction of body and soul would remain doubtful in fact—which would require Descartes to "need" the proof of the existence of body in order finally to obtain the definitive certainty of this distinction.

The cause of this misreading is easy to find. To suppose that the existence of body must be demonstrated in order that we may stop having doubts about such a separation in fact, is to confuse *the relation of essence and existence with the relations of essence and its properties.* Of course, essence is a possible: its relation with existence is consequently merely possible and this existence is a priori doubtful,[20] but the properties belonging necessarily to essence are in themselves necessary and indubitable for this essence, and consequently, they are ipso facto necessary and indubitable for the very existence (or for *the fact*) that essence designates as possible—whether this existence itself (this fact) is doubtful, possible, probable, or certain.[21] Descartes writes: "Even though we do not yet know certainly whether such a thing [corporeal substance—M. G.] *exists* in the world, nevertheless, because we have an idea of it, we can conclude that it *can exist,* and that in case it does exist, some part that we can determine about thought *must be really distinct* from its other parts."[22] The expression *can exist* concerns existence, which is problematic; the expression *must be* concerns the property of essence, which accrues *necessarily* to existence (which is also problematic) and is apodictic. Thus Descartes means: we now know in all certainty that in the case in which the substance exists, we would find in its existence the necessary and certain properties of its essence, namely, its real separation with respect to any other substance. But Gilson understands: only if substance happens to exist will the real separation of substance become certain in existence—although it was certain and necessary from the point of view of essence, it will remain doubtful from the point of view of existence. But such an interpretation goes against the geometer. Thus the existing triangle is only simply possible with respect to its essence: *it can exist;* but that the sum of its angles is equal to two right angles is a necessary property that *must exist,* meaning that we have to affirm it in all certainty of any existing triangle, from now on, if it ever existed, and even if actually, this factual existence is in itself, only doubtful, possible, probable, or impossible to establish. It is the same for body. Its existence is merely possible with respect to its essence, but since its real distinction with soul is a necessary property of this essence, *it must necessarily be a property of its existence, even if this existence remains doubtful.* It is therefore, from now on, not merely possible or probable, but indubitable. The impossibility to prove the existence of bodies does not subtract anything from its certainty, and the possibility to prove it does not add anything to it. On the other hand, the existence of body can be doubtful, possible, probable, or certain, according to the reasons that one could invoke about it. As a result, we could not say with Gilson that "the real distinction of soul and body would be only probable   .   .   . a conclusion at which we would arrive if we considered the case of imagination . . ." as long as we could not explain "the confused element of thought,"[23] lacking the substantial union. On the contrary, such a failure would leave the real distinction between the two substances necessary and certain. Moreover, the recourse to imagination has never served to prove the probability of the real distinction of soul and body, but only the probability of the existence of body—no more than the consideration of the idea of the essence of material things, which intervenes just before that of imagination in order to prove the possibility of the existence of these things, ever serves to prove the possibility of the distinction of body and soul. On the other hand, the recourse to this same idea allows one to establish *the necessity* of this distinction. In brief, Descartes has never applied the hierarchy of the possible, probable, and certain, which defines the main demonstrative stages of *Meditation VI,* to the proof of the distinction of soul and body, but only to the proof of the existence of body, and subsidiarily to its union with soul. And, in fact, we can ask ourselves whether the existence of a triangle in nature is doubtful, probable, or certain, whereas such a question could not be asked, for example, about the property of its angles, which will always remain, for anyone, necessary and certain. We do not add anything to the certainty of a triangle's necessary properties by discovering its existence; we do not add anything to the certainty of the body's property of being really distinct from soul (a certainty that becomes neither more nor less indubitable and necessary) by discovering the existence of body.

Of course we could be tempted to affirm that, in order for a triangular thing to have the sum of its angles equal to two right angles it is first necessary for this thing to exist. However, if it stopped existing, we would not say that it lost this property, nor that it stopped being triangular, but only that it stopped existing. And if this thing remains always merely possible, without our being able to say whether it will exist, we would not say that the property of its angles to be equal to two right angles is itself only possible and doubtful, and that consequently the geometer "needs" to demonstrate that the triangular thing exists in order to end his doubt and to establish that the property of this thing is not merely possible, but real.

Gilson adds, "the distinction of fact becomes real and completed once Descartes eliminates all the conceivable causes of the involuntary character of our sensations, except bodies themselves,"[24] which means that, if this enterprise failed, the factual distinction between body and soul would become doubtful. This is a conclusion that Descartes rightly and forcefully would have rejected. If our sensations were not caused by bodies, and if we could not establish the certain existence of bodies by means of them, only this existence would remain doubtful, and not the separation of soul and body, which would remain as certain as the equality of a triangle's angles with two right angles would remain for the triangle, in the case in which no triangle existed in nature. And if the certainty of the existence of body were given to us by another means, without the existing body being perceived as the cause of our sensations, we would be, in this case as in the other, just as certain that this existing body is really separate from our existing soul, since the properties of essence must necessarily be valid for existence. Thus we ought to conclude, as we have already indicated, that, if the existence of body could not be proven, physics would lose its existential character, and it would be difficult to differentiate it from "speculative geometry," but that it would not lose its geometrical character. Even if we denied that sensation is really caused by body, or that matter existed, there would result no gain from this for the physics of substantial forms (that is what the examples of Malebranche and Berkeley certify).

That the proof of the distinction of soul and body must precede the existence of bodies in the order of reasons is a necessity under many relations. In fact, only clear and distinct ideas can certify the reality of substances upon which existences depend. Moreover, in order to prove the existence of bodies by means of a foreign cause operating on us, it is necessary to establish that body is a reality foreign to us—which only the clear and distinct idea of the separation of substances, and not the sensation of the existence of bodies, can allow. The proof of this existence is therefore impossible without the proof of distinction. On the other hand, the proof of distinction owes nothing to the proof of existence and is established against the sensation of this existence. In fact, we are conjointly conscious of the existence of bodies and the union of my soul to a body by means of this sensation; if we started from sensation alone, it seems that we could never attain the conception of their distinction. Sensation "impedes" the knowledge of distinction, as we know. Instead of revealing it to us, sensation excludes it.[25] That is why common men, Scholastics, and generally all those who rely exclusively on the senses, starting from the existence of bodies such as it is given to them by sensation, cannot conceive that body is really separate from soul, and inevitably settle in a physics of substantial forms, although compromising the belief in the immortality of the soul. But the conclusion from being to knowledge is not valid. The true nature of things is revealed to us only by clear and distinct ideas. And if sensation and experience are necessary to certify definitively the existence of material things, their testimony has no weight and cannot be included as truth unless it is first qualified and determined in its limits and proper function by the understanding. Thus, the proof of the distinction of body and soul, a condition of the two following proofs use sensation and experience, begins by anticipating the conclusion to which sensation would lead if it were left alone. That is why, with respect to sensation, the principle of the limitation of its claims is established before the principle of the limitation of the doubts that it raises.

4. The Second Part of the Proof

The second part of the proof consists in distinguishing the modes of each substance, by means of their contingency with respect to the substance, and then separating the set of modes of one substance from the set of modes belonging to the other, as strictly as the substances themselves are separated among themselves.[26] These relations between substance and modes, clearly and distinctly established by *Meditation II,* receive their full objective validity here, by means of divine veracity. By means of this radical distinction, as much from their substance as from their respective modes, the complete separation of mind and body is established, and we can certify that nothing belonging to body belongs to mind, and vice versa. As an immediate result, substantial forms are abolished in the world of bodies.

This second part of the proof already introduces the proofs that follow. In fact, the description of thinking substance and its modes, on the one hand, and that of extended substance and its modes, on the other hand, converge toward the positing of the faculty of sensation considered no longer as merely a mode of the soul, meaning as "including some intellection," but as including in itself something "that does not presuppose my thought."[27] We rediscover here this intermediary that *Meditation II* has revealed to us, which on the one hand appears as attributable to the soul and excluded from body, and on the other hand is referred to body insofar as it contains something contradictory with intelligence. In brief, what is posited here before the nature of mind alone and the nature of extension alone is sensation insofar as it is the expression of *my composite nature.* And this set of three natures constitutes *human nature* in the broad sense, in opposition to *my nature,* in the narrow sense, meaning in opposition to this composite nature of which sensation is the immediate expression, and which is only one part of my total human nature.

CHAPTER XIV

Proof of the Existence of Material Things

1. The Premises and the Object of the Proof

As we have seen, the second part of the proof of the real distinction posits the premises of the proof of the existence of material things: i) thinking substance with all its modes and extended substance with all its modes are posited as completely foreign to one another—both are elements of an assemblage that, together with the composite substance, constitutes my nature in general; ii) sensation, which is first posited as a mode of the soul, is then perceived as enclosing something foreign to it and implying a cause that does not involve my thought.[1]

We are now concerned with determining what this cause is and whether it is body. Such is the object of the proof. If the proof succeeds—if sensation proceeds from bodies—then body exists. It will therefore become possible to seek in what consists sensation, which arises both from soul and body, and to ask how this double appearance is admissible, given that body has nothing in common with soul. The proof of the substantial union of my soul with a body—my body—will intervene at this point.

2. Statement of the Proof

Considering myself, I discover a mode of my substance, namely, the faculty of sensing, a passive faculty for receiving ideas. It implies an active faculty for producing them. This active faculty can be either in me or outside me. This active faculty cannot be in me, because it does not imply my thought, and because these ideas are given to me without my consent—they involve a constraint.[2]

The faculty is therefore necessarily outside of me, in a substance different from me, which must possess a formal reality equal to or higher than the objective reality of these ideas. If this formal reality is equal, the cause will be formal, and it will be the body. If this formal reality is higher, the cause will be eminent, and it will be God, or some other creature nobler than the body.[3]

But God has given me an extremely strong inclination to believe that these sensible ideas arise from corporeal things, although he has given me no faculty to know that they arise from him or from a substance nobler than the body. And God is not a deceiver. Consequently, corporeal things are the cause of these sensible ideas; therefore corporeal things exist.[4]

3. The Eight Elements of the Proof

We can break up the proof into eight elements.

The first element is the realization that there is a mode of thought in me that consists in "sensation." The character of this mode is to be revealed immediately to consciousness as passive. In fact, we have to distinguish between the passivity that is the real characteristic of all knowledge (even intellectual knowledge[5]) and the special passivity of sensation. The latter is the immediate object of spontaneous consciousness— in brief, a phenomenon for the natural consciousness of any man. On the other hand, the passivity of my intelligence in the knowledge of clear and distinct ideas, or in that of will, is not the object of spontaneous consciousness, but of a philosophical consciousness, which is reflective and acquired. Moreover, it is not merely experienced, as is the consciousness of passivity in sensation, but it is clearly and distinctly known. It is because the passivity of the understanding is not the object of natural spontaneous consciousness that the term "passion" is reserved by Descartes for all that concerns the impressions received by the soul from the fact of the modifications that occur in the brain to which it is united, for only these impressions are known immediately (meaning here, sensed or experienced) as passive.[6]

In this way the classification of ideas as *innate, adventitious,* and *artificial,* as given by Descartes in *Meditation III,* is confirmed at the level of common consciousness. In fact, this classification rests on the natural and spontaneous consciousness according to which innate ideas appear to me as such because "it seems to me that I do not derive this [the faculty of conceiving them—M. G.] from anything but my own nature"[7] and according to which adventitious ideas "seem alien to me and coming from outside . . . like a foreign thing sending and looking up their image in me."[8] Thus spontaneous activity does not account for the passivity of innate ideas, which arise from my own nature only because a being alien to myself (God) has impressed them on me from my birth, nor does it account for the innateness of the constitutive elements of sensible ideas (called adventitious), which are present from my birth, that is, once my composite nature has been constituted. Only philosophical reflection allows the natural light to reveal these two characteristics of clear and distinct consciousness.

However there is a difference of nature between the passivity of the understanding, which is affected by clear and distinct ideas, and the passivity of the soul, which is affected by sensible ideas, a difference of nature that accounts for the different way in which they are perceived by consciousness. The former does not alter the substance of the soul, for the idea impressed on me, as well as its cause (God), are of the same nature as my soul— meaning they are spiritual in nature. That is why they do not give rise to any sensation in me; and it is also why clear and distinct ideas appear to me as "derived from my own nature." On the other hand, the passivity of sensation implies an alteration of the substance of the mind due to the fusion of the latter with a foreign nature, and the composite substance, which arises from this fusion, is radically different from my purely thinking substance. That is why this passion is *felt* by the soul as "involving the consciousness of something foreign to intellection."

Malebranche's doctrine is completely opposite with respect to this point. There is no difference of nature, but a difference of degree between the passion that the soul experiences in the representation of a clear and distinct idea, and the one it experiences in sensible perception: the two representations are each accompanied by a passion due to the action of the idea on the soul, a specifically affective passion, which is extremely weak in the first case and extremely strong in the second. The extremely strong affection that accompanies the sensible perception of an object does not suppose an alteration of the nature of the soul by its intermingling with corporeal nature. It is of the same nature as the extremely weak affection that the soul experiences in the representation of a clear and distinct idea.[9]

These differences derive from a different conception of the human mind, which, for Malebranche, is only pure affectivity, and which receives its modifications from the outside only by means of ideas that are foreign to it. The intensity of the modifications is a function of the force by which the idea acts on the soul, touches it, and penetrates it. Under these conditions, we conceive that sensation cannot provide any point of support for any proof of the existence of material things.

The second element is *the reciprocal implication of passion and action,* an Aristotelian category that Descartes reintegrates into our understanding, along with causality and other concepts, as an innate idea known immediately by means of natural light. But he transforms it completely. For him it is one of these "notions" that are so simple that they themselves do not allow us to know anything existing[10] and are thus subtracted from metaphysical doubt. And it is also a relation of identity. The bond that links action and passion is, in fact, based on the principle of contradiction. It is of the same order as the one linking the mountain and the valley, since passion and action are, in reality, only two different names for one and the same thing. "I have always thought that action and passion are one and the same thing for which we have two different names, according to whether it is referred to the term from which action arises *(terminus a quo)*, or the term at which it terminates *(terminus ad quem)* or in which it is received, such that it would be repugnant for there to be a passion without action during the least movement."[11]

The third element consists in the affirmation that the active productive faculty of my sensible ideas does not presuppose my thought. From this we ought to conclude that it cannot be in me "to the extent that I am only a thing that thinks."[12] Here the definition of thinking as consciousness intervenes. If this active faculty involved my thought, I would know it, since nothing can escape my consciousness in my thought.[13] Let us note that this active faculty is said to be excluded from my thought, and not from thought. However, Descartes does believe that it is foreign to all thought. In opposition to Gassendi's opinion, and against all the great rationalists of the seventeenth century and the empirical idealists of the eighteenth century—Malebranche, Spinoza, Leibniz, and Berkeley—he does not think that in order to act on a thought it is necessary that the acting power must itself be a thought—in brief, that "only an intelligence can act on an intelligence, a mind on a mind." The a priori rejection of this axiom (the axiom of common measure) constitutes, for Descartes, an indispensable condition for the success of his proof.[14]

The fourth element, which is actually only an explanation of the first (the passivity of my sensations), is constituted by the verification of a fact in me: the fact of *constraint*.[15] It alone allows me to give an application to the universal principle of the necessary linkage of action and passion, and to institute outside of me an *active cause* in order to account for the passion in me. The role of this fourth element is therefore of primary importance. Because of it, the productive faculty of sensible ideas is definitively rejected outside of me. Thus a first conclusion is posited: the active faculty is posited in *a substance that is different from me.*

The fifth element is constituted by the recall of the principle of causality defined according to the formula of *Meditation III*: there is necessarily a quantity of formal reality in the cause that is at least equal to the quantity of objective reality in the idea. We therefore reach a second conclusion: this activity foreign to myself must either be *God* or a *substance nobler than body,* in which case it is an eminent cause, or it must be *body itself,* in which case it is a formal cause.

The sixth element is constituted by the appeal to *nature,* meaning to the presence in us of an instinctive and irresistible inclination to believe that the cause is body. If this inclination is veracious, body exists; and that will be the third and final conclusion.

However, is this inclination veracious? Is the criterion of constraint valid? The appeal to the notion of action and passion, to the definition of consciousness, to the definition of causality, was an appeal to clear and distinct ideas, whose objective validity is both evident and guaranteed by God. Inclination, meaning *nature* and *constraint,* are not clear and distinct ideas. Their objective validity must be founded.

This function is assumed by the seventh element, namely divine veracity. But how could divine veracity be entitled to guarantee a natural inclination and a sensible constraint? In fact, it guarantees the truth of clear and distinct ideas, which thus furnish the norms for truth. And very often these ideas are opposed to the claims of inclinations and sensation. It therefore seems as if divine veracity cannot guarantee the former unless it denies its guarantee to the latter.

The eighth element resolves this problem by indicating under what precise conditions natural inclination can receive validly the guarantee of divine veracity: when God has not given me the means to reveal the error of my inclination, such that I am inevitably led by it to a false judgment, if it were effectively deceitful; in fact, God who is veracious, has not wished to constitute me such that I would be infallibly deceived by my nature. The inclination that leads me to judge that body is the cause of the constraint of sensation must respond to this condition, for God did not give me any faculty allowing me to know that it is false and that these ideas do not come from body. This inclination is therefore necessarily veracious. Thus the conclusion, "body exists, as cause of my sensations," is certain.

The eighth element, the veracity of an invincible inclination that nothing can denounce as false, constitutes the fundamental principle of all demonstration within the sphere of "nature," that is, the sphere of sensation. This principle will govern the demonstration of the union of soul and body; it will furnish the criterion allowing one to determine what authentically constitutes my "nature."

It alone allows one to eliminate the objection of Gassendi and Hyperaspistes[16]—an objection Descartes constructs for himself several times during *Meditations I* and *III*: cannot an unknown faculty of my soul produce sensations without my knowing it?—without having recourse to the definition of thought through consciousness; in fact, God would be deceiving us if, leaving us ignorant of this faculty, he puts us entirely at the mercy of a fallacious inclination. It also replies to the objection derived from the illusion of dreams, since God has given us through reason the means to place into evidence the deception of dreams before the truth of wakefulness. It finally replies to the objection that denies all validity to the natural inclination from the fact that it leads us sometimes, in spite of our will, to error and evil, for God has specifically given us in this case, through reason, the means to distinguish this evil and error, and thus even to escape it.

This principle governs the method that will be followed in the sphere of the proof of the substantial union of soul and body, when it will deal with establishing and determining the validity of nature's voice, as criterion of the certain objective validity of the teachings of the senses relative to this union and to its internal necessities. In virtue of divine veracity, all teachings called "natural," for which we are not given any means to suspect their falsity, are necessarily true within the limit of their competence, without needing any further positive proof of their truth. In brief, everything that is *truly nature* is infallible. Reciprocally, everything that we attribute to nature and that we discover to be fallible or false, either by reason or otherwise, does not belong to true nature, but to something we arbitrarily introduce in it and that we falsely take for it—for example, the understanding, customs, everything that can be redressed and reformed by reason in our natural judgments—in brief, this third degree of sense that Descartes has specified as foreign to sensation itself.[17] Consequently, in order to found the validity of the criterion of nature that is itself infallible, we will have to dissolve the vulgar concept of nature by dissociating in it true nature from pseudonature; we will thus engender an irreducible residue of authentic teachings whose infallibility is guaranteed from the fact that no other faculty could place them in doubt nor supplement them. To the extent that it is unshakable for man, once it is stripped of what man adds to it arbitrarily, "nature" in its infallibility directly expresses within its sphere God's omnipotence, goodness, and veracity. This thesis will have a profound influence on Malebranche, and through him, on the doctrines of the French philosophers of the eighteenth century, relative to the infallibility of nature and instinct.

4. Discussion of Elements Three to Six (Definition of Consciousness, Constraint, Principle of Causality, Inclination, or Nature)

This proof is constructed with a rigorous geometrical precision.

Only one of its elements seems to be postulated, namely, the possibility of an action exercised on thought by a reality *without common measure* with it. This postulate is rejected as absurd by all the rationalists. However, Descartes does not institute it gratuitously. He does not deny the contradiction and incomprehensibility that it implies. But his theory of possibility resolves this difficulty because God's omnipotence is capable of doing what our understanding does not comprehend. If, on the other hand, God certifies in us in an undeniable manner that he has actually done the thing, we ought to bow to it, no matter what is the impossibility of our conceiving it. It therefore suffices to establish the indubitable character of the testimony that sensation brings to us on this point by means of reason, in order for the barrier raised by our understanding to disappear in the eyes of the understanding itself. In addition, this proof does not contain anything that contributes to establishing that body is different than soul, given that this difference is already established and constitutes a necessary condition of the demonstration of its existence. In fact, the fourth element of the proof, sensible constraint, proves only that sensation must have *a cause different from myself*; and the fifth element establishes by means of the quantity of objective reality that this different cause could be either God, the spirits, or body. This consequence is possible only because we know, by means of the prior proof, that body is a diffcrent substance from mc. Thus, we do not posit that body is different from me because it must be posited as such in virtue of the constraint exercised by the cause, but on the contrary we prove that body can be the cause of the constraint because we already know that it is different from my soul. Descartes is therefore much more demanding in this case than other idealists, who do not require, in order to establish the existence of a corporeal thing outside me, reasons other than the principle of causality tied to the realization of a constraint in myself (Fichte, for example).[18]

But does not the authentic teaching of nature, meaning the instinctive, infallible inclination that leads me to posit body itself, and not another reality as cause of the constraint, suffice to assign body as cause of my sensations, even if, lacking clear and distinct knowledge, I did not know that body is substantially different from my soul? Of course, it is unquestionable that common man, mired in the life of the senses, ignorant of the distinction of body and mind, attributes without hesitation the cause of the passivity in his soul to body, as a reality foreign to the self.[19] But Descartes did not wish to rest his proof on this sensation, because it would never have been able to establish the *real* and *substantial* character of the difference between body and soul. In this way, it is confirmed that the proof of the distinction of body and soul owes nothing to the proof of the existence of body, since I could not have any necessary and certain knowledge of the existence of body if I did not first know that it really differs from the soul. Without this prior knowledge, I could never assign it validly as a foreign cause acting on the soul, in fact, and consequently, I could never establish that it exists.

The relations between the fourth, fifth, and sixth elements—constraint, causality, and nature—pose several problems.

First, the criterion of constraint, which is necessary and sufficient in order to prove a cause of sensible ideas external to my soul, is incapable of determining (as small a task as it may be), not only what it is, but also what it could be. The definition of causality is required in order to bring forth a first determination, one that remains insufficient, since it leaves us with three different possibilities: God, the spirits, and body. The definitive determination of this cause is brought forth by inclination—meaning *nature*. Finally, this inclination concerns only the form of the sensation, meaning passivity or constraint. It does not concern its content, that is, it does not concern its objective reality or its character of obscurity and confusion—in brief, it does not concern its character of quality. Quality will be considered only in the proof of substantial union.

The use of the principle of causality in order to establish the relationship of an idea in us with a thing outside us, meaning in order to determine the objective validity of a representation, has been recommended as the only use that would be legitimate and efficacious, once *Meditation III* posited the problem of objective validity in its generality. It is through the intermediary of this principle, defined as the necessity for a quantity of formal reality in the cause to be at least equal to the quantity of objective reality in the idea, that the necessary objective reality of the idea of God has been established, since God is necessarily posited as the only possible cause of the objective reality of that idea. Thus, it became possible to confer indirectly, by the intermediary of divine veracity, the objective validity essential to all clear and distinct ideas. Descartes had himself expressly noted the necessity of such a general use of the principle of causality thus understood as an instrument of all proof aiming to establish the existence of things outside of me, with respect to God or to material things.[20] But the use of this principle is altogether different in *Meditation VI* and in *Meditation III*. In the proof of the existence of bodies, the externality of the cause is posited in virtue of the necessary relation between passion and action, not in virtue of the relation between the quantity of objective reality in the idea and the quantity of formal reality in the cause. It is the fact of constraint that allows the application of the causal relation. Moreover, the objective validity of this constraint is finally guaranteed by *nature*. But the recourse to constraint in order to establish the externality of the cause was radically excluded as illegitimate in *Meditation III*, which prescribed only the use of the principle of causality (as just defined) and consideration of the quantity of objective reality of ideas, toward this end. Thus, in the realm of the senses, the inquiry for the external cause of the idea is conducted and succeeds, through the criteria that *Meditation III* had rejected, in the realm of the understanding—meaning by following the "path" of common sense that had been abandoned for the path opened up by the principle of equality *(ad minimum)* of formal reality of the cause and objective reality of the effect. We ought not be surprised by this, because we know that the order of living things (which is the order of the existence of external things and my body) contradicts the order of pure intellect. The intervention of the principle of causality according to the definition given by Descartes is produced here, as the fifth element, only to specify the cause under three possible forms (God, minds, and bodies) without our being able yet to determine definitively which of the three causes ought to be retained. This determination is finally possible only because of the criterion of *nature,* which therefore, in fact, intervenes twice, once in order to guarantee the instinctive judgment that leads me to affirm, starting with constraint, the existence of a yet undetermined cause of my passion, and a second time, in order to guarantee the instinctive judgment that leads me to determine this cause by affirming that it is nothing other than body itself.

The proof therefore receives only limited support from the principle that, in *Meditation III,* allowed one to posit an adequate cause outside the idea. However, the general goal is the same in both cases. We are always concerned with discovering in the idea a character such that it seems *necessary* to attribute to it a cause existing outside it, therefore outside ourselves. But it is evident that the process that succeeds with respect to the idea of God cannot succeed with respect to sensible ideas. The principle of equal quantity *ad minimum* of formal reality in the cause and of objective reality in the effect cannot lead one to posit an external cause except in an extreme case—the case in which the quantity of objective reality is *maximum,* meaning infinitely infinite. Only then do we know immediately that the formal reality of the cause, which ought at *minimum* be the *maximum* (meaning infinite), is necessarily excessive with respect to the finite formal reality of our self, that it must be situated outside it, and that it is the very thing whose representation I have in my idea, since this cause cannot be more than its effect, since the representative content of my idea cannot be less perfect than what it represents, unless it is no longer its representation, meaning its idea—which is contradictory. Thus the application of this principle gives me necessarily in this case, both the knowledge of the externality of the cause of my idea to myself, and the certainty that I have a perfectly faithful knowledge of its essential reality, by my representation. In the present case, on the other hand, the objective reality of the idea is a *minimum,* since it is normal for sensible ideas to be at the extremes of being and nothingness, with respect to their representative content. Consequently, since the principle requires that the cause has at least as much reality as the effect, and not that it has either more or less reality, the formal reality of the cause can be as great as one wishes. As a result: 1) cause can be eminent; 2) we are referred to a multitude of possible causes between the *minimum* and the *maximum,* and we have no means of determining in this fashion which is the real cause among these possible causes, as was the case with respect to God; and 3) the soul can be conceived as one of these possible eminent causes, since it involves a formal reality greater than the objective reality of these sensible ideas. It is therefore necessary, in order to establish the nature of externality of the cause to myself and in order to assign body as this cause, to have recourse to other such criteria such as sensible constraint and inclination—in brief, to have recourse to "nature." And *Meditation III* contested the legitimacy of these criteria. We must therefore inevitably restore their validity within a sphere distinct from the sphere of the truth of clear and distinct ideas, namely, the sphere of the existence of material things. This restoration is now possible and legitimate because, since we are farther in the order of reasons, divine veracity has succeeded universal deception as the directing principle of the inquiry. By accruing upon the definition of thinking by consciousness, divine veracity destroys the first objection, based on the possibility for the soul to produce the objective reality of the ideas of the senses without knowing it. It destroys the others by legitimately guaranteeing "nature" (inclination) to the extent that it reveals to us the sign that allows us to recognize, among the apparent solicitations of instinct, the ones that truly belong to it, that are irrefutable, from the ones we lend to it gratuitously (pseudonature), that must be condemned.

The incapability of the principle of causality to base, in this instance, the objective validity of the idea on the quantity of objective reality, does not even derive from the fact that this reality is a *minimum* in the present case. In fact, we notice the same incapability whenever this reality has a finite magnitude, for example, with respect to the clear and distinct ideas of myself or mathematical objects. As we have seen, this incapability disappears only in one case—God's.

That is why objective validity is not conferred to clear and distinct ideas except through the mediation of divine veracity. In this way, if we know that they are real and that thus God is their author, as generally he is the author of everything real, we would not yet know whether their immediate cause is God, or another reality dependent on God. In fact, since the objective reality of all these ideas has only a finite magnitude, it can be explained by the formal reality of our soul, without our being able to affirm that our soul has produced it.[21]

In order to determine their cause, Descartes needed to refer to a special criterion, as he did for sensible ideas. And it happens that this criterion is also constraint, in this case, an intellectual constraint. As we have seen,[22] an idea, even an intellectual idea, is known by the understanding only because it is received there, meaning because it determines a passion there.[23] However, the constraint experienced by my soul because of an intellectual idea is of a different kind from the one that founds the objectivity of sensible ideas. It concerns the inflexible rigidity of their internal structure, and not the way in which I receive ideas, for I can, in opposition to what occurs in sensations, evoke ideas at my leisure. It is manifested by the resistance that the true and immutable nature opposes to all the efforts of my subjective thought in order to modify it, by either adding or subtracting something from it. I perceive immediately, because of this resistance, that "my thought does not impose its necessity on things, but is determined by the necessity that is in the thing itself."[24] In spite of its internal and immanent character, this necessity certifies that the cause that placed the idea in me is greater than me, from the fact that it constrains me, while the fact that no external cause ever constrains me to think of this idea or not (the evocation of the idea remains free) proves that these ideas have always been present in me, and that their cause could only have acted from within me in order to introduce them the moment my soul was created. Therefore this cause can only be God who, while dominating my thought, implants these ideas in it from its creation, at the same time that he implants in it the idea of infinity. In brief, the objective validity of this constraint is based on the proof of the existence of God as in *Meditation III*. In fact, this proof certifies that God's causality is exercised directly on my soul in order to imprint on it, as with a seal, the objective reality contained in an idea. To the clearly and distinctly perceived necessity of the clear and distinct idea whose true and immutable nature constrains my thought and whose validity is guaranteed by divine veracity, and to the natural light that solicits my free judgment to conclude that this constraint has its cause in God, there corresponds, in the order of sensible ideas, the constraint sensed by the natural receptivity and inclination that solicits my judgment to attribute the cause of this constraint to body—the signification of this constraint and the truth of this inclination being equally guaranteed by divine veracity.

5. The Limit of Being and Nothingness, the Objective Reality of Sensation and the Existential Reality of Body

The result of the demonstration of the existence of bodies seems to establish an intersection between two elements of the doctrine. The objective reality of sensation is, in fact, close to zero since it is at the limit of being and nothingness.[25] Moreover, the demonstration of the existence of bodies ends up by positing body as a formal, noneminent cause of this objective reality, that is, as a cause whose quantity of formal reality is not greater than the quantity of objective reality of the idea. Since this objective reality is close to zero, the formal reality of the body must also be close to it, in the same proportion. This conclusion is in agreement with the Platonic and Christian thesis, which is also the Cartesian thesis, according to which the matter of existing bodies is what is closest to nothingness, in the hierarchy of realities.[26]

But body is a substance; does not the formal reality of a substance have more perfection than either the formal or objective reality of its modes? Therefore does it not have more perfection than the objective reality of various sensible ideas? We would reply that what causes in me the objective reality of sensible ideas is not the substance of bodies, but the modes of that substance insofar as they exist and act on my body in virtue of the laws of the communication of movement. And sensible ideas refer only to modes and do not teach me anything about the corporeal substance whose idea, which is innate in me, is not introduced in my soul by the action of that substance. However, is it not the action of this substance that gives me the idea that *this substance exists*? Will we sidestep this latter objection by distinguishing between the essence and the existence of that substance? Would we say that it is this existence that is the sole cause of the action exercised on my soul? And is not the existence of bodies closer to zero than the essence of their substance, in the hierarchy of beings?

This argument makes no sense for Descartes, for he does not distinguish between the existence of body and the being of its essence outside us; and existence (the formal reality of the corporeal thing) is, with respect to our idea, meaning with respect to the essence of the thing in us, or to the thing objectively in our understanding, a perfection missing to the idea. The argument would make sense only according to Malebranche's principles, which posit essence as distinct from existence *outside of me,* and which affirm that the intelligible reality of eternal, infinite, immutable, uncreated essence, being an aspect of divine essence, wins out in the criterion of perfection over the existence for which it is the archetype, an existence that is finite, created, changeable, temporal, and contemptible.

There is a difficulty of conceiving under these conditions, in Cartesian doctrine, the equality it postulates between infinite smallness of the objective reality of sensible ideas and the formal reality of existing body, which is its formal, noneminent cause.

We have already encountered this difficulty when examining the first proof by effects. We have seen that, in all rigor, with respect to God, the principle of the equality *ad minimum* between the reality of the cause and the reality of the effect did not allow it, by itself, to posit necessarily in the cause the extra perfection of existence, which remained then merely possible, but not necessary. We are confronted with a similar difficulty here. In fact, whether we are concerned with the existence of God or the existence of material things, in both cases, existence always constitutes a perfection of which the representing idea is deprived.

To seek a solution on the side of the object, by attributing the objective reality of sensation to the action of one of the existing modes of extended substance, and not to the substance itself, is to fall into a purely verbal argument. On the other hand, we can get a glimpse of a solution, if, turning away from the object, we consider the subject. We can then verify that the objective reality of sensation is not the image of the existing thing, but only a *sign* of its existence, a sign that leaves us not knowing *what is* this existing thing about which we have no representation on this plane. The objective reality of sensation therefore has its correlate only in the existence of the thing, to the exclusion of the essence of the substance upholding it. And the cause is only a cause *ad minimum,* since it is not an exemplary cause, but only an occasional one.[27]

6. Discussion of Elements Seven and Eight (Divine Veracity, Criteria of the Veracity of Inclination)

The proof could not be concluded, here as elsewhere, without the intervention of the principle of divine veracity and the reasons that justify its use (elements seven and eight). The absoluteness of this principle allows Descartes, in *Meditation VI,* to justify its universal application, and at the same time to furnish the criteria determining the cases in which its guarantee is not legitimately applicable. This double use appears to be contradictory at first. However, it is not; in fact, since God is absolutely veracious, everything is true for the whole of his work, *as long as he is its responsible author.* Two consequences flow from this. First, when we err, the error is contingent, attributable to us alone, without any foundation in things (at least in the *maximum* of cases). Since it is contingent and dependent on us, it is avoidable and rectifiable. Since God did not wish it, he has placed at our disposal the means to recognize it, or to recognize that we are exposed to it. He has given us the means to escape it. As a result:

A. Everything toward which we are not led in an absolutely invincible and indubitable fashion cannot, as a whole, be recognized as true—meaning as real and coming from God—and consequently cannot be covered by his veracity; and we ought to use the means that he has given us in order to recognize what is indubitable by having contact with the authentic reality of which he is the author and which he thus guarantees necessarily. No true reality can, in fact, be deceitful.

B. When he has given us no means to suspect that an error is possible, nor any means to prevent it, avoid it, or correct it, we are in the presence of the *true reality* he has created and that he guarantees.

The first of these two consequences provides us with a criterion and a directive thread for the determination of the true "nature" (in the narrow sense of the term), during the proof of the union of soul and body. The second provides the criterion of the absolute truth of the invincible inclination that leads us to attribute to existing body the cause of the passivity of my soul in sensation.[28]

Divine veracity, as we have seen, extends not only to clear and distinct ideas, but also to a natural inclination. Malebranche, who criticizes the Cartesian proof, freely admits this extension.[29] As we have seen, it is regulated by some very carefully defined conditions. Nevertheless, the proof has seemed improper to some critics, who have restricted its legitimate application to the sphere of the ideas of the understanding.[30]

As we shall see, such a restriction does not seem justified, either by Descartes' principles or his texts.

As we have seen, the principle of divine veracity, the direct refutation of the principle of universal deception, substitutes the principle of universal truth for the principle of universal deception. It allows the inverse of the rule of doubt to succeed the rule of doubt. It extends unavoidably to the whole of the creation. That is why error, when confronted with it, appears scandalous and poses a theological problem: if everything is true, if God is veracious, how is it possible that I am deceived? Since everything of which God is truly the author is necessarily true and real, instinct and sensation, which he has created, must also be infallible, as is my understanding, when they are taken properly, that is, when they are authentic. Consequently, as in the case of the understanding, error can be produced here only through the ill use of my faculties, meaning because of the fact of my freedom (which would no longer be freedom if its proper use were imposed upon it). Indeed, the metaphysical discovery of divine veracity does not have as immediate and radical an effect on our attitude with respect to sensible ideas as on our attitude with respect to clear and distinct ideas. In fact, the disappearance of metaphysical doubt cannot alone confer on sensible ideas the complete evidence that the ideas of the understanding possess by themselves because of the nature of our mind. The intrinsic confusion and obscurity confirm the natural doubts that are justified by the fundamental errors of which they are the occasion in the sphere of the understanding, and even some indubitable errors within their own sphere. Divine veracity must therefore enter into battle with the natural suspicion that attaches to them. From this arises the necessity—and legitimacy—to undertake in its name the task of the reduction of doubts, to determine the zone of unshakable certainty coinciding with the plane of the true reality described by the region of the sensible, to explain error within this region by lifting the responsibility from God, and to trace rigorously the limits of the objective validity of obscure and confused ideas. Thus the justification of sensation, required by divine veracity, governs a process of dissociation whose aim is to obtain as an authentic residue the reality of the senses, such as God has given rise to it in us.

With respect to the natural inclination that is tied to constraint, the conclusions of the proof end up with a dual dissociation. On the one hand, we dissociate this inclination from what our understanding and our judgment add to it, in such a way as to isolate true natural instinct in its quasi-infallible authenticity; on the other hand, correlatively, we dissociate the legitimate affirmation of external existence—which is referred to our noncorrupted instinct—from the illegitimate attribution to the existing thing of sensible qualities foreign to it, an attribution resulting from the usurpation of our judgment. To the residue of reality that subsists in my sensible representation and to the true instinct stripped of what adulterates it, God, who is indubitably their author, must indubitably and *necessarily* give his guarantee.

In opposition to Malebranche's conception, Descartes' conception of ideas gets him to place clear and distinct ideas, and obscure and confused ideas, on the same plane, in the sense that for him they are all ideas in us, meaning modes of consciousness, and equal among themselves in that respect, but unequal with respect to the objective reality whose quantity varies from the infinitely large to the infinitely small; this conception imparts a great precision and a solid foundation to the thesis of the guarantee of sensation by divine veracity. For sensible ideas, like the works of God, are realities and consequently they are truths according to the two kinds of realities that are theirs, meaning not only with respect to their formal being, as simple modifications of my consciousness, but also with respect to their content, as objective realities. As small as their quantity of objective reality is, in this case, a quantity that is at the limit of being and nothingness, it is not a "pure nothing." It must therefore have a truth, meaning an objective validity that matches its infinite smallness. Divine veracity necessarily guarantees this validity even up to the point at which God is the author of this objective reality as he is the author of all reality.

7. Descartes' Indifference Concerning Certain Reasons Alleged against the Objective Validity of Sensible Ideas

The proof of the existence of bodies does not lead exclusively to the refutation of the objections against the reasons invoked for the objective validity of our sensible ideas. However it seems to require that this refutation be complete. And Descartes was satisfied, in this case, with eliminating only one objection: the objection against natural constraint and inclination. He neglects to respond to the others. Why does he limit himself in this way?

This neglect—or indifference—can be explained in two ways. First, Descartes has not insisted in *Meditation VI* on the objections that he now neglects, whether they aim at the vivacity of sensible ideas, or their presumed resemblance to material things (based on the fact that we cannot know the latter except through the former), or the presumption of the sensible origin of all ideas (based on the observation that sensible ideas are drawn from experience, that ideas are mostly formed by the combination of sensations, that sensible ideas are more used than other ideas, and that they are more able to express themselves). Second, Descartes himself does not believe in the validity of the reasons that these objections attack: the criterion of vivacity appears insufficient to him, since he prefers not to mention it at times, or he mentions it only subsidiarily, whereas he rejects the latter two objections, the one arguing for the similarity of the sensible idea and the material thing, and the one arguing for the sensible origin of all ideas.

8. The Role of the Proof in the Use of Physics as a Science Distinct from Speculative Geometry; the Objective Meaning of Sensible Variation *(Varietas)*

In any case, we see that, through the refutation of the critique of the principal reasons that found the objective validity of sensible ideas, Descartes has realized the aim he announced: to restore the validity of the senses only within a certain limit, not admitting all its claims, but not rejecting all of them either. The proof that justifies the judgments based on constraint and natural inclination renders back only a part of the objective validity that common people recognize for the senses, for although it confirms them in their capacity to certify to us the existence of bodies, it destroys radically, by means of the real distinction of the two substances that constitute one of its premises, the claim that the senses give us an image of things and that they are at the origin of all our ideas.

And this limitation is of extreme importance for physics. Since sensations, insofar as they are referred to their (nonexemplary) external cause as sensible qualities, must to that extent be explained by existing bodies, and since existing bodies are by their nature nothing more than an extension in width, length, and depth, these sensible qualities (hot, cold, dry, wet, sound, light, etc.) are nothing more than the expressions and signs in us of properties that are purely geometrical in the bodies themselves.

This conclusion attempts to found the geometrical character of physics as *the science of real existing things*. The proof of the real distinction of soul and body certified the necesarily geometrical character of all *possible physics*. The proof of the existence of bodies allows one to pass from possible physics to *real physics*—the physics of the world existing for our senses. In this way the dual method that will be imposed on this science is specified: l) it will have to attempt to discover, beneath sensible qualities, insofar as they express something of the real properties of different bodies, the corresponding geometrical properties that alone truly belong to them; 2) it will have to have recourse to the experience of the senses. Without the experience of the senses, possible physics would never become real physics. It would be reduced to the science of all possible relations of the modes of extended substance. This amounts to saying that it will never be able to be distinguished from "speculative geometry," and that finally, there would be no physics. In fact, what differentiates possible physics from real physics is what differentiates a science of bodies really existing from a science of merely possible bodies, which can be nothing more than a science of pure geometrical essences. Thus, we can explain that if an essentially geometrical character must be accepted for physics, it is as a sine qua non condition, no doubt a necessary condition, but not a sufficient one. In brief, it is a necessary *minimum*: "at least that is what we have to concede," specifies Descartes.[31]

Does this conclusion allow one to determine definitively the limit of the objective validity left to sensation? Is this *minimum* that my understanding must necessarily recognize as the property of things whose existence is revealed to me by the senses, the *maximum* that I can affirm with respect to them? Since bodies and their properties are nothing more than the geometrical determinations of extension, that is, ideas that are clear and distinct, must one not consider that sensations, being of spiritual nature, and what is more, obscure and confused, and being entirely heterogeneous to bodies, would not be able to serve in any respect whatsoever to determine *what are* these bodies? Must not the objective validity of sensation be strictly limited to a function certifying indubitably the mere *presence* of existing bodies? The extreme reserve with which Descartes expresses himself indicates that there is nothing to this: "However, they [corporeal things—M. G.] are *perhaps not entirely* as we perceive them through the senses, for there are many things that render this perception of the senses extremely obscure and confused, but *at least* we must confess that all the things I conceive clearly and distinctly there, meaning all the things, *generally speaking*, that are included in the object of speculative geometry, are truly there."[32] This extremely attenuated conclusion and the particularly noteworthy expressions that we have emphasized, announce that, though physics has indubitably a geometrical essence, it is not reducible to geometry pure and simple, and the recourse to the senses must allow one to introduce into it determinations through which it would be distinguished from geometry. To say that things in themselves are perhaps not entirely as we perceive them through the senses, is that not to understand that they also have some relation to them, and that, to some extent, the senses can give us a means to know something about them in addition to their simple existence? Moreover, the argument Descartes uses in order to limit the objective validity of the senses here does not concern their spiritual character (which would reject them outside of extension, by making them into modes of the soul, and would disqualify them completely as enabling us to know something about it), but concerns their obscure and confused character (which is repugnant to the essence of mind, meaning clear and distinct intelligence, and which they owe to the close mingling of soul and body). And it is by means of this mingling that *the variation of sensations whose particular combinations in each sensible perception imply the correlative particular diversities in existing bodies* has been introduced in my soul. Thus we already glimpse that although sensation cannot teach us anything relative to the true nature of bodies, and that although none of the properties of bodies can be anything other than geometrical, the objective validity of sensation is, however, not limited to certifying simply, in virtue of constraint, the existence of material things, but must include, in relation to what they are, a teaching that surpasses this pure and simple positing.

This teaching, Descartes indicates, is in contrast to the generality of the essences constituting the object of speculative geometry, *the particularity of existing bodies* that constitutes the proper object of real physics, for example, "the sun having such magnitude and such shape," or even "light, sound, pain, and other similar things . . . conceived less clearly and distinctly."[33] Are these elements belonging properly to the content of sensation radically false? Certainly they are "extremely doubtful and uncertain."[34] But God is veracious; he has placed nothing in me that is capable of deceiving me. Divine veracity has a universal range. If God has placed the senses in us, it is because he has given them to us as an instrument of truth, arming us at the same time with all the necessary faculties for avoiding the errors to which they might give rise. "It is certain that they [the particularities of existing things that the sensible given brings us—M. G.] are extremely doubtful and uncertain [. . .], nevertheless from the mere fact that God is not a deceiver, and that consequently he has not permitted any falsity in my opinions without having given me some faculty capable of correcting it, I think I can conclude with assurance that I have the means in me to know them with certainty."[35]

Thus divine veracity reappears again as the direct link to the determination of the limits and of the degree of truth, no longer for the senses in general, but for the *varied sensorium* of particular perceptions. Here also it guides us in conformity with the principles that it has given the force of law in the whole sphere of sensation: where doubt and error are possible, rational critique is always possible and redressing error is also possible. Inversely, where this critique is not possible and consciousness of error not forthcoming, doubt and error are impossible, and truth is certain.[36] These two principles emanate directly from one and the same dogma: the dogma of the infallibility of true "nature," based directly on God's veracity. In the one case, in which a critique is impossible, it is useless, because nature is given to us directly in its authentic and truthful nakedness: such was the case for my natural inclination to posit an external body as the cause of the constraint experienced in sensation; since no faculty has been given to me by the veracious God in order to contradict or suspect this inclination, it is certainly not deceitful. In the other case, in which a critique is possible, it is necessary, for nature is not given to us as such, but with a surplus of reasonings, interpretations, and judgments that do not arise from it. Such is the case, now, for the variation of sensible perceptions in which doubt arises naturally regarding the judgments of which it is the occasion. The veracious God then commands us not to impute to this sensible variation the errors we commit relative to the variation of the particular existing thing in itself. He also commands us to put into place the instrument of rational critique, with which he has armed us in order to dispel the false judgments that are revealed as emerging from the fallibility of our freedom. In this way a new truth proper to the senses will be revealed: the truth of its *variation,* a truth that answers to the veracity of its author. Finally, in this case, as in any other, this purification of the senses will be ipso facto a purification of the understanding. The understanding, by redressing its own errors relative to the nature of the particularities of existing physical things, will be able to recognize the latter faithfully, meaning according to their purely extended essence, by utilizing correctly toward this end the qualitative sensorial particularities that it wrongly attributed to them as their properties.

Once we have understood that divine veracity was only the expression of the identity between the objective reality of our ideas and God's reality or truth, we are compelled to presume that, as little objective reality as is enclosed by the contents of the various sensations, and consequently as easy as is error with respect to them, they must possess a *minimum* of objective validity corresponding to their *minimum* of objective reality. Consequently, we now have to judge that the various objective realities constituting these different contents must refer to diversities in corporeal things. But these diversities of bodies do not resemble the diversities of sensations; sensations are intrinsically obscure and confused, and are only their *signs*: the former are only geometrical and quantitative diversities that are knowable clearly and distinctly; the latter are only qualitative: "From the fact that I sense different kinds of colors, odors, tastes, sounds, heat, hardness, etc., I readily conclude that in the bodies from which all these various perceptions of the senses (*variae istae perceptiones sensuum*) there are some corresponding variations (*varietas iis respondentes*), even though perhaps these variations are not really similar to the perceptions."[37]

9. The Innateness of Sensation

Thus we understand that sensations are innate, even though they constitute the matter of all my adventitious ideas, for the material body I assign to them as cause would not be able to introduce them in me, since it is pure extension and it has no relation with them. On the other hand, they are always in me as qualities sensed by consciousness. They are originally given to me in and by the substantial union in order to constitute "my nature" in the narrow sense; they are innate to "my nature," in the same way that this nature is itself innate to my nature as a man, which includes the composite substance together with the understanding (and not innate to my pure understanding alone). It constitutes a primitive notion.[38] The various kinds of sensations (odor, color, sound, etc.) are themselves also primitive notions, and from *Meditation I* on, the analysis has isolated them as ultimate constituents unable to be broken, which have in this way the authenticity and simplicity of an element, in the same way as mathematical elements in the sphere of pure understanding are simple and authentic. They are innate ideas of "my nature," of the substantial composite, in the same way that clear and distinct ideas are the innate ideas of my pure understanding. And in the two regions, the terms "unbreakable constitutive element," "primitive notion," "immediate given," and "innate idea" are all synonymous. The action of the external body on my composite nature is only the occasion for the awakening in me of the sensations that are present from all time in my composite nature. What depends on the external cause is that such an innate sensation is awakened in me at such a time rather than at another, and that such and such innate sensations are grouped kaleidoscopically in such a particular fashion at the same moment for my express consciousness, in a way as to constitute the variation (*varietas*) of my perception. The resurgence of such innate sensations thus grouped is the sign that a particular existing body, with certain particular qualities, has entered, by its action on my psychophysical substance, in the zone of vital relations concerning my composite nature, and these relations are then specified with respect to that body according to certain perspectives. The particular qualitative variation of my perception, which allows me to grasp these specified relations immediately, without the intervention of reflection, to the extent that I experience them, is at the same time the sign for my pure understanding that certain correlative geometrical variations, given to consciousness by sensation, belong in themselves to the nature of existing body.

Thus, what is adventitious in sensible representation is the knowledge that such a particular material thing exists, having such qualities (of vital interest), but not the constitutive elements of the representation—whether or not we are concerned with the idea of the understanding (present under the geometrical forms of the objects being thought), sensible qualities assumed by this idea, or the vital meaning of these qualities and their dispositions. The adventitious core is the awakening in me, at such moments of time, in spite of myself, of such and such sensations, and the particularity of their combination.[39] *Meditation I* observed that there can be error only where there is fiction, and fiction only where there is combination. We have already noted above[40] that the classification of ideas as innate, adventitious, and artificial operates on the plane of common consciousness. Thus the adventitious idea was conceived as being due to a cause that appeared to "send and imprint its likeness on me."[41] The light of the understanding has dispelled this illusion while conserving in this idea an adventitious core that has just been specified. The innateness of the constitutive elements of the adventitious idea would be impossible if we believed, as does common consciousness, that the appearance of the idea in me was due to the action of the external body as an exemplary cause. It is possible, on the other hand, once this action is only the occasion of this appearance, and the idea is not the image but the sign of the particular existing body. When, on the contrary, we are dealing with ideas of the understanding, the cause of these ideas (which, in this case, is God or the essences created by God) is exemplary and imprints its resemblance on our mind. The idea is therefore completely adventitious in this respect, while being entirely innate, since this impression occurred at the same time my soul was created, and it remains forever immutable within my understanding. The idea is as immortal as my soul. In the realm of the senses, the innateness of the idea (which perishes at the same time as the composite substantial nature) has a connection with the following characteristics: unbreakable constitutive element, primitive notion, immediate given, sign, occasional character of the external corporeal cause.

10. The Determination and Limitation of the Objective Validity of Sensation

The same veracity that guarantees the judgment of existence that we bring to bodies in virtue of the constraint that sensation imposes upon us, guarantees, as we have seen, the judgment by which we affirm in them the geometrical variations that are yet unknown, as cause of the correlative qualitative variations of these sensations.

Beyond this limit, there is only doubt and error, for sensation, no more than the nature of bodies in general, cannot itself instruct us about the true nature of these particular geometrical variations, since it is a subjective quality, whereas body is a pure extension. But again, God, who is veracious, has given us the remedy for this: he has given us the reason which, through the critique of the senses, allows us to destroy the errors that we add onto the raw given, and thus to restrict our judgments to the limits of its competence. Thus the objective validity of sensation is completely established, determined, and precisely limited relative not only to the knowledge *that* material things exist, but also to the knowledge about *what they are.*

The conclusion with which we end up is then dual, according to whether we are situated at the point of view of the thing to be known, that is, at the point of view of physics, or at the point of view of the faculty that knows, that is, at the point of view of epistemology and the critique of knowledge. On the one hand, it is established that physics can attain the knowledge of *what* the particular existing things *are,* through the teaching of the senses, which must be correctly interpreted by the understanding in this respect. On the other hand, it appears that from now on the senses, considered in themselves and in their qualitative content, are not radically false and useless with respect to the knowledge of the diversity of existing things considered in themselves, but that they entail a certain objective validity—although limited—that the rational scientific critique must determine. In the same way that they testify that material things exist, while leaving us ignorant of their nature, they testify that diversities exist among them—diversities that they reveal each time by different qualities— without being able to teach us by themselves the true nature of each diversity.

Such is the way by which the proof of the existence of bodies allows one to determine the objective validity of sensation with respect to the existing body (as much from the point of view of the *quod* as of the *quid*) and its indispensable role for the establishment of real physics, meaning a science of particular geometrical objects (existing things) that is different from possible physics or from general (speculative) geometry. Thus we see that although the proof confirms the geometrical character of physics, it does not aim to demonstrate that character, but it aims above all to establish the unavoidable necessity for having recourse to experience, to an experience critiqued by reason.

11. The Dual Character of the Qualitative Element: a) Variation, b) Obscurity-Confusion; Twofold Reference to the Physical Reality outside of Me and to the Psychophysical Reality That the Self Attributes to Itself

The consequences flowing from the proof of the existence of bodies, by which we have been able to go from the knowledge of the existence of material things in general to the knowledge of the existence of the diversity of these things and their properties by means of the senses, have been developed by considering a new element, which until now was set aside, namely the qualitative content, the variation (*varietas*) of sensations. The proof of the existence of bodies in general used only the formal and extrinsic element of sensation—constraint. In conformity with his method of division, Descartes has separated two elements of sensation for science that, in reality, are only one: constraint and the variation of quality; and he has justified them separately by attributing a proper function to each. To constraint he has attributed the revelation of the existence of material things; to the diversity of qualities, the certain revelation of the existence of differences in these things. Divine veracity, which governed the discovery of these two functions by which the senses testify that they are an instrument of truth, receives, through the fact of this discovery, the satisfaction due to them. The senses thus appear justified in the totality of their constitutive elements.

We must note, however, that Descartes has set aside the constitutive element of quality, that is, obscurity and confusion, in order to consider only the character of the *diversity* of qualities. The analysis has therefore, in fact, dissociated sensation into three, not two, elements: constraint, variation in quality, and obscurity and confusion of that quality.[42] Thus we see that sensation is not yet justified in its totality and that divine veracity has not yet received adequate satisfaction, since the objective validity attributed to the senses, within the limits we have sketched, concerns only two out of the three elements. The remaining element, obscurity and confusion, appears as a residue that, in relation to this objective validity, seems to conceal essential falsity within itself, in some intimate and unshakable fashion. And is not God its author?

Consequently, should we not guarantee it in its intrinsic truth?

Divine veracity will therefore require another inquiry, in this respect. This inquiry will lead to the rehabilitation of this third element of the senses, from a certain point of view, and thus will bring to divine veracity the complete justification that its absolute universality requires. This rehabilitation will be possible only if we discover that this element also assumes a special function that confers upon it an absolutely certain sui generis truth, within the region that properly belongs to it.

What will be the direction of this new inquiry?

In order to know this direction, it suffices to observe that quality has only been considered up to now insofar as it is directed toward the object, meaning in its function of instrument that enables one to know the properties of various material things. It has been considered only in relation to the constitution of a real physics. In fact, variation (*varietas*) establishes a certain correlation (in spite of and beyond obscurity and confusion, which pits sensible qualities against the real properties of bodies) between the sensible differences of our perception of existing things and the geometrical differences of these same things taken in themselves,[43] and between the differences of the composite (psychophysical) subject and the differences of the thing itself: the one difference refers to the other difference, even though intrinsically they are heterogeneous and irreducible. But quality, on the other hand, deals with the subject at the same time, since it is a mode of my soul, even though it is repugnant to the latter's essence because of its intrinsic obscurity and confusion. And precisely this obscure and confused element is the expression of what is most eminently subjective, before *variation* and *constraint*. The new inquiry will therefore consider quality, not with respect to the appearance it shows the object, but with respect to the appearance it shows the subject, in this case, the *sensing* subject, meaning "my nature" (in the narrow sense), the composite substance I attribute to my self—which means that I am not talking only about "*my* soul," but also about "*my* body." We will then discover a new function in sensation, a function proper to quality considered as obscurity and confusion. This will be the psychobiological function, which entails a sui generis truth for quality—the truth of biological information with respect to the needs of the human body, a truth valid only within the limits of the human biological sphere, meaning of substantial union.

In brief, the qualitative element has a double aspect that it derives from a mixture of mind and extension. According to the one aspect, difference or *varietas* is referred to the proper difference of things in themselves, meaning to the *variation of their intrinsic geometrical properties*. From this point of view, obscurity and confusion, insofar as they are distinct from geometrical variation, constitute a purely aberrant element. According to the other aspect, obscurity and confusion, the qualitative as such, refer at the same time, and correlatively, to the *subjective variation of the needs of "my nature"* (of the composite substance of soul and body). This qualitative element, as confusion and obscurity, is constitutive of what is *sensed,* properly speaking, by which my soul can know immediately—or more exactly *experience*—the various alterations of the composite whole that constitutes my nature, and can react immediately to these in accordance with the requirements for the maintenance of the whole. This immediate knowledge, conscious instinct, is impossible without the *total* union of soul and body; and the totality, the substantiality of that union is the very essence of quality as *obscurity* and *confusion*.

The Cartesian analysis therefore accomplishes an extremely fine and thorough analysis of sensation. Constraint, diversity, and quality, properly speaking, finally are granted their respective functions and are invested with the sui generis truth of these functions. These truths cannot be safeguarded unless the functions do not overlap and, above all, unless the set of these functions does not overlap the function of the understanding, and vice versa. And even though the understanding seems to limit itself more and more, to the extent that it digs deeper within us, it discovers functions and orders of truth that are foreign to it and that it cannot supplant; and in fact it it becomes more clearly the supreme master of all truth, since without it, the distinction between faculties and elements of these faculties cannot be made, and it would be impossible for us to know them clearly and distinctly since, without this dissociation, the faculties would be confused with one another and would usurp each other's functions; moreover, through their mutual perversion, they would engender the somewhat mutual falsity of all the regions of knowledge—in brief, they would engender total confusion. In addition, to the extent that the understanding annexes other regions of diffcrent truths together with the region of the truth of the understanding to the realm of truth—truth of the senses in general, truth of constraint, truth of scnsible variation, and truth of obscurity and confusion—the domain of truth becomes coextensive with the whole of the domain of consciousness, considered as the sum of its different facultics, and in this way absolute adequation, which was proclaimed *ab initio,* is established between the universality of divine veracity and the universality of the elements or faculties of knowledge of which God is the author. The equating of reality and truth, which was at first posited only formally, thus receives the fullness of its content.

12. The Connection between the Consequences of the Proof of the Existence of Bodies and the Preliminaries for the Proof of the Union of Soul and Body

Through the consideration of quality (even considered simply in its most objective aspect, the aspect of the diversity of qualities), we already penetrate into a domain different from the one of the proof of the existence of bodies, namely, the domain of the union of soul and body. Once quality is considered in its content, whether we are concerned with the variation of this content or its qualitative aspect (obscurity and confusion), which constitutes the essence of what is *sensed,* of what is *experienced* as such, the substantial union is implied in things *(a parte rei).* That is why the preliminaries of the proof of the union of body and soul coincide with a development which, beginning with the conclusions of the proof of the existence of material things in general, draws consequences relative to particular existing things (sun, sound, light, etc.). In the same paragraph,[44] divine veracity is invoked for two ends: to justify the objective validity of the diversity of sensible qualities with respect to the diversity of particular material things existing outside us; to justify, subsequently, the truth of the senses relative to the conservation of the union of soul and body, that is, my various vital needs. And it is during the proof of the union that the role of diversity *(varietas)* of quality in the knowledge of the true (geometrical) diversity of material

things (a diversity not known to the senses) is fixed.[45] Only then is physics
founded not simply as a science of particular existing bodies in general
(*Principles*, pt. II), but as a science of the diversity of particular bodies
existing in our universe (*Principles,* pt. III and IV). This implication seems
natural since, on the one hand, sensible variation supposes *in veritate rei
existentis* the union of soul and body, and, on the other hand, truth relative
to physics (beginning with the experience of the senses) and truth relative
to psychology (as psychophysics, the science of my composite nature) both
arise simultaneously from the same process of dissociation that alone is
sufficient to exorcise an ambivalent error. Thus the passage from one proof
to the other is accomplished, as was the passage from the proof of the
distinction of body and soul to the proof of existence, by a continuous
train of thought.

13. Independence of the Proof of Existence Relative to the Proof of Union. Refutation of the Second Part of the "Paradox" Attributed to Descartes

But does not this linkage imply a vicious interdependence of the two proofs
that would compromise their logical perfection and demonstrative rigor?

Some have reproached Descartes for having embroiled the proof of
the real distinction of soul and body with that of the existence of bodies;
this arose, as we have seen, from a confusion between the relation of essence
and existence with the relation of essence and its properties. If we now
reproached Descartes for having embroiled the proof of the existence of
body with that of the union of soul and body, we would now be confusing
the order of conditions of science with the order of conditions of things
(as did Gassendi, when he noted that, in fact, soul stops existing and thinking
when body disappears, and denied Descartes' right to affirm that I can
conceive it as capable of subsisting without body because I conceive it
separately from body in my science).

In the same way, Gilson argues that, because it is impossible for
Descartes to conceive that *in things* a cause can be exercised on the soul
and determine a passion there, if the body is not substantially united to
it, we must conclude that *in science* the proof of the union of body and
soul is inevitably and viciously embroiled with the proof of existence: "The
question of knowing whether Descartes could prove the existence of the
external world without presupposing the union of soul and body, and
consequently this existence, is therefore reduced to the following question:
Can Descartes adduce sensations that do not suppose the substantial union
of soul and body? If he can, the two parts of the proof would be distinct;
if he cannot, the two parts of the proof will lead the whole proof into

irreparable confusion. What explains why Descartes thought he could have accomplished the proof is the purely formal character of the sensible element that he first took into consideration . . . the unforeseen and constrained manner in which sensations were produced in us. . . ." But this external character of sensation, even considered apart from the content, "cannot" be explained without a real union of soul and body. . . . "The passion of the soul, whose violence the soul suffers, already supposes the substantial union that Descartes will prove."[46] The whole strength of the objection depends on the meaning of the term "supposes"—*accepting that it is not possible for* the "suppositions" of science to be other than the suppositions of things. Sensations suppose the substantial union *in things*, since the former are impossible without the latter. Sensations would suppose the union *in science* only if their being posited *in science* would depend on the preliminary positing of the union of soul and body *in science*; that would be the case if the certain knowledge (or science) of the former would be impossible in science without the knowledge of the latter. Only in this case would the Cartesian argument be faulty; it would grossly violate the order of reasons.

That the union of my soul and my body is embroiled with the existence of bodies *in things,* and that in fact common man cannot perceive the one without the other, is what Descartes is the first to notice, when, describing sensation, he describes it to us at the same time as he claims that bodies exist and that I am united to my body. But this interdependence in things does not establish that the *proof* of existence and the *proof* of union are themselves interdependent *in science.* In fact, science establishes a chain of truths that are linked among themselves by the conditions that render these truths certain. But the conditions that render these truths certain are not those that in themselves render things real. That is why the order of science "considers only the series of things to know, and not the nature of each of them,"[47] and that it is "different from the order that is established between the things considered in their real existence *(prout revera existunt).*[48] It is precisely because the order of science produces *certainty* through the linkage of reasons that we can acquire the *indubitable knowledge* of the different order—the real order—which is proper to things, and whose science, when it is completed, gives us an accurate representation. Thus, first I know that I am, and that this truth conditions the certainty of other truths, namely, that God exists, that bodies exist, etc. But it is evident that in things, the existence of my soul is in no way a condition of the existence of God or the existence of my body. From the infinite perfection contained in the idea of God, I conclude the existence of God that is its cause; but although this first knowledge (of the content of the idea) conditions the second and its certainty, it is evident that the idea is not, in things, the condition of the existence of God. And we cannot accuse Descartes of committing a paralogism under the pretext that the idea of God, which serves to prove that God is its cause, already supposed, in things the divine causality that Descartes will prove.

And it is the same thing for the proof of the existence of bodies and that of union. Indeed, we base the existence of bodies on "this passion of the soul whose violence the soul often suffers," which Gilson tells us "already supposes the substantial union that Descartes will prove."[49] But this passion supposes it only *in things (a parte rei)*, and not *in science*, as an element used by it in order to render possible the necessary and certain knowledge of the existence of body, meaning as condition of the proof. Certainly quality (obscurity and confusion) is indissolubly tied, *a parte rei*, with constraint. But it is not so tied, in my science, at this point in the order of reasons. My science does not need to invoke it in order to achieve the certainty of its conclusions according to the order; it therefore has the right to set it aside.

Let us take an example drawn from the *Elements* of Euclid, about which Descartes tells us, "among those we believe to be the wisest men in Scholastic philosophy, there is not even one out of a hundred who undertands them."[50] In order to establish Pythagoras' theorem, it is first necessary to demonstrate that, in a right triangle, each of the sides of the right angle is a proportional mean between the whole hypotenuse and its projection on the latter. As a result, the square of each of the sides is equal to the product of the whole hypotenuse and its projection on the latter. We therefore only need to add the members of these two relations of equality together in order to perceive that the square of the hypotenuse is equal to the the sum of the squares of the sides of the right angle. It is evident that, in the figure at issue, each of the properties of the sides of the right angle suppose, *a parte rei*, the property of the hypotenuse that science will demonstrate. In fact, if this latter property were absent, the latter two would be, in things *(a parte rei)*, ipso facto, impossible. It is also evident that in things these three properties are indissolubly linked to one another as a simple unity. But the order of reasons requires for the constitution of certain science (geometry in this case) that I consider and demonstrate separately the property of each side of the angle, in order to unite them together later, to establish thus the property of the hypotenuse, which itself, as the unknown of my science, was separated from the two properties of the angle with which in itself it made up a unity. Euclid therefore proceeded in the same fashion as Descartes. He instituted his demonstration by means of properties "which [according to Gilson—M. G.] already supposed [*a parte rei*—M. G.] the property that he will prove." But no one thought that Euclid was guilty of circular reasoning. On the contrary, we do not see how this demonstration would be possible unless, *a parte rei,* the demonstrated property had been indissolubly tied for all eternity to the properties that serve in its demonstration and that, in science, must themselves be considered without the demonstration and separately from one another.

The necessities of the order that govern the certainty of science therefore require that we consider separately what is not separated in things: "If for example," writes Descartes, "we consider some body with extension and shape, we acknowledge that it is, *a parte rei,* something simple and unique; for in this sense, we cannot say that it is composed of the nature of body, of extension and shape, since these constituents have never existed distinct from one another. But in relation to our understanding we say that it is composed of these three natures, because we have first represented them to ourselves separately before we were able to judge that all three are to be found together in one and the same subject."[51] Similarly, sensation, *a parte rei,* unites in one and the same being—"simple and unique"— two elements (two "natures"): constraint, which refers to the existence and action of bodies, and quality, which refers to the substantial union. But for the certainty and necessity of my science, the order of reason allows, and even *requires,* that they be considered separately and successively by my intellect. Moreover, everything that has not been expressly posited in my science as certain truth in virtue of the ordered linkage of reasons is, for that science, a void of knowledge. Since the unavoidable link in things between constraint and quality has not been deduced as such, according to the order, it therefore remains as yet unknown (scientifically); similarly, the substantial union implied by quality is yet unknown (scientifically) to me. Since the unknown has not even been used surreptitiously in my proof, and only constraint, which is separate from it, has been used as a condition of it, the proof is correct and its necessary conclusion is legitimate: "The order consists only in that things proposed first must be known without the help of the ones that follow."[52] And as Descartes has warned us, he assumes that "those who will read [his] writings will know the elements of geometry, or at least, that they will have a mind capable of understanding the demonstrations of mathematics."[53]

No doubt, as we have seen, constraint, an argument proper for the proof of the existence of bodies, can also serve as an argument for establishing the union of soul and body. But, although it can be used toward two ends, that does not prove that the two ends must necessarily be interdependent, nor that the two arguments must be interdependent. First, constraint does not allow one to establish the *substantial* character of the union. Testifying only that the properly affective sensations the soul attributes to itself cannot arise from the soul alone, it requires one to conceive that the soul must be associated with an external cause, in order to be able to produce them. Moreover, existence and union are always distinguished from one another in such a way that union never serves to prove existence, even though it is, no doubt, given with existence in things *(a parte rei).* Finally, the fact that the cause or principle by which a science explains its object must be entailed, *a parte rei,* in this object, does not render science viciously circular, but merely possible. There is no begging the question unless the *knowledge* of what the demonstration intends to establish as explicative cause is arbitrarily supposed and used during the demonstration itself.

Thus Spinoza's attempt to "better" the Cartesian proof of the existence of bodies, in the *Principia Philosophiae Cartesianae,* by having it rest entirely on clear and distinct ideas, does not seem to us, as it does to Gilson, to prove that Spinoza has placed his genius at Descartes' disposition,[54] but rather that, with the best intentions, he has substituted his genius for Descartes'.

Cartesian rationalism does not consist in reducing the real into clear and distinct ideas, but in using the light of reason *in order to distinguish clearly* the different regions of the real (clear and distinct, obscure and confused) that imperfect knowledge most often *confuses.* That is how reason determines a sphere in which it alone must rule and another sphere, the sphere of composite substance, in which it must realize its incompetence and qualify another faculty of knowledge: sensation. But by recognizing its own limits, reason does not abdicate, for first, it exercises its function, which is to distinguish what is really distinct; then it alone confers on sensation the "certificates of believability" that impart to it a definitive certainty. In fact, it alone allows me to know God, his existence and veracity, and the necessity for me to acquiesce with what authentic sensation teaches me, since God has not placed anything in me that allows me to doubt it. It is reason itself that reveals to me that God's infinite omnipotence can create what I do not understand, and that the incomprehensibility of a fact—that of substantial union—could not make me doubt it once God took upon himself the task to certify it through sensation. On the other hand, Spinoza does not recognize any other valid instrument of knowledge than clear and distinct ideas. The understanding, instead of validating sensation, denies all its truth. My reason does not have as mission to distinguish the various regions of the real from one another in order to reveal that it is banished from one of them, but to expand itself into the absoluteness of its universal competence, through the subordination of everything with respect to the first common notion with which it is identified and which is God itself. It is therefore natural that Spinoza would think necessary the recourse to clear and distinct ideas alone in order to found the existence of body and the relation between body and soul. Clear and distinct ideas, by conferring an absolute validity to the principle of "common measure," exclude radically all reciprocal causality for one another: "Having no common measure between the power and forces of soul and body, the forces of the latter cannot be directed by those of the former. . . . How many degrees of movement can soul impress on the pineal gland, and with what quantity of force?[55] . . . What speed could it communicate to body?"[56] This is an argument that will be taken up by Leibniz, for whom the soul can only communicate to body either a null speed or an infinite speed.

We see that, in order to think about the relation between body and soul by means of clear and distinct ideas, we must give up their reciprocal causality, as does Spinoza; or else, in order to posit this reciprocal causality, we must give up thinking about this relation with clear and distinct ideas, as does Descartes. But in this latter perspective, Descartes would reproach Spinoza for having violated the requirements of clearness and distinctness, for, according to him, it is the worst confusion to wish to introduce clear and distinct ideas in a region that is foreign to it by nature. True clear and distinct knowledge distinguishes rigorously between the thinking substance, the extended substance, and the composite substance. What is proper to obscure and confused knowledge is to confuse them, and Scholasticism, which by its physics of substantial forms confuses the substance of bodies with the substance of my composite nature, introduces no less confusion than does Spinoza by applying clear and distinct ideas to my composite substance, although they are valid only for extension alone or thought alone.[57] Moreover, Cartesianism can go so far as to claim, in its own way, an integral respect for the principle of common measure. It is out of respect for this principle that Cartesianism refuses to conceive the reciprocal action of body and soul in the same way as the action of two bodies on each other. By creating the composite substance, God has created a common measure between the two realities (soul and body) which, by themselves, do not involve it. In this case, the incomprehensibility of the divine institution does not consist in authorizing a reciprocal action between two heterogeneous substances (contrary to the principle of common measure), but in that it has united substantially these two substances into a third, in order that, by means of this fusion, they become commensurable, although they are not when considered each separately.

The Cartesian doctrine is therefore perfectly coherent. To attempt to substitute in it clear and distinct idea for sensation is to misunderstand completely the role it assigns to human reason; it is to ruin the edifice from top to bottom. The conceptions of God's incomprehensibility, of possibility, of the limits of reason, and of the substantial union of body and soul form an indissoluble whole. But nothing is more opposed to the first truths of Spinoza's philosophy than this set, since the doctrine of the incomprehensible substantial union rejoins, through God's incomprehensibility, the theory of divine free will as principle of limitation for our understanding—which, for Spinoza, renders God into a despot.[58]

In conclusion, since the proof of the existence of bodies is no more embroiled with that of the distinction of soul and body than it is with that of their substantial union, we can say that the "Cartesian paradox" is only a myth. Descartes has not committed the monumental paralogism of which some reproach him, a mistake that would be extremely odd for such a powerful mathematician, a genius who is so attentive to the rigors of the methods of invention, to the techniques of demonstration, and to the requirements of order—or to quote his own expression (an expression of such modesty that it becomes ironic): for a man "who knows a little about geometry."[59]

14. Degree of Certainty of the Proof

These latter considerations allow one to determine exactly the degree of certainty of the proof of the existence of bodies. Coming late in the chain of reasons, the truth concerning the existence of bodies must appear as less evident and certain than the first truths, in virtue of the formula "*evidentior* (or *notior*), *quia prior.*" In fact, we have seen Descartes distinguish between degrees of certainty according to the function assumed by the truths in the order of conditions of certainty. For example, he establishes a difference of degree between the certainty proper to the knowledge of God and the certainty proper to that of the soul, which is comparable to the one separating the certainty of the knowledge of soul with that of the knowledge of body. However, we know that a series of deductive reasons is only a chain of successive intuitions, and that it is sufficient to go through this chain several times in order to render the recourse to memory useless and to capture the set as *uno intuitu,* such that the truth of the most composite reasons ends up almost as certain as the truth of the simplest reasons. Although some truths are more difficult to know than others, "once they have been discovered, they are not believed any less certain than the others." Thus it is more difficult to discover the property of the square of the hypotenuse than to discover that this hypotenuse is necessarily opposite the largest angle, "but once this has been recognized, we are as convinced of its truth as of the truth of the other."[60] The place occupied by the proof of the existence of body in the chain would therefore lead one to confer a less immediate certainty on it than to the other truths, but it would not make it such that this certainty be of another nature.

It would be a different matter if we considered its object; for the existence whose certainty is posited here is not itself grasped by a clear and distinct intuition, but is certified by an obscure and confused sensation, whose validity is demonstrated clearly and distinctly by the understanding. Sensation, which does not know the thing whose presence it certifies, has no rational evidence; it has only the evidence it borrows from the understanding. Thus, with respect to the existence of bodies, we do not have knowledge, properly speaking; we do not have intuition; but in fact, we have belief (even though Descartes does not use the word): a belief that nevertheless is both absolutely certain and absolutely rational. Relative to this point, some philosophers at the end of the eighteenth century (Jacobi and Fichte, for example) will agree with Descartes about the reality of existing things, the objects of my sensible perception, by professing that there can only be a sensation, a belief, whose validity is guaranteed by God,[61] but there can never be an intuition.[62] And it is clear that a truth affirmed in virtue of a belief, without intuitive knowledge, even if *we know* by means of the understanding that it is a truth, must be less certain for a Cartesian than the one we affirm in virtue of the intuition of a clear and distinct idea, no matter how rational and certain is its affirmation. Consequently, despite the necessity of its proof, the existence of body must not appear to us as certain as the existence of soul and of God, perhaps less so because it is not known first than because its knowledge, since it is not of an intellectual order, is not of the same nature: "Finally [writes Descartes in the *Summary of the Meditations*], I bring out here [in *Meditation VI*—M. G.] all the arguments from which we ought to conclude about the existence of material things; not because I judge them very useful, in that they prove what they do prove, namely, that there is a world, that men have bodies, and other similar things that have never been doubted by any man of good sense, but because, considering them closely, we come to know that they are not as firm and as evident as those that lead us to the knowledge of God and our soul, so that the latter are the most certain of the truths that can become known to the human mind. That is all I planned to prove in these six *Meditations*."[63] The reasons are less firm and evident because, although the linkage of reasons that constitutes the proof is the object of clear and distinct knowledge, what it achieves is not the intuition of an idea, but the validation of a sensation. Hence, this conclusion is mostly negative, since it certifies that sensation cannot deceive us in this case. And especially because we are not dealing here solely with intuitions of ideas, the affirmation of judgment is "less firm," for "only the great clarity in my intellect produces a great inclination of my will,"[64] and "I must always come back to this: only the things I conceive clearly and distinctly have the power to convince me completely."[65] This conclusion echoes the conclusion in *Meditation III*. Body is less easy to know than soul, not only because it is known through the intermediary of the soul, but also because its existence is known through a faculty other than intelligence.

Finally, we have already observed that, even though it is less certain than the knowledge of the existence of the soul and God, the knowledge of the existence of bodies, as established by the proof, belongs to the sphere of absolute certainties, since it is different by nature from the highest degree of moral certainty, than which it remains higher.[66]

15. Examination of Malebranche's Critique

This conclusion can be compared with Malebranche's, which agrees with Descartes' thinking that the existence of soul is infinitely easier to know than the existence of body, but argues against him that the essence of bodies is more easily known than of soul. And, pushing the thesis to the limit, Malebranche argues that one cannot give an exact demonstration of the existence of material things through reason. Such a demonstration would be possible only if we had a purely intellectual evidence of this existence, as we have of mathematical objects. Malebranche contests the invincibility of the Cartesian proof, by contesting the invincibility of the inclination on which it is based. If, in fact, the inclination is not invincible, it depends on our freedom and does not depend on God. But God only guarantees what depends solely on him; therefore God does not guarantee this inclination. Consequently, the existence of material things remains uncertain. Moreover, this inclination might not be invincible, for only the inclination of my will to judge an intellectual evidence as true is invincible, not the inclination to judge the constraint of sensation as true. I therefore remain free to affirm or deny that body is its cause. However, since God has not given us any reason to doubt it, "we have more reason to believe that there are some [bodies—M. G.] than reasons to believe that there are none."[67] Therefore the proof can only lead to a *likely* "belief."

Malebranche's critique gains strength because it is based on indubitable Cartesian theses, namely, that the proof of the existence of bodies does not involve purely intellectual evidence (intelligence resulting by constraining me to recognize the truth of a sensation without itself grasping the demonstrated reality by intuition), to the extent that it has less certainty than the other proofs, and that the inclination of will to affirm it is as great as the knowledge is clear and distinct: "ex magna luce in intellectu sequitur magna propensio in voluntate."

But for Descartes, likelihood has no place in philosophy, and a proof is properly a proof only because it ends up with a necessary and certain truth. Although it has less certainty than metaphysical truths and mathematical truths, this truth, which has been integrated into *science* in virtue of the clear and distinct linkage of reasons, is, as the division of *Meditation VI* into three stages proves it, not merely *possible* or *probable,* but absolutely *certain.*

The real focus of the debate is the invincibility of inclination.

For Malebranche invincibility is absolute in intellectual evidence, for when the object is known completely, the will cannot go farther and can no longer incite the understanding to new discoveries. It is therefore stopped necessarily and is fixed invincibly in its affirmation. When on the contrary, the object is not known completely, the will can always go farther and provoke the understanding to a clearer and more distinct knowledge. Its stoppage can therefore be only discretionary and provisional: its assent is therefore free and not invincible.[68] Consequently, even when we have no reason to doubt the object, but when we do not have a completely clear and distinct knowledge of it, the inclination to affirm it cannot be invincible; it remains entirely free. Such is the case when we affirm the existence of bodies.

For Descartes, the invincibility of assent is never rigorously absolute (as it is for Malebranche) in the sense that even with complete mathematical evidence, I can always, speaking absolutely, refuse my assent—for example, in order to prove to myself that I am free.[69] But beyond this subjective reason that is intended to reveal the subsistence of the form of freedom in the most necessary affirmations, assent is practically and in fact ("morally") invincible, when it is established that there are no possible objective reasons that can incite me to refuse it. As a result of this, practically, assent is hardly more ineluctable in the case of mathematical evidence, as in the case of the natural inclination to posit material things as the cause of the constraint; for having no reason to impeach it and no reason to subtract myself from it, the affirmation cannot not occur, except that, here as elsewhere, I can suspend it in order to prove that I am free. But this suspension cannot stop the object of the judgment from appearing absolutely certain. Thus, whether the reason for the invincibility is negative (namely, that God has not given anything that allows us to doubt it) instead of being positive (that God has placed us in the presence of a clear and distinct idea), that does not change the incontestable fact of invincibility. This invincibility manifests itself in the fact that "no man of good sense" can doubt the existence of bodies,[70] and that the artifice of hyperbolic doubt, which is contrary to God's veracity, was needed in order to suspend judgment, in the same way that we suspend judgment on the truths of the understanding, in any case.

Because this inclination is invincible, it does not, practically speaking, depend on my freedom; it depends on God, and consequently God must guarantee it. The existence of material things is therefore not merely likely, but certain. Moreover, the necessity or invincibility of the proof, even though it assumes the invincibility of the inclination, can be distinguished from this latter invincibility; for it is based on clear and distinct ideas that invest this inclination with the character of truth—the ideas of God, of his veracity, and the clear and distinct knowledge of the conditions that put this veracity into play. The true certainty of the existence of bodies does not arise from the natural judgment that we bring upon it, but from the reasons that validate this judgment, meaning from the clear and distinct knowledge that allows the philosopher to affirm this existence with a firmness unknown to common man: "Ex magna luce in intellectu magna sequitur propensio in voluntate."

Moreover, Malebranche, because of certain fundamental principles of his philosophy, lacks some of the instruments of proof that Descartes possesses. Sensation and passivity, constituting for him the very nature of the soul, are not alterations that alone can explain an antagonistic reality. Since God's omnipotence is not raised above the truths of our understanding (which are truths of God's understanding and impose themselves on his will), the principle of common measure takes an absolute value that does not allow anything other than a mind to act on a mind. Finally, the relation of creatures to God is defined in such a way that no action can be exercised on creatures beyond that of God. All the paths that would allow me to prove, by considering myself internally, that bodies exist necessarily as causes of my passivity are therefore blocked.

We cannot attempt a demonstration by beginning with God either, or more exactly, by beginning with his Verb, the source of all truths and source of the natural light by which all kinds of proof are rendered possible, for the existence of bodies depends on divine free will. Since it is not a necessary truth contained in the Verb, given that it is contingent with respect to God, we would not be able to deduce it necessarily.

With respect to the first point (sensation does not necessarily imply the action of a material thing exercised upon the soul), the Cartesian thesis cannot be compromised, since Descartes professes a completely different doctrine than Malebranche with respect to sensation and the nature of soul. It is the same for the second point (the absolute validity of the truths of the understanding and impossibility of all effective action of one creature upon another), since Descartes has a completely different conception of eternal truths, and since, moreover, he admits the effective action of one creature on another, in spite of continuous creation.

As for the third critique (bodies are not necessarily created), it is also inoperative. It could only be valid against Spinoza, who claims to derive from God the proof of the necessary existence of things said to be created. Like Malebranche, Descartes professes the contingency of creation, and like Malebranche, he could not conceive a necessary deduction for creatures beginning with God. But if we are concerned, not with proving the *necessary existence* of bodies, but with proving, beginning with myself, that I must *necessarily recognize* that bodies exist, the contingency of their existence in itself does not constitute an obstacle to exact demonstration, in this case. It is sufficient that the premises of the doctrine (theories of sensation, of eternal truths, etc.) constrain me to posit these bodies as existent *necessarily for myself,* because of the characteristics of certain representative contents that I discover, in fact, in my soul. That I am necessarily required to posit that bodies exist does not require me to agree that God necessarily had to create them. In this sense and to that extent, Descartes is authorized to reject the proposition that there cannot be an exact demonstration of the existence of a being, except for the necessary being,[71] even though he himself recognizes that the proof of the existence of bodies does not have the attribute of directly intuitive evidence that mathematical proofs and the proofs of God's existence have.

CHAPTER XV

Proof of the Union of Soul and Body

1. On the Proof of the Union; the Problem of the Truth and Falsity of Quality

The problem of the union of soul and body has already been mentioned on two occasions, first when Descartes turns toward the operation of imagination in order to find an argument for the existence of bodies, and then when, turning toward the senses for the first time, he discovers there the reasons to believe in the union of my soul with my body, along with the reasons to believe in the existence of bodies.

The hypothesis by which Descartes explains the operation of imagination entails the union of soul and body. But this hypothesis is not valid unless it is demonstrated that bodies exist: "I easily conceive that imagination can be thus, *if it were true that there are bodies.*" Since the existence of bodies is now demonstrated, the hypothesis in question acquires the force of law, and the union of soul and body becomes ipso facto, certain (with *absolute* certainty). However, Descartes does not himself draw this conclusion; he leaves it to his reader. That is because the problem is not simply to prove the union, but to prove its substantial character. And we have seen that the imaginative process could not establish this by itself. Moreover, we are concerned, of course, with proving both the existence of body and the substantial union of soul and body, and also— even more so—with accounting for the contents of the various orders of ideas[1] and examining "their certificate of believability." If we were satisfied with concluding the substantial union in the fashion just indicated, the problem of the validity of these contents would show no progress toward a solution. And the content of sensation has not yet been completely explained or justified. The problem of the validity and meaning of obscurity and confusion as such—meaning the qualitative—has not yet been resolved. The analytic order of reasons requires that this last element be considered and attached to the chain, in turn.

That is why the passage to the proof of the union of soul and body is not accomplished by going from the external results of the preceding proof, as for example by deriving the necessity of the substantial union from the certainty that a body foreign to my substance exists outside of me and acts immediately on it; for in this way the substantial character of the union would be established immediately, and the analytic order of the investigation would be broken (for this order consists in pursuing, a step at a time, the analysis of the contents of my ideas, by going from the simplest to the more complex, and the various existences thus posited along the way—my existence, the existence of God, the existence of bodies—are only correlates of the objective validity that the analysis necessarily recognizes for them). And, as we have seen if we consider sensible ideas, whose examination constitutes the proper task of *Meditation VI,* only three of their characteristics have been accounted for up to now, *constraint, objective reality,* and *variation of the qualitative content* (and this latter in an as yet incomplete fashion), but not the fourth, which is the most specific one, that is, obscurity and confusion as such—in brief, *quality.*

As we have seen in the previous chapter, the proof of the substantial union of soul and body begins to be developed in the same paragraph in which the consequences of the proof of the existence of bodies relative to what the senses teach us about the particularity of existing material things (the proper objects of physics, strictly speaking) are deduced. That is because these consequences concern the qualitative content on which the proof of union will be founded exclusively. But the proof of the existence of bodies, which bears on the objective validity of the objective reality of sensation, considers this content only under a single aspect—*variation*—in order to determine the objective meaning and interest with respect to the order of the truths of physics. Consequently, it indicates that sensation, although teaching us that there exist different bodies, and giving us variations particular to each of them, does not allow us to know *the true nature* of these variations, such as they are in themselves in the bodies existing outside me. It therefore leads to the elimination of the qualitative character (which, in the case of sensible idea, is assumed by the objective reality of the idea) as something false with respect to the formal reality of external things. It assures us, by virtue of divine veracity, that we have the necessary faculty for this elimination.

But once this demonstration has been accomplished, we rediscover in consciousness, as one of its incontestable givens, this qualitative residue which, although it is eliminated by physics as something false with respect to the external thing, something illusory with respect to bodies outside of us, does not exist any less in me (who am a true thing), as something positive and real.[2] If the qualitative variations respond to something geometrical and quantitative outside of them, something which is foreign to them, but whose presence they certify and leave indeterminate,[3] must they not also respond, in this self within which they are definitively confined, to some reality that upholds them, explains them, and justifies them precisely with respect to that by which they are excluded from body and geometrical and quantitative variations? In brief, although it is rejected outside the reality of bodies, qualitative variation is not rejected outside all reality— it remains real in me. And everything real has God as its author, and everything that has God as its author is true and is guaranteed as such by him. Consequently, divine veracity requires that we discover the truth of this qualitative residue whose reality cannot be denied.

This discovery is possible only if we redress the false opinions that we form with respect to it. But the correction at issue will no longer concern the knowledge of the external existing body, to which the senses refer, but that of sensation itself, which has its own truth and which is false only when, as a sensible quality, we convert it into a property of the thing. The investigation that begins then no longer concerns physics, but psychology—that is, *human* biology as a psychophysical discipline. It will reveal a new kind of truth that, in itself, has no relation with the truth of geometry and physics, nor with the truth of pure understanding. It will entitle a new instrument of knowledge, adapted to a sphere in which pure understanding is no longer competent, which consequently must be completely different from that of mathematics, physics, and the rational psychology of pure understanding. And this organ of knowledge will also appear—if not absolutely, at least almost always –as infallible in its own kind,[4] when we refer it to the truth for which it is intended. This organ is sensation considered no longer in its representative content, in its objective reality, nor even in its qualitative variation, considered as a sign of a geometrical variation, but in the obscurity and confusion in which it is given, that is, as quality. In modern terms, to an inquiry concerning the truth of the understanding will succeed an inquiry concerning the truth of what is experienced.

The fundamental error is to confuse the two orders. An error that is no less serious is to deny one of the two orders for the other.[5] And this second error is no less difficult to avoid than the first. In fact, we know that the sensation of union is destructive to the clear and distinct knowledge of the real distinction of soul and body, and vice versa, so that the philosopher has a great difficulty in obeying the teachings of sensation (of what is experienced) and in practicing true psychology, while the common man, given completely to this experience, cannot rid himself of the weight of sensible qualities in order to perceive the truth of body and to practice true physics.[6] But the understanding, by following the strict order of linkage of clear and distinct ideas, is required by divine veracity to validate the truth of what is experienced (which is irrational for it), by means of a rational proof, while delimiting its sphere exactly.

2. The Reappearance, at Another Level, of the Two Problems Concerning Error That Intersected in *Meditation IV* (Theodicy and Psychology); Fusion of These Two Problems with the Problem of the Intrinsic Truth of the Qualitative

The analysis will now be conducted on quality. Quality will be considered in itself, distinct from constraint, and from the quantity and variation of objective reality. We will seek to account for its constitutive nature and to discover its meaning, which, as in the previous cases, will have as result to assign it a correlate and a function at the same time. This discovery will entail, as previously, the refutation of the objections that attempted to destroy the reasons invoked in favor of its teachings.

It is with the greatest urgency that this justification is imposed, here as elsewhere, in order to safeguard the thesis of divine veracity. Given that obscurity and confusion—quality—have appeared until now as the result of the small quantity of objective reality that constitutes the content of sensible ideas, we may think that the properties and functions which have been granted to sensible idea with respect to its small quantity of reality and in virtue of its two other characteristics, constraint and diversity of contents, are sufficient to justify completely the truth of that idea, within the limits of its reality, and that, within these same limits, it has been fully satisfied by divine veracity, which guarantees it. But we must still know specifically if the qualitative as such can be reduced to the infinite smallness of the objective reality of the idea and can be completely explained by it. In fact, the qualitative, taken in itself, is distinct from the quantity of objective reality, and the constraint and variety of contents. As a given of consciousness, it is not reducible to the above, and the justification given to them is not ipso facto its own. Moreover, it appears as the incarnation of material falsity, as the place in which all possibility of falsehood and evil takes refuge and resides, independently of our freedom. The confrontation between this element and divine veracity seems therefore to reveal, within our consciousness, meaning within God's work, a kind of scandal similar to the one revealed in *Meditation III* by the confrontation of formal error with divine veracity.

Thus, we are not surprised to see reappear in this *Meditation* problems and desiderata similar to those in *Meditation IV*. In the same way that divine veracity required, in *Meditation IV,* that error be explained *in its somewhat technical possibility*—in its *psychological* occurence—such that in addition and at the same time it would be justified *in its metaphysical possibility,* similarly, obscurity and confusion of the senses—quality as such—must be explained (insofar as they are false or principles of falsity) in their technical possibility, such that, in addition and at the same time, they are justified in their metaphysical possiblity with respect to an altogether good and completely veracious God. The principle of divine veracity is therefore, in this case, a heuristic principle, the indispensable directive thread for discovering its explanation as a fact and its legitimation as a rule.

However, the explanation to be furnished with respect to the qualitative can no longer be of the same order as the one brought forth for formal error by *Meditation IV.* Formal error, stemming from our freedom, is positively only the work of man, and God is exculpated insofar as it is established that he is not directly responsible for it. Correlatively, error was recognized as *an evil for man* and expressed the nothingness in which man participates. Therefore error, in this case, has *no useful function for man,* and Descartes, as we have seen, at no time treads in the path of *felix culpa.* Error receives a semblance of function only outside man, to the extent in which it *is referred hypothetically to the whole work of the creation*—to the extent that God, having allowed it, is assumed to have accepted it in his work only because, when all is said and done, it was useful for the beauty of the whole (or at least, it would be unavoidable in the best possible whole). On the other hand, since obscurity and confusion, that is, what appears as false in itself with respect to our understanding, being a given of my consciousness that is present in me in spite of myself, cannot, in this respect, have any author in me other than God himself, for it does not depend on my freedom that this obscurity and this confusion are or are not in my soul. God is therefore responsible. Consequently, it seems impossible to have recourse here to my freedom in order to displace this direct responsibility and to refer it to myself. As a result, since God is veracious, the obscurity and confusion he has introduced into human consciousness cannot in themselves be radically false elements with no utility *for man.*

Thus, what is first of all recognized as intrinsically false, from the viewpoint of my understanding, will have to be recognized as such, during the progress of the analysis, not in itself and absolutely, but only *from a certain point of view,* meaning relative to the requirements of the purely rational knowledge required by the understanding alone. What is materially false for the understanding will have to, contrarily to what has happened for formal error, receive *a useful function for man and be recognized as not being an evil for man.* The qualitative is metaphysically justified with respect to divine veracity only to the extent that it receives a justification with respect to man's good. On the other hand, formal error was metaphysically justified only by reference to the whole of the creation, without ever receiving the least useful function with respect to man, in which it is nothing other than a pure shortcoming of his freedom.

Thus, according to whether he is dealing with formal falsity or material falsity, Descartes brings forth two completely different replies to the one alternative: Since God is veracious, either the false does not exist (since as such it is only an appearance) and God is therefore exculpated (since in creating it he has created nothing that in itself was truly deceptive); or else it exists, but then God may not be its author (its author might be a nothingness that has no cause, properly speaking), and God is exculpated, since he is not responsible for it. In the case of formal falsity, Descartes opts for the latter hypothesis. In the case of material falsity (obscurity and confusion) he opts for the former. Obscurity and confusion are intrinsically nothing false.[7] Considered in themselves, they reveal to us authentically the union of soul and body as substantial union, which is precisely the cause of what constitutes them as such, as qualities, which allows us to learn about their specific function, which is to serve toward safeguarding this union. Considered within this limit, they are veridical, and their claims appear legitimate. We must even recognize that they are irreplaceable, in this respect. Thus they are justified intrinsically with respect to man, and in this way justified metaphysically with respect to God, who is their author.

But in this way we would possess only one of the elements of the solution—the most important element, however. In fact, first, in spite of its intrinsic truth and its useful function, the qualitative remains as the opportunity for formal error, and we have to account for this, but no more than it was when produced with respect to the ideas of the understanding—formal error is not here consubstantial to the nature of idea. Here as there its cause is outside the idea, in the free judgment that confers on quality a competence it does not have. Judgement ends up by falsifying not only the knowledge of the understanding, but the very truth of the senses. The general solution discovered in *Meditation IV* with respect to the problem of formal error is therefore applicable, to that extent, to the error committed with respect to the senses, as it was previously applied to the error committed with respect to the idea of the understanding.

Moreover, we ought to note that the senses, if they are veridical by themselves in principle, are not always absolutely so. In some exceptional circumstances, they fail at their informational function and are intrinsically deceptive. It is impossible to justify these faults by means of their function, since they betray it, and it is impossible to justify them by means of man's freedom, since they do not depend on it. We will therefore need, in this case, a new investigation in order to legitimate metaphysically, with respect to divine veracity, the existence of such faults in the divine work. This inquiry will conclude with the justification of the senses: if they could not have been given an absolute infallibility, at least they have been given the greatest possible infallibility compatible with the terms of the given problem, in a world which is the best that we can hope for. Thus the infallibility of our understanding will be verified as superior, since it is not simply a relative *maximum,* but an absolute *maximum.*[8]

Thus we see that the investigation will be two-pronged. First, it will seek the determination of a certain validity in quality as such, which, without being, properly speaking, objective in the strict sense of the word, will be objective to some extent. In fact, this validity will concern the things outside me, not as they are in themselves, but insofar as they act favorably or unfavorably on my "nature" (in the narrow sense). We will thus discover the useful function of quality as such, a function that is purely biological (in the psychophysical sense of the term).

Second, it will investigate the problem of error, properly speaking, and will rejoin the themes of *Meditation IV* by adapting them to the sphere of the obscure and confused, with respect to the determination of the human factors (freedom, judgment) of formal error relative to sensible quality. As for the problem of the faults proper to the senses, which can be explained only through factors that are foreign to man and his freedom, it can only be resolved by the combination of the analysis of the psychophysical structure of man with the metaphysical reasons already invoked in *Meditation IV* (principle of the best).

3. Priority of the Latter Problem over the Problem of Error. The Search for a Substitute with Objective Validity for Quality (Reexamination of a Problem Treated in *Meditation III* at Another Level); Proof of Union. A Single Proceeding for the Passage from Dual Error to Dual Truth. Divergence of the Physical Path and Psychological Path with Respect to Quality

The first investigation is along the path of *Meditation III.* In fact, it is an attempt to seek whether an element of consciousness belonging to the sphere of ideas possesses an objective validity or not, and to what extent it does. This element, which here is quality, is conceived in its constitutive and specific property of obscurity and confusion. But this problem is more difficult than ever before, for we cannot find support in the elements that have allowed its resolution until now, whether elements from the sphere of clear and distinct ideas or from the the sphere of sensible ideas. These elements were i) the quantity of objective reality of idea, and ii) constraint— internal constraint (perceived by reason) with respect to the ideas of the understanding, external constraint (sensed) with respect to the ideas of the senses. Moreover, it seems that all the possible objective validity entailed by sensation has already been established, namely, its existential objective validity, which correlates with the infinitely small degree of its objective reality, specified by constraint, and particularized as many times as this objective reality offers different variations. Quality (obscurity and confusion as such) is not this objective reality itself, but simply the sign and the result of the infinite smallness of this reality for our understanding. It does not constitute the content of the idea, but the scrambled aspect under which it is presented to us.

Thus, objective validity, or the substitute for objective validity, which will have to be recognized for quality as such, could not be what we recognize for sensible idea in virtue of its quantity of objective reality. Yet the substitute for truth that we will recognize for it will have to have some affinity with objective validity, since that validity is what belongs to an idea and concerns, in some way, its relation with a thing outside the idea. But since constraint and objective reality are not suitable as points of support in order to establish such an objective validity, on what will the proof be founded? It will have to be founded on the only probative element that remains, namely, divine veracity. Until now, divine veracity did not intervene alone or directly. It invited us to discover elements of the proof without instituting itself as such an element. It intervened in the proof only through the interposed criteria it guaranteed: constraint, natural inclination to explain constraint by means of a cause, quantity of objective reality, etc. Now it intervenes alone, proving directly, without any intermediaries, the truth of the teaching of quality, from the fact that it guarantees that this teaching, coming from God, cannot itself be deceptive.[9] In brief, the proof has no support other than the commandment that divine veracity addresses to us to grant necessarily in principle and a priori to quality (to what is experienced as such) the validity and signification that it recognizes for itself, for the sole reason that God has placed quality in us.

Thus sensation, as obscure and confused quality, consulted integrally and authentically, will have to bring us some teachings on its meaning, on its own validity, and thus its constitutive nature, as the voice of nature itself (or God's voice). Consequently, the whole proof will consist in gleaning this teaching from *nature itself, taking care to leave it in its authentic original terms.* It is the only care that divine veracity leaves to our freedom, to our scientific effort, for this veracity guarantees only what God alone has placed in us, not what *we* could have added on to it. We cannot satisfy this requirement of authenticity unless we recapture this teaching in its nakedness, in some sort of original state, in a state that is most "sensible" and "express," meaning most immediate, primitive, barren, humble, but also most imprescriptible, and at the same time most outside all interpretation added by the *understanding*. For it is solely the voice of "nature" that must be heard. And "there is nothing this nature teaches me more *expressly* or more *sensibly* [our emphasis—M. G.] than that I have a body, that this body is ill when my sensation is pain, that it needs to drink and eat when my sensation is thirst or hunger," that "I am not lodged in it like a pilot in his ship, but that furthermore, I am conjoined with it so closely and mixed with it so confusedly that I am something of a unity with it"; for when it is wounded, or when it needs to eat or drink, I do not learn this clearly and distinctly as from the outside by means of the understanding, but know it confusedly and intimately from the inside, by means of my pain, my thirst, or my hunger. Whatever happens to my body, I do not perceive it merely as an accident that modifies it, but I sense it at the same time as a modification of *myself*—in this case, *my* body and *my* soul are one. These sensations are therefore "confused ways of thinking that arise and depend on the union and apparent mixing of mind with body." The sensations that teach me that my body "exists within other bodies, which I must seek or evade according to whether they are beneficial or harmful to my body"[10] are of the same order. In this way I see that the teaching of the senses has a specific function, and that this function consists in "indicating to my mind which things are useful or harmful to the composite of which it is part."[11] Thus God has placed sensation (obscurity and confusion) in me in order to give "a sufficiently clear and distinct"[12] consciousness to the substantial composite of soul and body that specifically constitutes "my nature," so that I may be able to safeguard it. And it is evident that the set of all these teachings is certain, since God, who is their source, is veracious.

Thus is discovered, for the fourth element of sensible idea, meaning for quality, the substitute for objective validity it accrues, namely, the value of biological information relative to my psychophysical nature, as well as the function proper to it, of assuring the preservation of that nature. If the qualitative aspect of the variations of objective reality of sensible idea is false when it is referred to existing material bodies so as to make it a property that they really possess in themselves (at most it is only the sign of their geometrical variations), it is true when we refer it to the function of quality in the psychophysical complex. A radical divergence between the two paths that the physics and psychology of sensibility will have to follow is thus established. They both start with the same sensible perceptions, but each must preserve from this perception only the element the other abstracts away. Physics eliminates quality in order to retain only the geometrical variations hidden under the sensible variations that denote them; psychology abstracts away the geometrical variations, which are able to be captured by clear and distinct ideas under the cloak of sensible qualities, in order to preserve of these qualities only what is obscure and confused in them—in brief, what is experienced in them that is properly qualitative.

At the same time the substantial union of soul and body is proven. But we see that this consequence, which is externally more visible than the other one, is only a correlate. It is like the external aspect of an internal primordial and deeper conclusion, concerning the clear and distinct determination of the nature and validity it is suitable to recognize, of that element of our consciousness that appears last in the methodical order of the analysis of the contents of our soul, namely, the qualitative sensible in general. We should not fail to note, finally, that constraint does not intervene in this proof, which is based exclusively on the teachings of quality as such. As we have seen, with respect to the union of soul and body, constraint can only establish the existence of an external body united with my soul insofar as body must collaborate with soul for the production of our internal sensations (pain, for example). Therefore it founds the union only mediately, without being able to establish its substantiality. What it founds is not so much the knowledge of the union, properly speaking, as the objective validity of our judgments concerning the existence of such a union in general, without this union being determined with respect to its mode, in this manner.

4. First Result: Revelation of the Nature and Cause of Quality. What Is Unable to be Analyzed and Unknown in Quality; Simple Intellectual Natures and Simple Sensible Natures

Let us now examine the results.

First, we obtain a *clear and distinct knowledge* of the nature of quality as *obscurity and confusion.* By teaching myself in an absolutely sure manner that I am united to a body, God or "nature" allows me to know in as sure a manner the reason or the explanatory cause for obscurity and confusion, for quality as such: "These confused ways of thinking *arise* and *depend on* the union and apparent mixing of mind with body."[13] This union is a close mixing, meaning a *substantial* union, and not a more or less accidental and external linkage. In this latter case, in fact, the union would produce no sensation, and we would be informed about our body only by means of clear and distinct ideas. It is because the soul is "really united to the body" that "sensations of pain and others of similar nature are not pure thoughts of soul distinct from body, but confused perceptions," for, "if an angel were united to a human body [a union that would be accidental, since angels are by nature without body—M. G.], it would not have sensations such as ours, but it would perceive only the movements caused by external bodies, and thus would be different from a true man."[14]

We rediscover here a characteristic already indicated: the simultaneous acquisition of a certainty concerning the external world (in this case, the substantial union of my soul with a body) and a certainty concerning the internal world (in this case, the nature of the qualitative: the essence of sensible quality and its irreducibility in any analysis, and therefore its irreducibility to clear and distinct ideas). In fact, what unites two natures, in themselves separate, to the point that they can no longer be distinguished, is necessarily obscure and confused.

We must not confuse a sensible idea, which is obscure and confused by nature, with accidentally obscure and confused ideas which are ideas of the understanding that have not been sufficiently analyzed, or have been obliterated through their confusion with sensible ideas. Nothing is more contrary to Descartes' doctrine than the Leibnizian conception according to which obscurity and confusion proper to the sensible depend on the weakness of our mind and would be resolved into clarity and distinctness for an infinite mind capable of pushing the analysis to its end, or rather dominating and encompassing all possible analysis at once.

Certainly, all obscure and confused ideas have been defined as a conception that involves in itself something that remains unknown.[15] And moreover, what allows its confusion with something other than itself, is precisely this unknown that it has in common with what is confused with it.[16] Sensible quality, to the extent that it is not suitable to analysis and remains unknowable in the end, seems thus to require assimilation to the obscure and confused idea of the understanding. But that is not true. The qualitative, which in itself is unable to be analyzed, has nothing in common with this provisional unknown that conceals the analyzable idea that remains unanalyzed. It is not because it is not reducible by analysis that we can confuse the qualitative with something else, and it is not because it contains something impenetrable to the understanding and hence unknown in this respect for it; it is insofar as the understanding does not recognize it clearly and distinctly as such, although it has the power to do so. The unknown which, in this case, allows the confusion of the qualitative with what it is not, is constituted by these elements which, coming from the understanding and from judgment, have massed together with quality in order to constitute this complex that we call sensible perception. Through force of habit and weakness of attention, these elements of intellectual origin are not recognized by the understanding as stemming from itself, because it has not been able to push the analysis to its end and discover their true nature and origin.

The radically unanalyzable character of the qualitative gives rise to the qualitative, on the contrary, as a simple nature or primitive notion (an immediate given), whose distinctive mark we can recognize from the outside, a mark which, once we know it, prevents us from confusing it with anything else.[17] There is therefore an obscurity and confusion of the content of our knowledge when this content is constituted by sensation (by quality) and adheres essentially to it. But our very knowledge of this quality can be either obscure and confused, or clear and distinct,[18] according to whether we come to grasp quality in its authenticity or not—that is, in its nakedness.

In brief, sensation allows me to know clearly and distinctly what it aims to teach me (for example, that fire burns one who touches it and that I must avoid getting too close to it; that when I am thirsty, my body needs to be refreshed; etc.).[19] Similarly, I can acquire a clear and distinct knowledge from sensation, by distinguishing it from the other modes of my thought and by ceasing to mix it up with what it is not, in particular by ceasing to make it into a property of bodies.[20] I can also acquire a clear and distinct idea, in philosophy, of the essence of sensation insofar as the understanding conceives it necessarily as issuing from the substantial union of two simple natures. But, from all evidence, nothing in all this makes sensation itself into a clear and distinct idea; on the contrary, I know from all that, clearly and distinctly, that it is obscure and confused, and why it is so. The analysis that separates it from what it is not does not dissociate it in itself; the understanding that conceives it *as a composite* does not take it apart. If it conceives it as a composite, it is not by taking it apart, but by perceiving, by means of clear and distinct ideas of the soul and body, that the unity of these two substances *can only be* a unity of composition. In itself, sensed quality remains opaque for the understanding, which can merely posit it only as such. Therefore, if the substantial union of soul and body can be called a primitive or simple notion, like thought and extension, it is insofar as, *in its own sphere,* it assumes for science, as a substance, the role imparted to all substance— meaning a first truth which does not depend on any other, and which, rendering all others possible, is self-sufficient. In this respect, it is truly what is most simple, with respect to the analysis; it is incapable of being taken apart for science, meaning for the psychology of sensibility. But it is not simple in the way that extension and thought are, since, contrary to these two absolute natures, it is intrinsically composite. If the notions of thought and extension are unable to be taken apart, it is because in themselves they are not composites. If the notion of substantial union is unable to be taken apart, it is because the very being of this composite substance is only constituted in virtue of this composition. Of course, by his omnipotence, God could separate the natures he has united into one substance, but then this substance would disappear. This substance is therefore truly unable to be taken apart in itself, and even if God's understanding, from which nothing escapes, can penetrate this obscurity and confusion, obscurity and confusion are truly proper to its nature in itself, since it results from the mixing of two antagonistic beings, and not from an incapacity for our understanding to accomplish a sufficient analysis. Thus it is not from within, through a direct penetration of its quality, but only from without, by sketching the outline of the sphere of sensation by means of the clear and distinct knowledge of other natures and their reciprocal irreducibility, that the understanding arrives at a clear and distinct idea of the senses, their competence, and limits. Even though the understanding penetrates intellectual natures that are completely transparent to it, it notices and critiques from without the sensible given that in itself remains opaque to it.

It seems therefore that we must apply only in a restricted sense what Descartes says about the simple intellectual nature to this primitive and simple notion of union (to the qualitative given), namely that our mind, as soon as it acquires the least idea of it, must, from that fact alone, know it completely, because otherwise we could not call it simple, but we must say that it is composed of what we perceive of it and what we do not know of it.[21]

We have seen that, even with respect to simple substances (thought, extension), we cannot claim to know them completely, meaning in all their properties, from the fact that we know them completely *as substances,* meaning as self-sufficient. However, this knowledge is sufficient so that we are no longer liable to confuse them among themselves because of properties in them that can as yet be unknown to us.[22] With respect to the senses, it is advisable to be still more reserved. To know quality clearly and distinctly as a primitive simple notion is to perceive by intelligence both that quality is irreducible to extended substance as well as to thinking substance, and at the same time that it includes in itself what we immediately perceive in it—that is, both its raw given and what we do not know about it, its "I know not what" that refers to its occasional cause,[23] or even to the rational link that attaches quality to the geometrical variation of which it is the sign, and that unites the needs of body with the desires that the soul experiences, etc.[24] Finally, we must not forget the aspect of material falsity that sensation dons for the understanding, which is incapable of penetrating and distinguishing in the latter what there can be of being or nothingness in it.

5. Different Aspects of the Obscurity and Confusion of Sensibles According to the Perspective of the Realm of the Understanding and That of the Senses

But do we not have two conceptions of sensible obscurity and confusion? *Meditation III* explains obscurity and confusion by the infinite smallness of the objective reality contained in the idea, sensation being at the limit of being and nothingness. The obscurity and confusion of the idea express, in this case, not the confusion of soul and body, but the confusion relative to the limit of being and nothingness. The judgment of objective validity stemming from the act of freedom, transforming this material falsity into formal error, only expressly translates this confusion of being and nothingness by affirming outside of us something that, in reality, does not exist.[25]

Is this conception able to be reconciled with the one constructing obscurity and confusion from the mixing of soul and body? It is clearly evident that they have no relation to one another, that the mixing of soul and body is not that of being and nothingness, since the existing body is not a nothingness, but a formal reality suited to the objective reality contained in sensible idea. In addition, we can legitimately conclude that since this objective reality is infinitely small, the existing body assigned to it as formal, noneminent cause can have in itself only an infinitely small formal reality, which is in agreement with the small degree of reality (the lowest in the hierarchy of beings) that Neoplatonist and Christian philosophy traditionally recognizes for this corporeal existence.

These two conceptions are therefore not at all equivalent, and it is impossible to reduce one to the other. However, they are not incompatible. Their difference stems from a difference of point of view, arising from their different places in the chain of reasons.

In *Meditation III,* sensible idea is perceived from the point of view of the understanding that passes all ideas in review by kinds. The interpretation of sensible idea is constructed solely in terms of its quantity of objective reality. Consequently, obscurity and confusion are perceived as stemming from the infinite smallness of this reality, which is at the limit of being and nothingness, such that the understanding cannot know whether there is something before it or not. Thus, we see that the obscurity and confusion of sensation appear at this level, not as adhering to its proper nature, but only as a resulting appearance, *for intelligence,* of the infinite smallness of the objective reality constituting its content. We therefore do not reach the essence of sensible quality in this way. We are dealing, not with its intrinsic obscurity and confusion, but with the obscurity and confusion that are entailed necessarily for intelligence by the knowledge it can have of sensation. In brief, we reach the obscurity and confusion that rule over intelligence in this respect, and not the obscurity and confusion that are in the sensible quality considered in itself as *permixtio*. We must wait until the chain of reasons has introduced us into the sphere of the union of soul and body so that we can conceive what, constituting sensation, accounts for its intrinsic obscurity such as it is in itself, and so that we can perceive that it is in this intrinsic obscurity that we grasp quality in its authentic character.

We see at the same time that *material falsity,* blamed on sensible idea by the understanding in *Meditation III,* is only a point of view of the understanding with respect to this idea. It appeared from the fact that the understanding considers that idea in the same way it considers clear and distinct idea, namely, with respect to its function of knowledge. But if sensation does not have this function, which is reserved for clear and distinct idea, if it has another function in which the intrinsic obscurity and confusion of what is "sensed" intervene as principal factor, ought we not, instead of blaming material falsity on sensible idea, blame the understanding for placing itself in a false point of view in order to judge sensible idea?

6. Second Result: The Intrinsic Truth of Quality. Interdependence of Physics, Psychology, the Medicine of Composite Substances, and Morality with Respect to the First Common Condition of Their Respective Truths

The second result specifically founds the intrinsic truth of sensation. This result has been obtained through divine veracity. As we have already seen at various stages in the analysis, it alone governs the correct constitution of the sciences bearing on material things existing outside of me (physics), as well as sciences bearing on our own composite nature (psychology of sensations and affectivity, medicine under one of its aspects, and morality). All these sciences now appear as interdependent with respect to the establishment of what primordially conditions their respective truth. We cannot satisfy the requirements of one with respect to this without satisfying the requirements of the others in this way.

That is why the preliminaries of the third proof (the proof of union), which allows one to found the sciences of what is experienced, have been introduced at the same time as the consequences of the second proof (which founds physics as a science distinct from mathematics) were developed. These consequences are summed up in the certainty acquired from now on that there is an element of truth usable in qualitative diversities, and that this element allows one to distinguish the different sensible ideas with respect to their objective reality, and to perceive thus the particularity of material things existing outside of me and signified by these ideas.

Divine veracity, which already guarantees our natural inclination to posit the existence of bodies, an existence which is the correlate accounting for the content of these ideas, also guarantees that something real from the point of view of physics (namely geometrical variations) is the correlate of these obscure and confused variations. Moreover, it guarantees that we have in us the necessary faculty to attain these geometrical variations by means of sensible variations, "redressing" what is false in our opinions relative to the real constitution of particular things.

But the expression "to redress my false opinions" has a double meaning: I can redress them with respect to *external objects,* which I believe I know truly by means of sensations, as I can redress them with respect to *sensations themselves,* whose true nature and true end I wrongly believe I know. This second correction, which is entailed by the first, constitutes precisely the essence of the proof of union, since the latter consists in discovering the authentic tenor of sensation (of what is experienced) in its indubitability, in order thus to impose its teaching as necessary, as harvested in its natural state.

Thus, sensible variation, which is without objective validity properly speaking, since it does not resemble in any way the variation of things outside of me, is discovered within the limits of its objective reality, as a dual truth: on the one hand, it is true with respect to physics as the indubitable sign of the existence of certain particular external things, and of their particular properties, which are knowable objectively through them by the understanding that is capable of interpreting it correctly; on the other hand, it is true from the point of view of psychophysics, in its subjective meaning relative to the necessary information for the life of our body. The function of biological information, which is the principal function of the senses, must not allow us to lose sight of its auxiliary function, which is to render possible physics as such, nor must it allow us to believe that physics involves a radical condemnation of all pure sensorial givens, since it merely condemns the prejudices grafted onto it. The destruction of the false judgments that are added onto the authentic sensorial given (for example, the destruction of the judgment that makes me posit that the sun is objectively the size of a plate, or that a star is as large as the flame of a candle[26]), although stripping the sensorial given bare, such as to strip it of all objective validity *with respect to the true nature and the true magnitude* of these existing things in order to leave it only its biological meaning, does not entirely deprive it of all its objective meaning. It allows me to take support from this given in order to discover the true ideas of these things, (in this case, the true idea of the sun such that it is in itself). The knowledge of clear and distinct ideas, which are objectively valid, thus arises from the rectification of false concepts starting with the sensorial given, that is reconciled with its authentic content. And the reduction of the "variation" proper to the senses (as the sign of a variation that is heterogeneous to it) to its true validity is linked, ipso facto, to the true science of the geometrical variation proper to the existing thing. Thus going from false physics to true physics is not going from sensation to concepts, but to inadequate concepts stemming from the understanding, insofar as it badly interprets sensation, to clear and distinct concepts that have become possible through the detachment of my mind with respect to the fundamental error that makes it mistake sensations for qualities of things. This conception will be rendered fruitful by Spinoza in a completely different setting. There is therefore an ambivalence in the falsity of our opinions stemming from our senses that corresponds to two different orders of truth: i) a falsity of physical order, in which the true properties of external things are misjudged because of the fact of their confusion with sensible qualities, of which they are merely the sign—in this way we would be missing *the truth of physics;* ii) a falsity of psychological order, in which the true nature and role of sensible quality are misjudged because of the fact of its confusion with clear and distinct ideas—in this way we would be missing *the truth of psychology.*

These two errors, as different as they may be, have one and the same source. Whether we are dealing with a bad phychologist, who gives these same qualities the objective validity that belongs only to clear and distinct ideas, or gives clear and distinct ideas the virtue of allowing us to know the things of sensation, the mistake is the same: it consists in confusing understanding and sensation. Once intelligence succeeds in dissociating them by means of its critique, and to get each of them to keep within their limits, the double error disappears. As a result we see that the faculty that the veracious God has imparted to us in order to correct our errors on the first plane is, ipso facto, the one that allows us to correct them on the other, and we see that I cannot reach the truth of my sensation unless I reach the truth of the understanding. Evidently, the problem of the truth of the understanding, of the possibility of physics on the one hand, and of the truth of the senses on the other (of the possibility of human psychology as psychophysical substance) are finally reduced for philosophy to one and the same problem, since the conditions that render possible for the understanding the discovery of the truths of existing bodies in general and existing bodies in particular, beginning with the sensible given, are the same that render possible for the understanding the discovery of the intrinsic truth of the senses relative to its function of biological conservation. Under these conditions it was rational that the proof of union, relative to the psychological truth of sensation, was introduced when the consequences relative to the meaning of sensible truths from the point of view of the truth of physics were developed, beginning with the proof of existence.

7. Consequences Concerning the Problem of Error

If the revelation of the truth of the understanding and that of the truth of the senses appear as indissolubly tied to one another, then the order requires that the truth of the understanding be the first to be revealed, for only when I am assured of the validity of the knowledge of the understanding can I trust in all certainty the conclusions that the understanding imposes upon me relative to the proper truth and function of sensation.

From this flows an important consequence concerning the theory of error. In *Meditation IV,* the order constrained Descartes to discover only a part of it: then he could treat only error with respect to clear and distinct ideas, in conformity with the necessities of the analytic order, which had not yet integrated realities in science other than those of the ideas of my understanding, and which consequently posited sensation simply negatively, as what, outside science, constitutes its main obstacle. *Meditation VI* reintegrates sensation in the sphere of knowledge, and in this way determines its reality and degree of truth, in proportion with its degree of reality. The chain of reasons has transported us from the sphere of pure understanding to the sphere of sensation, to the point of view of "nature" (in the narrow sense).[27] It is therefore with respect to "nature" that the problem of error will now have to be posed. And under this aspect, its formulation and solution appear at first to be the inverse of those developed in *Meditation IV.* According to *Meditation IV,* error arises from the fact that our freedom, surpassing the limits of the understanding, affirms what it does not know and, in particular, treats obscure and confused ideas (sensations) as clear and distinct ideas. The weight of error falls on sensible ideas. Of course, fallibility arises from our freedom, and if the freedom of my judgment were held to the limits of the clear and distinct, error would be impossible. But if there were no obscure and confused ideas nor sensations, this fallibility would hardly be manifested, since my will, having before it only the clear and distinct ideas of my understanding, could not be incited to bear on anything other than on the truth.

The point of view is now completely different. Sensation in itself is generally infallible. If we are deceived with respect to it, it is because we introduce into true and authentic "nature," into the truthful given of the senses, elements stemming from the mind, properly speaking, that is, from the understanding: "This nature effectively teaches me to avoid things . . . but it is the business of the mind alone to know the truth of these things";[28]

and if I am mistaken when taking the various perceptions of things as the truth of these things, it is because "I pervert and misconstrue the order of nature" by using sensations as "extremely certain rules" in order to know the essence and nature of bodies.[29] In brief, it is the introduction of "mind" (meaning pure understanding) in "nature" that *perverts* the original truth of the latter. This view is specified further in the *Replies to Objections VI*, where the third degree of sense, which contains the source of all errors, is attributed to understanding alone.[30] The thesis of the infallibility of good nature[31] is therefore completed by the thesis of the perversion of nature by reason, a final trait that in some respects foreshadows the doctrines of the end of the eighteenth century, a trait that Malebranche will highlight.

Perceived from the aspect of sensation, error therefore truly appears due to *the intrusion of reason in the domain of "nature."* If *judgment kept within the limits of sensation,* it could not fall into falsehood; but it goes beyond those limits by proceeding to affirmations that only the ideas of the understanding allow. The point of view is therefore truly completely inverted, since, in *Meditation IV,* error, perceived from the point of view of the understanding, was due to the intrusion *of sensation into the domain of pure mind,* since judgment was unable to keep within the limits of the understanding.

Although seemingly contradictory, these two perspectives are in reality only rigorously complementary. In fact, in virtue of divine veracity, everything instituted in us, in spite of us, is necessarily *within the limits of its truth* and *to the extent of its reality*—that is, with respect to the faculties of knowledge, to the extent of the quantity of objective reality enclosed by their ideas—*absolutely real and true.* Therefore, on the one hand the understanding, and on the other "nature" or the faculty of sensing, are, taken in themselves, absolutely and equally infallible. But these two faculties each have their own function, and an infinitely free will disposing of a merely finite understanding does not always have enough light nor enough power of attention to be able to judge exactly the difference between these heterogeneous functions and the respective limits that these faculties derive from this. It therefore comes to confuse them. From this arises a double error, which is basically only one, that consists *in adulterating reason by sensation* and *nature by reason.* It is natural that there be only one and the same remedy for these two errors, for a will enlightened by reason; and this remedy consists in rendering the understanding to itself by purifying it of sensation—which is equivalent to rendering sensation ("nature") to itself by purifying it of the understanding. Consequently, we must not be surprised if, by reestablishing the truth of "nature," the destruction of false judgments relative to the senses tends to establish at the same time the completely different truth of science.

This conception will be carried to its ultimate conclusion in Malebranche's philosophy, to the extent that, entering into conflict with other elements of the doctrine, it will engender a series of complications and inextricable difficulties of the highest interest for its theory of the union of soul and body (which is extremely different from Descartes'), complications and difficulties whose exposition unfortunately cannot enter into the scope of this book.

8. Extension of Divine Veracity to Nature, Considered as the Assemblage of Three Substances

Since it has an absolutely universal scope, divine veracity has governed, in all legitimacy, the inquiry oriented toward the justification of the qualitative as such.[32] That is why the proof of union, which is nothing more than the demonstration of the truth of the teachings of sensation, was announced effectively by proclaiming the extension of divine veracity to the whole set of the divine creation, meaning as much to all its spiritual and material ingredients as to their *reciprocal adjustments*, as much to the great universe, within which I exist, as to the small universe that I myself constitute, which is also an *assemblage* of material and spiritual ingredients: to that assemblage, to the macrocosm of the universe as to the human microcosm, is given the name *nature* (in the broad sense). "First, there is no doubt that all that nature teaches me contains some truth. For by nature, considered in general, I now only understand God himself, or else the *order* and the *disposition* [our emphasis—M. G.] that God has established in created things; and by my nature in particular, I understand nothing else but the arrangement or assemblage of all things that God has given me."[33] "*My* nature" and "nature" (in the broad sense of the two terms) are therefore here *God himself.* Thus the veracity of nature and of *my* nature is absolute in principle. In fact, we know that the whole reality of a created thing is such only through its participation with the Supreme Being and that truth is reciprocal with being, falsehood with nothingness. The perfection, reality, and veracity of the whole of creation are therefore nothing more than the perfection, reality, and veracity of God himself. The voice of nature is the very voice of God: "Therefore there is no doubt that everything nature teaches me contains some truth." Ought we not even say that everything it teaches me *is nothing other than truth?* That would be the case, if not absolutely, at least *maximally,*[34] if I did not confuse the teaching of nature with prejudices and interpretations that do not belong to it and that I attribute to it. If I am mistaken in this respect, it is not nature that deceives me—in the *maximum* of cases— but I myself that deceives me, because I do not hold to its authentic teaching, as I ought and could do. The expression *my nature in particular* is contrasted with *nature in general,* meaning the universe in which I live; but here it is taken in its widest usage, in contrast with my nature as psychophysical substance. It designates the set of all realities that constitute me: spiritual substance, extended substance, and composite substance of soul-body. It therefore encompasses, besides the extended part to which I am united, all the faculties of my consciousness and, in particular, all my faculties of knowledge: the understanding, the site of clear and distinct ideas; the senses, the site of obscure and confused ideas. Taken in itself, each of these faculties is veracious and infallible. But if we confuse them, they soon adulterate one another.[35] And this confusion, which the weakness of my mind renders possible, is actualized by my freedom, and is expressed by false judgments concerning the physical world (errors about the truth of bodies) and the psychological world (errors about the truth of the teaching of nature relative to the composite substance of soul and body). Fallibility arises, in this case, from my freedom, not from nature. It belongs to another part of the inquiry to examine how nature can remain infallible and veracious, although, if we understand by nature the set of all the faculties that constitute me, freedom, which is fallible however, must be included in it. We can foresee that this difficulty will be resolved by a further refinement of the concept of nature.

Be that as it may, divine veracity, whose knowledge is given to me only by my pure understanding, requires us in principle to believe in the infallibility of our lower faculty of knowledge, as much as in that of our higher faculty. Here as elsewhere, it provides us with two methodological criteria, which are already known, that caution its guarantee: 1) *Everything false is destructible by the power of our mind*—in this way God has given us all the faculties necessary to destroy the false interpretative concepts arising from the understanding and allowed us to recover from behind the screen of prejudices authentic nature in its nonadulterated tenor;[36] 2) *everything that resists the critical power of our mind is true*—when, having bared our sensible nature, we become aware that God has given us no means to suspect or to destroy its eventual falsity, we are assured that this nature is authentic and veridical and that its voice is the voice of God himself.[37]

9. Reduction to the Minimum of the Objective Validity Recognized in Quality; Sign and What Is Signified

However, the truth that divine veracity is called upon to justify here is a new kind of truth.

The truths taught by sensation are of various natures. First, I know that I am united with a body and that this union is substantial. That is a theoretical truth. Even though it is brought forth by experience, it is a speculative truth, for it is objectively true that in itself my soul is substantially united to a body. Second, sensation gives me biological information about what is harmful to or what is useful for the preservation of the sustantial composite. These are practical truths deriving their validity from their efficacy with respect to the end whose realization they make possible. Finally, by reuniting them with the former truths, these latter truths allow one to attain another truth, which this time is of speculative order, namely, that sensation possesses truly and in itself a nondeceiving biological function, which accounts for it and to which it is perfectly well suited: "These sense perceptions were given to me by nature only to indicate to my mind which things are useful or harmful to the composite of which it is a part, and are within this limit (*eatenus*) sufficiently clear and distinct";[38] this implies not only that they are intrinsically clear and distinct, but that they allow us to know with all desirable clearness and distinctness the reason they were made, that is, what I must pursue or avoid: "Nature teaches me to avoid things that cause in me the sensation of pain and to seek those that make me have some sensation of pleasure."[39] And none of these teachings, no matter how they are considered, possesses objective validity, in the precise meaning of the term. By objective validity, we must understand the property possessed by all quantity of objective reality contained in an idea to refer to a certain formal reality. However, the *quality* about which we are concerned here is not the objective reality of a (sensible) idea, but the aspect that this objective reality presents. Since this aspect is not itself a certain quantity of objective reality, it cannot refer to some formal reality corresponding to it.

Better yet, the union of soul and body to which the qualitative is referred specifically, excludes the distinction between objective reality and formal reality, since there is no distinction here between subject and object, but a fusion of the two into a single subjective-objective being. The qualitative is therefore, among the elements that science distinguishes in sensation, the one that is farthest from idea as copy referring to a model. It is what is experienced as such, the thing in which the dissociation between the representative and the represented is erased, in which is sensed the reciprocal penetration of soul and body. What gives us quality, through this deep-seated obscurity and confusion constituting it, is the substantial character of the union, that is, the closeness of the *permixtio*. It is the immediate experience of the fusion into one of two beings that are incompatible as a rule. Of course, sensation has an objective reality. By means of it we can conclude the existence of external bodies, as its formal cause. But here we are concerned only with the obscurity and confusion of the content, considered in themselves separately from this content, as its sui generis aspect in our consciousness.

As for the practical biological information relative to external bodies to avoid or seek, information that we derive specifically from quality, it has no validity, in the strict sense of that word, since it is foreign to the truth of things. It is referred not to the order of reality and truth, but to that of goodness (utility) and finality. Here we are concerned with a relation, not that of copy and model, but of sign and signified; better yet, this relation is not even that of sensation to existing body. Already, the objective reality of sensation, by referring us to the existence of body, without being able to give use the true picture of what it is, appeared less the representation than the sign of this existing body. Sensation thus truly manifested that it belonged to the circle of utility, of finality, of the living, by opposition to the circle of the real, the true, and the speculative, which is that of clear and distinct ideas. Only the latter possesses objective validity in the proper sense of the term (which must be conceived as the copy of an original, the effect of an exemplary cause). In other words, the minimum of objective validity, which is the relation of sign to what is signified, corresponds to the minimum of objective reality. And this relation of sign to what is signified is now reduced to the minimum of this minimum, since it no longer serves to signify the existence and the variation of a material thing, but only the relation of the external thing to our needs.[40]

All that we can affirm is that the teachings of quality (meaning the knowledge of the union which reveals to us the property that a certain body possesses of being united substantially with our soul, and the biological information that instructs us about certain possible effects of the action of external things on us) have a meaning that still preserves a certain affinity with objective validity. The givens of the problem imply that it was thus.[41] On the one hand, we could not be dealing with a true objective validity, which is conceivable only as a function of objective reality; and as we have seen, quality, as considered here, as simple aspect of this reality, is not an objective reality. But on the other hand, in virtue of the Cartesian definition of idea, quality, as an element belonging to the nature of a certain kind of idea, of a certain kind of representation, can have a validity only relative to what is outside me, and, in the case in which it has a validity, only if it is more or less related to what the idea is supposed to represent, meaning if it possesses a validity having at least an affinity with objective validity. Here this validity is that of the sign to what is signified, whether what is signified is the existing thing, or the relation of that thing to my vital needs.

10. On the Right to Extend the Guarantee of Divine Veracity and on the Truth of the Elements of the Assemblage with Respect to the Goodness of Their Assemblage (Final Utility): Divine Veracity, Reality, and Causality; Divine Veracity, Goodness, and Finality

The justification of this validity by veracity poses a problem.

The ultimate foundation of this veracity is, as we have seen, God's omnipotence and supreme reality, which, since it cannot lean toward nothingness, cannot lean toward deception. Therefore, everything existing in the world, since it can only be real, has God as its author and is, ipso facto, true and veridical. Can we say also that the qualities (meaning obscurity and confusion) existing in the world, having God as their author, are real and cannot be intrinsically deceitful? Certainly we can say this, if truly obscurity and confusion as such are *real*. But they do not constitute the objective reality of sensation, since, by hypothesis, we have separated them from it in order to examine them apart, as being, not this reality, but the aspect under which the latter presents itself in our consciousness. Moreover, the objective reality included in sensible ideas has already received, in the preceding proof, the objective validity that is due to it, through the positing of the existence of body; and it has received from divine veracity the guarantee that accrues to its truth in proportion to its degree of reality. Thus, since it is neither formal nor objective reality, but a simple aspect or appearance of an objective reality, which has itself already received all its validity of truth, the qualitative as much—meaning obscurity and confusion considered apart—*is not a reality*.[42] Consequently, how can divine veracity impart to the qualitative its guarantee, if the principle that legitimates this guarantee is that everything real *has God as* its author?

To see how Descartes has resolved this problem, we must first note that what justifies the qualitative is its capacity to teach us immediately about what is suitable for the substantial composite—in brief, its function or *finality*. No doubt the truth of the teaching that sensation gives me relative to my substantial union with a body is founded immediately by efficient causality: since the substantial union is the cause of the qualitative, the qualitative can consequently reveal this union. But this union, although *explaining* the qualitative, does not *justify it*. Can we not reproach God for having introduced in me, by creating this union, this obscurity and confusion, which are not realities but the fallacious mixing of two realities (mind and body), to which they are foreign and with respect to which they are false? But, if the qualitative (what is experienced) is the best means that can be given to my consciousness to preserve the body to which we are joined, and if this union had to be *substantial* in order to produce this indispensable sensation of quality, the substantiality of the union and this sensation that it renders possible are justified at the same time as a means with respect to an end—to preserve the body to which I am united. And is not sensation, because of the rapid and sure character of its information and localization, more apt to accomplish the task of preserving of the body than an understanding that is not substantially but accidentally united to the body? Of course, such an understanding could know by means of clear and distinct ideas what is happening in the body with which it is associated externally, but it would be subject, because of its finiteness, to delays, and to oftentimes insurmountable difficulties, which would not allow the useful or necessary reactions to intervene in the appropriate time. Is that not precisely the unfortunate intervention of the understanding in the sphere of sensation, which compromises the efficiency and truth of its teaching by "perverting" it?

That is the start of Malebranche's theses, which oppose, with respect to the preservation of the union of soul and body, the infallibility and promptness of sensation (giving us the results of infinite calculations involving God's infinite wisdom), and the inadequacy for this task of our finite understanding, which would fail in most of the cases, or would succeed only after long evasions and painful inquiries. But Malebranche does not judge that the union of soul and body must be substantial[43] in order for sensation to be what it is and to be capable of assuming all these tasks.

Therefore it is truly through its *finality* that the qualitative is justified. Until then the justification of the various elements of representation was always accomplished through the discovery of their *reality*: the objective reality of various ideas (God, clear and distinct ideas, sensible ideas) implying that God was their author and that they were thus true. Inversely, it was sufficient to establish that a phenomenon has no reality or cause (in the precise sense of the term—that is, in the sense of positive efficient power) to account for its falsity—thus formal error. Since the qualitative is not real, but an obscure and confused appearance spread over a mixed reality, it cannot be justified as a truth by its reality, nor consequently as caused by God, since, to the extent that causality is reciprocal with reality, it seems not to be capable of having a cause in the precise sense of the term. The cause of quality is not a reality (the formal reality of the thing outside the idea), as is the cause of the objective reality of an idea, but a union, a substantial linkage between two realities, for there is no reality in the composite substance other than the reality of its constituents. Thus the qualitative does not bring forth a teaching concerning the positing of any reality whatsoever (as does, for example, the objective reality of sensation, which implies the positing of the formal reality of the existing body), but a teaching concerning the avatar of two realities, soul and body, namely, their union and the substantial character of that union. That is why the validity of the qualitative is based on the relation that ties it, as a means, with the preservation of this composite nature, as an end, and not on its "reality"; from this results the institution of a relation of means to end between external bodies and my composite nature.[44]

The validity of the qualitative therefore no longer rests on its truth being supported by the reality of the idea, since this reality is attached by the principle of causality to the reality of the veracious God, author of all being, but on its function, in virtue of the principle of finality, which founds the relation of a biological order (psychophysical) established between the qualitative and the needs of the composite, on the one hand, and my proper nature and external bodies, on the other hand. That is why, although completely devoid of truth with respect to *the reality* of things, the qualitative is wholly true with respect to its appropriateness for the requirements of the composite whole. What divine veracity now guarantees in this case is not a truth based on a reality, but the perfect appropriateness of a means to its end. It guarantees the validity of the relation of finality between sensation and the substantial composite, the infallibility of the qualitative as a means. It guarantees that in principle sensation indicates to us, without risk of error, the food good for nourishing the body, the heat good for warming it, etc. In exchange, the infallibility and excellence of this element with respect to its end justifies God for having given it to us. Even if its obscurity and confusion are sources of error with respect to the knowledge of true reality, we have nothing to complain about, since after all, it was what was most appropriate for the end we have to pursue as a composite "nature"—since our intelligence reveals to us that sensible idea does not have as role to bring to us the knowledge of what is reality in itself. We can even say that when we accuse the senses of entailing some material falsity, we commit a formal error with respect to them, by bringing forth a false judgment about their nature and role.

It is immediately clear that divine veracity cannot bring forth its guarantee here, except in virtue of a completely different foundation from the one that until now justified its usage.

Until now, from the proof by effects *(Meditation III)* up to the proof of the existence of bodies *(Meditation VI)*, divine veracity was applied to things by the intermediary of their reality which, certifying their participation in God's reality, thus entailed their own truth. Each element of nature, considered one at a time, received the guarantee of divine veracity, as soon as we discovered some reality in it.

Now, on the contrary, since we are concerned with guaranteeing the perfection of a relation of finality, the excellence of a means with respect to an end, God must no longer be satisfied with founding the veracity of nature in each of its elements insofar as they are real, but he must found it in the *assemblage* of its real elements *taken collectively*. He must guarantee that this assemblage has been brought together in such a way that nature could not deceive us—meaning that the relations between my sensing soul with the body to which it is united and with external bodies acting on the latter are, in their totality, the best adapted to the requirements of our nature. From which arises the following formula about God's veracity (a formula completely different from the one found in *Meditation IV*), which bears not only on the *reality* of things, but also on their *disposition:* "There is no doubt that all that nature teaches me contains some truth. For by nature considered in general I now understand nothing else than God himself, or rather *the order* and *disposition* that God has established in created things; and by my nature in particular I understand nothing else than the *arrangement* or *assemblage* of all that God has given me."[45]

And it is evident that divine veracity cannot assume such a role as long as it is conceived merely as based on God's supreme reality and omnipotence, for such a foundation can only guarantee the truth of what is real, not the exact and infallible appropriateness of a certain disposition of the real to an end. Divine guarantee can only be extended to this assemblage insofar as God's veracity is related to his *goodness*. And Descartes has, in fact, always based divine veracity on God's goodness as well as on his omnipotence, so much so that it has often been believed that it rested on the former alone, although the latter was its principal foundation. Moreover, such a foundation is legitimate, since God, who is supremely perfect, must possess all the types of perfection, infinite goodness as well as infinite being and infinite omnipotence.[46] The principle of the best, which in *Meditation IV* was introduced only externally in order to justify metaphysically the presence of error in the universe created by a perfect, good, and veracious God intervenes here to allow an internal justification of sensed quality by means of divine veracity.

The dual root of the principle of divine veracity allows it to assume a double function: i) to found the truth of every reality (in virtue of the requirements of omnipotence), and then ii) to found the truth of their assemblage (in virtue of goodness). The application of the principle of veracity to the solution of the problem of the justification of obscure and confused quality, and generally to the problem of composite substance, would be impossible without the recourse to God's goodness, which appears as the final foundation of the proof of the union of soul and body. For although God's omnipotence renders admissible a substantial union of two substances that our finite understanding cannot conceive, it is his goodness that guarantees for our understanding the truth of the sensation issuing from this assemblage, in virtue of the intrinsic excellence of this assemblage.

Since "nature" is nothing other than God himself, and the infallibility of his voice is only the expression of its goodness directly emanating from God's goodness, nature is already to some extent, for Descartes, the guardian and divine "good nature" celebrated by the philosophers of the end of the eighteenth century.[47]

The sphere of the composite substance appears to be the sphere of internal finality; moreover this finality is the only one accessible to our finite understanding. It is guaranteed by God's goodness, which bases the idea of a general organization of the universe ("order" or "disposition" of nature) on the principle of the best. We ought to assume that this organization exists, without having even the least knowledge of it, for it escapes our limited minds.[48] Thus is confirmed that God acts in accordance with ends, but that his ends are impenetrable.[49] The size of the created universe, based on the infinity of divine omnipotence, must not lead us to exclude all kinds of ends from it, but must lead us to give up our search for them, and above all to give up conceiving them anthropomorphically.[50] In God's work, infinity must not suppress all characteristics of beauty and goodness, which necessarily imply a harmonious (and consequently teleological) organization, but it must require one to raise to infinity the idea of its beauty and goodness as one does for the idea of its magnitude: "It seems to me that we ought to observe two things. The first is that we ought to remember always that God's power and goodness are infinite, so that we can know that we ought not fear failing when imagining his works as too great, *too beautiful, or too perfect,* but that we can easily fail if, on the contrary, we assume in him some limitations or bounds of which we have no certain knowledge."[51] "The second is that . . . we ought not be too presumptuous, as it seems we would be if we supposed that the universe had limits, without being assured of that by divine revelation, or at least by extremely evident natural reasons, and as it seems we would be to an even greater extent if we were persuaded that God has created all things only for our use, or even if we claimed to know by the power of our mind what are the ends for which he has created them."[52]

Of the True and of the False in the Realm of the Senses, First Problem: Formal Error of Judgment—the Analysis of the Concept of Nature

1. From the Problem of the Intrinsic Truth of the Senses to the Problem of the Falsity of the Senses. Complication Arising for the Problem of Error Relative to Its Position in *Meditation IV*

In the two preceding proofs we have witnessed the discovery of the truth of the senses considered under its two aspects: the senses are true insofar as, by constraint and objective reality, they teach us indubitably about the presence of external things existing outside of us, certifying by the sensible *varietas* modifications that are not in themselves sensed; and they are true insofar as, through quality, they teach us infallibly about the substantial union of our soul with our body and give us, in a most secure fashion, the information necessary for preserving this union. In this way the positive portion of the inquiry is completed. In its broad outline, it corresponds, for sensation, with what *Meditation III* and the beginning of *Meditation V* were for clear and distinct ideas.

But the facts testify that the senses, in reality, deceive us often. Their truth therefore remains subject to question as long as this deception is not explained and the doubt it authorizes is not exorcised. We rediscover here, under another form, the problem treated in *Meditation IV*, the problem of error.

In this respect, the task of *Meditation VI* is more arduous than that of *Meditation IV*. The latter finds the question of the intrinsic truth of (clear and distinct) ideas completely settled. Divine veracity was sufficient for that. It needed only to appear in order to abolish, ipso facto, the only doubt capable of disturbing our certainty in this sphere, namely, the metaphysical doubt stemming from the hypothesis of the evil genius. Here the principle of divine veracity cannot settle the question by its mere presence. In fact, we are no longer concerned with clear and distinct ideas, but with obscure and confused ideas which have not been assailed by metaphysical doubt alone, but which are repugnant to the understanding, and which are naturally called in question by doubts based on facts. These doubts and these facts enter into conflict with the claim of divine veracity to be valid absolutely and universally. To pursue the inquiry, we must therefore appeal, this time, to the resolution not to doubt, but to persevere, in spite of the evidence to the contrary, in believing that everything in the world is true. Thus two problems are posed: 1) to complete the positive demonstration of the truth of sensation—toward this end we must give an explanation for the errors that appear to trouble sensation, such that sensation is in itself rehabilitated, at least within the limits within which its truth must be recognized; 2) to complete vindication of God, and, toward this end, to rehabilitate the senses, in order to confirm his absolute veracity. The two problems are tied indissolubly.

Thus we are brought back to the formulas of *Meditation IV*. The general difficulty is the same: "How to reconcile divine veracity with the fact that we can be deceived." This problem is rendered specific here under the following form: "How to reconcile divine veracity, which entails the universal truth of nature or of the senses, with the fact that nature or the senses can deceive us." We rediscover the same intersection as in *Meditation IV*. But here two solutions are possible:

1) To demonstrate that nature or the senses basically do not deceive us. If we are deceived about the senses, it is because we use our free will badly. There is then an intrinsic truth of the senses and a formal error of judgment. We return purely and simply to the doctrine of *Meditation IV*, with the intrinsic truth of the senses taking the place that the intrinsic truth of the ideas of the understanding occupied in this *Meditation*. The important question is then the rehabilitation of the senses.

2) To admit the intrinsic falsity of the senses, but to find that this falsity can be explained as to exculpate God (if not *absolutely*, at least *morally*). We rediscover here, as in *Meditation IV*, the intersection of a technical problem, relative to the explanation of a fact, and a problem of theodicy. But what is at issue is not the same: the falsity at issue is that of a given of consciousness, not that of judgment.

These two solutions shall be examined in turn and will converge toward the solution of the total problem.

2. First Problem: Formal Error in the Realm of the Senses. Analysis of the Concept of Nature; the Fivefold Reciprocal Perversion of Various Natures and Its Principle

The facts that justify doubt with respect to the senses are of two kinds.

There is first a falsity of our opinions stemming from the senses. There is also something of an intrinsic falsity of the senses, a failure with respect to their function. The first kind of error, the only one we have to consider for now, is the one that consists in taking sensible qualities for the properties of things. A lengthy analysis is not necessary to discover that this false opinion does not arise from the senses themselves, but from false judgments that I make with respect to them, which arise from the confusion of my sensation with the ideas of the understanding.[1] This confusion is extremely tenacious because it dates from childhood.[2]

There results from this a double error about the two natures that are combined in the substantial union, and that, joined to the latter, constitute the whole of my being (my nature in the broad sense). The first arises from confusing my composite substance with my mind alone: it is properly the confusion of rational, clear, and distinct ideas with sensible, obscure, and confused ideas. The second arises from confusing my composite nature with extension alone: it is properly the confusion of sensible quality with the real properties of things. This double error, an error of psychology and an error of physics, is the diffraction of a fundamental error about our psychophysical reality, that is, about *our nature* (in the strict sense of nature as an entity composed of soul and body). In fact, if confusing pure mind with my psychophysical being destroys the truth about the essence of my soul, if confusing pure extension with this same psychophysical being destroys the truth about the essence of bodies, the truth of my psychophysical being, of my nature (in the strict sense)—relative to the true meaning of sensation, to its true function and its appropriateness for this function— is itself destroyed by the confusion of this psychophysical being with pure mind and pure extension.[3] And this confusion underlies what are alleged to be the errors of the senses, and it underlies our condemnation of them. It is because of this confusion that I falsely interpret the sensible given and am mistaken about things. Moreover, from the fact of this same confusion and of the false interpretation it entails, I charge the senses with this error for which I alone am responsible, and I err about them when I accuse them of deceiving me. And, since God is the creator of the senses, it remains only for me to accuse God while accusing "nature." The sum of these confusions and errors adds up to what I call, in agreement with common usage, the "teaching of nature."

But is that truly the teaching of nature? In order to answer this question, we see how urgent it is to define what I actually mean when I say that *nature teaches me something.* Evidently, this teaching cannot be the one that common opinion imagines, for it could not include the interpretations that I myself add to the sensible given. Moreover, the nature that instructs me through original sensation (stripped of what the understanding gives to it) is not my nature in the broad sense (meaning the assemblage of three substances—thought, extension, and psychophysical substance— which constitutes the totality of my human being), but my nature in the strict sense (meaning my composite nature, the seat of the qualitative element in its purity and in its first authenticity). Everyday thought has no clear and distinct knowledge of my nature either in the strict sense or in the broad sense; it confuses them, just as it confuses the three constitutive elements of nature in the broad sense. Consequently, it confuses the various teachings it draws from each of them into one and the same obscure and confused teaching, and it relates that teaching to nature in the strict sense, meaning to sensation, properly speaking.[4] It thus "perverts" my nature in the strict sense, meaning both affective and instinctive sensation, which is irreducible to the idea of the understanding, as well as the sensible quality that is irreducible to the properties of extension: "I see that both here and in many other similar cases I am accustomed to pervert or confuse the order of nature, because although these sensations or sense perceptions were given to me only to signify to my mind which things are useful or harmful to the composite body of which it is a part, and are *within that limit sufficiently clear and distinct,* I nevertheless use them as if they were very certain rules by which I could obtain direct information about *the essence and the nature of bodies outside of me,* about which they can, of course, give me no information except very obscurely and confusedly."[5] If we refer to the considerations preceding this text, we can see that the nature whose order we pervert is physical nature, that is, the world of material things that are reducible to extension and movement.[6] We confuse this nature with the properties and laws of my nature in the strict sense, by lending sensible qualities to bodies, by imagining that they are separated by void, etc. If, on the other hand, we refer to the considerations that follow this text, that is, to the explanation of this perversion,[7] we perceive that the perverted nature is *my nature* in the strict sense as well as physical nature, and that the ideas of my nature as sensible ideas are perverted by assimilating them to clear and distinct ideas of the understanding, whereas sensible quality, which is its product, is perverted by converting it into a real property of bodies.

Hence everything is perverted, for this fundamental perversion of my nature is also the basis of the perversion of my purely spiritual nature, which is adulterated by confusing its clear and distinct ideas with the affections of the senses; and we have seen already that it was the purely corporeal nature that was corrupted because of the confusion of its true (geometrical) properties with sensed quality.

Moreover, each of these perversions is many-valued, and each is also only the inverse of another. Thus, the confusion of my nature *stricto sensu* with extended nature can lead either [on the one hand] to referring my (composite) nature to the physical nature of bodies—my human body is then reduced to a pure machine like the body of an animal, to modes of extension and movement (this is what materialists do[8])—or [on the other hand] to reducing physical nature to the standard of my proper (composite) nature—we then obtain the physics of substantial forms. From another point of view, the confusion of my nature in the strict sense with extension alone entails the confusion of clear and distinct idea with sensation, or quality. And this confusion engenders in its turn a many-valued perversion. In fact, we shall want either to reduce the ideas of the understanding to sensible ideas—we shall then profess with common sense and the empiricists that "I have no idea in my mind that I have not previously acquired through the senses"[9]—or we shall want to convert into clear and distinct ideas what is in the domain of sensation, that is to say, to explain by means of clear and distinct ideas everything that concerns the union of soul and body (such will be precisely Spinoza's error, which is condemned in advance by Descartes in his letters to Elizabeth).

Thus, what for the present I call "nature" when I say what "nature teaches me" is a notion that is false in five ways, resting on a fivefold confusion, which at bottom reduces to one. In fact, the four important confusions resulting from the two possible confusions of the composite nature with the soul alone, together with the two other possible confusions of this composite nature with extension alone, arise from the fundamental confusion between my nature in the broad sense and my nature in the strict sense. From this arises a pseudonature. In order to make it disappear, we have to accomplish a fivefold fundamental dissociation of nature, in the strict sense, from nature in the broad sense.

It is not as if my nature in the broad sense is always necessarily confused knowledge, the source of all perversions. Its confusion with nature in the strict sense, from which the whole problem seems to arise, is nothing more than the confusion of the latter with the other natures, whether intellectual or extended; that is, it is itself only confused knowledge of my nature in the broad sense. This is what certifies that originally the understanding of this latter nature is not less truthful than the others, and has a perfect clearness and distinctness. In fact, it is formed by uniting the authentic teaching arising from the various substances of which my whole human being is constituted. And since the assemblage of the three substances that constitute this being arises from the hand of the good and veracious God, it would be incapable of being defective in itself, nor the cause of falsity. Each of these constituent realities, understanding alone, extension alone, psychophysical being alone, teaches me a truth that in itself is infallible. And since God has assembled them together, and since his goodness has presided over their assemblage, in principle nothing can come of it except what is good and true. These teachings, each true in its own sphere, have not been intended by God to remain isolated from one another. Since he has brought them together, he did so with a view toward their harmony in the human being and for the good of those beings. Also, each of these teachings completes the teaching of the two others, precisely because none of them by itself can bring to man what the others give him. Given man's state in the world, it would be impossible to assure his life and happiness if he were reduced to sensation alone or to understanding alone. Without understanding he could not interpret the senses on the level of everyday life, and he would remain blind, for only the understanding sees;[10] on the level of science, he could not rise to the level of mathematics, which governs all science. In contrast, deprived of the senses, human understanding would be aware of nothing that would allow intelligent beings to guide themselves in the world of existences in the midst of which they are placed; they would see nothing of existing things,[11] whereas, on the level of science, they could never rise to the level of physics, as a science distinct from speculative geometry. Thus we must consider that the teaching of my nature in the broad sense is also in itself originally and intrinsically truthful, in the most absolute manner possible, as long as we take it as we should (meaning in its original state) by carefully distinguishing in it what arises from the mind alone, from extension alone, and from my composite substance alone.

3. Distinction and Harmony; Confusion and Perversion.
The Human Instruments of Distinction and Harmony.
Widening of the Problem of Limits

Hence it follows that "the whole science of man" will consist essentially in distinguishing clearly and distinctly the three substances that constitute me.[12] The result of distinguishing these elements will be to bring them into harmony and to put an end to their confusion, for confusion is no more harmony than clear and distinct discernment is reciprocal isolation. In contrast, it would by itself be enough for me to allow myself, out of the habits of childhood and without attention and reflection, to confuse these various teachings instead of distinguishing them one from the other, for them to destroy themselves reciprocally instead of perfecting one another—giving rise to a general commingling affecting my nature in the strict sense equally with my nature in the broad sense and the elements that constitute it. The confused hodgepodge of assembled elements is substituted for the harmony of the assemblage.

And it truly appears that no intermediary is possible between thus distinguishing the elements of my total being and producing in myself total clearness and harmony, and confusing them and reducing myself to absolute obscurity and disorder. We rediscover here the clean separation that Descartes established between science and what is not science, between the true and the false, between the pure and the impure—in brief, the "all or nothing" that will also be the maxim of Kantianism.[13] And, since there is no middle ground between knowing and being ignorant, between the clear and distinct knowledge of my nature, taken in the different legitimate senses of the term, and its complete misappreciation (an abyss of inextricable confusions): between harmony and disorder, given that a good action will depend on true consciousness and a bad action will depend on false consciousness,[14] the result is that there is no middle ground between the moral man and the immoral man. Here we come to the sharp Stoic separation between fools and wise men[15] (as we do, in Kant, between autonomy and heteronomy) if, as we will see later on, this absolutism in matters of morals was not made to give way a little, or at least to change its nature, in virtue of the fact that man lives in a universe whose perfection, which, of course, is as great as possible, is nevertheless only relative and not absolute.[16]

Attention allows this dissociation to be accomplished. When I confront my nature in the strict sense, in its ultimate purity and its original authenticity, I oppose it immediately to pure soul and pure extension, from which it is distinguished. As soon as I perceive the limits of these different regions, I perceive clearly and distinctly the limits within which I must restrict my various affirmations. By ceasing to transgress these limits, I obtain both the purity and the harmony of all the elements of my nature.

We see the problem of the *limites ingenii* that had been already treated in *Meditation IV* with respect to formal error in the realm of the understanding reappear here, along with this general solution of error in the realm of senses, an error that again presents all the characteristics of formal error due to my affirming will. That is because the problem of limits is tied indissolubly to the problem of formal error, the latter being always only an affirmation of will that transgresses the limits of a faculty of knowledge. In *Meditation IV,* formal error consisted in the transgression of the limits of the understanding by will. Here it consists in the transgression of the limits of the senses by will, a transgression that is extremely easy to accomplish, since the understanding, although it is finite, is almost without limits compared with the sensible faculty, which is extremely narrow.[17] And the circumstances of life bring about that man seems fated to be led to reduce by violence his whole faculty of knowledge to this lower, very narrow faculty, for the manner in which the body imposes itself on him from his childhood, the pressing care that it must have from him, and the delayed growth of the powers of consciousness and the understanding, lead him to attribute to body qualities that come from sensation, and to suppose that he receives all the knowledge he has of body from sensible ideas.[18] When, in the long run, the powers of the understanding have increased, habit has also with time taken root in us, and it takes us a great effort to break its bonds, a kind of wrenching in the opposite direction.[19] And yet, while the problem of limits reappears, it is only to spread itself even more widely. We are no longer concerned only to determine the "limits of our mind," but to determine the limit of all the realities that constitute man's being,[20] and the limits of the affirmations allowed with respect to them. We are not only concerned with the limits of its mental faculties, understanding and sensibility, but those of its material reality, since the validity of geometrical relations must stop at the limits of the sphere of psychophysical reality. Cartesian analysis demonstrates its novelty by not limiting itself to the breaking up of man's mind, but by extending itself to the breaking up of the whole of human reality—spiritual substance, material substance, psychophysical substance—without ceasing to base itself solely on the consideration of what I discover inside myself.

The result of this exhaustive analysis is, on the one hand, to determine the limits, the proper usage of each faculty, and to submit all of them to a discipline that renders natural light possible, the discipline of *pure reason;* on the other hand, it is to reestablish harmony between the three natures whose assemblage constitutes the whole of our human being, by this *just* and *precise* repartition of legitimate competences. We perceive here the union of two formulas. The first seems to anticipate Kantianism, which assures the discipline of faculties by determining their limits and their legitimate use, thanks to pure reason. The second seems to echo Platonism, which has recourse to rational knowledge in order to place in equilibrium the three constitutive elements of our soul and to allow a harmony based on justice to govern in it.

4. Conformity of This First Solution with the Solution of *Meditation IV*

By giving this definitive solution of the problem of limits, that is, by analyzing the concept of nature in such a way as to dissolve the concept of pseudonature so that I confront my authentic nature, a true and good nature, whose truthful language—namely sensation—is the voice of the guardian and veracious God himself, the problem of the intrinsic truth of the senses is resolved. At the same time the general problem of error in the realm of the senses is resolved. And it is resolved under two aspects: psychological and theological.

The psychological possibility of error is explained by a confusion of the senses with something other than themselves, which converts their intrinsic truth into falsity, a transformation for which I am responsible since I can avoid it. Of course, the urgent necessities of life and the habits that from childhood they unavoidably bring with them seem to excuse me. But, even though Descartes had no occasion to express his thought on the matter, we can assume that here, as elsewhere, God has acted for the best, given the problem that he had to resolve. In any case, he has given us, together with will, attention, and the light of the understanding, all the necessary tools for us not to allow ourselves to be deceived. The senses, such as God has given them to us as an immediate datum of consciousness, are intrinsically true. God is therefore exculpated of the fault with which he has been accused.

In this way the theological problem of God's culpability in the alleged error of the senses is resolved. God cannot be held responsible for the defects of what we commonly call nature, because the latter is only a pseudo-nature of which we are the sole authors, and which we have constructed with our confusions and our prejudices. True nature, of which God is the creator, is truthful. Our defective use of attention, that is, of freedom, is still what is alone culpable in this case. We discover here the exact correlative of *Meditation IV*, to which Descartes expressly refers.[21] The mutual confusion of understanding and the senses is identified in *Meditation VI* as the principle that corrupts the truth of the senses, just as it was identified in *Meditation IV* as the principle that corrupts the truth of the understanding. Here as there, the misuse of my freedom, my inattention, explains my failure and absolves God. And since *Meditation IV* we know that we cannot accuse God for having introduced into one of these three substances that constitute my nature in the broad sense the freedom by which error can be accomplished, for there can be no freedom possible without its possible misuse, and if this misuse is an imperfection, we must conceive that, in the universe considered collectively, slight imperfections are no doubt necessary for the greatest perfection of the whole.

Of the True and of the False in the Realm of the Senses, Second Problem: The Intrinsic Falsity of the Senses-Internal Conditions of the Psychophysical Substance. The Union of the Soul with Every Part of the Body

1. Relation of the Problem of the Intrinsic Falsity of the Senses to the Inquiry for the Internal Conditions of the Union of Soul and Body. General Principle of the Solution. The Two Problems with Respect to the Conditions of the Union (Union with the Body as a Whole, More Particular Union with One of Its Parts)

The solution of the problem of formal error in the senses does not, however, completely resolve the question of the truth of the senses. Another problem looms behind this problem, one about the intrinsic falsity of the senses. In fact, the senses appear deceptive in themselves when they allow me to sense as good what is bad for the preservation of my composite substance; nature is deceitful when it leads me to absorb what can destroy my composite substance. We must account for this defect that indicts God's goodness and veracity, since it arises outside the use of our freedom. In fact, it is God who has placed directly in us and without our consent these senses that deceive us. God therefore seems undeniably responsible.

This new problem is particularly difficult, since the method of solution used until now (the ill use of our free will) seems excluded in advance. And yet as in *Meditation IV,* the philosopher cannot escape the double requirement, to account for the technical possibility of this fact and to exculpate God. If he does not do both, the dogma of divine veracity is destroyed and the foundation of the sciences gives way.

The solution will be sought for along the following path:

1) We will reduce to a *minimum* the intrinsic error of the senses, which is imputable to the Creator; we will increase to a *maximum* the role of our freedom—that is, of our responsibility—in the falsity of the senses, which is the occasion for formal error in our exercise of freedom and which can at first sight appear to excuse it. To that extent God's responsibility will be diminished; it will become a *minimum*.

2) The technical possibility of this *minimum* of intrinsic falsity of the senses will be so explained as to reveal the absolute good of divine intention, which, given the terms of the problem, will have done, in this case, the *maximum* of what was possible and "desirable." Lacking an *exactly* perfect material realization—namely, the realization of a sensory-motor system whose information and reactions are always rigorously exact and impeccable in all circumstances—we have, no doubt, only an *approximately* perfect realization; but this *minimal* difference between what is absolute and what is approximate does not place into question the absolute and rigorous veracity of God, because the creative *intention* of God was *absolutely* good in this case. God's responsibility, which, under the first consideration, had already fallen to a *minimum,* now falls morally[1] to zero, since given that divine intention was absolutely good, it was impossible to do better. And we are not responsible for anything that is beyond our power.

Recourse to absolute goodness of intention, instead of absolute perfection of material realization, will finally be made in the sphere of human morality, in which the realization of the maximum possible by our action (relative and comparative nonabsolute maximum) will take the place of an absolute material realization, once it is inspired by an *absolutely good* intention—the intention directed toward the better, lacking the unrealizable absolute good. In this way the first conceptions of morality will be subject to a readily noticeable realignment.

Carrying out this solution (which is evidently of mathematical inspiration) will be complicated. It requires that two truths concerning the internal conditions of the union of soul and body be demonstrated in relation to one another:

1) *The union of the soul with all the parts of body,* which will be established when we will have discovered how the soul penetrates the whole body, in such a way that the body I call *my* body is united to *my* soul and that this body participates fully in the indivisible unity of my soul, as a *human* body.

2) *The more particular union of the soul with a part of the body,* which will be established by discovering the sensory-motive structure of

the soul-body substance, a structure that will be deduced from its principle: the union of the indivisible with a part of the divisible.

We rediscover here a characteristic feature that we have noted all along in the *Meditations:* the critical investigation of the immediate givens that I discover within myself and of the judgments that lead us astray with respect to them (determining the various kinds of objective validity, of the various kinds of ideas, explaining the psychological mechanism of the various kinds of errors, etc.), have as correlates demonstrations and affirmations about the existence of things outside my idea and to the proper nature of these things (existence of my self, the nature of this self, existence and nature of God, existence and nature of external bodies, existence and nature of the union of soul and body).

2. The Materialist Path: The Abolition of the Intrinsic Falsity of the Senses through the Abolition of Their Finality; the Reduction of the Nature of the Psychophysical Composite to Mere Physical Nature — Comparison with a Clock

There is indubitably some intrinsic falsity of the senses: "I am directly deceived by my nature." Thus the pleasant taste of poisoned foods leads me to eat them. In illness, thirst or appetite lead me to drink or eat things that can be harmful to me. The amputee believes that he still feels pain in the arm he no longer has, etc.[2] This is an altogether new difficulty.[3] If, in fact, nature itself deceives me, God cannot be exculpated. If the senses themselves are fallacious, I cannot revoke the doubt with which I have struck them down; and if God cannot be excused for having given them to me, my freedom can be excused for allowing me to be taken in. Recourse to the freedom of my judgment and to its ill use can no longer solve the problem. We must now discover a new approach in order to vindicate God and to validate the senses in spite of everything.

We first note that, in the case of the poisoning of food, my nature seems to be excused, for it leads me directly to eating the pleasant food, and not the poison that is mixed in it, of which it is unaware. And since my nature is finite, it cannot know everything.[4] However, this explanation cannot account for the other case, that of illness, in which it is truly nature that leads me directly to what is bad for me: God then appears, without remission, as responsible for the error.[5]

We could argue that God has created nature good, that it became corrupted later, and that the fault results only from the corruption of what he has created. But God does not stop being the author of everything happening in nature. His creation is continuous. He is therefore as much the creator of the corruption of nature as of its prior goodness: the blame for corrupted nature must fall wholly upon him.[6]

In attempting to exculpate God, Descartes takes another path, which, let us note, is not his, but the path of the materialists. It consists in dissolving the concept of "my nature," with respect to which the deficiency and fault are manifested, in order to reduce it to one mode among others of purely material nature. If, in fact, we understand by *my nature* simply the body-machine, that is, the assemblage of purely material devices by which the body moves and which mechanical laws explain completely—if we reduced *"the nature of man"* (in the narrow sense) to the *animal-machine*—it is impossible to speak of a deficiency. In fact, whether corrupted or not, this machine, constituted from modes of extension and movement, is always, in all cases, a physical phenomenon completely in conformity with the necessary laws of *physical nature* in general, meaning of the *material world,* instituted by God's immutable will.[7] We therefore cannot speak of fault in nature here, since everything happens as it should; as a result, we cannot speak of God's fault. In order to speak of such a fault, we must refer to something that is outside nature, namely, to some end that God would have had in creating a machine "that moves in all the ways it is accustomed to move." Thus, in order to state that a clock is faulty when it does not mark the hour exactly, we must refer, outside the material clock as it exists in "nature" (in the physical sense), to the intention of its craftsman.[8] But this intention is nothing real in nature. It is extrinsic to the thing considered. In other words, the finality we attribute to the clock, since it is nothing real within nature, cannot really constitute *its nature,* meaning an entity that would make of it a nature distinct from the universal nature with respect to the laws that it obeys. Consequently, the clock cannot be faulty with respect to its proper nature, *since it does not have any*—it is only a determination of material substance, only a mode of universal physical nature. It cannot be faulty with respect to universal physical nature either (meaning with respect to the world of bodies and its laws), since nothing in the clock has stopped being in conformity with it.[9]

At most we can say that the craftsman has committed an error with respect to himself by making something that did not fit the end he was pursuing. But surely he did not commit any error with respect to the clock, which is always what it must be, namely, modes of extension and movement necessarily determined by some laws. In this case there is no mistake *with respect to what is due to it.*[10] Thus God in no way deceives anyone (even if he has created a work that is defective with respect to the end that we attribute to him), and, in any case, he does not deceive his work (the man, in this comparison with the clock). He simply deceives himself. This is an absurd affirmation that would be allowed only if we knew the ends of God, the creator of the animal-machines. But these ends are impenetrable, whereas the Perfect Being would indubitably not be able to deceive himself. Hence the circumstances causing material machines in material nature to be destroyed and others to take their place, certainly have a sufficient reason, which we do not know, but which must be derived from the greater perfection of the whole.[11]

The principle of this argument is based on the theory of animal-machines. Reducing man's *psychophysical* reality to a machine (that is, to the merely *physical* reality of an animal), suffices to dissolve "the nature of man," so that it becomes the same as an animal's nature, a simple mode of material nature, deprived of individual substantiality, a pure determination of extension modified by movement. At one stroke, all the considerations of finality, on which rested judgments passed on man's nature by virtue of a deficiency in the means for attaining the end of that nature, are shattered into nullity. The mechanism of physical nature in fact excludes all valid appeal to finality. Under these conditions, what we call "the direct error of the senses" would be only an extrinsic denomination without weight. It would be without reality. God would be exculpated in this way.

We rediscover here an attempted solution modeled after *Meditation IV,* in which, in order to prove God's innocence, we established that error, despite its psychological reality, had no metaphysical reality, since it is not a privation, but a negation that does not entail anything positive. Here, in a sphere that is not that of reality, but that of finality, we attempt similarly to prove that error, an error alleged to be the direct error of the senses, has no metaphysical weight because it has no physical weight. It does not amount to a shortcoming in what is owed to *my nature,* because it does not amount to a shortcoming in *physical nature* in general, to which *my nature* is completely reduced. Although in *Meditation IV* error, suppressed as privation, remained on the metaphysical plane as negation and retained on the psychological plane a privative force with respect to my self, here it disappears completely.

In fact, it has no reality except in relation to some end. And from the point of view of finality, there is no other possible being for error except privative being; error is the privation of true information that is owed by the senses to this substantial composite whose safety it has as end. By suppressing the privative character of error, we therefore suppress error completely. This excessive and paradoxical gain has been possible only because we have withdrawn all real validity from the finality with respect to which the error is conceived. But at the same time we have destroyed all the truth of the senses. The latter cannot be conceived except with respect to the finality of the senses.

We find once again the pendulum swinging to the limit that marked the introduction of the general problem of error in *Meditation IV,* after the establishment of divine veracity. The swing to excess was manifested by positing the problem as: "If everything is true, nothing is false." Here, reducing the error of sensation to zero by dissolving our nature into physical nature, raises the problem with respect to the senses, according to the correlative formula: "If nothing is false, nothing is true." In brief, error is annihilated only because the notion of man in the strict sense is itself annihilated in its reality—that is, as a nature distinct from corporeal nature. Error disappears metaphysically because it disappears psychophysically, and it disappears psychophysically because we have denied that there existed a psychophysical reality.

3. Refutation of This Solution: a) through Its Consequences: Abolition of the Truth of the Senses Through the Abolition of Its Finality; b) Through Its Principle: Contradiction with the Demonstrated Truth of Substantial Union. Restoration of Finality to the Senses

This argument, which consists in vindicating God by removing the sensation he has created from all possibility of error, fails completely, since it subtracts sensation *only by subtracting it from truth in an infallible fashion.* Being neither true nor false, sensation would no longer have any meaning. It would have no meaning because it would have no end. But having no end, it would not have an efficient cause and any sufficient reason. Since it would still remain in the soul as an obscure and confused quality, as the principal source of errors of the understanding, we could say that God, by creating sensible quality, would have shown himself to be absurd or evil—which is contrary to the hypothesis. Thus if, in order to rehabilitate sensation, we remove from it the very notion of error, we merely condemn it more by removing any notion of truth from it; similarly, if we attempt to vindicate the good and veracious God by removing from the senses all biological signification, we do no more than overwhelm him.

But, in order to show that such a demonstration is illegitimate, there is no need to have recourse to its consequences; it suffices to consider the postulate that inspires it: the assimilation of the psychophysical nature of man to the merely physical nature of the machine. In fact, this postulate is contrary to a fundamental truth, which has been established previously according to the order in a sure fashion, namely, the existence of the substantial union of soul and body, constitutive of this composite whole I call "my nature" in the strict sense. This substantial union is precisely what prevents the identification of the human body with the body of an animal and all other bodies in the physical world; the latter are without real unity and constitute only precarious unities without reality within extended substance.[12] The reality of the composite whole therefore maintains its intrinsic validity with respect to finality. The relation of finality cannot be external, in this case, as is, for example, the relation of the clock to an end foreign to its natural reality (the goal of the craftsman: to indicate the exact hour); nor can it be nominal, meaning simply relative to the idea someone fashions for himself by relating it to the end for which he supposes it has been made. The finality has to be internal, since the end aimed at by the composite substance is internal to itself—it is its own preservation—and real, since it is *one with the substantial constitution of the thing.* And it is evident that, for this real nature, the false teaching that leads, by means of the destruction of the body, to the destruction of this very nature is an error *with respect to itself* and a lack *with respect to what is due to it.* Error is therefore a positive privation for which God is irremediably the responsible author. We find ourselves before the same problem once again.

The identification of my nature with purely material nature attempted to vindicate God. The refutation of the argument favorable to God allows something new to appear with respect to what preceded it. Until then, the attribution of a characteristic of falsity to things themselves, and consequently to God who has created them, resulted from a confusion arising from an error of the understanding engendered by the precipitation of my judgment. It sufficed to dissipate the confusion to see God's alleged fault disappear. Here, on the contrary, it is the argument which attempts to exculpate God that rests on a confusion due to a judgment badly enlightened by natural light. The confusion of my nature with the material machine, which constitutes the principle of this reasoning, is, in fact, the confusion of composite substance with extended substance alone. It therefore involves one of these fundamental errors arising from a lack of clarity and distinction in the knowledge of my nature which, identified vaguely with my nature in general, is taken confusedly at times for the three constituents at once, and at times for one of them.

Thus, after the confusion of my nature, understood strictly, with thought alone, which engenders the double corruption of the idea of the understanding with sensible idea and sensible idea with the idea of the understanding, we find ourselves in the presence of one of the two aspects of the confusion of my nature with extension alone. This confusion, when it occurs for my nature, corrupts physics by converting sensible qualities into properties of things; from this results the physics of substantial forms and the conceptions of animals as informed by a certain kind of soul. When it occurs for extension alone, which is the case here, it corrupts my psychophysical reality by assimilating it to physical reality: it identifies the human body, which is informed by a soul, with the pure materiality of the animal-machine; this is a confusion proper to Epicurean and materialist tendencies,[13] a confusion that Descartes, of course, condemns with vigor. It is impossible to save God's veracity by means of a confusion denounced by the natural light that this veracity guarantees.

4. The Internal Finality of Ensouled Beings Proved by the Substantial Union; the Reality of Ensouled Substance Is Incapable of Being Demonstrated by the Appearance of Internal Finality. Animal-Machine and the Human Body. Psychophysical Definition of the Finality of the Human Body. The Functional Indivisibility of This Body

The foundation of the refutation of the purely mechanistic explanation of the nature of the human body is the previously demonstrated truth of the substantial union of this body with my soul, a union that requires us to recognize a real value to the internal finality of this substantial totality. Moreover, we do not prove the substantial union by means of the finality of my body,[14] but inversely we prove the real finality of my body by means of the demonstration that it is substantially united to a soul.

As a result, if substantial union is impossible to prove, the presence of real internal finality is also impossible to prove, and if we prove that there is no, and cannot be any, substantial union, we prove at the same time that in the being considered, there is no, and cannot be any, real finality, but simply a purely mechanical combination, accounted for by efficient causes. That is why even though the animal-machine is externally identical to the machine of the human body, we must refuse it the real internal finality that we grant the latter, because, since animals have no soul, they are alien to all substantial union. Consequently, animals are refused the deep-seated indivisibility and numerical unity that characterize the human body. In fact, if soul is missing, "form of body" is lacking a substance distinct from extended substance, a true individuality, and everything is reduced to an endless circulation of material elements: "Human bodies are only *numerically the same* because they are informed by the same soul. . . . Provided that a body is united with the same rational soul, we always take it as the body of the same man whatever it may be and whatever quantity and shape it may have; and we count it as an entire body, provided that it needs no additional matter in order to remain joined to the same soul."[15] The numerical unity of a man's body does not depend on its matter, but on its form, which is the soul.[16] From this derives Descartes' reply to Gassendi in which he invokes finality in order to prove the animate character of living machines: "Everything that you relate to final cause can be related to efficient cause; it is the same for this admirable use of each part in plants and animals."[17] The production and preservation of animal bodies proceeds from the same causes, though more complicated ones, as those determining the configuration and subsistence of bodies.[18]

As a result there seems to be something of a split in the world of organisms that are said to be alive, since they are all placed into the category of pure mechanisms deprived of all real internal finality, except for one only—the human organism, which seems amenable to animism instead of mechanism. This split in the domain of living beings evokes the split that separates the first law of movement from the second and third, in physics.[19] It seems to oppose, in both cases, the principle of homogeneity and continuity. We understand that Leibniz had wished to reestablish this homogeneity by explaining by means of the same final cause the ordering of all machines, human as well as animal, according to the view that where there is internal teleological harmony, there is a soul; and since an effect of the same order must correspond with a cause of the same order, the cause of man's body (the extreme case of a series) is the same as that of the other cases in the series.

However, the problem is not so simple.

First, Descartes has, according to his doctrine, an infallible criterion for discerning finality where it is and for excluding it from where it is not: it is the presence or absence of sensation. The presence of sensation in us, by its teaching (whose truth is certified by divine veracity), reveals to us the reality of our substantial union with our body in our intimate daily experience and consequently the truth of the teleological relation that ties the senses to the necessities of the organism. There is no sensation outside men—the absence of sensation in animals certifies that they are only pure machines. If sensation is absent, soul is necessarily excluded, and correlatively, the substantial union that renders it possible and finality are excluded. And this absence of sensation in animals is a truth—if not a necessary truth, at least maximally probable *(maxime probabilis)*—and it is impossible to prove the contrary assertion, in any case.[20] In fact, sensation is a mode of soul;[21] consequently it involves intelligence. In order to have sensation, animals must have intelligence. And it is quite evident that intelligence is missing in animals, since they are deprived of speech; their actions have the perfection of automatons. Finally, they do not have the power to vary their reactions infinitely according to the infinite changes of events.[22]

Have we thus accomplished a split between the order of the animal-machine and that of the machine of the human body? Not in certain respects, that is, if we consider in the human body only the machine properly speaking, as distinct from the composite nature of soul and body. That such a distinction remains is proven by reflex actions and purely automatic movements, among other things.[23] If there is a split between the order of animal bodies and the order of human bodies, it is only in the sense that the human body is the only one of all the machines to be substantially united to a soul. But, taken in itself, this machine, with all its most ingenious devices, is explained, as is the machine of animal bodies, by purely efficient and physical causes—movements, impulsions, shocks, dilations, condensations, from which result the theories of the circulation of blood, of animal spirits, etc. From this arises the comparison of the human machine with a very complicated automaton. Under these conditions, there is perfect homogeneity between the same effects (animal-machine, machine of the human body) and the same causes (mechanism). Thus, real finality is no more required to account for the machine of the human body as a pure machine than it is for that of animals, and the union of this machine with the soul allows everything that is pure mechanism to remain in the machine.

But then where does this real finality, which is affirmed from the fact that the human body is united to a soul, reside in the human body? Not in the reciprocal relation of parts and not at all in the machine, which is sufficiently accounted for by pure mechanism, but in *the relation of the totality of this machine to an internal consciousness which is tied to it in such a way that a relation of means to end is established between this consciousness and this machine:* sensation is, in the soul, the means toward this end of providing for the mechanical necessities implied by the functioning and the preservation of the mechanical assemblage of the parts of body; moreover, the consciousness of sensation entails that the soul uses the machine of the body as an instrument in the process of satisfying the requirements of the preservation of that machine. Finality does not therefore reside in the assemblage or the mode of assemblage of the parts of the body, nor in the movements by which these parts push each other, *but in the relation of the soul to this assemblage, which is explainable mechanistically.* Sensation transforms the machine into an end and its simply efficient elements into means by the insertion of the soul into the body; but the true end is the preservation of the union of my soul with my body: it is in order to maintain this substantial union that sensation takes as end the preservation of dispositions of body that render this union possible. In brief, it is a finality of the assemblage of body and mind (a psychophysical finality), not a finality of the assemblage of body, which, in principle, introduces no finality into the physical realm. In fact, finality is the characteristic of *union;* it involves only *composite nature,* not the corporeal element of this composition considered apart from this union.

In that sense, we see that the indivisibility of the human body is not the characteristic of reciprocal linkage between the different parts constituting the whole organic mechanism, taken in itself, but only the machine's possession of the soul associated with it. Consequently, the real functional indivisibility of the human body results from its union with the soul, and there is no real indivisibility in animal-machines. Moreover, the indivisibility of the human body is not that of the machine, but that of *man,* given that the composite nature constituting it can only derive its indivisibility from the soul in it, since the soul alone possesses this property and is opposed in this way to extension, which is always divisible: "Our body, as a *human* body, remains always *numerically* the same while it is united to the same soul. *In that sense,* it can be called indivisible; for if an arm or a leg of a man is amputated, we think that his body is divided only in the first sense of body [physical—M. G.], but not in the second sense [psychophysical—M. G.], and we do not think that a man who has lost an arm or a leg is less a man than any other."[24] This conception of the indivisibility of the organism, which is proper only to an organism effectively *ensouled,* which contains a psychophysical finality and consequently is reserved for man alone, is extremely dangerous in its consequences, since if this finality is conceived as absent, indivisibility must disappear. Under these conditions, is it not sufficient to amputate the leg of a horse in order for the horse to be *less of a horse than any other?*

5. Material Conditions for the Insertion of the Soul in the Body. Human Death

Setting these consequences aside for the moment, we see, in any case, the extreme restricted sense of the expression "human body is informed by soul." We are not concerned with a transformation of the material organism; it is not as if a soul, by being incarnated in matter, made matter conform to it from the inside, according to its own force, so that it shapes it into an organism; this would introduce finality as a genetic factor and consequently as a factor explicative of the corporeal machine, which would cease being a pure mechanism completely, in even the least of its parts. We are concerned simply with an intimate association of the soul with the totality and the parts of the *whole* machine, as it is produced according to the laws of general physics. Thus physical nature would produce mechanically a very complicated machine, made such that a soul could *fit* it in some way, without having been a factor in the construction and fitting together of its parts. At the moment when it is inserted into the machine, the soul, by sensing the passion stemming from the action of the matter with which it is united, experiences a sensible joy that testifies to the suitability of the machine that purely mechanical laws have so perfectly made to receive it. Since this perfect manufacture of the machine is the first condition that originally allows the union of the soul with it, it results that the first passion is necessarily joy.[25] Once this insertion of the soul in the mechanism is accomplished, the union can subsist only as long as a certain integrity of this mechanism subsists: "We believe that body is a whole as long as it has *in itself* all *the dispositions required* to preserve the union."[26] "We always take [matter—M. G.] for the body of the same man . . . and we count it as a whole body, provided that it needs no additional matter in order to remain joined to the same soul."[27]

As a result we see that the death of a man cannot be conceived, under these conditions, other than by the same process that engenders the disappearance of the animal-machine—namely, by the dissociation of the physical machine in virtue of purely mechanical causes. In the case of the animal, this dissociation has no other consequence than the disappearance of the machine; in the case of the man, it entails, moreover, the rupture of the substantial union with the soul. Therefore, it is not the soul that by leaving the body removes from it the principle that maintains organic cohesion, but on the contrary, it is the mechanical destruction of this cohesion that leads to the departure of the soul and the rupture of the substantial bond.[28] The introduction of the soul into the machine and its departure from the machine do not in themselves bring about any modifications in the machine. The disposition and adjustment of parts remain the same, and yet there is produced a total internal transformation, in the strong sense of that word. It is from within that the organism, as it is mechanically constituted, is bonded in all its parts to a soul, meaning to a spiritual, teleological principle, which, sensing the vicissitudes of the mechanical functioning and the state of the machine through its union with body, uses the latter by applying itself, as with its own end, to the excellence of this functioning and of this state. This substantial union brings no more modifications in the structure of the physical body as such than transubstantiation brings into the physical structure of the bread of the host when it becomes the body of Christ. The incarnation and transubstantiation are therefore no more obscure than the substantial union of soul and body. On the other hand, the latter is no less obscure, and since we are concerned here with the deepest mysteries of religion, we are able to measure in this way the extent of the incomprehensibility of the union, meaning its inconceivability for our finite understanding, which can only conceive the radical distinction of substances.

6. Problem of the Negation of Functional Indivisibility in Animals

In spite of its perfect coherence, this doctrine contains a great difficulty, which, however, is not insoluble in certain respects. By making the real indivisibility of organic bodies the consequence of its union with a psychological principle, the doctrine denies not only real finality, but also functional indivisibility from the bodies of animals, and reserves it for human bodies alone. In this way Descartes not only contradicts common judgment—which is perfectly legitimate when a judgment based on natural light is opposed to it—but also the evidence of physiology. For if I judge that the body of a man is always the same body or the same man after one of his legs has been amputated, it is evident that the body of this or that animal also remains the same body and the same animal when a limb is amputated. It is no less evident that there is the same functional indivisibility in animal bodies as in human bodies, meaning that the removal of an organ renders defective the whole of the organism. Even if we denied all internal and immanent finality in the machine, are we not required to recognize this latter indivisibility for the machine as for the "human body"? And Descartes refuses to grant this because there is no defect in the machine unless we are assured that there is *an end* in this machine, which is the end of "having in itself these movements that we are accustomed to noticing in it"; but if this end is not really immanent in the machine, whatever happens, there is no defect in it. I simply notice that the absence of one of its elements does not impart as result the same convergence of movements as the one I commonly notice in it. Where common man believes that he perceives a functional indivisibility, there is simply the coincidence, according to the laws of mechanics, of efficient causes necessary to produce a certain composite phenomenon. There would be real functional indivisibility only if the functioning and economy of the machine were really, meaning intrinsically and immanently, the end of this machine. But this internal and immanent finality is there only when the machine constitutes itself as a "nature," meaning as a substance existing by itself, distinct from purely extended substance. And precisely, it constitutes such a nature only when it is united to a soul.[29] And we know, because of reasons invoked above, that there are no souls in animals. Therefore animals do not constitute a "nature"; consequently, they do not have a functional indivisibility. In contrast, we know, by means of a necessary proof, that such a nature exists—namely ours. Therefore our body, substantially united to a soul, constitutes something of a "nature" with the latter, and functional indivisibility, which is lacking to animals, must accrue to it necessarily. Thus we see that, if the corporal machine itself appears, from the fact of its union with a soul in a composite, substantial, sui generis nature, as possessing a real, proper totality and having the functioning of this whole as its proper end (that which founds its functional indivisibility), it is uniquely due to the fact that this whole and functioning of the machine appear as being really an end *for the soul* that is united to it.

In addition, the totality of the machine is an end for the soul only insofar as the totality has been united to it as already constituted, and to the extent that the soul perceives in this totality and in the perfect functioning of the machine *the end of that machine*—in brief, to the extent that *it lends to the machine* an internal finality. As a result we see that the totality of the corporeal machine and its good functioning is not in itself (that is, having abstracted away the soul) *the end of the machine,* and that there is not really any internal finality in the machine considered in itself, but that everything happens as if the machine acquired this finality and became its own end for itself once it is united to the soul in a single and *same nature* of which it becomes the end. At the same time, we see that it is the *end of the soul* only insofar as the soul, linking itself to the machine, considers the totality and integrity of the functioning of that machine as being effectively *the end of the machine.* Thus finality is possible here, not as finality in my soul alone and for my soul alone, nor as finality in my body alone and for my body alone, but only as the finality of my composite nature of soul and body, taking this body as the real end for the *psychophysical* whole and consequently transforming in this nature the relations of parts to whole in the machine of the body itself.

We then understand why Descartes, when he speaks of the indivisibility of the human body, designates it as indivisibility of *man,* since there is no functional indivisibility of the material machine of man's body, having abstracted away the union of that machine with a soul in a substantial nature. It is the union with a soul *that transforms into a teleological relation,* with respect to the totality of the body, the purely mechanical relation in itself of the parts assembled in this totality, and it is thus that the corporeal mechanism acquires a true functional indivisibility. In fact, because of the union with soul, the functioning of the machine, which was rendered possible by the mechanical assemblage (such as it was already constituted by its parts in the totality), becomes for the soul, as does the totality itself, an end that must be assumed. At the same time, the reciprocal adjustment and play of these parts, without which the whole as result is not possible, is metamorphosed into an indivisible set of means that are linked indissolubly together, and into an end that they condition. Thus we see very clearly why animal bodies, although presenting an organic structure almost identical to that of the material machine of the human body, are entirely devoid of functional indivisibility, because of the fact that they are not tied to any soul in a composite substantial nature.

7. The Incommensurability of Soul and Body, and Finality; Finality and Corporality of the Soul

All these considerations allow one to advance further into the secrets of the deep mystery of the union of body and soul, of the extended and unextended, of the divisible and indivisible. In fact, we see that if, on the one hand, the union of soul with body does not change anything with respect to the material structure, or the real disposition, or the very substance of the parts of body (insofar as they remain extended), on the other hand it radically modifies the foundation of that structure into something somewhat relational. It transforms the foundation in some manner from within, and one part at a time, in its most intimate details, by introducing a new relation between its parts and between the parts and the whole—the relation of internal finality. This modification, which operates along the whole thickness of the fabric of body, is truly substantial. However, it leaves intact both the external appearances of the machine and the proper substantiality of the constituents of the human body, for although it is penetrated by mind as soon as mind instills its finality into the most recessed parts of the fabric of body, body does not cease to be purely corporeal—these assembled parts of matter do not cease to be pure extension. And, although it expands itself into matter as much as possible and mixes itself as intimately as can be conceived, the mind, infusing itself through its finality, does not cease to be pure mind. We see also that, because of this total metamorphosis of the relational structure of the fabric of body when mind penetrates it with finality, the union of body with my soul is truly a total mixture. Since finality is spread throughout body, into its infinitely small parts, the soul thus is present absolutely everywhere, in the whole as well as in the parts. Moreover, body, which is divisible by nature because of this finality with which the soul invests all its organization by uniting with it, contracts something of spiritual indivisibility, under the form of this internal finality, of this functional indivisibility that founds its individual unity as a human body, a unity that remains intangible, no matter what part may be amputated. At the same time, it does not cease being divisible, because it remains extended materially. Reciprocally, the soul, by expanding its indivisibility throughout body by its finality, is united to the whole divisible extension of body—in its length, width, and depth. However, it does not cease being indivisible, for the teleological relation that it expands throughout body is itself nothing extended or corporeal, and consequently, nothing divisible. Even though it extends to the whole as to the parts of body, this relation cannot itself be divided or localized in the former or in the latter. Consequently, we conceive that soul *can have extension without being extended* in the composite nature, and that, by this extension, it attributes to itself a matter that is not thought. Thus is explained the well-known and often misunderstood passage from the *Letter to Elizabeth* of 28 June 1643: "I beg [Your Highness—M. G.] to feel free to attribute matter and extension to the soul because it is no more than to conceive it as united to the body; and once you have formed a proper conception of this and experienced it in yourself, it will be easy for you to consider that the matter attributed to the thought is not thought itself, and that *the extension of that matter is of different nature than the extension of that thought,* because the former is *determined to a definite place, from which it excludes all other bodily extension, which is not the case with the latter.*"[30]

If the substantial union founds the teleology of human nature and the finality of the human body, finality gives us the key to explain better the fact of substantial union, such as it is given to us—not that we can thus render intelligible its possibility, which is not amenable to any clear and distinct idea, and which our understanding will never conceive, since it contradicts the real separation of thinking and extended substances, and since it rests solely on God's omnipotence, which is capable of accomplishing what is repugnant to our clear and distinct ideas.

What appeared to have condemned such an enterprise a priori is the incommensurability of the two available terms. This lack of common measure is for materialists, as well as idealists, the proof that the substantial union of body and soul, as well as their reciprocal action, is only a pure appearance. Gassendi has forcefully described the aspects of this incommensurability, which is related to the aspects under which Descartes himself considers the fusion of the two terms. For the aspect that interests us presently, the union of soul with the totality of body, Gassendi's objection is particularly forceful: "It still remains to be explained how this union and apparent intermingling or confusion can convince you that you are immaterial, indivisible, and without extension, which . . . must have some magnitude or extension however small it would be. If you are wholly without parts, how can you mix or appear to mix with the most subtle parts of that matter with which you assert to be united, since there is no mixture unless each of the things to be mixed has parts that can mix with one another? And if you are completely discrete, how can you be confused with this matter and compose a totality with it? And since all composition, conjunction, or union is accomplished between parts, ought there not be a certain proportion between these parts? *But what proportion can be conceived between something corporeal and something incorporeal? . . .* Moreover, ought not all union take place by means of the closest and most intimate contact of things united? But . . . how can a contact take place without body? How will that which is incorporeal attach itself to something corporeal, in order to join itself and to be joined reciprocally, if there is nothing in the incorporeal by which it can join the other or be joined to it?"[31]

To this pressing argument, which is subscribed to in principle by Malebranche, Spinoza, Leibniz, and Berkeley, and which is essentially founded on the principle of common measure, Descartes merely replies that one cannot compare the mixing of two bodies, as diverse as they might be, to the mixing of body and mind, because [in doing so] one is concerned with two completely different kinds of things: "For although the mind is united to the whole body, it does not follow from that that it is extended along the whole body, because it does not belong to mind to be extended, but only to think." The mind does not need to have parts in order to conceive the parts of bodies.

Descartes is the first to subscribe to the total incomprehensibility of the union of two substances: "You do not contradict me at all," he emphasizes. In fact, my understanding conceives only the reciprocal exclusion and not at all the union of the substances. This union is a fact that we notice, not a truth of essence that we conceive in its intrinsic possibility. But although he judges that we must not violate the principle of common measure, he affirms that this principle must not prevent us from admitting the reciprocal action of two substances on one another, in spite of their incompatibility, since it is taught to us by the facts. Does not the substantial union confer upon them this homogeneity and commensurability that they do not possess by nature? Finally he believes that most of the questions posed to him do not need to be resolved in order to prove what he has asserted.[32]

It has often been thought that Descartes was satisfied with these purely negative observations, and that since the incomprehensibility of the union of the two substances rendered it conceivable for God alone, all further explanation must be set aside a priori. However, Descartes did not assert that this union is inexplicable, but merely that it was very difficult to explain.[33]

And the theory of mixing by finality constitutes an original and positive attempt to explain this union, under one of its aspects: the union of the soul with the totality of the body. The explanation will be completed when Descartes will have accounted for the other aspect: the more particular union of the soul with a certain part of body.

From all evidence, finality responds well to the requirements of the first part of the problem. Both inextensive and indivisible, but capable of extending itself to the whole extension of the human body without dividing or materializing itself, it furnishes an *intermediary* between the spiritual and the corporeal, the indivisible and the divisible, without which we could not explain the reality of their mutual interpenetration. As a relation of intellectual order that is neither mathematical nor extended, nor mechanical, nor quantitative, a suprageometrical incorporeal form that instills its proper indivisibility into body in order to give this body a unity that renders it indivisible like the soul itself, not localizable here rather than there, finality allows the soul to penetrate the body so that it constitutes a whole with it, up to the final extremities of body. Thus the soul subsists everywhere in this body, as a complete, indivisible, and incorporeal unity, even though it is impossible to dissociate it from the deepest and most intimate structures of that body. That is why the human body is organized and sensibilized up to its least parts, and it is why the soul "constitutes a single totality with it," and can "sense" pain once the "body is wounded," even though "it is only a thing that thinks."[34] This explains why, when some part of the human body is removed without putting an end to the assemblage of the whole, the soul, even though it judges the whole diminished in its extension, does not judge it diminished as a human body, any more than it judges itself as diminished;[35] this also explains that the union ceases when the assemblage of the parts of the body ends. Consequently, when Descartes speaks either of the aptitude of the soul to be united to the body, aptitude by which it may be said to be corporeal, or of the natural aptitude of body and soul to be substantially united in a man,[36] or of the disposition of the body to be united with a soul,[37] he understands, in part, the capacity that the soul has to penetrate body with finality, and in part, the mechanical dispositions of the parts of the body that are such that the soul can instill among them the relation of finality. However, finality does not give rise to homogeneity and common measure, strictly speaking, between the two radically heterogeneous substances. It only constitutes a substitute for commensurability, for its property and role as intermediary are precisely to preserve the very irreducibility of the two mixed elements within the mixture that it renders conceivable to us in certain respects. This role of teleology as intermediate factor of the union by means of the functional indivisibility of the human body is specified clearly in article 30 of Part I of the *Treatise on the Passions: "That the soul is united to all parts of the body conjointly.* But in order to understand all these things more perfectly, we must know that the soul is really joined to the whole body, and that we cannot, properly speaking, say that it exists in one of its parts to the exclusion of the others, because it is one and in some manner indivisible, owing to the disposition of its organs, which are so related to one another that when one of them is removed, it renders the whole body defective, and because it is of *a nature that has no relation to extension,* nor dimensions, nor other properties of the matter of which the body is composed, but only *to the whole assemblage of its organs,* as it appears from the fact that we could not in any way conceive half or a third of a soul, or what extension it occupies, and because it does not become smaller by cutting some part of the body, but removes itself completely *when the assemblage of its organs is dissolved.*"[38]

As deep as these Cartesian views are, they are not sufficient to dispel all obscurities.

We must first note that if the deep-seated incomprehensibility of the union of soul and body does not exclude in principle all attempts at explanations that are accessible to human understanding, as we have said, it must, however, limit them unavoidably. Of course, to discover an element that reestablishes a certain common measure between soul and body, a common measure between finality, on the one hand, and the suitable disposition of the parts of the machine, on the other, is something that contributes toward rendering their union more intelligible. However, the unintelligible character of this union and the deep-seated incompatibility of the substances united seem to be indispensable requisites to account for the irremediable obscurity and confusion of my nature, in the strict sense—that is, of sensation. Everything that tends to reestablish some homogeneity behind the heterogeneity of the two substances tends to go against the theory that bases the existence in me of obscurity and confusion on this heterogeneity. No doubt the relation of finality offers the advantage of introducing a homogeneity between the two terms such that it allows each of them to preserve their heterogeneity in the mixture. But the fact that, because of finality, the union is accomplished between them without any alteration being produced in one or the other, if it allows us to conceive that they each preserve their nature while being mixed substantially, does not lead us to conceive how they can thus *jumble up* one another, so as to engender obscurity and confusion—quality, properly speaking. This obscurity and this confusion do not certify that they remain unaltered in the mixture, but that they are in themselves profoundly contaminated by one another, to the extent that they meld intimately in a composite nature, in which properties that are repugnant to one another unite, from the point of view of the composing elements.

This difficulty can be perceived from another perspective. Finality, as principle of explanation of the substantial union, accounts for the penetration of soul in body, but not the inverse penetration of body in soul. In fact, that thought contracts some kind of extension, from the fact that it is instilled in the whole extension of body through the relation of finality, has nothing in common with the alteration of the nature of the soul in qualities, meaning in obscure and confused sensations. On the contrary, there is nothing more spiritual and intellectual than this relation of finality that is introduced in all the parts, up to infinity. The penetration of extension by mind, by means of finality, therefore gives only a partial explanation of the substantial union. This explanation, in order to be completed, should entail an explanation of the penetration of soul by body, accounting for quality. But is not this impossibility to explain everything precisely the requirement of the doctrine of the incomprehensibility of the union?

A second difficulty derives from the way Descartes presents his thesis, notably in article 30 of the *Treatise on Passions,* cited above. In this text, the functional indivisibility of body appears as an intermediary through which the soul is united to the machine. But we know, from the *Meditations* as well as from letters (*To Mesland, To Dinet,* etc.) that functional indivisibility is the privilege of individual real unities, which are themselves possible only through the union of a body to the soul that informs it. But how can the functional indivisibility that results from the union with soul, and is not a property of the machine in itself, appear at the same time as the property of the machine in itself that renders the union possible? From all evidence, Descartes, while rejecting real internal finality for machines that are not united to a soul, is required all the same to recognize that, in order for a machine to unite with a soul, it must in itself offer certain dispositions that agree with the finality of the soul and that render the union possible.[39] He tells us that when "the required dispositions" disappear, the union ceases. And the very interdependence of the gears of the machine, with respect to its proper functioning, is the most indispensable of these "required dispositions." However, in virtue of the Cartesian conception of physics, this correspondence of the dispositions of the machine with the *idea* of a disposition with a view toward an end, a correspondence that is at the foundation of the real agreement of the set of these material dispositions with the soul (meaning with the end that the soul pursues in the union), would not imply the least real internal finality in things. The interdependence of the gears, which renders possible the proper functioning of the whole, and without which the latter could not be converted into an end with respect to the gears, which are themselves promoted to the function of means, does not attest to any real indivisibility as long as the machine is considered simply as a fact of physical nature not united to a soul—for example, as in animals. In the material world, this functioning and assemblage of elements of the machine are considered simply as a combination, in itself precarious, resulting from the mechanical play of efficient causes, not as a real end with respect to which the lack of one of the gears appears as a lack to what is due to it. Such an interpretation becomes possible only when the soul, by uniting itself with the organism, makes the functioning of the organism—which in itself is a result of a purely mechanical act—an end for itself, such that it appears at the same time as the end for the organism and as the reason for the assemblage of its parts. The substantial union of soul and body therefore simply requires that physical nature in general engenders, according to the laws of mechanics and by the play of efficient causes, independently of any final cause, a material result such that the soul can be united substantially with it, can invest it with the character of end with respect to the soul and with respect to the constitutive parts of the machine, to the extent that the soul is completely penetrated by the *nexus* of finality and that it reveals a functional indivisibility.

And it is evident that such an agreement between the mechanical effects of physical nature, namely, body considered as pure machine, and the conditions required for the incarnation of a soul in this body, is not accomplished by chance, and that we must have the transcendent finality of God intervene more or less explicitly in this case: he has wished that, by the laws of mechanics alone, machines having parts arranged in such a way that they have dispositions in agreement with the requirements of a union of soul and body, meaning a relation of means to an end, be engendered and preserved. But do not animal-machines offer in themselves these dispositions required for a union with a soul? Do they not present the same characteristics of organization and interdependence of parts among themselves and with the whole, allowing, in principle, for a soul to be united with them, by transforming the purely mechanical relational relation of their elements into a teleological *nexus,* conferring upon them functional indivisible unity? Why do such "dispositions" remain unused? This is a question that remains unanswered.[40] In this difference of destiny reappears the incomprehensible division between animal organisms and human organisms, a division that we had suppressed by the reduction of all animal bodies, including the human body considered in its pure materiality, to simple machines. This unfathomable mystery merely refers us to the inscrutable abyss of God's wisdom, to the impenetrability of his ends, and to the certainty based on the knowledge of his perfection—that everything, in his work, is for the best "collective."

CHAPTER XVIII

Of the True and of the False in the Realm of the Senses: Internal Conditions of the Psychophysical Substance-More Particular Union of the Soul with a Part of the Body

1. Reemergence of the Problem of the Intrinsic Falsity of the Senses because of the Confirmation of the Finality of the Senses. Relation of This Problem to the Problem of the More Particular Union of the Soul with a Part of the Body. General Characteristics of the Demonstration and of the Principle of the Solution

The previous demonstration attempts to safeguard the specific reality of the nature of the human body—that is, "my nature," in the strict sense—against a ruinous argument which, under the pretext of exculpating the senses from all error, radically suppresses their truth, by destroying their nature completely for the benefit of *physical nature in general.* We can understand that the confusion of these two natures is as fatal when it is produced for the benefit of extended nature as when it is produced for the benefit of nature as psychophysical composite: in the latter case, true physics becomes impossible; in the former case, the true psychology of sensation is ruined at its foundation.

The restoration of *my nature* (psychophysical) before physical nature in general, a restoration that is based on the incontestable fact of the union of soul and body, allows the founding of the reality of the intrinsic finality of the composite, and has revealed the teleological relation as the condition of possibility of *"the union of the soul with every part of body."* In this way the internal finality proper to the human body was explained, and the informational function of sensation with respect to the totality of the

157

union (meaning definitively with respect to the body whose conservation is posited as its end) was justified. Finally the veracity of the informational function was guaranteed by divine veracity.

But as soon as sensation was reinvested with this informational function, we find ourselves again before the problem of the error of the senses, which had disappeared with the materialist thesis that removed all real teleological signification from the senses, and which consequently, had removed all relation with truth, as with error. Since my nature is real and fundamentally distinct from a simple extended mechanism, the intrinsic error of the senses is real. The latter constitutes a lack with respect to what my psychophysical being is due: God who has created this being is responsible for the fault. The question reappears then, under an infinitely more difficult form than previously, namely, "how can God's goodness not prevent man's nature, taken in this way, from being faulty and deceptive?"[1]

This problem will only be resolved by investigating further the conditions of the real union of soul and body.

This further investigation will result in the demonstration of the conditioning of the *"more particular union of the soul with a part of the body."* Here again Descartes remains faithful to the characteristics of analytical method. The examination of the validity of faculties ends up positing correlates outside those faculties. The justification of the reality of the informational function of the senses in general, against the materialist thesis, has its correlate in the demonstration of the role of teleology as a factor in *the union of the soul with every part of body.*[2] The justification of the truth of the senses in the exercise of that function will have as correlate the determination of the factors of the *more particular union of the soul with a part of body.*[3] In conformity with the principle of the division of the difficulty, Descartes attacks separately each of these two aspects of the substantial union.

The demonstration of the more particular union of the soul with a part of body, which amounts to describing the ways and means by which the soul becomes ready to exercise its function as the safeguard of the composite (action of the soul on the body, and inversely), attempts here, beyond its most immediately visible goal, to justify *conjointly* the truth of the incriminated faculty (the senses) and the veracity of God who guarantees it. This duality of the inquiry is the rule with respect to error. We will have to combine the psychophysical explanation (no longer the psychological explanation as in *Meditation IV*) together with the metaphysical explanation.

With respect to the first point, the discovery of the sensory-motor mechanism by which the senses can assume their function will allow one to establish that the errors imputable to the senses are unavoidable because of the difficulty of the problem imposed upon God. With respect to the second point, we will show that these errors are reduced to a *minimum* by God's wisdom and goodness. In most cases the senses tell the truth; since error is an exception, God's fault, if there is a fault of God, is consequently itself the exception. But since the givens of the problem made it impossible to avoid this exception, since God could not have realized a better solution, the subsisting falsity appears as the *minimum* required for the *maximum* of truth, and God is already, in principle, thus excused. Moreover, in conformity with the second corollary of his veracity,[4] according to which God always places a remedy next to the evil he has permitted, he has armed us with all the faculties necessary for preventing, recognizing, and redressing error. God is therefore excusable in four ways: by the immensity of the difficulty to conquer, by the technical elegance of the solution that has allowed the difficulty to be conquered as well as possible, by the goodness and wisdom exhibited by the choice of the most advantageous solution for our nature, and by the care he takes by placing at our disposition a surplus of auxiliary means necessary to escape the minor disadvantages of the chosen psychophysical mechanism. Thus (as in *Meditation IV* with respect to formal error, relative to the ideas of the understanding), the mechanism of the error of the senses, the goodness and innocence of the veracious God, and the technical means of which man disposes in order to avoid this error, are revealed at the same time.

Here, as before, the investigation is governed by an extreme multiplicity of intentions and goals that intersect. This complexity is masked, however, by the external goal, namely, to establish how the soul is more particularly united to a part of the body; the deep goal is to establish the *certificates of believability* of the senses,[5] while exculpating God once more, through the discovery of the means he has used in order to resolve a particularly difficult problem.

2. The Meaning, According to the Order, of the Present Demonstration of the Indivisibility of Soul and the Divisibility of Body. The Second Aspect of the Problem of Incommensurability

It is the very difficulty of the problem that actually constitutes the essential proof of God's innocence. Divine omnipotence cannot change the given of the problem that it proposes for itself and that supposes, in order to be resolved effectively, the success of something that seems impossible: to unite closely, with a view toward their reciprocal action, two radically heterogeneity beings—the divisible and the indivisible. What will excuse God of the accidental defects of sensation will be the unavoidable constraints that these two terms, because of their deep-seated heterogeneity, subject upon the divine solution, by preventing God from achieving anything other than the best possible, in spite of his omnipotence and goodness.

The union of the divisible with the indivisible was already implied in the union of the corporeal and the spiritual such that it was rendered conceivable by means of the finality that allows the union of my soul with every part of body. But there we were concerned simply with explaining the total union of the two substances, while, in turn, the fact of this union proved the reality of the teleological function. In this way the problem of the *general sensibility* of the human body was resolved. Since no part of body is not penetrated by soul, we can explain that the harm to any part of body is perceived by the soul in sensation. Thus we can conceive, by means of finality, the penetration of the indivisible throughout the whole mass of the divisible. Now we are concerned with a completely different problem: the problem of the exercise of a causality of the soul on its body, the soul being considered as the center that suffers and acts. What is in question is the *pilot* that guides the ship, not because it is lodged in it and sees it from the outside, but because it is intimately—and substantially—united to it. The problem of generalized sensibility makes way for the problem of the sensory-motor relation. And this problem is, in some respect, the inverse problem, since the indivisible must be considered here, not to the extent that it diffuses to infinity in the mass of the divisible, but as wholly concentrated in a part of the divisible that is as small as possible, in order to be united particularly with it, as with an afferent or efferent center of movement. But a part of the divisible, no matter how small, is always divisible, for there are no atoms. Therefore, we do not see, in this material divisibility in which a final part remains always unassignable, an indivisible point that is congruent to the indivisibility proper to mind. This is an insurmountable difficulty as a rule, which Leibniz will resolve—or appear to resolve—when he places at the basis of corporeal divisibility (reduced to a confused appearance) the fundamental indivisibility of an atom, which, since it is no longer material, is congruent with the indivisible soul and exactly identical to it: *atomon spirituale,* the monad.

As long as we were concerned only with proving the reality of the teleological function and with conceiving, through it, the total union of the two incompatible substances, the difficulty ranged only over the incommensurability in general of the spiritual and the corporeal. Now that we are concerned with explaining how, in fact, the very exercise of that function is possible, the difficulty concentrates on this particular aspect of incommensurability that concerns the divisible and the indivisible. Consequently, we understand that the order of reasons requires one to establish, in a certain fashion, at that place in the chain, that the indivisibility is the fact of the soul and that the divisibility is the fact of the body.[6]

This proof is given by intelligence, sensation, and imagination. Intelligence allows me to know immediately that my soul is in itself one and indivisible; sensation allows me to know that, when the soul is wholly united to the totality of the body, it remains physically the same whole, even when it perceives that its body is diminished by one of its parts. Finally, while my intelligence teaches me that, in spite of its division into faculties, the soul itself is never really divided but remains wholly in each of them, imagination teaches me that, on the contrary, there is no unity of the purely material body that I cannot fragment to infinity.[7] The necessity of that demonstration at that point in the chain of reasons gives it its meaning.

The indivisibility of soul and the divisibility of body are not demonstrated for themselves here. Of course, in this way, we increase our knowledge of the two substances. We unveil the absolute unity of our soul against those who would want to divide it into faculties;[8] we prove that it is completely different from body. We give ourselves the means to establish, as does the *Discourse* and the *Summary of the Meditations*,[9] that soul is immortal. But these consequences, which Descartes indicates here (except the final one), have only a subsidiary interest for him. With respect to the complete difference between the two realities, Descartes even remarks that that is something that he has already "sufficiently learned elsewhere."[10] The whole rationale for this demonstration consists in putting into place the two incompatible elements that God must unite as his task, in order to permit the reciprocal action of body and soul—to posit the terms of this problem of geometrical metaphysics (to unite the divisible with the indivisible with a view toward their reciprocal action) which surpasses in difficulty all the problems of quadrature that human geometry may present. And the fabric of our nature, in the strict sense, stems from the solution that God, in an incomprehensible manner, has discovered for this problem.

However, by trying to pierce the secret of this metaphysical geometry, will not the understanding be boldly confronting what is most incomprehensible in the incomprehensible?

When we were concerned with knowing how the spiritual, the indivisible in general, could be diffused throughout the corporeal mass on which it has conferred its unity without ceasing to remain itself, the understanding had succeeded in scaling the obstacle of incommensurability by conceiving how the relation of finality between all the parts of body to infinity was instilled. But now we are concerned with (a concern of greater difficulty) the more particular union of the indivisible with a privileged part of the divisible, such that the former is informed about what happens in the latter, and such that they can act on one another.[11]

We are not surprised to see Gassendi emphasize the incomprehensibility of that second kind of union in terms no less pressing than when he objected to the first: "If you are not greater than a point, . . . how can you be united with the brain, or some minute part in it, which . . . cannot be so small that it does not have some magnitude or extension? . . . Since pain is an alteration or cannot occur without an alteration, how can can something be altered, that, being less divisible than a point, cannot be altered nor cease to be what it is, without being completely annihilated? Moreover, since pain comes from the foot, the arm, or several other parts together, must there not be in you several parts in which you receive it variously, lest this sensation of pain be confused and seem to come from one part alone? But, in a word, this general difficulty still remains: to know how something corporeal can make itself felt and have anything in common with what is not corporeal, and to establish a proportion between the one and the other."[12]

Fortunately, for this second kind of union, things are as they were for the first: we do not have to understand, but to accept a fact, meaning the practical results of the solution realized by God. Sensation places this solution before our eyes as a fact upon which our reflection can be exercised. The understanding can therefore discover the theoretical givens in it; it can even, by relating the given experiences to one another (one by immediate sensation and the other by clear and distinct knowledge of the corporeal mechanisms of extension alone), understand, if not the act of union itself, which escapes it unavoidably, at least the result, that is, the set of processes to which God has given rise in order to render possible the reciprocal action of soul and body.

That is why, when Descartes speaks of his "explanation of the union between the soul and body,"[13] he does not refer to a theory that would render the inconceivable conceivable, for we will never be able to understand that a divisible part is united to an indivisible. He merely describes the material devices by which God's omnipotence, in fact, by means of this union, has been able to render possible within my composite substance a constant and sure knowledge of what happens for the indivisible in the divisible. We would then discover that, given the present terms, indivisible and divisible, better devices could not have been invented, and that their disadvantages, which are unavoidable in virtue of the nature of the terms to be united, are the least evil.

3. Description of the Sensory-Motor Mechanism of the Psychophysical Substance; Its Interpretation with Respect to God

The description of these devices shows how, in fact, the *parts* of this divisible body are arranged in order to allow, on the one hand, the body to act on the soul (which is *without parts,* since it is indivisible), and on the other hand, the soul to act on the body. We notice first that mind does not immediately receive impressions from all the parts of body, but from only one: one of the smallest parts, which is situated in the brain. It is the pineal gland, which Descartes does not name here.[14] We then note that it is through this impression that the mind senses something, and that the variation of this sensation depends on the variation of the disposition of this small part, and not on the variation of the disposition of all the other parts. We note that the movement of a part of body accomplished by means of another part, which is very distant, can also be accomplished by means of any other intermediary part. Thus the nerve that terminates in the foot can be pulled from the foot; it then pulls like a cord on the small part of the brain in which it ends, and my nature makes me sense a pain in the foot. But the nerve can be pulled from the leg, thighs, or loins, and it would then be pulling on the gland in the same fashion, and my nature would make me sense the same pain in the foot.

Since each sensation of my mind corresponds to a new disposition of the gland, and to each new disposition corresponds a movement that is its cause, there can be only one sensation corresponding to each of the movements that modifies the gland. For example, the movement that the nerve going from the foot to the brain impresses on the gland can only give me either the sensation that I have a pain in the foot, or the sensation that I have a pain in the brain, or the sensation that I have a pain in some place on the way from the foot to the brain. God could have chosen to establish nature in such a way that it gave me one or the other of these three sensations, on that occasion, but the requirements of the mechanism excluded the possibility that it could have given me all of them at the same time. And God chose to give me the sensation that I have a pain in the foot. Thus the illusion of amputees is completely explained: no matter from where the nerve is pulled, there will always result the same movement, and from the same movement the same impression on the gland, and from the same impression on the gland, the same sensation, that is, in this case, a pain in the foot. The thirst of a dropsical person and all pathological, deceptive, and harmful appetites are explained similarly.[15] If we now consider God's choice, namely, that the pain tied to the movement of my gland is sensed in the foot, and not in the brain or in some other point on the way from the foot to the brain, we perceive that it is most proper and most commonly useful for the preservation of the human body, when the latter is in full health, and that "in this respect, we cannot either desire or imagine anything better."[16] It is the same for all the other appetites and tendencies. No doubt when the movement of the brain is caused by the nerve starting from a place other than the foot, I am inevitably deceived by my sensation, which can only be the pain in my foot. But this occasion is extremely rare, and from all evidence, it is preferable that I am deceived exceptionally rather than in most cases. It is the same for the dropsical man: "It is better that [the dryness of the throat—M. G.] deceive on this occasion than if, on the contrary, it deceived always when the body was well disposed; and so forth for the other cases."[17] We see that this explanation of the union of soul and body is as unmetaphysical as possible. It does not concern the solution of the principle of the possible union of a part of the divisible with an indivisible—which is beyond the means of our understanding. It merely gives a psychophysical interpretation of the facts based completely on the *physics* of the human body and on experiences, which present a finished solution.[18] Consequently, it escapes all the objections of Gassendi: How can an indivisible be united to a part, and even an infinitely small part, of the divisible? How can an indivisible receive various sensations arising from the foot, arm, and several other parts together without their being confused into one, and without seeming to come from only one part, etc.?[19] These problems, according to Descartes, are beyond theory. Let us note that God has resolved them practically. Hence, it is sufficient to limit ourselves to consider in physical and psychophysical fact what we can grasp experimentally about the implications of the solution.

4. The Latent Hypothesis of the Metaphysical Point

However, it is incontestable that the interpretation of the fact allows to appear, as in a filigree, its conformity with the hypothesis of a union of the divisible and indivisible, in which the soul is considered as an indivisible point—*a metaphysical point*—whose union with a part of the divisible is conceived only to the extent that this part would be a *physical* point that is as close as possible to a *mathematical* point. The image of the metaphysical point plays, in the conception of the "more particular union of the soul with a part of the body," a symmetrical role to that played by the teleological relation in the conception of the general union of the soul with the totality of the body. We must note that these two ideas will be used by Leibniz in the various conceptions that he constructed for the internal union of soul and body, conceptions that are completely different from Descartes'.

From all evidence, this hypothesis governs the whole economy of the theory. The structure of the machine is presented, in fact, as a bundle of threads going from the periphery in order to converge on the center. It is in this physical point situated in the gland, a point that is as close to being an indivisible as a physical point can be to a mathematical point, in which we conceive the indivisible soul to be present. It is therefore an instantaneous indivisible movement[20] (exercised from the periphery to the center—and vice versa in the action of the soul) that pulls the quasi-indivisible physical point and determines a corresponding indivisible sensation in the indivisible mind to which it is joined—the same indivisible sensation being tied always to the same indivisible movement. But the line going from the periphery to the center is itself divisible into an infinity of parts or points by which the indivisible movement terminating in the center is communicated in an instant. Whatever is the point of departure of the movement, meaning the number of points that are subject to that movement, from the origin to the center, the movement in itself is always the same. And since the indivisible sensation that is attached to it is the same when this movement remains the same, the sensation is necessarily indifferent to the initial point of movement and to the number of parts that the movement moves, in what is divisible between the initial point and the terminal point. Since the projection of an infinity of the point of a radius on the center is always only an indivisible point, the impression of the physical point to which the soul is attached remains identical, and so does the indivisible sensation of the soul, whatever is the initial point of the movement.

Thus, in virtue of the necessary geometrical relations that link the indivisibility of a point to the infinite divisibility of the line it terminates, and the indivisibility of soul being identified with the indivisibility of a point, God was constrained:

1) to limit to one and the same indivisible sensation the effect that the movements, having as many possible different points of departure as there are possible points on the infinitely divisible path of the nerve, can produce on the soul;

2) to choose, consequently, among this infinity of different points, the one suitable to relate this identical sensation, in order to realize the best one.

The difficulty of the problem has completely governed its solution, which consists *in combining geometry with the principle of the best.*

In *Meditation IV,* formal error was based on the presence, in our soul considered alone, of a disproportion due to the union of a finite understanding and an infinite will. It was explained by a *psychological mechanism* of transgression of the limits of knowledge that the ill use of human freedom put into play. In *Meditation VI,* the intrinsic falsity of the senses is based on the presence in our psychophysical substance of a disproportion between the divisible and the indivisible that are united in it; it is explained by a *psychophysical mechanism* of a more or less perfect accommodation between one and the other. The difficulty that arises from this disproportion poses a problem, not for the human creature, as with the disproportion between our understanding and our will, but for

God. Except that God is not weak and imperfect, like man; all-powerful and all-good, he reduced to the *minimum* the defect resulting from this disproportion, through the most elegant possible solution, stemming from a superior geometry. In any case, the more particular union of the soul with a part of the body, through the union of a part of the divisible with the indivisible, is symmetrical, in the sphere of the intrinsic falsity of the senses, to the union of the finite understanding and the infinite will, in the sphere of formal error. Finally, psychophysics is connected to the theological problem of God's innocence in the same way that rational psychology was, in *Meditation IV*.

5. The Nature of the Union of the Three Substances That Are Constitutive of My Nature in Its Broad Sense

The explanation of the mechanisms that condition the more particular union of the soul with a privileged part of the body completes the general theory of the union of soul and body. In order to encompass man in his totality, we must reintegrate nature *stricto sensu* according to the two modes of its conditioning, such as they have just been described—in the "assemblage" that constitutes the whole of human nature (nature in the broad sense) and of which it is only an element. In brief, we must perceive it united with extension alone and with thought alone.

How must one represent this latter union?

Must we conceive that there is a *part* of my soul that is pure thought, a *part* of my body that is pure extension, and another *part* that would be the union of soul and body? Do we not observe that many thoughts have no correlatives in the modifications of my body, and that the functioning of many organs of my body is automatic, uncontrolled by will and consciousness? Thus, Jean Laporte, observing that, for Descartes, the total nature of the human being involves, in addition to composite substance, pure soul, and pure extension, judges that, as a result, nature *stricto sensu* leaves aside a part of the life of the mind and a part of the determinations of our body.[21]

Of course, in one sense, it is true that "in opposition to Spinozist parallelism or Leibnizian preestablished harmony, the Cartesian union does not concern the whole life of the mind and the whole behavior of the body."[22] We must note, however, that the soul is united to all the parts of the body and that "we cannot properly say that it is in one of the parts to the exclusion of others because it is in one and in some manner indivisible."[23] Therefore we would be mistaken if we believed that a part of our body is foreign to the union. Consequently, and in agreement with the deep-seated unity and indivisibility of the human being, we cannot conceive the union and distinction, in man, of the three substances that constitute him, as an external adjustment of juxtaposed parts.

Being "one and in some manner indivisible," the human body could not be divided into two parts, one of which would be an extension mixed with soul, and the other a pure extension not penetrated by soul. This latter part would, in fact, be judged by me as belonging to the material world outside my body, and not to *my* body, for I consider only what is penetrated by my soul as being of my body. Thus, because of its indivisible unity, my body can only be *wholly* psychophysical substance, under one aspect, as it can only be *wholly* simple extended substance, under another aspect. In fact, none of its parts are not extended in length, width, and depth, divisible to infinity, completely and strictly subject to geometrical relation and to laws of general mechanics, etc.[24] But, on the other hand, none of its parts are not penetrated by soul. That is why my soul perceives sensibly the injury to any part of the body whatever, feels pain once the normally unconscious organic functions are disturbed, and experiences a general diffused well-being (coenesthetic)—*joy*—when this functioning is satisfactory and once the soul is inserted into a body perfectly disposed to receive it.[25] Of course, the automatic functioning of the machine is explained for my body in the same way that it is explained for animals, solely by mechanisms that arise from extension alone, but there is a basic difference between the human mechanism and the animal mechanism, which is that the former is at the same time the seat of general sensibility. All the involuntary and unconscious comportments of the human body cannot make what is outside my nature *strictu sensu* be anything of my body, since the former is reciprocal with the latter.

We can, in some way, discern in nature *stricto sensu* something like three concentric zones: the narrowest is that of the comportments amenable to conscious will (by the action of the soul on the pineal gland); the second, which embraces and overlaps the first is that of the zone of the comportments in general amenable to the sensory-motor apparatus whose center is the pineal gland—these two zones belong to the more particular union of the soul with a privileged part of body; the third, which is the largest, is that of generalized sensibility—it describes the plane of the union of the totality of the soul with the totality of the body. And it is evident that what is excluded from the first zone is not thus excluded from the second, and what is excluded from the first two is not excluded from the third, meaning rejected outside my nature *stricto sensu,* into purely physical nature. That *general sensibility* arises from the union of soul with the totality of the body and overlaps the zone of the more particular union of the soul with a privileged part of body is the evident result of certain texts. The elementary sensations of pain, hunger, and thirst are explained by the fact that "I am conjoined very closely, and so confused and mixed [with the body—M. G.] that *I seem to compose a single totality with it.*" These sensations are "confused ways of thinking, which arise and depend on the union and apparent mixing of the mind with the body."[26] The more particular union of the soul with a part of body concerns the immediate exercise of the functions of the soul on the body—in brief, the soul as it is substantially united with body and also as pilot of the body and presiding over the relational life of the human being. From this arises *differentiated sensibility,* and from it arises the sensory-motor apparatus, connected to the pineal gland, that places the complex instrument necessary for a changing and varied information, and the eventual response of the motive will,[27] at the disposition of the soul. It is the same for the soul, which is indivisible, but not simply "in some fashion" like the human body—meaning by being borrowed, in virtue of a union with an indivisible being that informs it—but by essence and absolutely. In virtue of this deep-seated indivisibility, it is impossible that the soul involves two parts, of which one would be the understanding alone, and the other composite substance; it can only be altogether, under one aspect, substantially composite (and consequently, sensation), and altogether, under another aspect, thinking substance (and consequently, understanding alone). In fact, the soul is always altogether in each of its faculties.[28]

6. The Simultaneous Resolution of the Problem of Psychophysics and of the Problem of Theodicy; Parallelism with *Meditation IV*

Through the explanation of the more particular union of the soul with a certain part of body, the task that fell on the final part of *Meditation VI* is completely fulfilled. The double problem of psychophysics and metaphysics that the intrinsic falsity of the senses posed—a problem parallel to the double problem of psychology and metaphysics posed by formal error—receives its perfect solution: on the one hand we know a (psychophysical) mechanism that explains the fact of this falsity, and on the other we have a theodicy to account for its metaphysical possibility.

God, who has made the best, is exculpated: "I notice that since each movement that occurs in the part of the brain from which the mind receives impressions directly can only produce in the mind a certain sensation, we cannot desire or imagine anything better than that this movement should cause the mind to feel that sensation, of all the sensations the movement is capable of causing, which is most proper and most commonly *[quam maxime et quam frequentissime—M. G.]* useful for the preservation of the human body when it is in full health. And experience shows us that all the sensations nature has given us are such as I have just stated; and hence there is nothing in them that does not show the power and goodness of God who has produced them."[29]

Indeed, God does not assure an absolute infallibility, but only the greatest possible infallibility within the frame of conditions within which they had to be instituted. However, the difference between this *maximum* possible and the *maximum* absolute is almost insignificant: it is a *minimum*. In fact, on the one hand, the likelihood of mistakes by one and the same sense is exceptional; on the other, the defect of a sense does not lead to that of others, so that the sense can be immediately compensated for and rectified by the normal functioning of the others. Moreover, God has given us memory and reasoning, through which control and correction are always possible, and most often easily accomplished, as long as one wishes them.[30] God has therefore, in some way, made up for—made up for *maximally* and even superabundantly—the *minimal* difference that separates the absolute *maximum* and relative *maximum* (which alone is possible) of infallibility. We must consequently conclude that, if we always used with sufficient care the faculties God has given us, we would never be deceived with respect to the senses.

Thus the responsibility for error is referred almost entirely to man: man's responsibility approaches the *maximum* of this absolute responsibility referred to him with respect to error in the realm of the understanding. The error that we commit, even on the occasion of an intrinsic defect in one of our senses, is finally a formal error, which has its source completely in our judgment, which, here also, is due to the weakness of our nature— meaning to the ill use of our freedom. The fact that God can be the cause of one of the rare failures of our sensory apparatus does not prevent error, when it is produced, from depending almost completely on our freedom— that is, from falling almost *exclusively on ourselves*. The conclusions of *Meditation VI* with respect to the realm of the senses therefore rejoin, if not "absolutely," at least "morally," the conclusions of *Meditation IV* relative to the realm of the understanding. Moreover, the results of the two *Meditations* are equally symmetrical in relation to the faculties that they consider respectively, as well as in relation to God himself: the sensible faculty is veridical, within its own limits, as is the understanding considered in its sphere, and thus, here as there, God's veracity, that has given rise to them in us, is entirely confirmed.

It remains for us to ask why God, who is supremely powerful, has nevertheless constructed, by uniting two incompatible natures, a nature for man, which he could not not make subject to mistakes, even occasionally. *Meditation IV* happens to have answered this question in advance. First, we do not know what are God's ends. Second, we ought to think that what is imperfect in details must, because of the necessary perfection of the divine work, contribute to the perfection of the totality. As for whether God could not intervene directly in order to obviate the exceptional errors that result from the constitutive dispositions of my nature, that is to forget that God's will is immutable and that he acts according to general laws: "God has made our body like a machine, and he wanted it to function like a universal instrument that would always operate in the same manner, according to its own laws. Accordingly, when it is functioning well, it gives the soul items of knowledge that do not deceive it; but when it is not functioning well, it still affects the soul in accordance with its own laws, and there must result from this some knowledge such that the soul will be deceived. If the body did not furnish this knowledge, it would not behave in a uniform manner, according to its laws, which remain the same in all cases. And then divine immutability would be defective, since God would not be allowing the body to act in a uniform manner, while the modes of behavior and the laws would not vary."[31] Thus God has acted for the best according to some general, immutable ways, and thus the exceptional defects in his work are explained. Moreover, these defects can, in turn, be used in the totality, as elements that contribute to the beauty of the whole. All the principal traits of the Malebranchian and Leibnizian doctrine about the simplicity of paths, the optimism according to the double meaning of the best *(optimum)* and of the most desirable *(optabile)* are there.[32]

7. Epistemological Considerations. The Termination of the Chain of Reasons. The Perfect Congruence between the Demonstrated Truth of the Universality of the Givens of Our Consciousness and of Their Assemblage, and the Necessary a priori Universality of the Guarantee Assumed by Divine Veracity

In the same way that, in the sphere of errors of the understanding, *Meditation IV* completed its double task of psychology and metaphysics with epistemological considerations, in the sphere of errors of the senses, *Meditation VI* completes its task of psychophysics and metaphysics with indications about method. In this latter case, as in the former, knowledge of the mechanism of error furnishes the means to avoid it. The intrinsic error of the senses can be avoided by the comparison of the various sensorial givens, through the recourse to memory and to the understanding. In particular, the illusion of dream that served as argument for generalized skepticism is dispelled by the understanding that reveals to me the incontestable reality of tightly linked phenomena.[33] Assured by all these controls, "we should no longer fear to encounter falsity in the things most commonly represented to us by our senses."[34]

The chain of reasons therefore ends with the refutation of that by which it began, that is, by the refutation of the hyperbolic doubts arising from natural errors and illusions of which the senses are sometimes convinced.[35]

Divine veracity has been able to handle its reductive task. It has been able to handle the exception which,under its various forms (error with respect to the ideas of the understanding, error with respect to the senses) seemed ruinous because of its preemptory universality. The universality of God's veracity does not put an end to error; but it certifies itself, in spite of the latter, in two different ways: 1) God is not directly the author of anything other than the truth, the truth of the understanding as well as the truth of sensation. 2) He has never wished for error, and when he had to allow it, on the one hand, no doubt he allowed it for the benefit of the whole—a better end about which we have no knowledge; and on the other hand, he allowed it while always giving us the means to recognize it and redress it. From this derives the corollary that we are sure of the truth when we have no means to recognize the possible falsity of a judgment and to effectuate a possible redressing, or when all the means have been used and spent effectively to prevent or rectify the error.[36] The presence of these means is a supplementary testimony to the goodness and veracity of God. If I am deceived, it is because the urgency of the action (a diversion) and the weakness of my nature lead me to be precipitous in my judgments and to make ill use of the freedom that I must thank God for having given me.[37]

Because of the guiding light that divine veracity has brought to reason, it has been able to fulfill its double mission to discover the mechanisms of our knowledge, by determining their respective limits, and to justify God by founding their proper truth. We perceive, at the same time, that each of our faculties is in itself veridical, and that the errors that they commit occasionally stem from the fact that we confuse them reciprocally—that it is sufficient to distinguish them (which is the essential matter of our science),[38] in order to see each of them clothed with the objective validity that belongs fully to them within the *limits* that are theirs, inside the regions within which they are competent.

But if the confusion of the understanding and the senses distorts the truth of the understanding, as it distorts that of sensation, if the dissociation of each faculty is the condition of all true knowledge, this precise discrimination does not prevent their collaboration. The suppression of the confused mixing of the faculties does not substitute for it their reciprocal isolation. On the contrary, it establishes between them the harmony of a mutual cooperation in which claims and competences are recognized to each for the sphere proper to it. The understanding would no more be able to inform us of the existence and of the variations of existence of material things, than sensation would be able to inform us about their existence and the diversity of their true nature; our understanding would no more be able to inform us about the vital relations that link my composite nature to the existing bodies surrounding mine, than sensation would be able to teach us anything about the necessary relations that link the properties of essences among themselves. But, in the same way that imagination aids the understanding in geometry, by allowing it to construct figures in sensible intuition and by giving it the support of symbols, the senses aid the understanding in physics by revealing to it real existences and the variations of these existences, referring it to the geometrical and mechanical relations that, among all that are possible, must be retained for the explanation of the world. Similarly, the understanding governs the imagination and rules the senses; by means of its critique and its controls, it is capable of redressing the errors of interpretation that sensation may commit, and of aiding my "nature" (in the strict sense) in preserving my life—which allows the conception of the possibility of a medicine that is both rational and concrete, meaning one based on experience and going into the sense of "my nature."[39] Finally, whether we are dealing with the senses, imagination, or the understanding, it is always my understanding that knows, the eye of intelligence that sees.

Thus divine veracity is certified twice: 1) by the intrinsic truth of our faculties (which are heterogeneous to one another), considered apart, outside of their reciprocal confusion; 2) by the total and integral truth, covering at the same time the domains of speculation and life that result from their clear and distinct collaboration. The intrinsic truth of things and of all our ideas, as lowly as they are, taken one at a time, and the truth of their assemblage, have permitted the principle of divine veracity to *fill the plenum,* and to certify in God's work a perfection such "that we cannot desire anything better," a reality that responds completely to the perfection of its author. The intrinsic truth is supported by objective reality; it is based on the causality, that is on the omnipotence of God. The truth of the assemblage is supported by the utility of his disposition; it is based on finality, that is, the goodness of God. Omnipotence and goodness are thus the two final foundations of divine veracity considered under its two necessary aspects, on the one hand, as the ultimate principle of the truth of mathematics and physics and, on the other hand, as the ultimate principle of the truth of concrete medicine, of the psychology of passions and of morality.

8. Relation of Absolute Divine Freedom with a) the Realm of the Principle of the Best, and b) the Impossibility of Creating More Than the Relatively Best. Primacy in God of the Perfection of Willing over the Absoluteness of His Decisive Power

Because of this subjection to the principle of the best, has God not appeared as subject to an order, while he has been posited as the free author of an order that rules all things without being ruled himself?

The general theory of possibility answers this question.

First, although God has realized the best *for us,* he could have done it freely, without being forced by this best. However, we must have considered that human nature, as imperfect, is not justified except in a universe that itself was collectively *(collective)* the best, not for us, but in itself. Thus we believe that God could only create what is best in itself, which appears to limit his power. But God is infinitely powerful, free and incomprehensible, only because he is infinite or perfect. To refuse to recognize that he must necessarily act under the idea of the perfect, is precisely to destroy the very foundation of this infinite omnipotence, which is limited (in appearance) only because it is perfect. To assume that God can act imperfectly and not realize the best is to admit that his infinite omnipotence can be limited and impotent. In fact, evil or the lesser good entails nothingness and to lean toward nothingness is to limit the power of one's will.

There would then be two orders of evil and good, as there are two orders of true and false, the one that God has freely decreed as eternal truth, valid for our understanding, and the other that flows necessarily from the infinity of his omnipotence, and that is thus uncreated and has an absolute validity in itself. This order could not limit his omnipotence, since it flows from his own infinity and does not impose itself on his infinity as an external rule of the understanding. Thus results this formulation: "Although God is indifferent with respect to everything, he has nevertheless decreed this necessarily, since he has necessarily willed the best, even though the best is such by his will."[40] This doctrine agrees with the doctrine of the identity of transcendental predicates, unity, truth, and goodness, to which, as we have seen, Descartes subscribes.[41] We cannot object that by conceiving omnipotence thus determined and based on the perfect we impose upon it a rule stemming from our nature, since the idea of the perfect is in us only because God has himself impressed it on us, and since we know that the objective reality of this idea in us is necessarily in conformity with the formal reality of the Perfect Being himself (which is both its efficient and exemplary cause). The idea of the good referred to that idea therefore has full objective validity; it is a divine norm that is opposed to the idea of good of anthropocentric essence, which has allowed us to judge the good and the evil of parts through their isolated comparison, while their goodness can only be assessed in relation to the totality.

But the question has another aspect. Why has God created only the relative best? Do we not limit his infinite and free omnipotence when we state that he *cannot unite* the indivisible and divisible except by this human sensory-motor system, which is only the least possible imperfect system?

No doubt his omnipotence would be limited in this way if he were not himself the author of the indivisible and divisible substances and of their incompatibility. Since he is their author, it would contradict his omnipotence if his will, unstable and contradictory, suppressed an incompatibility that makes them into really distinct substances, after having established this incompatibility in order to meld them into a single inseparable nature that he would no longer have the power to separate.[42] Moreover, the institution of the separate substances, and of their union according to the principle of the best, belongs to the one and the same simple act of divine will creating the world; divisions are introduced in this act only by human science, which, here as elsewhere, distinguishes that which, *a parte rei,* is only one. This indivisible act, which can never be directed toward nothingness, must maintain through the combinations it realizes the immutability of the eternal truths it has instituted, which are the constitutive elements of its work. Since the incompatible reality of substances to be united belongs to these eternal truths, it could not therefore be abolished by God's omnipotent will, which would then contradict his omnipotence and infinity. Here again, the impotence of divine will to modify the terms of the problem and to discover a solution that is only imperfect at the *minimum,* is, in reality, only the direct expression of his infinite omnipotence.

The analysis of the Cartesian monument therefore reveals a remarkable coherence. But if, diverted from the contemplation of the completed work, we let ourselves stray over spontaneous impressions suggested by a free reading, if we relate in some way the object—the completed work—to the subject that realized it, we experience the sensation that Descartes was divided between two tendencies. On the one hand, being preoccupied with founding the autonomy of a purely mathematical physics he emphasizes what God's incomprehensibility calls for with respect to absolute freedom conceived as decisive power free from every kind of rule, supreme power over *yes* or *no,* over action or inaction, over doing one way or another. Thus he separates radically science and theology, the material world and teleology from one another. On the other hand, he is preoccupied with integrating human experience (formal error, sensation) into the total system of philosophy, and affective psychology and morality into the system of sciences; he reintroduces finality, theodicy, and consequently theology (even though the latter is natural theology) into the created world through the principle of the best. As we have seen, this last task is closely linked to the first; instead of contradicting the first task, the last completes it. The impenetrability of God's ends suffices to immunize physics with respect to the teleology that was necessarily invoked to safeguard divine veracity, the ultimate foundation of all science. This does not prevent man—who must elevate himself to the consideration of the whole of the universe, and must conceive it in accordance with the idea of the perfect, which is implanted in our finite natures by God himself—from perceiving the world as completely enclosed by finality. From this arises an optimism that founds the notion of Providence. This optimism, governed by infinity itself, cannot fail to be felt as contrasting with the total indifference of a divine freedom without rules. God's incomprehensibility, whose foundation is never anything other than his infinity or perfection, is defined in the perspective of this optimism as a function of the idea of the perfect. Divine omnipotence then seems to us as limited by the imperative requirements of perfection. No doubt, as we have seen, this limitation is the contrary of a limitation, since that by which omnipotence seems limited is its *infinity itself,* such that the impossibility against which it is pitted is only the impossibility to be limited. No rule external to the omnipotence of will is imposed on it in order to restrain it, but the rule, if there is a rule, stems from this very will as the direct expression of its infinity—meaning of its limitless omnipotence. This does not prevent the infinity of freedom from being conceived as *the absoluteness of a decisive power,* as the power to pronounce arbitrarily *yes* or *no,* for God cannot subscribe to nothingness—he cannot will to deny being. There is therefore, in this case, a primacy of the idea of the perfect or of the essence of infinity over pure freedom. Whether this primacy emerges at the basis of divine will, imposing itself in virtue of its nature of omnipotence without limit, or whether it is imposed externally through the constraint of a dominant understanding, as in Malebranche or Leibniz, that is, of course, more than merely a nuance. But, in one or the other hypothesis, the fact of this primacy does not remain any less indubitable.

9. The Twelve Principal Truths in the Chain of Reasons

Here concludes the deduction of the "principal points" of Cartesian metaphysics, according to the analytic order of reasons.

The chain includes twelve basic truths:

1. The absolute certainty of the existence of my self as thought (a truth that is both subjectively and objectively necessary).

2. Certain knowledge of my nature as pure intelligence; criterion of substantiality (a truth that is still only subjectively necessary).

3. Certain priority of the knowledge of soul over the knowledge of body (a demonstration—which is still only subjectively necessary—of the principle that the consequence from knowledge to being is valid).

4. Necessarily objective validity of the idea of the perfect, or absolutely indubitable existence of God as both efficient and exemplary cause of this idea in me (a truth that is both subjectively and objectively necessary). From this point on, all the demonstrated truths will be both subjectively and objectively necessary.

5. Indubitable existence of God as self-cause and creator of my being.

6. Certainty of divine veracity: immediately certain objective validity of all clear and distinct ideas; presumed objective validity of other ideas to the extent that they enclose some objective reality; conversion of all the subjectively necessary truths of my science into objectively necessary truths, or truths of things.

7. Compatibility of divine veracity with human error (solution of the problem of theodicy).

8. Knowledge of the mechanism of human error: human free will, source of formal error (solution of the psychological problem). This truth and the preceding truth constitute the solution of the problem of error relative to the ideas of the understanding.

9. Consequence of our certainty concerning the objective validity of clear and distinct ideas: conversion of these ideas into essences; absolute certainty that the properties of these essences (of mathematical things or of God) are the very properties of things; from this results the validation of the a priori proof of the existence of God—the absolute certainty of the necessary existence, hence eternal existence, of God.

10. Objective validity of the necessary distinction of substances: absolute certainty of the real distinction of soul and body.

11. Objective validity of sensible ideas within the limits of their objective reality and of their realm: A) objective validity of the objective reality, of the constraint and variation of sensation; sensation as the indubitable sign of the existence of material things and of their differences in themselves; material things as occasional indubitable causes of sensation—the absolute certainty of the existence of bodies. Different degrees of absolute certainty.

12. B) Objective validity (substitute for that validity) of quality (of obscurity and confusion)—absolute certainty of the substantial union of soul and body: i) union of the soul with every part of body; ii) more particular union of the soul with one of the parts of body. Solution of the problem of error in the realm of the senses.

CHAPTER XIX

Some Consequences Concerning Medicine and Morality: Medicine and Morality as Techniques of the Good for the Present Life

1. The Realm of the Principle of the Best over the Objects of Medicine and Morality

The works of God, namely, nature in the broad sense (universe; man in general as assemblage of three substances—extension, thought, and psychophysical mixture), and nature in the strict sense (substantial union of soul and body), as we have seen, are governed by the principle of God's goodness, which the excellent order and arrangement of their constituent elements express immediately. Divine veracity extends to these complexes, not only in virtue of the reality of their constituents, which renders God their necessary author, but in virtue of divine goodness, the warrant of the benevolent intention that has presided over their composition. The truth of the biological teachings of the senses, arising from the substantial union, applies to the optimal appropriateness, to the needs of the composite, of the structure imparted to this latter by the goodness of the Creator, and not to the objective reality of the kind of thought (sensation) that results from this union.

Consequently, all these assemblages are ruled by *the principle of the best,* which is identical to the Providence that governs things. It is the principle of the best that, with respect to the created universe in general, accounts for man's existence as a disproportionate union of an infinite will and a finite understanding. In fact, it is what justifies error (which arises from this disproportion) and thus justifies the disproportion itself, by presenting it as contributing, in some manner that escapes us, to the goodness of the whole. It is also the principle of the best that, in my composite nature, leads God to unite substantially a part of the divisible to the indivisible by means of a psychophysical structure such that the senses fulfill their function in the best way possible for us; this structure is thus justified, despite the weakness that it exhibits on occasion.

The impenetrability of God's ends does not allow us to specify these ends, nor the details of their realization; but God's perfection reveals to us in all certainty that God does nothing in vain, that he aims toward the accomplishment of certain ends, and that these ends are always the best.

Certain consequences follow from that for the two disciplines that concern, not simple realities (extension alone, understanding alone), but complexes of realities, namely medicine and morality.

2. Reduction of Morality to a Technique Comparable to Medicine

We should be surprised to see situated on the same plane the two disciplines of medicine and morality, which are traditionally so distant from one another. No doubt they can both admit of a technique intended to realize a certain end, and both consequently imply a theoretical science of which this technique is the application. But medicine is fundamentally defined by that technique (therapeutics) which must be a perfect adaptation of means to an end—to heal the sick and to preserve health. It does not have to justify this end, which, for it, is beyond question, and which, on the contrary, justifies it. It seems to be completely otherwise for morality, which is less preoccupied with seeking to realize a certain end than to determine what this end must be, namely, to seek whether in some case we ought to act under the idea of an end.

But, in fact, Cartesian morality does not deal with this latter problem; it resolves it by dismissing it. Natural light, along with natural instinct (both guaranteed by divine veracity), reveal to us immediately, without the least doubt, that our end is happiness in the present life. It remains for morality only to furnish the technique capable of realizing this: "There is no person who does not desire happiness, but there are some who do not have the means."[1]

From this point of view, morality is altogether comparable to medicine. The latter may even be, in some respect, part of the former, for health is one of the necessary goods for our happiness here on earth. Morality is related to medicine in yet another way: it concerns only the present life, and since the principle of this present life is the composite substance, the latter will have to be an object common to both disciplines. However, medicine aims only at the integrity and preservation of this very substance— consequently it aims at the body—while morality aims at this substance only insofar as it is associated in me with a pure understanding as a primordial element of my contentment—consequently it aims at the mind. Concerning itself with contentment, it cannot, in fact, aim at anything other than the contentment of my mind,[2] for whether this contentment depends on body or not, it always concerns my mind, in the same way that it is always my soul that sees, even though it does so through the intermediary of the eyes.[3]

Morality is therefore the technique that must determine in what way I must act in this life in order for my soul to be full of contentment, in spite of the fact that this soul is not only pure mind, but is also substantially united to a body that plunges it into a natural and social world whose vicissitudes are infinite. We see immediately that morality, like medicine, can only be a technique that makes use of a theoretical science.

This science could concern either the object or the subject. With respect to medicine, it concerns the object; our concern with the knowledge of physics, or mechanics, is "in order to render myself master and owner of nature . . . to enable me to enjoy without labor the fruits of the earth and all the wealth to be found there," and to preserve my health, "the foundation of all the other goods of life," in order to render myself "wiser and more clever"[4] through medicine. It concerns the subject, when it attempts to determine how each thing can contribute to my contentment. In this case the concern is not with the knowledge of the truth of each thing, nor even with foreseeing specifically all the accidents that can befall on them;[5] the concern is about psychology, self-knowledge. In fact, the soul is content when it believes that it possesses a good. But its opinion in this respect is often confused. Passion leads it to believe that certain things are better than they truly are. The soul takes the trouble to acquire these things and loses the opportunity to acquire some other goods that are more genuine. The joy it extracts from the latter reveals the former's defects. The soul is then deceived and unhappy. The union of soul and body is often the cause of these illusions; but the pleasure of the mind alone can also induce us into false appearances, although rarely (for example, the pleasure of slandering). The soul must therefore evaluate the true magnitude of each pleasure—which can only be accomplished according to the rule of reason—by measuring the pleasure by the magnitude of perfection that it receives and that thus produces the pleasure in it.[6] Psychology thus appears as an instrument of morality, and morality as a medicine of the soul, even though it does not concern medicine, properly speaking, since it does not concern the fight against pathological problems (psychiatry), but concerns using some "remedies"—in the general, not the specifically medical sense of that term—against the current illusions of normal man, illusions that are harmful to his happiness.[7]

3. The Naturalistic and Quasi-Atheistic Character of Cartesian Morality

In Descartes' works, this naturalism, which subordinates morality completely to the positive sciences and renders it into one of their applications, pure and simple, is related to the absolute separation of the domain of philosophy from the domain of faith. Philosophy is the most "truly good and important occupation of men, as men."[8] It deals only with natural man,[9] meaning man such as the light of nature constitutes him, outside of what supernatural light can reveal to him: "Faith teaches us about the nature of grace, by which God gives us a view of efficacious truth and raises us to a supernatural beatitude." Consequently morality is concerned only with teaching all one needs "to take joy in natural beatitude,"[10] which concerns the present life and not the future life. Descartes therefore places himself deliberately in the point of view of the ancient philosophers "who, unenlightened by faith and knowing nothing of supernatural beatitude, considered only the goods we can possess in this life; and it was among these goods that they were trying to discover which was the supreme, that is, the principal and the greatest good."[11] Descartes also wishes to determine this supreme good *for each one,* that is, the good that, for each person, in this life, all at once, responds to one's own nature, is within one's reach, and is the greatest good.[12] But, under those conditions, philosophy gives no help toward the pursuit of the supraterrestrial good, for man's salvation, or for what a Christian considers as the only end of his life. Being placed solely from the point of view of the ancients, it is valid for them, as pagans, as well as for Turks and for Christians. Since it does not pose the problem of man's end, it does not ask whether his true end is terrestrial (natural beatitude) or supraterrestrial (supernatural beatitude through the salvation of the soul). It notes that natural reason prescribes the former and faith prescribes the latter. It postulates their equal legitimacy without even posing the problem. It does not ask whether the exclusive pursuit of the one excludes the pursuit of the other, or whether they risk interfering with or limiting each other. No doubt, for Descartes, this agreement cannot be placed into doubt, for what the natural light teaches indubitably, supernatural light cannot belie, since both emanate from the one and same veracious God. Moreover, since the happiness of this life, such as philosophy determines it, rests on the most perfect possible usage of the faculty by which I most resemble God (namely my free will), it renders me as similar as possible, to God on earth,[13] and it establishes a natural agreement between my will and his that could only help, it seems, for the Christian disposition of my soul. The optimism based on the principle of the best can only confirm such a harmony.[14]

This does not prevent natural light, meaning philosophy, from referring me exclusively to happiness on earth, to the certainty of an indefinite betterment of the human condition (by means of the transformation of nature by science), to an arithmetic of pleasures intended to fulfill my contentment,[15] and to the positive dreams that will be those of the eighteenth century in France and of the *Encyclopédie*. It does not point to heaven. Although, in order to open up the road to truth, it prescribes me to close my eyes and shut my ears, it guides me on the road to the good by returning me to the terrestrial world, in which I take root through my senses and passions, so that I can live in comfort and can enjoy its "wealth" maximally. It does not call me to the hereafter, does not sublimate me into the intelligible world, in accordance with Plotinus' statement: "to return home, we must close the eyes of the body and open those of the soul."[16] It discovers that the passions are all good; that their good usage gives a sweetness to this life;[17] that without the passions, I would not hold to life;[18] that life on earth has some good; that the goods outweigh the evils; that these goods are certain, while the goods of the future life are doubtful; that the ante is too valuable to risk in an uncertain bet; that a good *in hand* is worth more than two *promises*. . . .[19] To rephrase according to the *Meditations*, we have no reason to complain about the fact that God has given us a body and senses. "We cannot either desire or imagine anything better," even *for us*. In such a world, Malebranche's painful question seems incomprehensible and almost shocking: "Lord, why have you given me a body that fills me with darkness?"[20]

4. Confirmation of This Character in Spite of Denials by Descartes

It is true that Descartes has contradicted himself at times, and some of these occasions were at a few days' intervals.

He began by stating the contrary to Elizabeth herself, affirming that after death, the soul is capable of enjoying an infinity of contentments that cannot be found in this life.[21] He specified to Huyghens that the clear and distinct knowledge of the nature of our souls assures us that after death they will enjoy pleasure and happiness much greater than those we enjoy in this world (except if our souls have shown themselves to be unworthy). And this truth, taught by religion, touches us still more because of the fact that natural reason persuades us of it "by extremely evident reasons."[22] Should we admit that Descartes does not say the same thing, depending upon whether he is consoling a correspondent affected by the death of someone near to him,[23] or demonstrating some prudence with respect to a high-strung woman who, pushing to the extreme the logic of a doctrine, considers suicide reasonable and would perhaps be capable of doing it actually?

One thing is certain, in any case, namely that, although Cartesianism can truly be turned toward Christian edification,[24] as Bérulle saw, it can also be turned toward a eudaemonistic morality; and in fact Descartes has opted toward the latter. His consolations with respect to Huyghens have scarcely any support in the system. We can hardly see how the clear and distinct knowledge of the nature of soul can assure us that it will enjoy greater felicities after death and that the body is an obstacle in this respect. The disappearance of body entails the disappearance of all the passions, and of all the sensations; and all the passions are good.[25] "Our soul would not wish to remain joined to its body if it could not feel them."[26] The love and intellectual joys that can then subsist alone appear to natural light, in the plane of this life, as deprived of the color and heat of the passion that would render them "ravishing."

That is why in this life the love of a God worthy of that name must not remain purely intellectual, but must become sensitive; it must be able to "pass through the imagination, in order to come from the understanding to the senses." Only under that condition can knowledge of God through natural light be said properly to make us love him. Perhaps Christian revelation had as one of its ends to lower God, by means of the Incarnation, so as to render him similar to us and thus to allow us to love him through passion. In any case, only the force of our nature is capable of having arise in us, without having recourse to religion, such a passionate love for God. Of course the soul must be detached from the commerce with the senses in order to represent to itself the truths that excite the love of God, but "it can communicate this love to the imaginative faculty," in order to make a passion of it; it suffices that we imagine this love itself, meaning our union with God, in order that the idea of this union, exciting "the heat around the heart, causes an extremely violent passion," which is "the most ravishing and most useful that we can have relative to this life."[27] Thus the love and intellectual joys that natural light reveals to us here on earth appear truly bland as long as they are not increased by passion. Natural light therefore does not seem to give us by itself the least idea of the superior felicities that would await the soul separated from the body in the other world. It is already too much to expect that we can derive hope from it. Descartes is consistent with himself when he states that faith alone can reveal to us the sweetness of celestial beatitude.

Finally, in order to exorcise the idea of reasonable suicide, Descartes sets aside all the classical arguments, more or less colored by religiosity, that were upheld by Plato, Epictetus, and Plotinus.[28] His two arguments concern the certainty that here on earth goods outweigh evils, and the uncertainty of supraterrestrial happiness; the arguments are of eudaemonistic order and belong to a calculus of pleasures that, according to him, conditions the contentment of the soul. This calculus combines a certainty that produces the resolution of will and a limitation of our will with respect to certain goods that depend on us; thus our happiness always remains in our hands and becomes beatitude. Free will is able to decide, in this case, only in virtue of the proper interest of the reasonable being, and not in virtue of motives that are foreign to this interest and to ourselves, that belong to God (Plato) or to some higher order, such as to destiny, etc. (Epictetus).

Thus there is a great contrast between the natural, intellectual asceticism that conditions a science completely based on the purification of the understanding with respect to the sensible, and the clever, calculatory eclecticism of a morality that is careful to assemble, according to the maximum possible for us, satisfactions of various origins and natures. That is because we are concerned with satisfying a soul that is not the soul of an angel, but that is rooted in a body and is only partially pure understanding. This soul could not fulfill its possible contentment if it wished to set aside deliberately the satisfactions of its composite nature in order to be contented with the joys of pure thought alone. Reason therefore requires that a place be made for the pleasures arising from body, for we are concerned, once again, solely with the fulfillment of satisfaction.

Science itself is justified through the contentment it brings: material wealth and the joys of pure mind.[29] It is not as if it must be cultivated uniquely for this end, for these preoccupations would lead us to enclose ourselves into this or that particular science according to whether it responds more specifically to the whims of our personal utility or taste. We would then be breaking the unity of science into smaller, isolated disciplines. We would be thus going against a rationally understood eudaemonism. In fact, it is by cultivating pure science *in its unity* that we can elevate ourselves to this cleverness that permits our action to be perfectly adequate for *all* occasions. It is the conquest of this *unitary* science that alone can "increase the natural light of reason so that in each circumstance of life the understanding shows to the will what side to choose."[30] The petty specialists who are busy resolving minor difficulties retain small understandings that are ill-equipped for life. The vast mind that aims at a unitary science realizes these particular ends infinitely better than they do, without pursuing them expressly: "The advantages that we derive from science in life . . . the pleasure of the contemplation of the true in this life, is almost the only happiness that is pure and not troubled by any pain."[31]

5. Subordination of Stoicism to Epicureanism in Cartesian Morality

In contrast with science which, if not by its motive, at least by its conditions, requires intellectual asceticism and refers us to Plato and Saint Augustine, morality (which could at most refer to the *Philebus*) places itself, in the name of its eudaemonism, under the patronage of Epicurus (an Epicurus not according to the caricature drawn in legend, but according to his truth verified by history,[32] an Epicurus corrected by Zeno[33]) and not under the patronage of Plato.

That is why the Stoic elements of Cartesian morality, which are so numerous and so visible, as well as those related to Christianity, are introduced only in order to satisfy the ideal of Epicurus. If we need to distinguish between things that depend on us and those that do not, and thus to rise above the latter, it is because we thus escape the deceptions and evils stemming from fortune—it is because we can thus make the greatest contentment of our life dependent on us alone, and consequently we can acquire beatitude, as opposed to happiness, insofar as the latter always depends on chance (luck). This contentment would depend only upon us if it results effectively only from our certainty of having used our free will as best as possible. And it does result from this certainty, since the latter is necessarily tied to the consciousness of the strength of our soul, our self-possession, our mastery over things and passions, our internal perfection, and since this consciousness necessarily engenders a deep satisfaction.[34] If we needed to detach ourselves from the pleasures arising from the body, in order to devote ourselves more to the pleasures arising from the soul, it is because the latter are always under our power, are not fleeting, deceptive, and of little magnitude, as are the former.[35] If there is only a single virtue, firmness of will, from which all others proceed, it is because all the happiness of my life depends on this virtue alone.[36] If, persuaded about the immortality of the soul, I detach myself from the pleasures tied to the body (which is perishable) and from all the goods arising from fortune (which are nothing with respect to eternity), it is in order to devote myself better to these spiritual pleasures, which, having their origin in the soul, can be immortal like it and subsist unalterably during the course of this life; it is because I can represent the events of this world to myself as the acts of a play whose happy or sad vicissitudes can be turned into pleasures for my present life.[37]

Of course, Zeno was right to consider that the supreme good is virtue, for each man can possess it particularly, since it resides in his free will. But virtue is the goal only subsidiarily, as is the bull's-eye in a target shoot: we aim for it only to win the prize, meaning pleasure.[38] By eliminating pleasure, Zeno could only recruit "melancholics, or minds completely detached from bodies." Epicurus therefore is not wrong in affirming that the end of our actions is pleasure, meaning the contentment of the mind. In fact, nothing would obligate us to do good deeds if no pleasure were derived from them. Virtue must therefore be defined with respect to its aptitude for having us reach the goal of action, and not by itself. Man's happiness involves two elements: on the one hand, honor, riches, health, and everything that does not depend on us, and on the other hand, the satisfaction that results from the sensation of our perfection, when we are conscious of being masters of ourselves, firm in our actions, and indifferent to external ills. That is what depends on us and what we commonly call wisdom or virtue. It is certain that he who can add the first category of good to the second has more beatitude than he who has only the second. However, "a small container can be as filled as a larger one"; that is why "since the contentment of each is taken to be the plenitude and accomplishment of one's desires according to reason, the persons most barren of the first goods can be as completely content and satisfied as those who enjoy both the first and second goods, even though they do not enjoy as many goods." And since only that contentment is in our power, seeking the other is superfluous.[39]

6. Difference of Principle between Stoic Morality and Cartesian Morality. Comparison of the Container. Medicine and Morality in Stoic and Cartesian Philosophy

Is that not simply and purely a return to Stoicism? We must not forget that, for the Stoics, the end is also happiness, and that virtue is prescribed as the necessary and sufficient means for obtaining it.[40] And if Cartesianism in its turn also defines virtue as the exclusive search for pleasures coming from the soul, insofar as they alone depend on us, and as detachment from the corporeal pleasures, how is Cartesianism different from Stoicism?

First it differs in that it does not completely absorb beatitude into virtue;[41] it remains an end distinct from the latter. It then differs from Stoicism by its definition of virtue, which is not the exclusive search for only the goods of the soul and the radical detachment with respect to corporeal goods, but a conditional renouncement, in the case in which circumstances forbid them from us. We are concerned with obtaining the maximum of contentment of which our soul is capable, and not to reduce this capacity, to practice the restrictions of the Cynic, to make a small container out of a large one, in order to be able to fill it more readily. Descartes does not prize "these small containers that three drops of water can fill."[42] The goal of reason consists, on the contrary, "in knowing exactly how much each thing can contribute toward our contentment." The more actions bring us perfection, the more they are virtuous and bring contentment to the soul, "which is our internal testimony that we have gained some perfection."[43] We must therefore determine the correct magnitude of all the goods that we believe ourselves capable of attaining by our conduct and use our utmost care in obtaining them; and if fortune prevents us from attaining them, we will have the satisfaction of having lost nothing through our fault, and we will take joy from the entire beatitude that is in our power.[44] A calculation is therefore necessary: since we are ordinarily required to deprive ourselves of some perfection in order to have others, we will have to choose the best. Since the perfections of the body are the least ones, they will have to await the others. That is why we can say that "generally there is a way to be happy without them."[45] The words "there is a way" and "generally" signify that, although this is often possible, it is not always possible, nor obligatory, nor desirable, and that this is in spite of it all. Even if the goods of the body are only "to be esteemed [and not to be honored and praised],"[46] these goods and the sweetness of the passions[47] are to be attained when one can have them. Right reason, from which right action flows, will integrate them into their place in the order of values; it will introduce them into it by accounting for their magnitude and precariousness in the arithmetic of happiness. That is why neither health, not life, nor the passions are indifferent things: health is the foundation of all the other goods that we can have in this life;[48] life involves so many more goods than evils that it would be irrational (and even immoral, whatever is the opinion of Zeno and Seneca[49]) to put an end to it voluntarily;[50] the passions are all good and must be cultivated under the guidance of reason.[51] Whoever would neglect the goods of the body, whoever would "extirpate" the passions, would be sinning against virtue; he would be adding to the evils of corporeal origin that he would have imposed upon himself the sadness arising from the internal reproach of not having done what he should have done.

The detachment with respect to external goods is therefore only one of the factors of the arithmetic of maximal contentment. It first allows me to fill the container to the maximum, by having me avoid the illusory overestimation of these goods and to create thus a real deficit, in some way, by seeking them to the detriment of the greater goods. It then allows me, above all, to reduce the capacity of the container to my capacity to fill it, without ever rendering the capacity of the container smaller than my capacity to fill it. In fact, if I renounced a priori all the external goods that my reason reveals to me as able to be attained without having to deprive myself of others, I would render my container smaller than my capacity to fill it. If, on the contrary, I detach myself from these goods, not in order to forbid myself from seeking them, but in order to maintain the plenitude of my contentment when they happen to reveal themselves,[52] I would have an infallible recipe for making the capacity of my container never exceed my power to fill it, in all circumstances (without ever bringing its capacity to below my power). Finally, this plenitude of contentment will always coincide with my conscience, which is satisfied, having acted as it should have acted.

Thus we see that action cannot be understood by Descartes in the same way that it is understood in Stoicism. Of course, they both place duty in action enlightened by science, and not in contemplation; both also recommend belonging to oneself. But if I thus become God's equal, for the Stoic, it is because I am sublimated into the tension of the universal soul, which saves the total nature from dispersion, through the tension in which the act altogether folds upon itself[53] and tears my soul from external ends and dispersion. The affirmation of self is only a stripping of self for the benefit of the order of the world, and an indifference with respect to any external ends. For Descartes, on the other hand, belonging to oneself involves, no doubt, the acceptance of the immutable decrees of divine will and the submission to reason, but it is not a blind submission to the order of universal nature and indifference to external ends; on the contrary, it is a submission of nature to my will, which is capable, because of science, of modifying nature and of rendering myself master and owner of it. Belonging to oneself is not a baring of the self by free will, but the affirmation of free will in each person; it is this affirmation and not the fusion with the universal order that renders each individual into the equal of God, a person *who is not one of his subjects.*[54] Since it does not reside exclusively in the act of adherence to the order of the world, virtue, which becomes an effort to know in order to act efficiently on things and on myself, gives its full validity to what was only subsidiary for the Stoics, namely to the choice between preferable things: what is at issue is to "measure exactly the magnitude of the goods" in order to determine the choice of what will render us happy; no choice will be able to go against this arithmetic, under the pretext that it is ordered of us by a so-called destiny that is beyond us. Virtue will therefore be defined by the science of the best choice and, lacking this science, by the effort toward the science with a view toward the best choice; it suffices for me to be conscious of this effort in order to be protected from regrets and remorses that could arise from choices that the future reveals as unfortunate ones.[55]

Since it is turned toward an end external to virtue, and since it requires an action modifying material nature as much as my own nature, asking the exact sciences to illuminate these means, Cartesian morality is truly a technique, an applied science. It is thus opposed to Stoic morality. Originally proposed as a technique (for happiness), but substituting virtue over happiness as an end and detaching the subject from any external realization, Stoic morality, in fact, denies the problem of technique, for the problem of ends.[56] If it presupposes theory, it is not to discover in it a technique of actions on things, an application of science, but to determine by it *the character* that our action could and should assume, namely, the character of not having any end other than itself, not to aim toward realizing an external end, but to accomplish itself according to form—that of right intention. That is why medicine and morality are, for the Stoics, two disciplines that are incapable of assimilation in the final analysis,[57] while, for Descartes, they are completely comparable.

In brief, Descartes' morality is the opposite of quietism, of a morality of submission and renouncement; it is a morality of expansion and conquest that aims at domination over things. If it incorporates some elements of abstention and detachment, it does so as means, not as ends, with a view toward reinforcing thus the unshakable firmness of a will completely given to the progress of knowledge, allowing the more and more tight subjection of nature to the commodities of human life.

7. The Problem of the True and the Problem of the Good; Inversion of the Perspectives of Metaphysics According to the Perspectives of Morality; the Primacy of Life over Speculation and of the Composite Substance over the Thinking Substance. Philosophy as the Servant of Life. The Absolute Union of Science and Wisdom from the Metaphysical Point of View; Their Tendency to be Dissociated from the Moral Point of View. Excommunication of Tradition by Science; Use of Tradition by Morality. Internal Conflict in the Moral Technique. The Drama of Cartesian Morality

We thus see that the problem of the good is not posed in the same terms as the problem of the true, as it is, for example, in Malebranche and Spinoza. With respect to the true, composite nature is a radical obstacle. In order to reach the true, man must conduct himself as a disincarnate being— as an angel. That is not so for the good, for the substantial union is not, or at least is not necessarily and always, an obstacle to the attainment of the good. That is because although the true (which concerns essences and eternal truths) is the object of the understanding *alone,* and in no case the object of the composite substance, the good that concerns *this life* is defined as well, and even above all, with respect to the composite substance, whose existence precisely constitutes my life. That is why what can appear as a good of pure understanding, the love of God, for example, arising from natural light, is not a genuine good of this life until it is integrated with the sphere of the union of soul and body as a passion. That is why the hierarchy among the goods, based on the exact evaluation of their magnitude, meaning of the magnitude of perfection they bring to me (upon which depends the magnitude of contentment) is not at all comparable to the Malebranchian relations of perfection. Since the good is the beatitude or contentment of which I am the master, it matters little whether this contentment draws its origin from the understanding alone or from my composite substance, for the beatitude in question is that of this life, and not that of my supraterrestrial life. We thus conceive that the foundation of morality is not religion, in any way. Descartes' morality, which is immediately practicable by a Turk or a pagan, is the morality of an atheist.[58] At the most, God intervenes in order to establish the harmony and fundamental order of the world, which are necessary for the preservation of my composite substance; and the certainty of its existence allows it to establish in me a detachment with respect to the external goods, which is sufficient to allow me to escape the deceptions of fortune.

This conception of "natural beatitude" explains the importance of the composite substance. For, if we are placed in the point of view of *felicity in this life,* the composite substance plays a greater role than the understanding alone, even though the contemplation of the truth is the most ravishing of pleasures here on earth. In fact, is not health the most important good of this life, since it is "the foundation of all other goods"? We understand that, under these conditions, Descartes recommends us "not to devote too much time to metaphysics,"[59] since it is not what is essential for him, as it is for Malebranche and Spinoza. On the other hand, metaphysics would be what is essential if the happiness we ought to seek were completely suspended on the vision of intelligible realities that pure understanding alone is capable of conferring upon us—if we needed to tear ourselves away from the present life as much as possible, by means of thought. In fact (beside religion), metaphysics alone is capable of allowing us to do this. It is otherwise if philosophy must serve only to enlighten me here on earth in order to go forth with assurance in this life and to procure the maximum of happiness for myself. Metaphysics is then required only in order to found science, and science, in turn, is only required in order to increase my "wealth." To become "master and owner of nature" means that man, composed of a soul and a body, by the power of the understanding, will subdue physical nature for the satisfaction of the needs of his psychophysical substance. That is why "to attend to physics and sensible things" is the most important thing: "It is the occupation that we ought to wish most upon man, because it is the source of all the wealth of life."[60] To give oneself to metaphysics in too great a degree would be "extremely harmful" for man, "because that would impede him from devoting himself to the functions of the imagination and the senses."[61]

Thus is explained one of the contrasts we observe between morality, on the one hand, and physics and metaphysics, on the other. Although the latter two are constituted by making a *tabula rasa* of tradition, by deriving their truths from the linkage of reasons alone, morality, on the contrary, which no longer moves within the domain of the certain and of pure reason, but in the domain of the probable, of sensation, of the experience of things and of men, expressly follows from a *tradition*—the tradition of the ancient moralists (Aristotle, Zeno, Epicurus) such as Descartes perceives them through the works of Plutarch, Cicero (*Tusculanes, De officiis, Paradoxes, De finibus,* etc.), Seneca *(De Vita beata),* the moralists of the Renaissance, Christian Stoicism, or the wisdom of Montaigne and Charron. It is, to a certain extent, eclectic and syncretic, as is this tradition (it combines Zeno and Epicurus, as well as Christian beliefs). No doubt this syncretism is directed by an enlightened reason and an autonomous judgment, but we are no longer concerned with "exact science." We rediscover here between science and wisdom (which gives rules allowing the person most devoid of intelligence, as well as the most erudite to achieve beatitude[62]) the separation to which Descartes seemed to put an end, and which, as had correctly noted Gilson,[63] was one of the characteristics of the moralists of the Renaissance, particularly Montaigne and Charron. But we must add that, for Descartes, it is pure reason itself that, after having determined in an absolutely necessary and certain fashion the constitutive elements of our being, the various kinds of knowledge of which we are capable and their respective limits, traces the contours of this sphere in which sensation and the verisimilitude of opinions must decide.

If philosophy is completely directed toward this last goal—to render us happy here on earth—if it prescribes for us to spend little of our time on pure understanding, or understanding together with imagination, that is, on metaphysics and mathematics, so that we are free to spend the maximum time on the functions of imagination and the senses, it would seem that, in this perspective, the psychophysical substance, among the three substances constitutive of our nature, must become the object of a dominant preoccupation. In brief, the perspective of morality overturns the perspectives of science. Although in fact, it is the science of extension alone (mechanistic physics, pure mathematics) that governs all of philosophy and constrains it to be enclosed within the sphere of understanding alone—regardless of whether we are concerned with elaborating on it or with founding it—this philosophy and science finally are justified, in the eyes of philosophy itself, only through their utility in life; and philosophy, giving the fullest meaning to the adage "Primum vivere, deinde philosophari," finally reverses completely, on the plane of what is useful, the hierarchy that it had founded for the plane of what is true, by now placing composite substance at its summit. In fact, it is in relation to this substance that our happiness in the present life tied. It is the basic fact to which we are referred in order to found a *useful* science and to determine the rules of a happiness that is necessarily first defined with respect to this life *here on earth,* since the latter is nothing more than the union of my soul with a body. The subordination of that fact itself to something that would be eccentric to it and would be situated *beyond* my life is never what is at issue. From this arises the contrast with Malebranche, who is not satisfied to account for this fact with respect to the life here on earth, meaning through the help that the soul can bring in order to safeguard the body (because of its union with it), but who justifies it also, and above all, with respect to the life of the soul after death, meaning through the function of salvation of the body with which I am united, as an instrument of expiatory pains drawing me in this life from the merits that could influence my supraterrestrial destiny. In Descartes, terrestrial life—and consequently its happiness—remains considered in itself and for itself, since philosophy excludes from its speculations all the considerations, relative to original sin and to supraterrestrial life, that would stop making this life the true end of reason.

However, the fact that the contentment issued from the composite substance supposes science, and that, for science, the composite substance is an obstacle—that science finally unfolds according to the rational order of reasons—necessarily masks the primacy of the composite substance and creates an apparent conflict between the intellectual asceticism of science and the eudaemonism of morality. It remains no less true that all of science only contributes toward allowing us, through the knowledge of extension, thought, and the psychophysical substance, to give comfort to the latter, either by increasing material wealth, or by indicating to us the means to eliminate the emotions and passions that can be harmful to our terrestrial felicity, for the benefit of those that can increase it. Philosophy is no longer the servant of theology, but the servant of life here on earth. It is a servant without being enslaved, for it can only serve if it stems from pure reason alone in its very constitution.

But it remains for us to know, precisely, whether this morality-science can be constituted, whether the technique of happiness can suffice for its end, can furnish every man whatsoever a practical law indicating to him what it is suitable for him to do or not to do in every circumstance,[64] "encompassing in all cases and for all reasonable beings the same determining principle of the will."[65] We shall see the effort of the Cartesian technique aimed toward the determination of the matter of action finally miscarry to a large extent, and moral philosophy turn toward the opposite pole (that of form and intention: Stoicism) without ever being able to attain it and to fix itself on it completely. That will be the drama of Cartesian morality, which is played across the inextricable complication of a provisional doctrine which heralds a definitive doctrine that must replace it, and of a definitive doctrine, which, on the contrary, confirms and consolidates, once and for all, the morality that we thought to be provisional.

Some Consequences Concerning Medicine and Morality: Three Ideas of Medicine and Morality

1. The Impossibility of a Rigorous Medical and Moral Science; the Necessity for a Substitute Science

As we have seen,[1] medicine and morality at first present themselves as techniques applying a certain science to the realization of ends that concern our present life. Both concern themselves with human nature, meaning with the substantial composite of soul and body, associated with pure understanding. As a result, the matter offered to them is intrinsically obscure and confused. No doubt medicine involves in part a science of body as pure machine, and this science, a simple development from physics, involves only clear and distinct ideas. But insofar as it addresses itself to the human body, which is distinguished from the animal body by its substantial union with a soul, it is confronted with sensation. It is the same for morality, which is concerned with the problem of the passions, the eminent expressions of the psychophysical substance. In a more general fashion, morality defined as science of life, "allowing man to distinguish the true from the false in order to see clearly with respect to his actions, and to walk with assurance in this life,"[2] poses problems about how to conduct oneself, which most of the time cannot be resolved by the knowledge of clear and distinct natures, since the problem is not about essences, but about existences and existential circumstances known by means of the senses. Are not human science and morality impossible to constitute as sciences under these conditions, since there is no rigorous science of such natures? In the absence of such natures, am I not required to suspend all my judgments? But then my will, not being able to be enlightened in its choice will remain irresolute and will not act.

Moreover it is evident that such a hypothesis is excluded by life itself, which requires action, and by reason, which teaches me that my will has been given to me not only to direct my understanding toward the knowledge of the true, but to assure, at each instant, the preservation, the happiness of this life, and in a general fashion, my felicity. The search for science is only justified by the utility of the science for life, since the good depends on the knowledge of the true. That is precisely why our conduct ought to be ruled by the knowledge of the true.[3]

Consequently, although our will is required to suspend its judgment as long as the understanding is not able to perceive the true, it is not allowed to suspend its action in life, nor to suspend its judgment on what it ought to do, for the requirements of life cannot suffer any delay.[4] It would thus be lacking in its function since its irresolution, bringing it to stop acting for the good, would lead it inevitably toward defeat and toward the bad of our life.[5]

Therefore, *to certainty,* which is the imperative of speculation, will succeed unavoidably the acceptance of *risk,* which is the imperative of morality. In fact, although my will is infinite, my understanding is not; it is inadequate for the infinity of infinitely complex occasions of which my life is composed. From this results the need for my will to pronounce judgment in these occasions, without having clear and distinct ideas with respect to them. Life therefore requires will to pass over the requirements for absolute truth of speculative science, and even though it is incapable of illuminating its elective function using this truth, it is still required to accomplish this function.

The *assurance* that the will cannot find in the *certainty of science,* it will find in itself, in the *firmness of its resolution.* This firmness that will enable it to confront risk is therefore the substitute for the certainty that science alone could have given it and that would have enabled it to dispense with risk. Because of it, I can realize *morally* what science could have enabled me to attain *absolutely:* "To go forth with *assurance* in this life."[6] But this "assurance" is not the same here and there, for, in one case, it proceeds from the suppression of risk and, in the other case, from the power to face it.

Finally, since will cannot be exercised without the intervention of the intellect, because, although the understanding can be without will, will cannot be without the understanding, it will impose on the understanding the problem to enlighten it as best as possible, given that a science is impossible in this case. Since moral will is reasonable will, an attempt will be made, therefore, to limit risk *maximally* (through the calculus of probabilities—it is a calculated risk); lacking absolute certainty, it will tend toward moral certainties, whose degree of certainty, as we have seen, can be extremely great (as, for example, with the moral certainty of a completed decoding). Firmness, the disposition that the soul derives from will alone, will tend toward certainty, a disposition that the soul derives from science alone—from which arises the necessity for reason to install a morality that will be a *substitute for science.*[7]

The case of medicine (of the medicine of the substantial composite), which is also a science turned toward the practical, must be basically analogous.

2. Various Kinds of Substitutes

But what would this substitute consist of?

As we may realize, this whole perspective is governed by the initial postulate that if there is a science of medicine and morality, it must be of mathematico-deductive kind and must come from the understanding alone.

The truth that the disciplines concerned with life require as knowledge are those of the means by which one can realize the supreme ends of this life: the health of the body, the contentment of the soul. In brief, truth here is what is useful. From the point of view of the understanding alone, what is useful resides entirely in the exact sciences (mathematics, physics, and mechanistic medicine) and in their practical applications: the invention of machines that lessen human work, anatomical and biological discoveries that allow for the betterment of the well-being of the body and its maintenance, etc. On this level, medicine appears as involving a science as speculative as physics, namely, human anatomy-physiology as exact science, together with the practical applications it entails. Morality also appears completely governed by the knowledge of the truths of physics, mechanistic medicine, in particular. It is this conception that is evident in the famous passage from the *Discourse:* "If it is possible to find some means to render men wiser and more skillful than they have been until now, I believe that one must seek it in medicine."[8] That is also what Descartes understands when he conceives that the most perfect morality "presupposes the complete knowledge of the other sciences,"[9] and that it can be treated "exactly."[10] From this point of view, practical truth fits completely into exact theoretical truth.

It is the lack of ability to satisfy the needs of life, on this plane, with respect to the mathematico-deductive ideal, that will define the substitute for science. Given that we cannot derive the usefulness of the exact sciences, will directs the understanding to discover some biologically and morally useful knowledge, which is of a different order than the technical application of exact science and situated on a plane that is radically heterogeneous plane to that of speculative truth. It is discovered on the plane of life itself, of daily experience, of sensation, insofar as this whole realm, being that of the union of soul and body, constitutes a sphere apart from other spheres, whose teachings contradict the truths of pure understanding. We already know that in this sphere *truth* is not concerned with the *nature* of things, but with the *biological usefulness* of these things with respect to our composite nature. Sensation, passion, all these modes of obscure and confused sensibility have as unique role to furnish us, in this respect and in this respect alone, true information that is foreign to the truths of pure science, but that is guaranteed by divine veracity. Medicine and morality are the disciplines required by our condition of man united to a body. From this point of view an inquiry whose sole object will be a practical truth, of another order than the theoretical truth presented by the system of exact sciences, can be founded. It is this inquiry that will constitute the substitute for the true science.

But even though they are completely different from the sciences of clear and distinct ideas, how can these disciplines be called their substitute, since in the region of the union of soul and body, pure understanding is incompetent and must give way to sensation, the only organ justified for the true knowledge of life? We are dealing here with scientific disciplines of an entirely different kind, not with degraded rational sciences, but with sciences that can be perfect within their own kind, that are autonomous with respect to their object and the nature of their organ. They are also capable of leading us in an assured fashion to an uncontestable truth— that of sensation. They are rational in their own fashion; for although they do not have clear and distinct ideas as their objects, they lead us to clear and distinct knowledge with respect to sensation as such, whether we are concerned with receptivity (sense and sensation, properly speaking) or affectivity (passions, properly speaking). They use rational critique in order to rediscover the authentic teaching and function of sensibility in general (sensation, passion), hiding behind habit, prejudice, and ignorance. They lead us in this way to the proper use of these sensations and passions, which have been given to us for our good. Science—but a science other than mathematics and physics—therefore returns here to illuminate the acting will. Reason, if not immediately, at least mediately, through its power to restore to original sensation its integrity, appears always as the guide of will. The formulation "Omnis peccans est ignorans," or "He who judges well acts well,"[11] thus receives again a full justification. A sample of such a science is given to us, as it concerns morality, by the *Treatise on Passions*. Above all it concerns the affectivity stemming from the union of soul and body, an obscure and confused matter. It uses the rational critique to reveal its true teachings and true function; it destroys illusions, habits, and prejudices in this respect.[12] It entails a complete certainty. It allows the proper use of the passions, which, in themselves, "are all good."[13] It guides the will toward the best equilibrium of body and soul. It is truly a science.

However, does this science happen to satisfy the will fully? For this, it would have to attain more than merely general rules. It would have to furnish us, with respect to *each case* likely to occur in daily experience, the means to discover the exactly appropriate formula for action, that is, the knowledge of what is useful to do in order to assure both the preservation and happiness of our life. And the immense complexity of the events of life makes it impossible to determine for all possible occasions what is useful (either biological or moral), whose knowledge is indispensable for will, in order for it to act well. At most we can formulate general principles, which are no doubt the object of certain knowledge, but which cannot determine in advance what ought to be the content of our actions. And will, solicited by life, cannot abstain itself as long as it does not possess what is true, what is capable of determining the matter of action. Abstention is not required except in the domain of the speculative search for truth. Since it is constrained to act, will solicits reason to illuminate it, even though reason cannot succeed in presenting to it the true (in this case, the true good). Consequently, lacking this, the understanding has to furnish it a substitute. We find again, on another plane (the plane of psychological and psychophysical knowledge) the primitive problem of a substitute to be discovered for science.

Medicine (of substantial union), and above all morality, will have to furnish a substitute, not only for exact, mathematico-physical knowledge (which we have seen is impossible to realize), but also for a large number of indispensable, clear, and distinct items of knowledge concerning the realm of sensation and life, items of knowledge that these two disciplines are incapable of bringing to us, for they are overwhelmed by the immensity and particularity of their matter. In order not to lack will, they have to pursue their achievement as practical disciplines, in such a way that they are able to embrace the whole field of possible occurrences, in spite of the fact that it goes beyond the certain knowledge of the true. Thus, the clear and distinct knowledge that constitutes the final object of a complete certainty will be the assured rules that it is suitable to prescribe for a will destined to speak out at all costs in a field in which intelligence cannot reach either mathematical evidence or, in a general way, the clear and distinct knowledge relative to what is useful in the multiple occurrences taking place within the sphere of life. In each case, we would then be substituting principles that prescribe for us to be satisfied with what is probable, for the truths that cannot be discovered. But, since truth remains the ideal guide of the acting will, these principles require us, at the same time, not to cease striving toward truth—to get as close to it as possible. In brief, they order us to be satisfied with judgments as certain as possible, instead of and in place of certain judgments ranging over absolute evidences of mathematico-physical order, or clear and distinct knowledge of the passions and of their utilization, as well as opportune reactions of our will in such or such cases. Lacking a scientifically good (medical or moral) conduct, we will have to choose "the best possible."

The completion of these sciences of practical essence in principles prescribing the "best judgments possible,"[14] instead of and in place of "good judgments" that are generally outside our reach, is fully in agreement with the order that governs the world within which we have to live and act. In fact, God has given rise to this world and governs it through *the principle of the best*. In this world he has realized a combination that attains a *maximal* approximation, but not an absolute perfection and infallibility. In such a domain, man evidently does not have the power to do better than God himself. Where God has realized in the world, and for man in particular, only approximations, only "the best possible," man, who is finite, would never be able to attain, with respect to what concerns him, the absolute of infallible science and perfect behavior. A fortiori, he will also have to be satisfied with the order of his actions as the best possible, or the best approximation and best judgment; he will have to limit himself to attempt constantly to better his judgments by using reason.

3. Three Possible Ideas of Medicine; the (at Least Partial) Failure of Medicine

With respect to the preceding, we must expect that the rational disciplines concerning life, its preservation, and the happiness of the soul in the present life (beatitude) are conceived as functions of three very different ideas: according to the idea of an exact science, of mathematico-deductive kind, derived from physics; according to the idea of a psychological and psychophysical clear and distinct science having as basis the certainties of sensation (which is in itself obscure and confused), in the realm of the psychophysical substance; according to the idea of a body of assured general principles, intended to substitute for the (at least) partial absence of these two sciences and capable of guiding us in the midst of our uncertainties.

Medicine was above all and first of all conceived by Descartes as a development of pure physics.[15] It analyzes the structures and movements of living bodies by reducing them to a pure machine, in which everything is explained by the mechanical laws of the material world.[16] It has, as object, ideas as clear and distinct as those of physics, properly speaking. It attempts to act on the body by mechanical means.[17]

But such a conception appears inadequate, in the long run. In fact, the human body is not merely a machine. It is characterized by its union with a soul, from which it derives its "form" and its indivisible unity.[18]

Descartes was consequently required to take note of the abyss that separates the animal-machine and the human body.[19] He seems to have emphasized more and more the opposition between the physics valid for matter alone, and the psychophysics proper to man.[20] The physics of the animal-machine in general must have appeared to him as merely a preliminary to the physiology of man in particular,[21] since knowledge of animals is incapable of introducing us to even the humblest of human medicines, in virtue of the irreducibility of man to animals.[22] It appears most likely that Descartes began with medicine as pure physics, in order to elevate himself to a medicine of the substantial composite;[23] it also appears that one of the main reasons for his admission of his partial failure with medicine[24] was the increasing conviction that purely mechanistic conceptions were not sufficient to elaborate medicine, since the human body was not simply pure extension, but also psychophysical substance. There are therefore two conceptions of medicine in Descartes, one common to animals and men, situated on the plane of pure physics, and the other specifically human, situated on the plane of the union of soul and body.[25] On this latter plane, which is that of obscure and confused ideas, there can be no question of a medicine based on "infallible demonstrations,"[26] which can be treated "exactly,"[27] a medicine preoccupied solely with knowing clearly and distinctly the mechanisms of extension alone. We will need to turn toward sensation. In order to know it clearly and distinctly as something experienced we will need to find again this obscure and deep instinct of preservation (or, according to the Stoic expression, of accommodation of oneself to oneself and to external nature), which manifests the finality conditioning the union of the totality of the soul with the totality of the body and which stems in us from the principle that regulates the constitution of composite substance, namely, the principle of the best. It is this accommodation that is noted in the principal effect of the passions, which is to "incite and to dispose the soul to want those things for which they prepare the body, so that the sensation of fear incites it to want to flee, and that of courage incites it to want to fight, and so on."[28] That allows us to say that "the passions are all good."[29] And since they are that by which the soul holds onto life,[30] their reasoned use appears to be a condition of the maintenance of this life, that is, the health of the body—the health of the body being the condition for the joy of the soul.[31]

That is how one explains Descartes' statement to Burman that the best medicine is the one that sets man in nature, nature taking care to reestablish the equilibrium.[32] This is an anticipation of the modern conception that sees pathological manifestations as defense reactions in the organism. The nature to which Descartes entrusts us here could only be the substantial composite, which alone speaks to us through sensation (of thirst, of hunger) and through passions, and alone involves this accommodation of itself to itself and to things, in which the goodness of God is expressed directly. It could not be physical nature, whose laws can produce the animal-machine, but whose laws are indifferent to its perservation, while the machine itself is deprived of any principle of preservation and individuation.

We find again, in this trust in natural instinct, the Stoic optimism of the theory that bases the structural constitution of our composite nature on an action of God inspired by the consideration of the best.

The infallibility of sensation relative to what is good or bad for our psychophysical nature, to which pure understanding must reasonably rely, heralds Malebranche's theory, according to which instinct imparts to man's soul at each moment, under the form of sensation, the solution (in principle infallible and instantaneous) of a problem that involves the infinite and that, surpassing the possibilities of our limited understanding, translates immediately in us the results of a divine calculation entailing infinite wisdom.

Even though it is turned toward sensation, instinct, passion, and obscurity and confusion, this medicine of the substantial union remains based in reason. It is the rational philosophical critique which, allowing us to know clearly and distinctly the irreducibility of the psychophysical to the physical and the incompetence of pure understanding in the order of the questions of human life, sets aside the rational pseudomedicine that muffles nature's voice, under a jumble of abstract concepts. Therefore it is natural *(stricto sensu)* medicine that allows us to find again the rock or clay of natural instinct, beyond the prejudices that hide it.

It remains for us to know whether such a medicine, of which Descartes gave so few samples,[33] can be effectively constituted as a science, in an order that is its own. The advice given to us to consult nature, which is the best medicine, seems to be a dismissal of all scientific medicine, of any kind whatsoever.[34] Descartes himself noted that in illness, nature can deceive us about what is good for our body (it leads a dropsical man to drink, for example).[35] How then can one counsel the ill to drink and eat (which makes them worse) rather than to follow repugnant medical regimens.[36] It seems therefore that medicine must remain an empirical art of trial and error, of probabilities, and of judgments that are as best as possible. And we would discover in this the second substitute for science to which we would necessarily be referred by a will that is required to act in the events of life. We would thus encounter a third idea of medicine: the idea of a substitute, not of a pure physics of animal bodies, but of a certain science of the composite substance. But Descartes did not give us any doctrine in this respect. The failure of his efforts in medicine seems to have incited him toward the greatest caution, in this case, and seems to have deterred him from sketching the theories that he will not hesitate to sanction for morality.

4. Three Ideas of Morality. Provisional Morality and Definitive Morality

Morality is presented with more clearly defined characteristics. Here Descartes thinks that he has succeeded, whereas he recognized his failure with medicine.[37] We can more clearly outline the three kinds of morality among which he has wavered.

We have seen that morality had first been conceived as an exact science,[38] which presumed the completion of mechanistic physics and medicine, for which it is the final development.[39] Wisdom, which is its aim and ultimate principle, depends on the Supreme Good. The latter is the knowledge of the truth through first causes.[40] This knowledge, to which the *Principles of Cartesian Philosophy* gives us the means to accede, must allow us to reach the highest degree of wisdom, meaning the fifth degree.[41] That is a first idea of morality.

However, since morality has to come last in the chain of sciences, and since the will is not able to abstain from acting as long as science is not completely constituted, it is necessary, in order for us to be drawn out of irresolution, which is the worst of evils,[42] that the understanding propose to the will some direction, *in the meantime*.[43] This is the noted provisional morality, the substitute of science. This substitute is not, in any case, presented as *a replacement for science*, but as a practical set of maxims; this set of maxims is nothing at all like a science, but it holds the place of science for the will, as long as science is not yet constituted. This morality is conceived as preceding the definitive scientific morality, not only in time, but according to the order of the method, and for as long as it appears necessary to the search for the truth governed by that method. Finally it is proposed as needing to disappear when the truth is acquired.[44] However, Descartes' "exact" and "perfect" morality was never written. Must we believe that, up to the end of his life, Descartes never ceased to treasure the project, and that, in his mind, his philosophy remained incomplete with respect to this point?[45] That the provisional morality had to disappear altogether before the definitive morality?[46] That if he had not yet written the definitive morality, it is because of contingent reasons, lack of time and money necessary "to accomplish all the experiments he needed in order to justify and support his reasonings"?[47]

The above opinion appears unlikely.

Would not a morality (like a medicine), which would be of purely mathematico-physical kind, violate the interdiction against applying the understanding alone to the substantial composite? Here, as with medicine, Descartes--facing a problem that concerns neither an animal possessing only a body, nor an angel possessing only a soul, but a man, meaning a creature with a soul substantially united to a body--could only have treated it in its essential features by situating himself on the plane of confused and obscure ideas. He must therefore, for metaphysical reasons, and not for external reasons, renounce the idea of a perfect morality, meaning an exact morality, having for object only clear and distinct mathematico-deductive ideas drawn from physics, in the same way as "mechanics" and the medicine of animal bodies. Similarly, in medicine, and for the same reason, he had glimpsed the necessity to renounce a science of pure mechanism, in order to substitute for it, or at least to append to it, a discipline turned toward the psychophysical substance and deriving its support from sensation. But while he fails in medicine, he succeeds in morality. The *Treatise on Passions of the Soul* will give us a morality drawn from the knowledge of facts that are essentially psychophysical, the passions; it thus constitutes a true treatise of the substantial union.[48] Hence it has as object obscure and confused ideas, for "experience enables one to see that they [the passions—M. G.] are of the number of perceptions that the close alliance between the soul and body renders obscure and confused."[49] From this results the fact that the treatise unfolds on a different plane from mechanistic physics, which has no object other than clear and distinct, mathematically determinable, ideas. Descartes is responding to a second idea of morality.

This inquiry remains no less strictly rational since it pursues a clear and distinct, completely certain, knowledge of its object, even though the object is intrinsically obscure and confused. We therefore have a real science, in this case, even though it has no relation to mathematics. That is why Descartes wrote that he "wished to explicate the passions not as a rhetorician, nor as a moral philosopher, but as a natural philosopher."[50] This does not mean that he wishes to explain them only through physics, meaning through the physiology of the body,[51] but that he wishes to consider them from the point of view of a savant, meaning according to a rational method seeking evidence appropriate, as always, to the very nature of the object, which here is intrinsic obscurity and confusion. Similarly, Malebranche does not claim to reduce the givens of faith to truths of physical order, when he states that he considers them as given facts, in the same manner as the physicist considers the facts of nature in his domain.

Moreover, to the certainties about obscure and confused ideas emanating from the substantial composite, the *Treatise on Passions* adds certainties concerning the clear and distinct ideas belonging to the understanding alone. Although the seat of passions is human nature in the strict sense, meaning composite substance, the movement of passions cannot be understood except within the conception of human nature in the broad sense, meaning as the assemblage of composite substance, the understanding alone, and extension alone.[52] The certainty of the science of passions is completely assured once we carefully distinguish between the three elements and what stems from each of them. Also, this science assembles items of evidence of different kinds, some purely rational ones concerning either extension alone (physiological mechanisms),[53] or the soul alone (various functions of the soul, the emotions stemming from it alone, such as contentment, which comes solely from within, etc.),[54] and others that are above all sensible, concerning the sensation of passion itself.[55]

We understand, in this way, how Descartes could have said, with respect to this discipline, which however is not an exact science, that "the truths of physics are part of the foundations of the highest and most perfect morality,"[56] and that "a notion such as physics, which he has attempted to acquire, served him well in establishing the certain foundations of morality."[57] For not only does physics allow the constitution of mechanistic physiology, which is indispensable for the knowledge of one of the fundamental factors of passions, but it allows the definitive establishment— by a decisive verification—of the metaphysical truths upon which the entire economy of the *Treatise* rests, meaning the real distinction of substances, the existence of bodies, and the substantial union. Moreover, mechanistic physics is alone capable of giving us a proper idea of the immensity of God's works and of our own smallness. In this way it destroys anthropomorphism. It dissuades us from wishing, as do the Stoics, to become God ourselves, and it incites us to unite ourselves to his omnipotent and omnibenevolent will.[58] But making use of physics to establish the foundations of morality is not to reduce morality to a more complicated physics, meaning to a mechanistic physiology and medicine.[59] Morality requires metaphysical truths: God can do all, does all, is infallible, and we ought, therefore, accept in good will, as if sent by him, all that happens to us; moreover the soul is immortal. Similarly, morality has recourse to the truths of daily experience: that man cannot subsist alone.[60] Uniting these various items of knowledge, some metaphysical, some physical, others purely psychological, and others psychophysical—items of knowledge that possess their own certainty (even though these certainties are of differing orders)—into a system, morality applies to this system its principles, which are no less certain, concerning either the end—meaning the infallible determination of what is useful— or the absolute goods (determination of the true good by the rational distinction about what depends on us and what does not depend on us, determination of absolute felicity by the domination and good use of the passions), or concerning the means—meaning the infallible determination of what is useful—or the relative good (knowledge of the techniques allowing one to accede to what is truly good, use of the psychophysical mechanism of the passions in virtue of the certain knowledge that procures science for us, etc.).[61]

Considered thus, can this morality, which is completed by information drawn from the *Correspondence (Letters to Elizabeth, To Chanut, To Christina,* etc.), be viewed as a substitute for the perfect morality of the *Discourse* and *Principles,* a substitute that comes at the end of Descartes' philosophical career to take over for "the provisional morality," for lack of something better?

In one sense, no, since what is at issue is a true science, having its own complete certainty, and since any other science of the kind is impossible, in fact, and inconceivable, in principle. Far from being a substitute for the definitive morality, it is the definitive morality itself, the morality that replaces once and for all the provisional morality of the *Discourse.*

In another sense, yes; it seems, in fact, a substitute for the superior ideal (which is unrealizable) of a morality founded on the exact sciences and completely governed by mechanistic medicine. It is even presented as a kind of compensation for a disappointment that is felt.[62] The opposition that Descartes establishes, on this occasion, between medicine, in which he thought he would find the key to a morality and in which he failed, and morality, in which he succeeded, but by a means altogether different than with medicine, proves that the *Treatise on Passions* cannot at all be considered a medical treatise, even though it uses the expression "remedies" for the passions.[63] Finally, what confers on this morality the character of a substitute is that, although it puts an end to the provisional morality, it does not do so by abolishing it, as did the discovery of exact science, but by incorporating it.[64] And since the maxims of the provisional morality had sense and legitimacy only in relation with the idea of an exact, mathematico-deductive, not yet realized morality, the "definitive" morality of the *Treatise on Passions* seems to fill with respect to the exact morality the same function of substitution that the provisional morality, properly speaking, filled. The only difference appears to be that, being convinced that the exact science of morality is impossible, we know that the substitution assumed by the replacement morality loses its provisional character and acquires a definitive character.

This transformation (into permanent maxims of the maxims that are conceived originally only in relation to a provisional status required by an uncertainty of fact) therefore truly proves that morality could not have been constituted definitively except by definitively installing man in the status of the provisional and the uncertain. But must we think that this juncture is imposed by the avowed impossibility of an exact science of morality? In one sense, yes, for if this science were possible and were realized, the provisional and the uncertain would cease to exist. In another sense, no, for in the absence of an exact science ranging over clear and distinct ideas, from which we would be able to deduce an "exact" morality, the science of passions (even though it has, as object, sensations, things that are in themselves obscure and confused) is capable of bringing to us clear and distinct knowledge and complete certainty. In principle, it could therefore be conceived by itself as the possible foundation of a morality capable of tearing man definitively from the uncertainty that constrains him to use precarious and always revisable probable judgments.

But none of this is the case. From the above we ought to conclude that the final installation of man in the state of precariousness is imposed on the morality based on the science of passions from the fact that this science is insufficient to allow us to leave this precariousness. Before the avowed impossibility of attaining a certain knowledge concerning the multiple occurrences of life and before the urgency of the replies that my will must bring to them at once, each time, this science deals with finding, elsewhere than in this knowledge, a certain principle that can render assured my conduct, within this sea of uncertainty. The provisional morality of Part III of the *Discourse* instituted its maxims with respect to the state of ignorance and uncertainty that we had before having undertaken science. The morality of the *Treatise on Passions* and the *Correspondence* institutes its maxims with respect to the state of ignorance and uncertainty in which it perceives that man must necessarily remain with respect to the relative truths of life. It feels itself incapable, in the sphere that is its own—that of authentic sensation and experience—of furnishing a knowledge of these truths, which, dispelling all doubts, would inspire will, at each opportunity and unequivocally, to infallible decisions that are in agreement with the circumstances. Better yet, it incorporates to its own science the very consciousness of this unavoidable ignorance and erects it as the principle from which it deduces its maxims. Therefore, if the *Treatise of Passions* and the *Correspondence* consolidate as definitive the maxims of provisional morality valid for any state of theoretical uncertainty, it is not only because we lack a possible exact morality (according to the first idea of morality), but because of the possible demise of morality as the science of life (according to the second idea of morality), meaning we lack the power to constitute this discipline within the realm of the relations of my nature (pure understanding united with a nature *stricto sensu*) with the existing world that surrounds me. This morality assumes less the substitution of the deductive-mathematical science than it draws from itself that by which it substitutes for its own inadequacy. It is the proper substitute for itself.

In fact, it is capable only of furnishing some certainty with respect to extremely general truths and principles: for example, about our true good (self-contentment, which is entirely active, stems from virtue, issues from the soul alone, is known clearly and distinctly, is without any excess or defect, and is more powerful than all the passions); about the strength of the soul (condition for virtue); about the techniques for increasing that strength; about the knowledge of truth (without which the strength of soul is worthless); and about the various general remedies for the passions, etc.[65] But it cannot give rise to any determinate ethics, since it is not able to go from these general truths to particular truths that teach us what is materially useful to do in each eventuality. These eventualities are infinite in number and infinitely complex, and our intelligence is limited and often defective; it is so because what is at issue are existences or circumstances of existence about which only experience can teach us, whereas our understanding is made for knowing essences only. Thus, our ignorance, as well as our uncertainty, are unavoidable. Ignorance and uncertainty—such was the state of man before the beginning of the method, a state that, considered as provisional then, required a provisional morality. This state is now related to the extremely restricted limits of our possibility with respect to the science of life; it appears as having to be permanent, and must, consequently, render permanent the rules that a merely provisional certainty imposed.[66]

Thus the second idea of the science of morality as certain science based on the authentic givens of the psychophysical sphere and their relation with pure soul—in opposition to the first idea of a mathematico-deductive moral science drawn from the "exact" science of the whole of *things*—makes way for a third idea.

We must return finally to the principle of the best. Since no science, neither mathematico-deductive nor psychophysical and empirical can reveal to us what is the true good in each case, there remains the science that furnishes a general principle that is always within reach and that teaches us what we have to do in this state of ignorance. This principle no longer prescribes for us to seek to know the true, in one way or another, in order to act well, but to be content with what appears to approach it so as to act as best as possible. Just as in the *Discourse,* we will substitute for "it suffices to judge well in order to act well," the formulation "it suffices to judge as well as we can in order to do the best that we can," meaning in order to acquire virtue. Virtue and the beatitude that accompanies it—in brief, the supreme good—no longer therefore reside in the possession of the true, from which good action would invincibly result, but in the effort to attain it.[67]

5. The Principle of the Best in Divine Action and Human Action; from a Technical Morality to a Morality of Intention

Since the supreme good does not consist for us in the possession of the absolutely good in itself, but in the effort to attain it, the principle of the goodness of action no longer resides in the excellence of the matter of the act, meaning in the thing it realizes, but in the excellence of the intention that animates the will, meaning in the intention to realize the best. We see then that man's good will resembles God's will, and unites itself with it in this intention. Divine will, as we know, does not tend toward anything other than to realize in the creation of this complex world, not the absolute good, meaning a work that is entirely perfect, but the *best possible good.* It is, in this way, absolutely good by itself, whatever the degree of perfection of its work, a degree that it would be rash to attempt to express precisely, in any case. Thus the will of God, which has created senses that are fallible at times, is excellent in virtue of its *intention*, since it could do no better (and since it has solved the problem of the more particular union of the indivisible with a part of the divisible by obeying the principle of the best). Similarly, illnesses are no doubt what is best in order to allow the composite nature to avoid the dangers that threaten it. The principle of the best, which governs both the work of God and human morality, therefore imparts the key to all the problems that, dealing with the realm of composite substance, are given to man in his sphere of life.

By this definitive refusal to place the foundation of the morality of actions in the knowledge of what is true (the mathematico-physical true concerning the nature of things, or the psychological and psychophysical true concerning my soul and the biological and psychological utility of things and actions), Cartesian morality seems to have changed its orientation radically. It was first conceived as a technique derived directly from the scientific knowledge of the universe, and the value of an action was consequently placed wholly in its *matter,* since the action is not good except in virtue of the excellence of its results—the excellence of its results being guaranteed by the possession of what is true. Contrary to the conceptions of the Renaissance moralists, wisdom became a tributary of science. It was therefore impossible, on this plane, to admit the conjunction of error and good, however slight it might be. But once the value of an action is given, not in its material result, but in the nature of the want that inspires it (the want to act for the best), whatever the result, the conjunction becomes possible. Virtue and good, which until now were tightly linked to the truth of judgment, from which good action depends, meaning the matter of the action determined by the knowledge of the true good, are now dissociated from the nature of the matter and reported under the form of action. Whatever the various occurrences, the possible degree of our error, our virtue remains whole once our *intention* is good: the action may be good even though its matter is intrinsically bad and rests on error. Wisdom is once again dissociated from science; the man most lacking in understanding is capable of virtue.[68] Moreover we have a universal a priori criterion of the moral value of action since the determination of this value is independent of the apprehension of the results; in contrast, with respect to the morality derived from science, the value of an action, residing completely in the success of the technique, cannot be estimated except by the apprehension of the desired result. Thus, the impossibility as a rule and as a fact of the science, in which morality would arise as the technical application of the science, leads one to substitute for right action issuing from the knowledge of what is true, right action issuing from the internal disposition of a will tending toward the best; this has as result the transfering of the value of the content of the act to its form, meaning, as Kant would say, to "the character of the will" in action.[69]

6. The Order of the Good and the Order of the True. Distinction, but Not Opposition, between the Two Orders. The Impossibility of Returning Entirely to a Morality of Intention. The Ambiguity of Cartesian Morality

This seemingly radical about-face appears to destroy the rupture between the order of the true and the order of the good, which began in the *Discourse*. There, already, the duty of will seems different depending upon whether what is true or what is good is at cause. In the first case, the abstention of judgment is obligatory as long as the truth is not perceived; in the other case, action is obligatory even if the true does not reveal itself to us, since life requires action and the worst evil is to remain irresolute. Thus Descartes opposed the contemplation of truth, to the use of life, the first requiring abstention in the absence of all the evidence, and the latter requiring a decision of will, not only if the true, but even if the probable escapes us.[70] That is why some have been able to assert "that there exists a power of determination internal to will and even, in certain cases, a duty of determination independent from intellectual knowledge."[71]

This separation will be confirmed by the interpretation Descartes gives to the act of faith. He distinguishes between doubt in the matter of the understanding and doubt in the matter of the will. As long as the understanding has no proof that God exists, it can only doubt it; once it has a proof, it can no longer doubt it. The only question for the understanding is whether it can or cannot doubt it; there is no question of whether this is something it is allowed or prohibited to do. However, will, an elective faculty, must choose; and even if the understanding commands it to doubt, it has to affirm God, for it would be to sin greatly if one were to remain in doubt about such an important subject for life. Thus faith concerns only the will.[72] Therefore, the following statement seems justified: "Life gives will the task to exercise continually its choice; that is why we see it decide in the order of action even without the assistance of the intellect."[73]

Incontestably there is a certain distinction between the order of the good and the order of the true. But this distinction in no way supposes their dissociation.

First, the about-face we noted previously is not completely accomplished. The accounting between the value of the action and its form remains partial. If the effort toward the best, which defines virtue, founds the morality of the act, that is because of the results of this effort, for it assures us a contentment without excess or defects, it rids us of regrets and repentences, and it frees us from the subjection with respect to goods that do not depend on us, etc. If the virtuous form of the action seems to justify the action, it is on the condition that this form be justified also, not by the matter of the particular actions it governs, of course, but by the happiness that flows from the attitude it imposes. We therefore do not end up with a pure morality of intention.

Moreover, knowledge of the true remains always *in principle* the foundation of the final good. The value of the virtuous action remains attached to the true by the intermediary of the intention that gives it its value, since virtue is virtue only through permanent effort toward the highest approximation of the true. The most solid and most perfect contentment will always be the one that derives from an action inspired by what is true.[74] In brief, it is the imperative of the true that, founding our effort toward the best, imparts all its moral character to the act that this effort engenders. The morality of the action stems less from the will accepting a duty to act, even in the absence of all certain or probable knowledge, but from the fact that it accomplishes this duty in a certain way, meaning by doing all that it can to draw its inspiration as much as possible from what is true—meaning to use reason.[75] In addition, even the duty to act in spite of uncertainty and ignorance does not stem from will, but from reason. Reason alone, in fact, teaches us that it is preferable that will follows a doubtful opinion and acts, rather than abstains, when it lacks certain knowledge. Moreover, it commands us to change our opinion once we have found a better one, and it commands us to do everything in order to seek a better one.[76]

Thus, even in absolute doubt, will never decides *without the assistance of the intellect.* But, on the other hand, it happens that will often has to decide *without the assistance of science,* meaning without clear and distinct knowledge. How could it decide without or against the intellect, since, although the understanding can conceive itself without the will, the will cannot conceive itself without the understanding? The order of the good would not be radically different from the order of the true unless reason, capable of teaching us the true, were incapable of teaching us the good. And the order of the good would belong to will alone, if will alone taught us the good and duty. But will does not teach us anything; it merely chooses among what is presented to it by the faculty of knowledge, meaning the understanding in general.

Therefore, if the will is an internal power of determination, it is not a faculty of duty. It does not reveal to our consciousness the imperative we must realize; it is not the source of practical knowledge. In brief, it is in no degree a practical reason. The reason that governs here is the reason that knows: theoretical reason that divine veracity guarantees. Will is only a free arbiter; it is not autonomous, for it is not legislative. It tends naturally toward the true in order to affirm it and toward the good in order to realize it, but it must wait for the understanding to make its presentation; the requirement to act while lacking the knowledge of the good does not come from it, but from the outside, namely, from the necessity to attend to life or its happiness, necessities that the faculty of knowledge allows one to perceive. And it is this very same faculty that also reveals to us that it is a greater evil to remain paralyzed by doubt, than to risk a decision, in this case. The understanding is what commands both risk and resolution. Moreover, whether we are concerned with the true or the good, it is always will that decides, since it is will that judges; but in the domain of science, in which truth can be attained, it can be satisfied only with what is evident and certain, whereas, in the order of conduct, in which the knowledge of the true is often outside our reach, but in which reason tells us evidently that will is required to pronounce itself and cannot indefinitely delay its decision, it must be satisfied with approximations. In both cases, the use of reason is maximally required, but in the latter case, it is much more delicate and uncertain.

In this way we understand that, although faith is in the domain of will, since will must assume the risk of an affirmation in the absence of clear and distinct knowledge, will does not derive from itself the motives to pronounce itself. Here still, the decision remains rational and the understanding governs. Will would not be able to decide if the teaching of faith ever contradicted natural light;[77] in order for it to decide, there must be reasons to persuade it: "I say that each person's thoughts, that is, the perception he has of a thing, must be for him the rule for the truth of that thing, that is to say, that all the judgments he makes about it should be in agreement with that perception in order to be good. Even in the matter of the truths of faith, we should perceive some reason persuading us that they have been revealed by God, before deciding ourselves to believe them. And while those who are ignorant do well to follow the judgment of those most able, concerning the things that are difficult to know, it must, nevertheless, be their perception that teaches them that they are ignorant and that those whose judgments they wish to follow are less so; otherwise, they would do ill to follow them and would be acting rather like automata or animals than men."[78] Grace itself is not conceived as a kind of internal commotion that would dispose our will to believe blindly, but as a light that illuminates, as does reason in its domain, except that this light is supernatural, whereas the light of reason is natural.[79]

7. Inextricable Difficulty of Cartesian Morality; Three Reasons for This Difficulty

The inextricable difficulties of Cartesian morality, and to some respects also those of medicine, appear finally to derive from three causes:

1) The problems of medicine and morality, as disciplines concerning my composite nature, end up by erecting against each other two requirements of Cartesianism, which originally were not antagonists and appeared reconcilable. On the one hand, the only valid knowledge is that of clear and distinct ideas, and human action must be governed by the understanding; on the other hand, the matter of knowledge and action is nature *stricto sensu,* meaning fundamentally and irreducibly obscure and confused ideas, and these ideas are given as practically infallible in their own domain. The reconciliation operates easily as long as the understanding is limited to rendering to instinct its authenticity, to recognizing a privileged validity for it in its own sphere, and to allowing it to operate according to its natural range of movement; moreover, instinct is like a psychophysical transposition of what remains pure mechanism and pure physics in animals. But once the understanding is required to govern instinct, in order to metamorphose the action of the psychophysical being into reasonable action—meaning to substitute wise and reflected actions for the natural and unreflected reactions of sensible life, whether we are concerned to obviate some troubles with the psychophysical nature, such as it came from the hand of God, through rational knowledge and reasoning, as with medicine, or whether we are concerned with *deliberate* action, as with morality— the conflict between the two requirements appears inevitable, for pure understanding is compelled to intervene in a sphere for which it is not made—its domain being that of essence, not that of existence. Thus there

results an oscillation that, after having absorbed wisdom within science, ends up by dissociating it almost entirely, since we admit that moral good can coexist with a total theoretical error.

2) Descartes, constrained to rely on substitutes for a science that is in fact impossible to constitute or complete, has not expressly distinguished between the different kinds of knowledge with respect to which these substitutes must be constituted. On the one hand, it seems that practical science must be reduced to the substitute for a mathematico-deductive science involving medicine (itself restricted to the study of corporeal mechanics) and the integral knowledge of the material world. From this point of view, the discipline instituted by the *Treatise on Passions* tends to appear like the substitute for this perfect and geometrically scientific morality, which remains an unrealizable ideal. This discipline is what will give us, lacking the medical secret of longevity and wisdom, the means not to fear death any longer.

But on the other hand, the *Treatise on Passions* largely proceeds from another kind of science, which is an authentic rational science (but not a mathematical science): it is the science of sensibility (affectivity, instincts, tendencies, emotions, passions, etc.). This science also involves assured clear and distinct knowledge (which has as object obscure and confused sensation instead of clear and distinct ideas). It therefore cannot be considered as the substitute for any other science, because, in this domain, no other science can boast of doing better or even doing as well. We are concerned with a realm that is no longer that of pure understanding, of essence and mathematical truth, since it is the realm of the psychophysical substance, of sensation, and psychophysical truth (relative only to existence and to utility for life under all its forms). Moreover, this science of passions is not an approximative science dealing only with the probable. It attains an absolute certainty, although it is not founded on as firm and as evident reasons, as are the mathematical sciences. As we have seen, absolute certainty has several degrees, of which the lowest degree is still, by nature, irreducible to the highest degree of moral certainty.

However, this science of passions is far from furnishing, in its domain, all the truths necessary to morality, and we must recognize that it will never be able to furnish them. That is why this science must be expressly reduced to discovering the general principles that allow morality to be constituted even in the absence of these truths. This is where appears the necessity to propose, instead of the certain truths that are indispensable for each occurrence, certain, but general, rules prescribing us to resign ourselves, for each of these occurrences, to the probable, to our best possible judgment, and not to an absolutely good and sure judgment. This is where the substitute for science truly appears. It is established with respect to the rule of the determination of the useful for the multiple particular cases answering to the multiple urgencies of life. The study of the passions, considered in the spirit of the natural philosopher, cannot determine the useful or discover the true relative to the useful except in a general fashion. And will is not exercised except by particular volitions that require a true knowledge of what is useful at each time. Since such an infinitely diverse knowledge is impossible, we must be content each time with probabilities and approximations, with a substitute for knowledge. Lacking the true, the understanding is then requested to determine the probable. And for the cases in which probability itself cannot be attained, it reveals to us that putting one's all on an action based on a risky conjecture (an entirely doubtful conjecture) is still better than abstaining. The probable that we wish to determine concerns only the truth relative to the useful, and not the truth relative to the nature of things. Thus the only true substitute conceivable is not a substitute for completed physics, but finally a substitute for the "science" of the useful, or of the good, such as it has been sketched in its generality by the *Treatise on Passions,* which was not able to pursue it to a singularity.

3) Descartes is led to reverse, almost completely, the fundamental principles of his morality. If, in fact, the substitute that the *Treatise on Passions* furnishes us can be confirmed as perfectly exempting us from science itself, that is because felicity here on earth is represented as able to be attained completely outside the possession of the true, through the simple *effort* of a will agreeing to be satisfied with a substitute for science and deciding to do its all to be inspired as much as possible with what is true. Obedience to this principle of effort satisfies a priori the requirements of the *totality* of particular cases. A morality of the form of the action is substituted for the technical truth of its matter, as necessary and sufficient condition of beatitude. In some respects the reversal is complete, since virtue is compatible with error, and good action is compatible with a bad theoretical judgment.

All these considerations about medicine and morality do not offer, in their totality, the philosophical tension, rigor, and certainty that everywhere else characterize Descartes' thought.

However, we should observe that they develop outside the system, such as it is drawn by the *Meditations,* as consequences that the *Treatise on Passions* and the *Correspondence* consider partially, or by fits and starts. The dream of a rigorously scientific solution to the ethico-medical problem was formed before the system was methodically completed. The failure of this dream is less the failure of the system than the objective verification of some of its necessary results. The complexity of our nature in the broad sense rendered unavoidable the entanglement of perspectives, in this matter.

What we have called Descartes' successive failures, in this chapter, is perhaps, in the end, an ever more precise revelation of this entanglement, an always more varied awareness of the limits that experience imposes on the different orders of science, depending upon whether the science concerns it more or less. Nothing prevents us from believing that if death had not prematurely stopped him, Descartes would have been able to organize systematically these ultimate consequences of his doctrine. In fact, he did not have the time to realize the great *Treatise on Man,* in which he hoped to investigate thoroughly, among other problems, the metaphysical problem of knowing "whether angels and the thoughts of men have the power to move bodies."[80]

CHAPTER XXI

Conclusions

1. The General Economy of the *Meditations*

Considered as a whole, the six Cartesian *Meditations* seem to constitute a complete sphere in which the first three and the last three are opposed as two hemispheres separated by divine veracity.

The first hemisphere is under the rule of the principle of universal deception. This principle imposes the set purpose to doubt everything, even what our mind, by nature, considers invincibly as indubitable—namely, clear and distinct ideas. In this absolute realm of error and doubt, the Cogito registers a narrow, but piercing exception of fact. A battle begins between the principle of rule and the exception of fact. It ends with the defeat of the principle and the victory of the exception. First reduced to a point in the midst of the darkness of doubt, the light of the Cogito, increasing in some way upon itself, finally encounters the infinite God, which is other than myself and which, destroying the dark fiction of universal deception, illuminates the whole sky, from one horizon to the other, through the supreme splendor of absolute veracity.

We then enter into a new world. The law of the second hemisphere is the negation of the one that rules the first. It imposes, against the set purpose to doubt everything, the inverse set purpose to affirm the truth of everything, even what, for my understanding, is by nature the most doubtful thing possible—namely the senses.

However, in keeping with the symmetry of the Cogito in the hemisphere of the false, for the hemisphere of the true, in this absolute realm of certainty and truth, a narrow, but infrangible exception of fact is registered: human error. It punctures the light of universal veracity with a dark point, as the Cogito punctured the darkness of universal deception with a point of light.

Here as there a battle begins between the principle of rule and the exception of fact, but it ends, this time, with the victory of the principle. Divine veracity, overcoming the exception introduced by error, succeeds in safeguarding its spotless integrity, whereas it effectively restores to the senses a truth that matches exactly their quantity of objective reality.

God's work is revealed, consequently, as a block of reality without any cracks, as a block of total truth, and the infinitely small difference that separates the approximative truth of sensation from absolute truth, required by God's absolute truth, is made up for by the always possible intervention of the understanding, reasoning on past experiences and comparing the givens stemming from different senses among themselves, with a view toward a mutual control. Thus, God's work, through the plenitude of its reality, appears rigorously adequate to the imprescriptible truth of its author.

To the hypothesis of the evil genius, which plays the role of a principle of segregation, of elimination and purification, in the first three *Meditations,* responds, in the last three *Meditations,* the dogma of divine veracity, which is a heuristic principle, an organ of reintegration, and a rule of discipline. It draws in advance a kind of empty space that will be filled completely by the various realities that constitute the full block of the divine work, which cannot give rise to what is false, since it contains only the real. The filling of this space is accomplished by the assemblage of elements restored one at a time, according to their own substantiality (understanding alone, extension alone, composite substance), with respect to nature in the broad sense, or the universe of human consciousness—according to the exact quantity of objective reality of ideas, according to the strict competence that they derive from their reality and the nature of their authentic function. But, reciprocally, if the dogma of veracity is a warrant, a heuristic principle, or principle of reintegration, because of this plenitude of reality and truth, it is also justified and confirmed because it reveals this reality and this block of truth whose discovery it allows. If the exception of error could not be surmounted, if the truth of the senses could not be established rigorously within its sphere, the givens of my consciousness would finally remain rebellious to the supreme requirements of my understanding, which, through the intuition of the idea of God, imposes on me the dogma of absolute veracity. The system would no longer close upon itself. It would be annihilated. Therefore nothing is more deeply inscribed into the system than the intervention of divine veracity in the problem of error and in the problem of the validity of the senses; nothing is more closely associated with the other parts of the doctrine than the theory of the substantial union of soul and body, often wrongly considered—beginning with Spinoza— as an extra, outmoded element that is foreign to the living spirit of Cartesianism. Once we perceive the true complexity of reasons, we understand the truth of the Cartesian statement that if one element were lifted from the doctrine, the doctrine would be destroyed completely.

2. The Two Panels of the Diptych

If we pass through the Cartesian itinerary from beginning to end, we seem to see the perspectives reversed. Originally, we were concerned with substituting the rule of *good sense,* another name for the understanding, for the rule of *common sense,* another name for the power of the imagination.[1] The enterprise then seemed completely governed by an ascetic exercise that dissolved the obscurity and confusion of what is sensible for the clarity and distinctness of the intellectual, and attempted to establish science through the ruin of prejudices, of which the fundamental principle is that *everything true comes from sensations or senses.*[2] According to that perspective, man, gathering together all his energy, untwists the coils of his habits through a great effort and abstracts himself from what constitutes him specifically as man—meaning from his composite substance, the locus of obscurity and confusion, the obvious source of his blindness and disorder—in order to attach himself exclusively to understanding alone and to extension alone—realms illuminated by pure natural light. Metaphysics and the exact sciences appear to constitute the final ends of philosophy.

This picture has always passed traditionally as the summary of the whole Cartesian enterprise.

But it constitutes only the first panel of a diptych.

Faced with the truth of science, we see the truth of life established, in fact. As author of composite substance, the qualitative, or obscurity and confusion, God must guarantee its truth insofar as he founds its reality. But this truth is completely heterogeneous to the truth of the understanding, which concerns solely the nature of things. If, with respect to the nature of things, sensation is pure falsehood, clear and distinct ideas are no less falsehoods with respect to experience, in which the close union of soul and body is expressed. However, sensation possesses truth only when it is taken in its authenticity. We must therefore strip from it the clothing that it borrows from the understanding, in the same way that previously we had to strip rational nature of the borrowed clothing with which the senses covered it. The contrast between clarity and distinctness, and sensible obscurity and confusion, cannot therefore appear as the contrast between what is true and what is false, or between being and nothingness, but as that of two orders of reality or two irreducible truths—as the opposition between two heterogeneous ways of being. Once the understanding has taken a clear and distinct knowledge of their specific nature, these two truths cease to destroy each other in order to compose themselves harmoniously, but without ceasing to oppose each other. It appears then, that it is just as contrary to "good sense" to state that *all the truths of life are able to be captured by the ideas of the understanding alone,* as it is to state that *everything true comes from the senses.* That is the point where the perspectives seem to be reversed. If philosophy has as object "man *qua* man," this signifies not only that it must have recourse to natural light alone, but also that its final end resides in the composite substance of soul and body, for it is through the composite substance, and through it alone, that I am "man."

Philosophy does not therefore consider metaphysics and science as ends in themselves, but as simple means with respect to this present life, which is such only through the interweaving of my soul and my body—in brief, it sees in them only better means with which to assure my terrestrial happiness. Far from requiring me to abstract myself definitively from the sensible to enclose myself forever within the field of pure intelligence, it invites me to devote most of my time "to the occupations of the imagination and the senses," and not to turn away very much from them for metaphysics and pure mathematics. Thus, through a seemingly unexpected reversal, composite substance, this obscure and confused experience that was originally the object of a major excommunication, is installed into first place for our needs, while relegating the understanding alone and extension alone to last place with respect to our preoccupations.

It is this contrasting perspective that is sketched in the second panel of the diptych.

Is this a reversal of perspectives? We could affirm it as a reversal only if good sense—natural light—had stopped governing, only if we forgot that Descartes had already thought out what he had written to Elizabeth in 1643, as early as the *Studium Bonae Mentis,* in 1619,[3] and only if Descartes had not, from the *Discourse on Method,* justified his philosophy and science through the establishment of the "wealth" that they could procure for our life here on earth.

These two contrasting perspectives are, in truth, only two means of conceiving one and the same being: beginning with the *terminus ad quem* or the *terminus a quo.* In order for life to flourish, we must dominate things; in order to dominate things, we must construct science. In order to *succeed* in science, we must, however, forget its utility for life, for "the legitimate fruits that we could attain" would be compromised if these concerns about utility protruded "into the midst of our studies."[4] The exercise of science involves detachment from life, as long as the exercise lasts.

But to want to *succeed* in science we must want to *undertake* it, and the will to undertake science supposes a sufficient reason derived from the excellence of science as a means for our end. Therefore, whoever would allow himself to be sterilized by science and cut himself off from life by mathematics, would be contradicting the reason that requires our scientific effort, would be missing the goal that natural light assigns to us, and would be failing to be virtuous. Symmetrically, whoever wishes to live and understand his life must discharge the concepts of the understanding alone, the concepts that retain speculation and the exact sciences, at the exclusion of all other concepts. But whoever would allow himself to be engulfed by the common usage of life, by closing off his access to science because of prejudices arising from slavery to the senses, would be missing the goal that natural instinct teaches, which is precisely the same goal that natural light teaches, from its perspective, namely, the happiness of this life. One thing is certain, namely, that science could never mislead us or turn us away from our natural ends, *as long as we go through the entire cycle.* The understanding, when it is consulted in full, after having led us toward mathematics and the exact sciences in general, introduces us to the sciences of the substantial composite, and compensating each with the other, teaches us about the rights of sensation after having established those of the understanding. Thus, after having given us the means to govern things through the exact sciences, it fulfills its task by procuring for us the means to govern ourselves, through the sciences of experience.

In virtue of the complexity of his nature, man is therefore called upon, in order to realize himself fully as man, to furnish two exactly opposite efforts, the one consisting of liberating himself from the senses in order to arrive at science, and the other consisting in liberating himself from the subjections and habits required by science, in order to rediscover life and to govern it according to true reason.[5] This dual movement, if it is required by natural morality, is also, as we have seen, required by religious life. The latter requires an effort in order to become detached from the senses, an effort that permits the highest truths, the source of intellectual love, to be attained; at the same time, it requires an effort to impress on my brain the concrete and distinct image of my union with God—this cerebral impression releases the mechanism of the passion of love (heat around the heart, etc.).[6] Religious life is therefore, in part, only detachment from body, liberation of pure mind, and pure spiritual love; it is also, in part, a voluntary reincarnation, in my body, of this pure mind and love, under the form of passion.[7] Moreover, this duality appears in conformity with the conception of Christian life as an imitation of the life of Jesus. In addition, we should note that this religious life, such as it is described in the *Letter to Chanut,* is the one arising from natural religion, since it is concerned with the love of God rendered possible by natural light. But, as Descartes himself notes in this letter, through his allusion to the Incarnation, the case of revealed religion is not substantially different from that of natural religion, for there also we must detach ourselves from the senses in order to conceive the highest truths of faith, and have recourse to imagination in order to give strength to sensation. Revealed religion merely renders the task easier: the supernatural light of faith helps us to grasp the highest truths, and the "mystery of the Incarnation, which lowers God so as to render him similar to us," allows us to imagine more easily that which, by its infinity, appears to "have nothing imaginable in it." Beyond the Christian philosophers to whom he alludes here, no doubt Descartes has thought about the *Exercise spirituels* of Ignacius of Loyola, and in particular about the *Première contemplation* of the *Premier jour de la seconde semaine (De l'incarnation),* in which the imagination represents according to the various senses, in a vast fresco worthy of Dante, the created universe within which operates the Incarnation of the Son of God.[8]

3. The *Nexus Rationem* of the Various *Meditations*

This overview confirms what the exposition of Cartesianism according to the order has revealed to us along the way.

Contrary to an extremely widespread opinion, this order is not unilinear. The reasons are not threaded to one another like the pearls of a necklace. Descartes does not merely speak to us of a *series,* but of a *nexus rationem*. This complexity of a *nexus* is present from the beginning and increases with the unfolding of the long chains.

It appears as early as the instauration of radical doubt and the passage to the absolute certainty of the Cogito. First, the hyperbolic doubts stemming from natural reasons for doubt are exorcised by the progressive breaking up of contents into their simplest elements. Metaphysical doubt, which then strikes at these elements and is instituted by means of the fiction of the evil genius, suddenly confers a considerable extension to the breadth of the analysis: the latter bears on the whole of consciousness, and not simply on its contents. It distinguishes in consciousness between the contents and the form of my thought in general. In this way only, I can conceive that what I perceive in myself as true for me (for example, that two and one are three) might have no truth in itself. But also in this way, I can free myself definitively from doubt, for the existence of my thought, insofar as it is a necessary condition of all representation of any content whatsoever, cannot be denied, whatever is the falsity of all the possible contents. Although, on the plane of natural thought, certainty is necessarily attached to the final constituent element (the mathematical element), in virtue of its simplicity, on the plane of philosophical thought, certainty is necessarily attached to a residual element (the thinking self), not simply because it is incapable of being broken up, but because, as a necessary condition of thinking about what is or is not able to be broken up, it cannot be eliminated by abstraction. The simplicity of the Cogito is therefore not at all of the same order as that of the mathematical element, even though the two are residues of analysis. The certainty of my thinking being does not flow from its simplicity; on the contrary, the certainty of its simplicity flows from my certainty that it exists, because, since it is what operates the abstraction, it cannot, by hypothesis, abstract itself away.

This distinction between what is necessarily true for me and what is necessarily true in itself, based on the distinction between the form and content of my thought, is not erased by the fact that I enclose myself in the Cogito. On the contrary, it governs all the rest, for the great, and even the only question, is to seek whether and how I can "get out of myself," meaning whether I have in me ideas that have objective validity—in brief, ideas such that I can affirm in all certainty that the ideas in me are in conformity with models existing in themselves outside of the ideas. This distinction is made from the first reflections the Cogito makes about itself. Of course, when I say that I exist because I think, I am in possession of some knowledge that is not merely subjectively necessary, but objectively valid, for the thing I affirm as existing is nothing other than the affirming subject. But once I attempt to know what I am, I who am—the split between this knowledge of myself as necessarily true for me, and what is outside this knowledge of myself as really true in itself—appears; I do not yet know whether the purely thinking and intellectual nature I necessarily attribute to myself is truly the one I possess in itself. Thus, the Cogito, in spite of its initial simplicity, supposes a *nexus;* not only it is possible only through the conjunction of an empty principle ("in order to think, one must exist") and an experience, but it involves a reason of the knowledge of my existence and a reason of the knowledge of my essence, which are both tied to one another and dissociated from one another—they are tied, because I know what I am by reflecting on the very manner with which I have posited that I am in a previous reflection; they are dissociated, because the one gives me a subjectively necessary and objectively valid knowledge, while the other gives me only a subjective necessary knowledge of still uncertain objective validity. On the one hand, through the Cogito, I know that I am and I know that it is *absolutely impossible* that I not be, since I think;[9] on the other hand, I know that I necessarily appear to myself as a pure mind, and that it is absolutely impossible that I do not appear thus to myself, but I do not know whether it is absolutely impossible whether in itself I am something else. However, I know that I am prohibited from speaking about what I do not know or do not yet know, and consequently, to split hairs about what my nature could be in itself: "I do not know this; I am not now discussing that question, since I can only give my judgment on things that are known to me."[10]

The subsequent examination of the objective validity of our ideas, in *Meditation III,* involves a new *nexus.* Since the hypothesis of the evil genius is the condition of the doubt striking at clear and distinct ideas, the first path offered is to refute that hypothesis and, toward this end, to demonstrate God's existence, in order to restore, in a scientifically certain manner, to the universality of our clear and distinct ideas, the objective validity that our mind attributes to them invincibly by its nature, without any proof. But I know God only through an idea, and I can only prove his existence if his idea has objective validity. I am therefore constrained to use a second path, which consists in seeking the foundation of the objective validity of the idea, without having recourse to God. That is a direct path, which leads me to examine methodically, one by one, the various kinds of ideas, by order of their increasing quantity of objective reality, so that I can see whether some, or at least one of them, possesses necessarily an objective validity. The result of this progressive inquiry is decisive, since I end up discovering that there is indeed an idea in me, the idea of God, to which it is impossible for me to refuse this validity. This idea necessarily has outside of me its real correspondent; it is in conformity with it, and it allows us to know it. But with respect to the proposed goal, which concerns the whole set of our clear and distinct ideas, it is an extremely meager result, since the proof is constructed for only one of them. However, this idea is specifically the idea of God, and it happens that the objective validity obtained for it can ipso facto be attributed to all the others, through the intermediary of universal veracity, which is assured from now on, since I know that God exists. In fact, it is one and the same thing to establish the objective validity of the idea of God and to prove that God exists. The goal that we proposed to ourselves by an indirect path—to restore as a block to all clear and distinct ideas the original objective validity that the understanding attributes to them, by refuting the evil genius— is therefore attained, we dare say, by the detour from the direct path, which attempts to reestablish this validity through the examination of ideas taken one at a time, without refuting the fiction preliminarily. It is, consequently, both true, as Descartes says, that I have proven God's existence "on the occasion" of an inquiry bearing on the objective validity of my various ideas, and that I have proven this objective validity, or truth, of my ideas, "on the occasion" of an inquiry aiming to prove that necessarily God exists.[11]

Meditation IV presents another nexus. Since God is absolutely veracious, the universe he has created can only be absolute and total truth. However, man, who takes his place in this universe, is the plaything of error. Therefore we must either renounce universal truth, which amounts to annulling the refutation of the evil genius, or deny error, which is contrary to fact. In this latter case, moreover, since everything is true, nothing would be false, and human science, unable to be differentiated from its opposite, would be as imposible as in the hypothesis of universal deception, in which, everything being false, nothing would be true. To renounce divine veracity and to deny the fact of error, are therefore two eventualities that are equally excluded. In order to found science, we have to establish the possibility of what is false in opposition to what is true. In order to found the possibility of what is true, we must, in spite of the presence of error, save divine veracity. From this stems the juncture of two problems, one metaphysical: how can error be possible as a rule with respect to a veracious God? and the other psychological: how is error in fact possible within the human soul? The solution of each of these two problems must be such that it agrees with the solution of the other. On the metaphysical plane, human error, from God's point of view, is only a limitation in man; it is pure nothingness. On the psychological plane, human error, from man's point of view, is only a privation for man; it is something positive. The privation from man's point of view must be reconciled with the simple negation from God's point of view; this is accomplished through a continual oscillation from the metaphysical plane to the psychological plane, and vice versa. Since it is a nothingness, error cannot properly have any cause, for there are causes only for what is real. But there is a real act of judging, of which error is the epiphenomenon and which has its cause in the reality of my free will. The epiphenomenon, the mirage in which nothingness is erected as being, arises from the disproportion between the infinite reality of this will and the finiteness of my understanding. Thus, even though all cause implies the reality of its effect, and error is a nothingness, it is possible to discover the explanation of error by means of a cause, without introducing the least reality to it, for the discovered cause is not the cause of error, but that of the positive act of judging. Error has no other substratum than a nothingness in me, than the metaphysical void opened for our infinite will by the finiteness of our understanding.

The psychological solution certifies the metaphysical solution. The responsibility for error derives from my freedom, and not from God, whose veracity is thereby saved. God's perfection finally induces me to consider that error, which he has simply permitted, contributes to the greater perfection of the whole. On the other hand, God's incomprehensibility prevents me from knowing, and even from seeking, in what way he obtains the best: his ends are impenetrable.

Meditation V, which derives for all clear and distinct ideas the consequences of divine veracity, also presents a remarkable complexity, since, treating the essence of material things and God's essence as one and the same problem, it rests entirely on the identity and the difference between these two kinds of essences. Since they are in us as clear and distinct ideas, they are, in this respect, on the same plane, and justifiable by the same conditions. The properties that we discover in them as necessary must be attributed no less necessarily to the things themselves, since the previously acquired demonstration of divine veracity constrains us to recognize an objective validity for them. Thus, God's existence, which appears to me clearly and distinctly as a necessary property of his essence, must be recognized of him, in itself, as certainly as the properties that we know clearly and distinctly, of any geometrical figure whatsoever, must necessarily belong to it.

But, in contrast, since it is an idea of infinity, whereas mathematical ideas are only ideas of finite things, the idea of God is radically set apart from them, since it alone can have existence among its necessary properties.

We discover in this way that the properties of mathematical essences and the properties of God's essence have a necessity of different origin. For, if the *clear and distinct ideas* that reveal them [the above properties] to us are all equally impressed in us by God's freedom, mathematical *essences* and their properties are alone instituted by divine will; God's *essence* and the necessary properties it encloses are by contrast uncreated and necessary for God himself, with which they are intimately united, in virtue of the definition of his omnipotence. This intimate knowledge of divine being is the highest of the truths of things *(veritas rei)*, which does not prevent it from being secondary and derived, as a truth of science *(veritas rationum)*, since it has no objective validity except in virtue of the proof by effects, and it loses all its certainty if it is separated from it.

Meditation VI, which derives the consequences of divine veracity for sensible ideas, offers the most complicated *nexus* of all: it is a *nexus* of *nexus.* On the one hand, the understanding rightly rejects the truth of these ideas, because of their very obscurity and confusion; on the other hand, the knowledge it has of God's veracity constrains it to admit that these ideas must be true to the extent that they are real. In fact, God must be their author, since he is the only possible creator of what is real.

In this way, with respect to obscure and confused ideas, an inquiry parallel to the one that characterized *Meditation III* arises: it is concerned with founding the truth of these ideas, meaning to discover something outside of me that corresponds with what objective reality they possess in me. We find again the juncture proper to this kind of investigation: we attempt to found the objective validity of ideas, and we attempt to prove an external existence (in this case, the latter is not that of God, but that of the body). Since sensation, the obscure and confused idea, is located in a soul whose essence is the understanding, and which in addition contains imagination and senses, the inquiry concerning its objective validity will have to be accomplished according to the descending hierarchy of these faculties. The examination of the understanding and imagination prepares the definitive solution in two ways. On the one hand, it establishes, through the understanding, the possibility, and then, through imagination, the probability, of material things; on the other hand, by emphasizing the incapacity of these two faculties to go beyond the *possible* and the *probable* in this respect, it reserves to sensation, meaning to affective passivity, the privilege of bringing about *certainty* with respect to the existence of bodies. Sensation therefore enjoys, in this case, with respect to the other categories of ideas, a similar privilege to that which the idea of God enjoyed in *Meditation III:* in the same way that this idea was the only one to entail necessarily, in virtue of the principle of causality, the existence of an external thing (God), to which it refers, sensible idea is the only one to entail necessarily, in virtue of this principle, the existence of an external thing (body), from which it stems. But, the objective reality of the idea of God, since it is the *maximum,* admits of a *maximal* objective validity, which allows me to know with the *maximum* of clearness and distinction compatible with my finite mind, the thing to which it refers; the infinitely small objective reality of sensible affection allows me to know through it the *minimum* about the body to which it refers—in fact, I only grasp its existence, and its nature remains completely unknown to me.

This first *nexus* will be entangled with another. If sensible ideas have some truth, they are no less obscure and confused, and in this respect, they are the occasion for error. But divine veracity is opposed to the fact that God has instituted such opportunities for error. We find again here, with respect to the senses, the problem of error, with the entanglement proper to it. How is human error possible with respect to God? How is it possible, in fact, in man? These are closely interlaced metaphysical and psychological problems.

The two inquiries, the one that bears on objective validity, and the one that bears on the metaphysical and psychological possibility of error, must intersect here. Since they each presuppose an intersection, there is a crisscrossing of intersections, and the *nexus* is fourfold.

But sensory error is also double: it can be formal error, due to the rashness of my judgment, or a material falsity stemming from a breakdown of my composite nature, of which I am not responsible. The problem of error must therefore double itself here: to the solution offered by *Meditation IV,* which is suitable for an error of which my freedom is the source, must be superimposed a solution suitable to a falsity of which God alone is responsible. This solution will consist in intersecting a psychophysical scheme (more particular union of a part of the divisible with the indivisible) and a theodicy (composition of the world according to the principle of the best), which will account for the intrinsic falsity of the senses while absolving God. Added to the two others, this new crisscrossing will give rise to a sixfold *nexus.*

4. Cross-Checkings and Correspondences. The Multifunctionality of the Demonstrations

Thus constituted by a kind of tight counterpoint, the doctrine involves an infinity of cross-checkings and correspondences.

The analysis of the piece of wax, which, in *Meditation II,* attempts to verify the thesis that the soul is more easily known than the body, involves a dual segregation that, rejecting the sensible (of the idea of my nature as well as of the idea that founds the knowledge of bodies for me), is the prelude to the doctrine of the substantial union of soul and body. The conditions of the clear and distinct ideas of a thing as substance happen to form the basis for the external determination of the real essence of substances. The conditions of the knowledge of external objects by perception already prefigure the articulations of the future proof of the existence of bodies. The process of segregation that allows me to obtain the knowledge of my existence and that of my nature happens to reveal the criteria of real distinction and modal distinction, that is, the foundation of the doctrine of substances, at the same time as these two items of knowledge. This same process, setting aside the contents of consciousness in order to consider only its form, prepares the investigation of the contents that characterizes *Meditation III:* it responds to the doubling of the first principles, the Cogito being the principle of certainty for consciousness considered in its form, and God being the principle of certainty for what is real that falls within this consciousness, meaning for all contents. The inquiry into the objective validity of my knowledge with a view toward determining the foundations of the various orders of science is wedded to a metaphysics turning toward the proof of existences (soul, God, and body). God's infinity and incomprehensibility furnish at once the positive principle of all truth and the principle of the limitation of all my knowledge: it is the incomprehensibility of the objective reality of the idea of the perfect with the finiteness of my self that founds at the same time the certainty of the existence of the Supremely Real Being outside myself, and the impossibility for me to encompass it within the limits of my understanding. From this results simultaneously the positing of an upper and a lower limit. It is impossible for me to know God adequately, to penetrate his ends. Moreover, it is impossible for me to refute sensation, in the sphere proper to it, by means of the understanding—to know through the latter what the former reveals to me, to deny in the name of the requirements of my intellectual thought the substantial union of soul and body (which is merely experienced, for it manifests God's omnipotence, freed from the impossibilities conceived by my intellect); it is one of the expressions of this incomprehensibility that limits my intelligence.

With respect to the problem of the certainty of the various kinds of ideas, the cross-checkings are no less numerous. That the ideas of the understanding are unable to be broken up, furnishes, in *Meditation I,* an external reason for certainty, which my mind naturally grants them. This certainty is then explained from within by *Meditation III,* which reveals that these ideas have a (finite or infinite) objective reality, such that my understanding perceives immediately this reality in them and thus cannot doubt that they are not nothingness. In its turn, the obscure and confused character of sensible ideas is explained with respect to the same understanding by the infinite smallness of their objective reality, such that the understanding is incapable of knowing whether they are being or nonbeing. We understand, under those conditions, why pure understanding places them naturally into doubt and must legitimately reject them when it wishes to hold only to what is certain. Nevertheless, since this infinite smallness is not reducible to nothingness, it must have an objective validity in itself, no matter how small, for all objective reality always agrees proportionally with an objective validity. The understanding, which seems at first to have to rebel against the recognition of any objective validity whatsoever for obscure and confused ideas, must, once it knows that what is true is reciprocal with what is real (and what is false with nothingness)— that God is the author of what is real—recognize that the obligation, imposed by the dogma of divine veracity, to seek a certain truth for these ideas once we recognize an objective reality in them, as little as it is, is founded in the nature of things. Divine veracity, divine reality, objective reality, intrinsic truth of ideas (rational, as well as sensible ideas), appear in this respect as interchangeable concepts. Finally, the objective validity recognized of sensible ideas is effectively proportioned to the infinite smallness of their objective reality, since these ideas do not resemble at all the material things to which they refer, of whose existence they merely inform us. Correlatively, this existence of body, the formal cause of this infinitely small objective reality, is the most humble and least noble of all the formal realities that we can conceive. Moreover, the obscurity and confusion of sensible ideas, which were only characterized extrinsically, from the point of view of the understanding, as an impossibility for the latter to distinguish being and nothingness in them, receive an intrinsic foundation, as they are characterized as mixture of soul and body. The qualitative is not simply an appearance of things that are really clear and distinct, perceived confusedly because of the weakness of our understanding. An infinite understanding that would succeed in perceiving clearly and distinctly the *minimum* of objective reality contained by sensible idea, and in being sure that it is not a nothingness, would not put an end to the obscurity and confusion proper to that idea; it would only know it clearly and distinctly as an irremediably obscure and confused reality.

From this complexity of *nexus* also flows an extreme polyvalence of demonstrations. A multitude of accessory conclusions proliferates around their principal axis. Thus, the analysis of the piece of wax, intended to confirm the primacy of the knowledge of soul over the knowledge of body, proves at the same time the purely intellectual character of the knowledge of external things—which are *known* only because they are *understood (intellectae)*—the constitutive role of idea in the perception of objects, the exclusion of sensations outside of what represents the essential nature of objects, for us, etc. The demonstration of the objective validity of clear and distinct ideas entails laterally the solution of the problem of their origin and founds the doctrine of innate ideas. The solution of the problem of the intrinsic falsity of the senses as a function of the conditions of a privileged union of a part of the divisible with the indivisible, in *Meditation VI,* entails the demonstration of the indivisibility of the soul. It also confirms the irreducibility of the soul to extension; consequently, it confirms its substantiality. It establishes the unity of its faculties under their apparent distinction and it founds the principle of its immortality, etc. This polyvalence has enabled what is accessory to mask what is the principal result. Thus, some have believed that the analysis of the piece of wax had as goal only to establish the doctrine of primary and secondary qualities, that the demonstration of the indivisibility of the soul had no other goal than to establish its substantiality and its irreducibility to body, etc.

The closeness of the network of which this *nexus* is constructed, and the extreme polyvalence that results from it for each of its elements, imparts to the Cartesian text a unique density and intensity. Leibniz has likened God to a savant author who puts the most matter in the least volume. The comparison can be redirected, and the Descartes of the *Meditations* can be assimilated, for philosophy, to a Leibnizian God.

5. The Analytic Order and the Real and Concrete Character of Analysis. Philosophy and Geometry. Cartesian Philosophy and *Elementar Philosophie*

The constitution of the Cartesian *nexus* operates uniquely through analysis. Analysis unravels a knot inextricably raveled by common knowledge. Since reasons are disposed uniquely with a view to promoting an absolutely certain science, their order is governed by the conditions of certainty in the knowing subject, and not by the conditions of things in themselves and the order of their real generation. We could then believe that they give rise to a purely abstract linkage.

However, nothing is less artificial or more concrete than this philosophy, which is completely deduced according to the analytic order. If the necessities of the *ratio cognoscendi,* which determine this order, although differing from the necessities of the *ratio essendi,* do not contradict them, but allow them to be revealed by discovering the truth of things, it is because philosophy, in order to obey the rules of the understanding that govern the conditions of my certainty, does not cease to be governed at the same time by the real itself. For Descartes this applies to philosophy as it does for mathematics. Mathematics is justifiable, for its order of discovery, by necessities that derive, no doubt, from subjective conditions of certainty, but which, at the same time, derive closely from the nature of their object. Thus they are not condemned to be an empty and abstract linkage, by the fact that their order first satisfies the conditions of a valid human certainty. On the contrary, they reveal, in this same way, the authentic realities to which they are applied: mathematical beings and their properties.

Descartes has told us expressly that his philosophy is no more than the application of mathematical intelligence, not to the reality of extension alone, but to the set of realities that are discovered by consciousness. His demonstrations proceed everywhere from the spirit that moves Euclid, Apollonius, Archimedes;[12] they can only be grasped by those who have a sense of mathematical demonstrations.[13] The *Six Meditations* are only the metaphysical answer to the fifteen books of Euclid's *Elements.* If the notions they treat could be supported by imagination, as are the concepts of geometry, instead of being contradicted by it, the *Six Meditations* would themselves be simply some books like those of Euclid. However, the human mind is required, in order to clutch the thread of intelligence, to break, by means of a powerful effort, the contrary and pernicious charm of the imagination and the senses; the same human mind must also superimpose upon the rational process of demonstration, which attempts to convince, a psychological process of intellectual ascetic exercise, which attempts to persuade. From this arises the dual aspect of the enterprise, which is, under one aspect, a metaphysical geometry, in the fashion of a modern Euclid, and under another aspect, a spiritual elevation, in the fashion of the Neoplatonists, Plotinus, and Saint Augustine.[14] This ascetic exercise is indispensable, not only to set aside the senses that "obfuscate" us, but in order to break the bonds of prejudices and habits that corrupt us with respect to the purity of the idea of the understanding and to the purity of sensible ideas.

The geometer discovers in the field of pure extension a great number of real and true beings *(entia vera et realia),*[15] having properties and sustaining necessary relations among themselves—beings and relations imposing themselves to his consciousness as a given that he classifies: rectilinear figures, triangles and parallelograms, rectangles and gnomon, circles, etc., and the various solids that constitute the contents of the fifteen books of Euclid;[16] similarly, my intelligence, running through the field of mind, discovers there a number of beings: self-consciousness, thoughts, ideas, volitions, inclinations, and various kinds of ideas.

In order to construct his science in certainty the geometer considers separately the properties of mathematical beings, by going from the simple to the complex, so as to integrate them a little at a time into his science under the form of demonstrated propositions; in this way he appears to contradict what these mathematical beings are in things *(a parte rei),* since in themselves all their properties are given in them at once, are incapable of dissociation, and are reciprocally tied to one another.[17] Similarly, the analytic order of the *Meditations* dissociates into separate elements that which in things *(a parte rei)* are only one. It first dissociates consciousness from all its contents in order to prove its existence and nature apart. It dissociates the form of ideas from their objective reality, and then objective validity from objective reality, in such a way as to prove the objective validity of ideas by establishing, by means of the a posteriori proof, the objective validity of the idea of God—the equation between truth and reality. Then, having reduced the aberration phenomenon that seemed to threaten this equation, and having instituted the confirming equation between what is false and nothingness, it demonstrates the objective validity of mathematical demonstrations from the fact that all clear and distinct ideas, having received an objective validity in virtue of the preceding equations, are instituted as essences. The necessity of essences is thus validated; and the a priori proof of God's existence, which supposes the validity of demonstrations based on this necessity, is itself validated. The philosopher then turns toward the properties of sensible ideas, in the same way that, after having demonstrated the properties of straight lines, the geometer turns toward those of the circle. He demonstrates these properties by circumscribing and limiting them, dissociating in these ideas, like the geometer and his figures, the elements that are indissolubly tied together there *a parte rei:* objective reality, constraint, variation, and quality.

Philosophical discovery therefore closely imitates geometrical discovery. Intelligence does not cease to apply itself to a reality that is imposed on it. Its whole initiative consists in discovering the order according to which the elements present all, at once in the real, will be dissociated, in such a way that the properties demonstrated one at a time impose themselves on our mind, which is then incapable of removing itself from the necessity obligating it. And, as we have seen, the eminent superiority of philosophy over mathematics arises from the fact that, instead of supposing the objective validity of the truths that human understanding presents to it as such, philosophy demonstrates this validity in the course of its process, in one of the theorems (the first a posteriori proof for God's existence) that is a part of the chain.

Thus, by stripping itself of its spatial *integumentum* in philosophy, intelligence, which is present in mathematical thought, far from being extenuated into proceedings without contents because of this universalization, becomes capable, on the contrary, of equaling the totality of what is real, of embracing it in all of its realms. But since these realms are not all reducible in themselves to the clear and distinct, rational knowledge must sometimes range over objects that cannot be converted into clear and distinct notions, and that must be grasped clearly and distinctly as intrinsically obscure and confused. This total apprehension of the real, according to its own articulations and characters, is therefore possible only by the preliminary reintegration of its various elements in their authentic specificity. From this arises the primacy of the effort of decomposition and dissociation: "It is the almost common vice of all imperfect knowledge to assemble several things into one and to take them all for the same; that is why we must, after having taken the trouble to separate them, distinguish them from one another through a more careful examination."[18] We are concerned, above all, to put an end to the reciprocal usurpation of the various faculties, or rather—in order to avoid the word that Descartes rejects[19]—to the overlapping of the various kinds of ideas. That is one of the traits that particularly reconciles Descartes and transcendental philosophy as *Elementar Philosophie:* to dissociate the constitutive elements of knowledge in order to obtain them in their intrinsic purity, to establish "their certificate of believability,"[20] to assign the limits of their compentence, and to allow the discipline of reason, which prohibits these limits from being crossed, to govern. Or, according to the vocabulary of a more recent philosophy, to dissociate some distinct irreducible "realms," within which certain kinds, certain methods of knowledge, rule at the exclusion of all others: the realm of the understanding alone, the realm of extension alone, and the realm of sensation, or of the composite substance alone.

The recomposition of the authentic real operates by itself, once the confusions between the notions are dissolved, confusions from which result the usurpations of competence. The original harmony internal to the (human) microcosm, the harmony imminent to the macrocosm, and the reciprocal harmony of the two can be seen vividly, once the mind perceives clearly and distinctly the elements that compose them in their irreducibility.

6. The Philosophy of Clear and Distinct Ideas, the Limitation of Rationalism

This ideal of a perfect distinction between the elements (to which Descartes has given successively the names, simple absolute natures, and primary notions—God, soul, body, composite substance, understanding, imagination, sensation, free will, etc.) fully justifies the doctrine as a philosophy of clear and distinct ideas, as long as this expression refers less to what is known than to the subject that knows. Descartes has never claimed to reduce all of reality into clear and distinct ideas. This reduction is possible for only a part of what is real. He has only wanted to obtain a clear and distinct knowledge for all elements of the real, whatever they might be in themselves. There are elements in the real that are in themselves obscure and confused; Descartes is concerned with distinguishing them clearly from elements that are in themselves clear and distinct, in order to obtain a clear and distinct knowledge of them. Thus, we have a clear and distinct knowledge of sensation, which is in itself obscure and confused, when we distinguish it clearly from clear and distinct ideas, and we conceive that it is irreducible to the latter. We have, on the contrary, a completely obscure and confused knowledge of it when we treat it as a clear and distinct idea, and we attribute to it a competence it does not have, as do the followers of common sense and the physicists of substantial forms. This obscurity and confusion is not any less when, falling to the other extreme, we attribute to clear and distinct ideas capacities that belong only to sensation—as do the Spinozists, and all those who, reproaching Descartes for being unfaithful to his own point of view, wish to qualify clear and distinct ideas so as to account for everything that concerns the union of soul and body. To do so is to demonstrate a confused knowledge of sensation, to ignore the limits that, enclosing clear and distinct ideas into their proper realm, prohibit them from overflowing onto another. Descartes cannot be accused of "dissolving" his original "point of view" in this case, as an excellent writer has thought,[21] unless this point of view required the reduction of what is real itself into intrinsically clear and distinct things, although it requires only clear and distinct knowledge of what things are intrinsically, whether they are clear and distinct, or obscure and confused.[22]

This undeserved reproach stems from an intemperate and abstract rationalism attributed to Descartes in virtue of an exaggeratedly subjectivist interpretation of his doctrine. Descartes' original idea is not that of the limitless omnipotence of human understanding, but of its absolute power within certain limits: "Definire limites ingenii"—such is, as we have seen, one of the first concerns of the *Rules*. There is therefore, in this case, a proper measure that finds its correlative and support in the doctrine of divine incomprehensibility. The latter, entailing that God is exorbitant to myself, assumes a double function: i) to found the objective validity of my ideas by demonstrating that God exists necessarily outside myself, with his necessary veracity and immutability, and ii) to limit the field of the necessities of my own understanding by subordinating them to the omnipotent will that has instituted them from the outside (which is thus exempted from them). Sensation is specifically established on God's incomprehensibility, since sensation is possible only through the union of soul and body, which is conceivable only in virtue of this infinite omnipotence, as omnipotence capable of uniting in an incomprehensible manner what my understanding judges impossible to unite.

7. The Authenticity of Cartesian Rationalism. The Problem of Limits. The Extreme Scantiness of the Realm of Sensation. The Rational Determination of the Irrational as Such. The Subordination of the Irrational to the Suprarational

However, this limitation of rationalism must not push us to another extreme and have us conceive Descartes as an agnostic, a fideist, an empiricist.

Of course, the substantial union of soul and body is, for Descartes, an acceptance of fact. And this fact seems irrational since it shocks reason in two ways:

1) It is inconceivable, for it unites what reason conceives necessarily as separate.

2) It implies for sensation a measure of truth (whereas clear and distinct ideas seem to require the domain of the true to be limited to themselves), and even the privilege of a truth that reason itself is incapable of reaching (when no truth knowable to man seems to be foreign to reason).

But a fact is without force by itself, from the point of view of mathematism. Therefore it would be without validity, unless reason certified it as authentic. And the two obstacles that could have brought reason to doubt this authenticity are overcome by reason itself: the first (inconceivability) vanishes before the idea of divine omnipotence, by which the understanding conceives as possible in itself what appears impossible for our finite understanding; the second (relative to the truth of sensation and the privilege it enjoys on the plane of life) vanishes before the idea of divine veracity by which reason sees itself constrained to grant truth to what necessarily has God as author, no matter how small its reality.

If the understanding must accept the reality of sensation, it is in virtue of the intellectual knowledge it has of God, his incomprehensibility, his omnipotence, and his veracity. The privilege that the incomprehensibility of God allows to be recognized in sensation, in the realm of the union of soul and body, does not at all imply the resignation of reason, since it is reason itself, through the intermediary of the knowledge it has of God, that qualifies sensation, determines its domain, and traces the limits within which I am authorized to trust it. If reason did not reveal to me that God, by means of his omnipotence, can make what I do not understand,

I would be torn between speculation and life, intelligence and sensation, between two reciprocally opposed dogmas or skepticisms. I would have to deny life in order to affirm reason and God; or deny reason and God in order to believe in sensation. If reason did not reveal to me that God is veracious, and that since he is the ultimate cause of sensation, he cannot deceive us by putting sensation in us, the belief that I would grant to sensation would be gratuitous and without foundation. Finally, I would be incapable of tracing the limit that determines the field of its validity. As for Pascal, reason remains the ultimate court, even in the case where sensation decides, for it alone can confer on sensation the full permit that gives it its authority.

Moreover, God's incomprehensibility is itself contained in a proper, and even strict measure. It is strictly determined, as we have seen, by reason itself. It is not unknowability, since God is the best known thing in the world, meaning the thing most clearly and distinctly known.[23] It is not unintelligibility, for it is through the intellection of his idea that we know that he is incomprehensible, an intellection that requires us to recognize rational necessities in him that are eternally immanent and do not depend on his free will, as do mathematical truths: for example, it is impossible that God is not, that he introduces nothingness in his being or in his action (he cannot create nothingness, independent beings, void, atoms; he cannot deceive, etc.). And our understanding conceives at the same time that these necessities, even though they are imposed on God, do not constitute in him a negation of his freedom, since by violating them God would be limiting his being and consequently his power, therefore his freedom, for to be free is to have a power without limits.

Thus, God's incomprehensibility, while limiting our reason, confers upon us an infallible principle of judgment with respect to the creative possibilities of the Author of our origin. The infinity of power that elevates God beyond what is comprehensible does not make God the refuge of the irrational. God remains the object of a strictly rational knowledge, and sensation, even though it is based on the incomprehensibility of the infinite being, is not at all qualified as a path giving access to what is divine.

Of course, rationalism seems limited by the recognition of the rights of sensation, and by the positing of a sphere in which it reigns as master, in which reason cannot supplant it, in which it is like a language that God speaks directly to us, as directly as, in the other sphere, he speaks with reason, and in which it is "an instinct" symmetrical to the rational "instinct" in its realm[24] (certainly, not possessing absolute infallibility, as the latter does, but possessing, in its own realm, a quasi-absolute infallibility). It has been placed in us by God's goodness, which has decided, in virtue of the best, to make us perceive it in a particular part of the body rather than in another—meaning where it can generally be most useful to us; it is protective. We can trust it almost completely; it is a "good nature," the immediate expression of divine goodness. Through the intermediary of Malebranche, and after having suffered several metamorphoses, due to the combined influences of Spinoza and Leibniz, this doctrine will result in the philosophies of sensation and good nature that characterize the end of the eighteenth century.

However, in spite of this historic lineage, the Cartesian conception (even though it attributes to sensation in its own sphere an incontestable truth and a function in which it is irreplaceable) confines sensation within very strict limits. Moreover, in opposition to Pascal and the mystics, it limits its revelations to the circle of my needs and my terrestrial subsistence. Founded solely on the substantial union of soul and body, sensation sees its competence rigorously restrained to the psychophysical domain. It could only be an experienced testimony relative to the state of my body. It does not allow me to go out from myself, to communicate intimately with nature, in the broad sense. It is only the language of my human biological needs. In the vast universe of the Creator and of created things, there is sensation only in man. Neither material nature, nor animals (which are entirely reducible to extension alone), nor God, nor pure minds or angels (which are entirely reducible to intelligence alone) are capable of sensation. Sensation therefore limits man, to man alone, or rather to his human body existing within other bodies.

Under these conditions it would be absurd to conceive that sensation could be permitted some hidden communication with nature in the broad sense and with God—that it could lead us toward the great metaphysical truths. What in God surpasses the possibilities of our understanding is able to be grasped as a rule only by a higher reason, in the same way that properties that remain hidden to us in a mathematical figure are knowable only through the understanding as a rule.[25] It would be as absurd in the case of God, as in the case of mathematical truths, to conceive that sensation can ever make up for the deficiencies of our rational faculty. Grace, as we have seen, is in itself nothing more than a supernatural light, conferring a supreme clearness and evidence to the reasons to believe in the obscure things that are revealed to me.[26] Knowledge of God's existence, of his principal attributes, is of purely natural and rational order. Sensation can only speak to me about my existing body, and never about God. On this point, Malebranche will develop, against Pascal, a most orthodox Cartesian doctrine, except that he will render medicinal grace into a sensation, not a supernatural light.

The fact that sensation is explained by substantial union, and that its sphere is thus restricted to extremely small dimensions, also has the consequence that we cannot see how sensation could subsist once the union from which it derives all its being is destroyed. We can perceive no other plausible hypothesis on the immortality of the soul than Spinoza's: only the subsistence of pure intelligence after the destruction of body.[27] For Malebranche, for whom sensation is a property of every finite soul, whether it is tied to a body or not, the sphere of sensation is already much larger. With respect to this theory, we conceive that it can subsist, once body is annihilated, and can be aroused by occasional causes other than by cerebral disturbances.

Thus, valid only for an exception, namely, for the case of a soul substantially incarnate in a body, for the time of that incarnation, and being qualified in its narrow domain only by permission of the understanding, sensation must, for Descartes, in spite of its privilege, be inscribed into the frame of a most rigorous rationalism.

However, this rationalism is not absolute, for sensation renders man into one of the most extraordinary exceptions within the universal whole. In fact, of all things, sensation is the only one that is *strictly* human. No doubt freedom makes man an exception, since it allows him, in some respect, to escape the laws of the physical world; but freedom is also the property of all minds, finite and infinite, whereas sensation is the exclusive property of human minds existing in the world. Moreover, man is the only being capable of misusing his freedom; he is the sole arena for error and sin. At first view, this is a shocking exception, given that man is in a world whose absolute veracity is governed by divine absolute veracity. This error is itself rendered possible by the duality of sensation and understanding in man. Of course, if human understanding were infinite like human will, no error would be possible; but would error be produced with a finite understanding, if sensation did not present to will, as objects of possible judgment, ideas that the understanding must consider from its point of view as being in themselves materially false? Furthermore, is not sensation, in its own sphere and with respect to the function specific to it, subject to mistakes that add to the scandal of formal error, the scandal of an intrinsic falsity for which man is not responsible? Cartesian rationalism openly allows for this irrationality of sensation. Instead of reducing it or erasing it, Cartesian rationalism founds sensation as irreducible.

Its whole effort consists in inserting sensation within the whole of God's work, with the other phenomena that are an exception to rationality (formal error and intrinsic falsity) as elements that are indispensable to the perfection of the whole—in brief, to have the point of view of suprarationalism prevail over that of irrationalism. It is concerned, in some way, with an external rationalization, accomplished through a combination of God's incomprehensibility and perfection. Perfection founds a theodicy that justifies sensation, its intrinsic and accidental falsity, and formal error in general, by means of the finality based on the principle of the best. God's work is the best possible, not only because it involves only what is real (since God can only create what is real), but because it is combined for the best (since God is essentially good).[28] Sensation and error are thus necessary conditions for this optimal whole. But, on the other hand, God is incomprehensible, and his ends are impenetrable, so we cannot go beyond the general principle that everything has a reason to be thus and not otherwise. The details concerning ends escape us; they could only be perceived by an infinite understanding, by God himself.

Malebranche's and Leibniz's theologies will work on the same canvas, and they will develop this conception that Descartes has wisely avoided. He rejects any penetration into God's counsels—we know his ridicule of Saint Thomas and his familiarity with angels;[29] he avoids entering into the problem of creation—a formidable problem, given its own principles. For, if the perfection of the Creator implies that his work is itself perfect, if God cannot direct his will on anything other than being, the question remains whether God's work should not be as infinite and perfect as its author, such that one could not be distinguished from the other. From this arises the necessity, according to Malebranche, to affirm that God's work is distinguishable from God because it is finite and imperfect, the simplicity of paths implying and justifying its imperfection, whereas, in spite of its finiteness, it is rendered worthy of its Creator through its union with a divine person; or, according to Leibniz, from the above arises the necessity to affirm that God's work is distinguishable from God, not because it is finite and imperfect, but because its perfection is of another order, being the perfection of what is composite, which is the *maximum per minimum,* whereas its author possesses the absolute perfection of what is simple. Descartes eludes the problem by another means, which, as we have seen, leaves the problem indeterminate. The principle of the best is sufficient for him to justify the apparent defects of the world through a general formula of optimism (taken from the Stoics and Saint Augustine), to which Leibniz will subscribe, but which Malebranche will seriously restrict.

Descartes' rationalism is therefore rigorous, not because it is absolute (meaning because it reduces irrational elements to what is rational, in which the irrational elements become irrational only in appearance), but because it determines completely, through reason, the irrational elements that we believe we are capable of discovering in the work of God (error, sensation) and in God himself (incomprehensibility).

8. The Essence of Cartesian Idealism. Critical and Dogmatic Elements of Cartesian Idealism

There remains the question of idealism. In it also, Descartes takes a balanced position. His idealism does not consist in reducing all things to ideas, or even in conceiving the world as produced by my thought. He is, above all, essentially critical. He attempts to establish the objective validity of our ideas, and he supposes that this validity can consist only in the real correspondence of ideas with external things existing in themselves. In order to prove this correspondence, he appeals uniquely to a necessity that I discover in myself. He then attempts to establish that this necessity is not just valid for myself, but in itself. This certainty cannot be procured for me unless the necessity that I grasp from inside me is revealed invincibly as a necessity imposed by things, that is, by something other than myself— God, who exercises the irresistible constraint of an infinite other on my finite self. Cartesian idealism therefore appears as a methodical progression toward realism, toward the positing of things in themselves that are reflected in me: God, essences, minds, bodies.

This duality is manifest in the conception of idea. On the one hand, idea is conceived according to the spirit of geometry, as an entity which is valid by itself, and which, enclosing the reason of the object, decides the legitimate affirmation that I can make with respect to the latter. It is the point of view of mathematism: the thing is justifiable from the idea— from knowledge to being is a good inference. On the other hand, idea is defined as the reflection of an external thing; reduced to the state of a simple picture, it has "fallen" from the primitive perfection proper to this existing thing. This conception of idea as passion and copy truly appears to refer to realism, the copy being conceived as the effect of that of which it is the image. We seem to return here to the conceptions of common sense, to the adage that from being to knowledge is a good inference.

We cannot fail to attribute these two definitions to the conflict of two tendencies, to two eras, to two forms of thought, to two antagonistic philosophical attitudes, the one Copernican, and the other anti-Copernican. But it is beyond doubt that the system tends to unravel the conflict by submitting realist affirmations to the jurisdiction of the idealist point of view.

First, the conception of ideas as copies of an original is only phenomenological. In itself, it entails neither realism nor idealism. It is concerned with describing the idea. Descartes thinks that the idea is given to consciousness like the image of an external thing (the word *image* should not be understood in the restricted sense of "sensible image"). This proper character subsists in the idea after we have abstracted the judgment that decides or rejects referring it effectively to such a thing. Even if I bar myself from judging that the sensible idea of the sun is in conformity with the thing outside it, and even if I know that this conformity is only a myth, this idea does not cease to be given in me as the image of the sun. Similarly, the idea of God is announced as an intellectual image of a reality outside of me, which would be the original or archetype, even if I refuse to affirm to myself that God exists, in fact, in that respect. The realist affirmation appears only from the moment when we are concerned with defining the truth of the idea, instead of merely describing the idea. The latter is, in fact, conceived as effective conformity of the idea to the external thing existing in itself outside of me. An idea is true when it is really that for which it is given immediately in our consciousness, namely, a reflection, an image, of that thing in itself that it represents. For pure idealism, on the one hand, a representation is true when it, in virtue of a necessity due to the constitutive structure of our mind, imposes on this mind a content of consciousness as sensed reality, perceived at the same time in a determined intuition of space and time, and referred unconsciously by my thought to an other simply conceived by me. On the other hand, the idealist point of view reappears in Descartes' conception of the reason that legitimizes the judgment of the conformity of the idea to the thing. In fact, this reason could not reside in the representative character that defines the form of all ideas, as common sense believes, but in the intrinsic character of the content—clearness and distinctness. Thus, the truth of the idea is independent from the representative character (the character of copy) that constitutes it as such—the formal attribution of this idea to the external thing, like its reflection and its effect, is no longer the consequence of certain properties of the idea, once the said representative character is abstracted away. Idea then has an intrinsic truth that exempts me from referring to its effective correspondence with a reality outside it; on the contrary, it authorizes and guarantees this possible correspondence. We reach here the idealist point of view of mathematism, which subordinates being to knowledge. But this intrinsic truth of idea is not imposed on us, in turn, as objectively valid, except insofar as I am assured that it possesses an objective validity, meaning that I know that it expresses in me the essence of a thing or its nature such that God has instituted it in itself, independently of me. We are therefore referred to a higher realism, the realism of essences, to which all existences are reduced. Cartesian idealism is therefore, above all, in the eyes of its author, the only possible point of view and legitimate method to found realism solidly.

In this way we can measure the chasm that separates it from critical idealism. Of course, it is brought nearer to it because of its mathematical inspiration, because of the ends it pursues—to prove the objective validity of our ideas in order to found science, to separate the regions of knowledge that common sense confuses, to allow the discipline of pure reason to rule, and to prevent the transgression of limits. But it is distinguished profoundly from it, through its method and its results.

The foundation of objective validity is not sought for in the analysis of the internal mechanism of our knowledge of the object. Where this analysis appears (for example, in the example of the piece of wax), it leaves this validity doubtful, because neither the faculty by which knowledge is constituted, nor the necessary structure of the latter, are sufficient to constitute the thing itself, which is not reduced to the representation (phenomenal reality), but conceived as a thing in itself outside the latter. Therefore, we must prove in addition, in order to found this validity, that something real in itself corresponds to ideas that are the condition in me, of the representation that I have of it, in brief, to prove that the foundation internal to myself, of my possible representation of the thing, namely, the clear and distinct idea that is in my understanding, reflects in me the fundamental condition of the very thing outside of me, that is, its essence. We must also establish that, to the sensations correspond, outside of me, the existence of the thing whose presence is attested to by these sensations. For Descartes, to prove the objective validity of ideas is nothing other than to prove realism—what Kant calls transcendental—starting with idealism—what Kant, rightly or wrongly calls problematic.[30]

Moreover, since this goal cannot be attained save by demonstrating the existence of a real God outside of me, the original and archetype *(instar archetypi)* of the idea I have of him in me, to prove the objective validity of ideas in order to found science supposes the institution of all metaphysics, and constitutes in some way both alpha and omega. Thus metaphysics is completely governed by the problem of knowledge, whereas the problem of knowledge, which is first posed in critical terms, is finally only resolved by a dogmatic metaphysics. Descartes' position is very particular; he is the only one of the great pre-Kantian rationalist philosophers to have all of philosophy depend on the problem of knowledge (in opposition to Malebranche, Spinoza, and Leibniz). In this respect, he is closer than all of them to Kantianism; but, since he does not conceive any other possible solution to this problem than a metaphysics that Kant would judge eminently dogmatic, he is radically opposite to him. Of course, it is by beginning with and through my mind alone that I can discover the foundation of truth, but it is not my mind, but something other than it—God—which constitutes this foundation.

9. Descartes' Point of View and the Point of View of Contemporary Phenomenology

A Cartesian could indeed reproach Kant for his own a priori dogmatism of science. There is no *epoche* in Kant. Kant's point of departure is not the doubt that strikes all of science, but on the contrary, it is the indubitable certainty of the sciences already constituted. It is concerned less with knowing *whether* science is possible, than with knowing *how* it is possible. The question, *quid facti,* is at first decided affirmatively, and the preliminary acceptance of fact allows the question of rule *(quid juris),* which alone is at stake, to be solved. Experience, as a set of phenomena ruled by laws (meaning the postulate of Newtonian science), is the phenomenon whose possibility founds the certainty of the conditions that the *Critique* is required to recognize of it. Since science is certain, Kant is concerned to pierce its secret in order to see whether metaphysics could not, by appropriating a science to itself, transform itself into science. The effect of this attempt at extrapolation is to introduce into philosophy the Copernican reversal, the formula common to the revolutions of the various sciences, and the measure of their success. By effectuating this reversal for philosophy, the *Critique* destroys the pretensions of any dogmatic philosophy to be valid as a science.

In some respect, we are back at the level of the *Rules,* which aimed at nothing other than to extricate from some already constituted certain sciences (geometry, arithmetic, the analysis of the ancients) their formula for success, in order to extend it to all other human speculations. No doubt the *Rules* do not themselves pose the problem of the *Critique,* the problem of the possibility of sciences, which is considered only in the *Meditations.* But the *Meditations* is situated at a higher level than the *Critique,* since it poses the problem of knowing, not only *how* science is possible, but *whether* it is possible. The question, *quid facti,* is no longer decided by omission, so that we can resolve permanently the question, *quid juris.* The point of departure is no longer the certainty of science, but the metaphysical doubt that strikes at it. The solution is sought in a sphere that transcends the sphere of science, and that of the given world of finite essences and sensible realities.

That is why Cartesian philosophy is, in this respect, closer to the phenomenology of Husserl, than Kantianism. Kantianism remains immanent to the sphere of the world, and phenomenology reproaches it for not having succeeded, nor even attempted, to transcend it.[31] On the contrary, the *Meditations* is well situated in this realm that is superior to Kantianism, in which Husserlian phenomenology attempts to establish a relation of foundation to what is founded, between a philosophy that knows the origin of the world, and all worldly knowledge in general. This philosophy also attempts to rediscover, beyond the sedimentation deposited by prejudices, habits, language, and philosophy, the *thing itself (die Sache selbst)*, to bring to light the heterogeneous realms of our consciousness, to dispel the confusion that mixes them up and that renders almost unavoidable the contrariety of two congenital tendencies in man: that of science, which he derives from pure understanding, and that of life, which he derives from the substantial composite.

It even seems that through *epoche,* established by means of metaphysical doubt, Cartesian philosophy is even more radical than Husserlian philosophy,[32] since it is absolutely transworldly, although Husserlian *epoche* is only the suspension of the thesis of the world, within the worldly attitude. Husserl does not have any metaphysical doubt, whereas Descartes, who does, does not ignore the Husserlian suspension of the thesis of the world, when, for example, describing idea as given as a picture reflecting the thing, he posits at the same time that we do not know whether what is signified as picture is *effectively* the picture of a thing. Husserl identifies *ab ovo,* without proof, *being* and *being for us:* he decides by means of a gratuitous postulate what Descartes institutes as a fundamental problem. Descartes' idealism is installed, from the start, in the sphere of the highest problems. During a congress on phenomenology, Fink noted that, among the gratuitous postulates of Husserlian phenomenology was the identification of *being* and *phenomenon* (meaning *being for us*), which supposes that the appearance, with respect to that which appears, is determined by the subject rather than the object. He noted that this supposition, which implies the revolution accomplished in Western philosophy by Descartes and Leibniz, "is not experienced as a problem" by Husserl.[33] This is a problem that seems insoluble if the phenomenality of the phenomenon can never be given as phenomenon. And Descartes, in *Meditation III,* has experienced this problem, by attempting to answer the question, by what right can one affirm that *being for us* is *being* itself? By what right can one affirm that what our mind constrains us, by its necessities, to posit as the *thing itself* is *this thing* itself? He attempts to establish that the phenomenon—in this case the clear and distinct idea of the infinite—is truly the phenomenon, that is, the immediate and authentic appearance in us of the very thing, meaning of the infinite, in flesh and blood. Thus, he makes the phenomenality of the phenomenon penetrate into science, that is, into the phenomenon. However, idealist revolution is only inaugurated by Descartes, since the solution with which he ends up is an ontological realism. *Being for us* is the thing itself only insofar as it reveals authentically a *being in itself,* which remains as different from the *being for us* as the thing is from its picture—*instar archetypi.* We will have to await the whole development of idealism in order to conceive that this phenomenon—whether it is in us or outside of us—is in itself completely constituted by the subject. That is the task of Fichte's *phenomenology*, which, as post-Kantian philosophy, resolves, with respect to the premises of Kantian transcendental philosophy, the problem that the post-Husserlians wanted to or claimed to resolve, with respect to the premises of the Husserlian transcendental philosophy.[34]

Thus Descartes, as Fichte, Hegel, and Husserl had announced, truly appears as the first source of the current of transcendental philosophy. This does not prevent him from having inspired the great Cartesians, and from being the principle of the reflective and analytic French philosophy, which concludes with Maine de Biran, by way of Malebranche, Condillac, and the ideologues; and it does not prevent him from being at the root of the English and French Enlightenment, of encyclopedism, of positivism, and of the philosophy of the scientific spirit, under its various forms, from Fontenelle to Léon Brunschvicg, through Condorcet, Compte, and Cournot.

From the small, dense, and laconic book of the *Meditations,* which has often been ill understood, in spite—if not because—of the accumulation of commentaries, has flowed the rivers of modern philosophy. When a book is that rich, it suffices for us to glimpse only a small part of its riches, in order for it to manifest an infinite wealth.

Appendixes

Appendixes

1. The Cogito and the Notion "In Order to Think, One Must Exist"[1]

(Cf. vol. I, chap. iii, sec. 1.) Descartes has many times given to the Cogito the look of a reasoning: "I noted that there was nothing at all in this 'I think, therefore I am' that assures me that I am saying the truth unless I see clearly that in order to think, one must exist" *(Discourse,* 4th pt., VI, p. 33, and X, p. 515). But in *Replies II* he rejected having derived this first notion from any syllogism: "The major premise, 'everything that thinks exists,' is taught to him from what he experiences in himself, namely that unless he existed, he could not think" (VII, p. 140); cf. also Spinoza, *Principia philosophiae Cartesianae.* In conformity with this reasoning, the text of *Meditation II* does not present any trace of reasoning (VII, p. 24; cf. also V, p. 136).

On the other hand, two years after the *Replies (Principles,* I, art. 7 and 10), there appears an exposition based on the premise "in order to think, one must exist": "When I said that the proposition, 'I think, therefore I am,' is the first and most certain that presents itself to one who governs his thought by order, I did not deny that we needed to know beforehand what is thought, certainty, existence, that 'in order to think, one must exist,' and other similar things; but because these are such simple notions that by themselves they give us no knowledge that any other thing exists, I did not judge that we had to list them there." Here Descartes was taking up his reply to one of Gassendi's *Instances:* "In order to know that one thinks and that one exists, we must know what is thought and existence, but you have rejected everything from your mind." Descartes' reply was: "I have not rejected the simple ideas or notions that contain neither affirmations nor negations, but only the judgments in which there can be error or truth" (IX p. 206). The Cogito would then suppose the major premise, "in order to think, one must exist." From this arises the controversy between Huet and Régis. The premise, in any case, is admissible only as involving no judgment and being nothing more than a pure and simple intuition. The first point is contestable; also, an intuition, by nature, escapes doubt. But Descartes doubts notions such as "the square has four sides, and three plus two makes five"; these are intuitive items of knowledge, as is proven by the examples of Rule 3 of the *Rules*. Some conclude from this that Descartes commits a *petitio principio*. Others, like Hamelin, admit the reasoning and reject the *petitio,* because they retain only a concrete major premise (the thinking self) and they call reasoning the movement that makes the mind go from the intuition *Cogito,* to the intuition *Sum*. But such an interpretation neglects the major premise previously advanced by Descartes, "in order to think, one must exist." Then, what right do we have to call "reasoning" the "movement of thought" that goes from *Cogito* to *Sum*? Properly speaking, Hamelin's interpretation rests less on a direct exegesis than on an indirect, extremely contestable inference. He says that if the Cogito is not a reasoning, it is a judgment. Is it a Kantian synthetic judgment? But then this kind of certainty would not be able to account for analytic judgments. Is it an analytic judgment? But then there would be no motive to refuse to make it into an abbreviated reasoning, since analytic judgments are as a rule the conclusions of reasonings. What is wrong with this dialectic is that it neglects the essential question, for it might be that, for Descartes, the kind of necessary connection he is dealing with does not enter into either the Aristotelian analytic judgment, or into the Kantian synthetic judgment.

In order to resolve the problem, we must therefore attend precisely to the givens: 1) Descartes refuses to consider the Cogito as a reasoning. He has, in fact, accomplished a philosophical revolution against the Scholastics and would not himself submit to its proceedings. 2) Why then does he present the Cogito under the form that he denies to it, on at least three occasions *(Search after Truth, Discourse, Principles)?*

On the one hand, the Cogito is a statement of fact. Hamelin himself recognizes that "those who refuse to see in it a syllogism have the sense of an important truth, since there is in the Cogito something of a fact." When Descartes insists on this character of fact, he presents the Cogito under a form as distant as possible from any reasoning. Expressions like "I could not deny that I had knowledge of my own mind, since it was so present, so conjoined to me" (IX, p. 241), or "direct impression of divine clearness over our understanding" (V, p. 136), reveal this character of fact, so as to allow the conception of an entirely receptive attitude of the soul in the intuition, according to a certain ontological realism of Augustinian origin.

On the other hand, is not a pure factual given always devoid of intrinsic necessity? If I simply note in me a sequence of elements, I could still conceive without absurdity the separation of this linkage, even if it would express fundamentally a real necessity emanating from God's will (as Berkeley will think). But we have here an unusual fact, which infinitely surpasses the order of empirical statements, since we grasp immediately in it a *necessary* link between *Sum* and *Cogito.* I do not persist in observing that every time I think, I exist, but it suffices that I think once, in order to perceive that I exist, in this respect, *necessarily.* Not that I possess necessary existence, of course, nor that I think necessarily, but that I must necessarily exist, if, *in fact,* I think: "This proposition: I am, I exist, is true *necessarily,* every time that I pronounce it" (VII, p. 25). The major premise, "everything that thinks exists," is taught to him from the fact that he experiences in himself *"that it cannot be* that he thinks unless he exists" (VII, p. 140). What Descartes perceives clearly in himself is that he thinks, but, above all, *the impossibility of thinking without existing.* Thus it appears that the text we hold for a reasoning is derived as naturally as possible from the text in which Descartes refutes the thesis of reasoning: "I noted that there was nothing at all in this 'I think, therefore I am,' that assures me that I am saying the truth, unless I see clearly that *in order to think, one must exist"* (VI, p. 33).

From the above, we can conclude: 1) that Descartes gives the Cogito the look of a reasoning every time he wishes to emphasize the necessary character of the linkage it contains; and 2) that in spite of this "look," the Cogito is not a reasoning. What is it then?

The Cogito is the apprehension of a necessary, singular truth of the same nature as that of a mathematical truth. This is evident since it is an intuition of intellectual thought, and the latter is the domain of necessary linkages of the mathematical kind. But its evidence goes beyond the evidence of mathematics, because its object is no longer the idea of extension (which is incapable of certifying immediately its objective existence), but pure thought, which ipso facto posits such an existence. It is only through its hypermathematical essence that the evidence of the Cogito can serve as criterion for all knowledge, even for mathematics.

How is this apprehension accomplished? The proposition, "in order to think, one must exist," that conditions it is not a major premise. In fact, when he refutes Gassendi, Descartes uses this proposition in order to show that it conditions the major premise "everything that thinks exists." Moreover, it is, for him, one of these "simple notions that by themselves give no knowledge of anything that exists," or "that imply no negation or affirmation." In other words, there exists innately a relation between the simple notions "thought" and "existence" such that although *existence* can be conceived without *thought, thought* cannot be conceived without *existence.* This unilateral necessary relation can be found everywhere in mathematics—for example: *line* and *straight line, line* and *curve, triangle* and *isosceles,* or *right* or *scalene.* In fact, *line* can exist without straight line but not the contrary. This necessary relation is not the same as contingent

relations that are alien to the understanding—as, for example, *black circle.*[2]
Later on, some philosophers even considered this necessary unilateral
relation as the fundamental relation of mathematics. And when the
understanding conceives these relations, it absolutely does not know whether
they are applicable (or, to use Cartesian terminology, when I formulate
these simple notions, I do not know whether they correspond to some
existence, being, or essence, outside my thought, or not). There is no *straight
line* without a *line,* but does there exist a *straight line* and a *line?* I do
not know. There is no *thought* without *existence,* but does there exist both
a *thought* and an *existence?* Before the Cogito, I do not know. What is
certain is that *if* there is a straight line, there is necessarily a line, and
if there is thought, there is necessarily existence. But this existence must
be *guaranteed* to me with respect to extension and must be given to me
with respect to thought; nothing can make up for the *fact* or the act that
gives it to me. What is also sure is that this existence cannot be derived
from this preliminary notion, but that, inversely, I could not derive the
necessity of this notion from the raw fact of its given existence. A necessity
and a fact that complete each other, but that could not *be derived* from
each other, are united indissolubly in the Cogito.

Therefore, the proposition "in order to think, one must exist" has
nothing in common with the major premise "everything that thinks exists,"
for the proposition contains no existence, and we could not extract any
existence from it through analysis. It plays the role of a principle of thought,
like the principle of causality or the principle of identity; it renders a certain
act of thought intrinsically possible. In that respect, it is the *condition*
of my judgment in the Cogito; thus, it can legitimately figure as such before
the Cogito: since in order to think, one must exist, it is sufficient that
I perceive myself thinking in order to perceive myself as necessarily existing.
If we suppressed this preliminary condition and gave ourselves the Cogito,
there would no longer be a necessary linkage, but the statement of an
actual coincidence between my thought and my existence; I would have
a judgment completely unworthy of the understanding, a simple
psychological observation, something analogous to the imaginative linkage
of *black circle.*

But, we would object, has not Descartes doubted these mathematical
relations, to which we are assimilating this preliminary condition, when
he rejected the simplest notions such as "a square necessarily has four sides,"
and "two plus three are five"? Let us understand that doubt precisely:
Descartes is not contesting the unavoidable internal necessity of these
notions, but their objective validity. He asks whether there actually exists
a square outside my thought, some existence or essence responding to the
necessity I experience in myself ("do I know whether there is no earth,

heaven, extended body, shape, and place, but that I nevertheless have sensations of all these things, etc.")? Therefore, as long as I refuse to bring a judgment attributing to these notions present in me, an existence outside of me, I cannot be deceived. That is so even for the lowest kinds of imaginative ideas (goat, chimera): "with respect to ideas, if we consider them only in themselves, they cannot be false, properly speaking" *(Meditation III)*. Mathematical ideas would therefore be situated on the same plane as the notion "in order to think, one must exist," if their extensive character did not almost invincibly call for a judgment of existence outside of us. But the question can be posed the same way with respect to these examples (even though they contain a relation other than unilateral linkage): "if there exists a square, it necessarily has four sides; if there exists a numerical essence corresponding to the numbers of *my* thought, then two and three necessarily make five outside *my* thought, as it does in it, etc.," or more generally, "if there exists an extended substance, all the innate mathematical notions of my understanding are true." Does it exist? I do not know. And I cannot know this, not only before having conceived the Cogito, but also before having conceived the necessary existence of a veracious God. On the contrary, with respect to the notion "in order to think, one must exist," it suffices that I pose the question "but does there exist a thought?" in order to realize, in this very way, that I think, and thus to furnish to the notion the existence that renders it applicable and confers to it objective validity.

Moreover, if the notion "in order to think, one must exist" conditions, in the fact of the Cogito, the consciousness of the necessary linkage of *Cogito* with *Sum,* the fact of the Cogito conditions, through the intermediary of that consciousness, the express consciousness of the notion that renders it possible: "this author demonstrates that he does not know *how truth is to be sought for*, when he maintains that to go from the general to the particular," replies Descartes to Gassendi, "we must go from the particular to the general. . . . Thus when we teach a child the elements of geometry, we would not have him understand that, when we remove equal parts from two equal quantities, the remainders remain equal, or that the whole is greater than its parts, unless we showed him some examples and some particular cases" (IX, pp. 205-6). And it is evident that Descartes— who is perhaps thinking about the examples that the Socrates of the *Meno* submitted to the *pais*—has never thought (cf. *Principles,* I, art. 13) that these examples can render possible the principle they render knowable, nor that the proposition "the whole is greater than the part" is an empirical truth, nor that it has anything at all in common with the major premise "all the totalities are greater than the parts." It is because the whole *cannot* not be greater than the part that the child verifies it [the whole not being greater than the parts] in the examples and is elevated to the consciousness of this *necessary* principle. Here, as elsewhere, the conditions render the facts possible and the facts render possible the knowledge of the conditions. And the act, or the fact by which thought knows itself, as well as the existence unavoidably linked to this knowledge, is necessarily conditioned by the immanent content of thought, since everything that thought knows, even in an adventitious manner, is innate to it (III, p. 418), and since, moreover, nothing necessary can be furnished by a fact, but only by a true and immutable nature. Descartes recalls this, from the beginning of his *Replies to Objections VI:* "It is indeed true that nobody can be certain whether he thinks and whether he exists, unless he first knows what is thought and what is existence; not that this requires a science reflected upon or acquired by demonstration . . . , but it is sufficient that one know this through the kind of *internal consciousness that always precedes the acquisition."* In order to acquire the knowledge of *Cogito ergo sum,* we must already possess thought and its internal laws, and we must have put some of them to action. The latter thus become manifest to thought, which is revealed at the same time to itself, and they acquire with the certainty of their applicability to an existence, the certainty of their objective validity.

But whether it is a major premise or not, is it not sufficient that the notion "in order to think, one must exist" conditions the Cogito in order that it is more clear than the Cogito and substitute for it as foundation of all knowledge? No. Descartes replied to the Scholastics, who reproached him for having given to the Cogito the place that accrues to the principle of identity and noncontradiction, that, "the word *principle* can be taken in several senses; it is one thing to look for a common notion so clear and general that it can serve as principle to prove the existence of all beings *(entia), to be discovered later.* It is another thing to look for a being whose existence is known to us better than that of any other, so that it can serve as a principle in order to know them. In the first sense, it can be said that the principle of contradiction is a principle, and that it can generally serve, *not to make known the existence* of anything else, but simply to confirm its truth once known, by such a reasoning: 'it is impossible that that which is, is not; and I know that such a thing is; so I know that it is impossible that it is not.' This is of little importance, and makes us no wiser. . . . In the second sense, the first principle is that our soul exists, because there is nothing whose existence is more manifest to us" *(To Clerselier,* 1646, IV, pp. 430 seq.). By analogy, we can apply, mutatis mutandis, what Descartes says about the principle of identity to the notion "in order to think, one must exist." It also does not serve to make known "the existence of anything" and could not play the role of principle in that respect. However, the case is only *analogous,* and not the same. Since it is purely formal, the principle of identity allows us to go only from existence to existence, or from thought to thought: "I am, therefore I am"; "I think, therefore I think." It also "does not make us any wiser" and merely "confirms the truth of what I know." But, the notion "in order to think, one must exist" possesses some content; it is no longer the tautology of the necessary link of existence with itself, but the necessary unilateral relation of thought with existence. Therefore it conditions, in the Cogito, the necessity of the link between existence and thought, once they are given. I think, I exist—that is manifest—but because I know that in order to think, one must exist, I also know that *it cannot be* that I think if I did not exist (VII, p. 140), such that "there is nothing in this 'I think, therefore I am' that assures me that I tell the truth, unless I see clearly that, in order to think, one must exist" (VI, p. 33). And, in fact, how could Descartes admit that the most scientific truth is stripped of this intrinsic necessity that renders mathematical truth into preeminent truth?

2. Nominal Definition and Real Definition of Thought and Idea

(Cf. vol. I, chap. iii, sec. 6.) In the plane of common sense, as in the plane of science, the more attributes I know of a thing, the better I know it. Thus an empirical or *quid nominis* definition allows me to know a thing with greater certainty as it enumerates more of its characteristics. Moreover, in geometry, I know a figure better as I demonstrate more properties of it, starting from its real definition.

In the first case, there is no clear and distinct knowledge, and progress consists solely in that the interlocutor reduces his risk of error with respect to the thing I intend designating to him by a certain word.

In the second case (geometry), there is progress in clear and distinct knowledge.

To confuse the rational demonstration of properties starting from the real essence, with the enumeration of properties realized in fact, is to confuse real definition with empirical or nominal definition—that is what happens when, reducing the former *quid (quidditas)* to the latter *quid (quid nominis),* we place the true definition of thought in the empirical enumeration of its modes, and not in the intelligence that constitutes its whole essence.

We can conceive that in the writings intended for teaching—as, for example, in the *Geometrical Summary of Replies II*—Descartes, in order to be sure that he is well understood, begins by a series of definitions *quid nominis* and, in particular, by a definition *quid nominis* of thought (on *quid nominis* definition, cf. *To Mersenne,* 16 October 1639, II, p. 197). These definitions are intended to be received without difficulty "so that, if we denied some of their consequences, it [synthesis—M. G.] enables one to see how the consequences are contained in the antecedents." The expression "I understand by," which introduces each of these definitions, attests to their nominal character.

The properties of thought that are enumerated empirically receive their rational status when we demonstrate, in virtue of a necessary linkage, that they belong to the considered essence. The empirical definition is then changed and appears as a necessary, clear, and distinct truth—in brief, a scientific truth. There is then a progress in scientific knowledge, since I have gone from knowledge of essence to that of its properties. On the one hand, I perceive that these properties can be attributed to thought from the fact that they involve a certain kind of intellection; on the other hand, I perceive that they must be attributed to it, because, given the intellection they involve, they cannot be without thought, although thought can be without them. Similarly, *line* can be without *straight line* or *curve,* while *straight line* or *curve* cannot be without *line.*

Therefore, in the order of the thinking thing, there is instituted a construction of the beings of thought, in virtue of rational and necessary relations; this is completely comparable to the construction instituted by geometry in the order of extended things, with respect to mathematical beings. Malebranche's argument to exclude my soul from the realm of clear and distinct ideas—*there is no rational science of the soul, as there is a rational science of extension; there are no Euclids of psychology*— is therefore without validity for Descartes, for he himself gives rise to this rational science of the soul (or rather of its essence, as thinking essence or pure understanding) and proceeds like a Euclid of psychology. There corresponds to the attempt to reduce the knowledge of existing matter to a science of mathematical relations, an attempt to reduce the knowledge of the thinking, existing thing (captured as an actual essence in the Cogito) to a clear and distinct knowledge of rational elements and necessary linkages. But although physics must in principle be referred wholly to mathematics, for there is nothing other than pure geometrical extension and movement in matter, psychology must not, and cannot, be referred wholly to rational psychology, for Descartes. There is, in fact, a region of the soul that is not pure thought, but substantial union of extension and thought. In this region sensation, and not clear and distinct idea, reigns. The empirical science based on sensation that Descartes admits for only one region of the soul—that of composite substance—Malebranche extends to the whole soul. On the other hand, Spinoza extends to the whole soul the purely rational science of clear and distinct ideas that Descartes rejects for the region of the soul united to body and confines in the region of pure understanding. What relates Descartes to Husserl is the common conviction that there is a possible rational science of things of the soul, bearing on essences, which is completely comparable to the rational science of mathematical things, and *at least* as certain and evident as it. Moreover, Husserl, like Descartes, was a mathematician before becoming a philosopher.

In the *Geometrical Summary of Replies II,* the definition of idea that follows the definition of thought confirms the external and nominal character of these definitions. There idea is defined, in fact, "as the form of any of our thoughts by the immediate perception of which we have knowledge of these same thoughts, such that I cannot express anything by words, when I understand what I say, without the very fact making it certain that I have in me the idea of the thing signified by my words." Here idea is therefore only what is properly conscious in all the modes of consciousness, whether these modes are intellectual or not. Ideas are considered here, psychologically, in the most external fashion, "only insofar as they are ways of thinking among which I do not recognize any difference or inequality, and that all appear to proceed from me in the same manner" (*Meditation III,* VII, p. 40, ll. 7-10). They are this "certain form of intellection" that allows images, sensations, and volitions to be referred to thought as modes. But since the essence of consciousness as intellection is still unknown, and in no way indicated by the preceding definition of thought, these various ways of thinking cannot as yet be conceived as "kinds of intellection"— even though the word "to understand" *(intelligendo)* appears near one of the phrases. In *Meditation III,* the definition of idea is different, more strict and less vague: ideas are only those of our thoughts that represent to us a thing by means of a picture—in brief, that have, at least at first sight, a representative content, an *objective reality.* Thoughts whose content is not representative, but volitional or emotive, for example, are immediately excluded from the circle of ideas (VII, p. 37). This second definition prepares for a third. An idea is not truly an idea unless it actually represents something outside itself—in other words, unless it has objective validity. And only ideas that my understanding cannot doubt naturally (if not metaphysically) as having objective reality can have objective validity. Such is the case with clear and distinct ideas. If, on the contrary, this objective reality is doubtful, for example, if I do not know whether cold or hot are realities or negations, my understanding is required to exclude, at least provisionally, such ideas from the circle of ideas, for an idea without representative content or objective reality represents nothing and is not authentically an idea; it is a pseudoidea. That is why my understanding affirms naturally that clear and distinct ideas are the only ideas that allow me to know things with certainty and evidence. We end up thus with the definition of idea by essence: an idea is what has objective reality such that I am immediately assured that it is truly representative of the thing. Ideas are then said to be essences, "true and immutable natures," and these essences belong to pure understanding. What follows will establish that where there is a minimum of authentic knowledge of objects, there is a minimum of objective reality and, reciprocally, that any objective reality, as little as it is, entails authentic knowledge.

This third definition of idea is completely different from the first. It opens the path for the Leibnizian definition that will eventually posit the criterion of idea in the analysis and verified compatibility of its content (of its objective reality, Descartes would say), in order to discover whether the apparent content is a being or a nothingness; for example, the representative content of the idea of the number greater than all other numbers, of the idea of the most rapid movement possible, etc., is a nothingness. From this we must conclude that these are pseudoideas. It is evident that this third kind of definition no longer owes anything to psychology.

The first definition is a definition of elementary psychology. The second is, we may say, phenomenological. It describes the sense of the phenomenon, the idea insofar as it is presented to us as referring to a thing of which it is a copy, without our having to affirm that it is indeed its copy, and without our knowing whether it is its copy: the thesis of the world is held in abeyance. It is here, and not in metaphysical doubt, that an *epoche* identical to Husserl's is manifested.

The third is metaphysical. It is accomplished through the evaluation of the quantity of objective reality, a quantity that determines the degree of truth.

It is worthwhile to note that the psychological definition of *Objections II* was naturally accepted as the most genuine definition by the weakest Cartesians—Arnauld (*Des vraies et fausses idées* [Paris, 1843], chap. 23); Dom Robert Desgabets, the disciple of Malebranche (who understands nothing of Malebranche) (*Critique de la Critique de la Recherche de la Vérité*, 1675)—although it was rejected by the great Cartesians—Malebranche and Leibniz. The latter attacks this definition as if he discerned, or claimed to discern, Descartes' true doctrine (*Animadversiones,* I, sec. 18, *Philosophische Schriften Leibniz,* ed. Gerhardt [Berlin, 1880], IV, p. 360); *Meditationes,* 1684, ibid., p. 424; against Desgabets, *Letters to Foucher,* 1686, I, p. 386).

3. That One Knows More Things about God Than about the Soul

(Cf. vol. I, chap. v, sec. 20; vol. II, chap. xxi, sec. 6.) God is the best known thing, more known than the thinking self, since we know more of his attributes than of our mind (VII, pp. 52-53; IX, p. 42).

This assertion appears to contradict the following text from *Replies V:* "There is nothing for which we know more attributes than our mind, since, to the extent that we know attributes of other things, we can also count them in the mind of the knower, and therefore his nature is better known than the nature of any other thing" (VII, p. 360; cf. also *Principles*, I, art. 11; *To Mersenne,* July 1641, III, p. 394, ll. 22-31; and above, vol. I, chap. iv, sec. 2). Consequently, to the extent that I know more things of God, I know more attributes of my mind. Therefore, I could not know more properties of God than of my soul.[3]

The solution of this difficulty could be as follows: the things that I grasp in God are such that I know them only to the extent that I perceive through them that my soul does not have sufficiently ample faculties in order *to comprehend* them. Therefore, the attributes I know in God could not imply as many attributes in my mind. Therefore, I know more things about God than about myself. In brief, here again the incomprehensibility of the infinitely infinite renders God into a privileged case.

4. Cartesian Radicalism and Transcendentalism

(Cf. vol. II, chap. xxi, sec. 9.) In a brilliant study, "La question du point de départ radical chez Descartes et chez Husserl" (in *Problèmes actuels de la phénoménologie,* Brussels, 1951, pp. 11-30), Thévenaz defends the thesis—which is also Heidegger's —that Cartesianism, instead of continuing the revolution from which transcendental philosophy has arisen, has cut the flow of transcendentalism and has diverted French philosophy from it. Nevertheless, Thévenaz believes that Cartesian radicalism is at least as worthy as Husserlian radicalism. In that respect he ceases to be of the same opinion as Heidegger.

There are two ways of minimizing the Cartesian revolution in Germany. Either, with the school of Marburg, we see in it a timid approach to Kantianism, a *Vorgeschichte,* or else, with Heidegger, we see in it a regrettable accident that has retarded the coming of the only true philosophy—which is the German one. Fichte, Hegel, and Husserl (to cite only these three German greats) have been on record as opposing these two judgments. They saw in Cartesianism the most fruitful revolution of modern times, and the authentic source of transcendentalism.

Thévenaz defends his thesis by demonstrating that Husserl was mistaken about Descartes' doctrine when he thought that his proceeded from it:

I. First of all, the historical context is different. Descartes does not find any science already constituted before him. He founds *ab ovo* a completely new science. He examines reason itself, and his enterprise is metaphysical, as is verified by metaphysical doubt. Husserl, like Kant, finds before him science already constituted. He asks only how is it possible.

He does not put it into doubt, nor does he put reason into doubt. He reflects on it and institutes, at the level of logic and theory of knowledge, a transcendental inquiry that is not at all metaphysical. Descartes seeks for the beginning of what is not yet there; Husserl seeks for the beginning of what is already there.

II. The process of radicalization is different. In Descartes, the *epoche* makes possible *attention,* through which consciousness grasps itself by having the world disappear. The point of departure is at the heart of the attentive, intensified, centripetal "I." And the self, whose "essential structure is attentiveness,"[4] thus gets a first hold on existence. In Husserl, the *epoche* is only a transformation of *intention,* by which consciousness, instead of losing the world, reveals it, by capturing it as intention or consciousness of senses. The point of departure is in the intentional "I," in the term of the centrifugal end. In Descartes, it is a grasping of self in which the liberated consciousness of everything acquired forges ahead along a linear path, without repetition or renewal; in Husserl, it is a perpetual renewal of what has been experienced and thought, in order to give it a meaning— it is a circular path around the point of departure.

III. In Descartes, the Cogito is the coincidence of consciousness with itself. It does not mark the appearance of a new object. It has as aim only to transform into apodictic and metaphysical foundation the self-consciousness that always accompanies the consciousness of the object, but which escapes the attention. For Husserl, since consciousness is centrifugal by essence, the true origin is not understood except as an increasingly complete recuperation of the world, in the transcendental perspective of constituent intentionality, up to the point of coincidence with transcendental consciousness with the totality of its intention—that is, with the world. This end perhaps may never be attained, but may always be aimed at, because of the perpetual shifting that intentionality and reduction maintain between consciousness and itself, between the natural and the transcendental.

IV. The departure from zero, implied by the Cartesian Cogito, supposes the discontinuity of time. From this stems a mechanistic recomposition, one piece at a time, of the universe, according to a rational order, and a linear time—the time of physics, a time without past; from this arises a consciousness without history. The act of phenomenological unfolding implies, on the contrary, what is already here, a past, a history: to aim at what is before is to aim at an end. There is a latent reason to be transformed into patent reason, a latent past prefiguring the future, which will reveal it as past. This *Urstiftung* is *Nach-* and *Endstiftung.* The beginning is the final goal. Everything is already accomplished; salvation is a priori, although it is always present in Descartes, either immediately available to the act of consciousness, or to the attentive will in instantaneous evidence.

These are therefore two completely different lines of thought. If transcendentalism, in spite of the considerable influence of Kant, was never able to take hold in France, we owe this to Descartes.

This vigorous analysis abounds in fine and penetrating remarks, in brilliant and striking formulations. It certainly comprises part of the truth. Of course, Descartes is not Husserl, and Husserl is not Descartes, or anyone else.

But if Descartes is truly as he is said to be, if his principles contrast to that extent with those of Husserl, we would still not have established that he turns his back to all transcendental philosophy, for the latter has many other representatives: Kant, Reinhold, Maimon, S. Beck, Fichte, Schelling, etc. The Cartesian Cogito is not *intention,* but is Kant's or Fichte's Cogito? The conclusion seems disproportionate to the premises.

Moreover, these premises are often themselves contestable.

Descartes is also in the presence of an already constituted and certain science: geometry, arithmetic, the ancients' analysis, and the algebra of the moderns (Cossists). He attempts to discover the formula that allows these sciences to succeed in order to apply it elsewhere and thus to revolutionize the whole of human knowledge. His scruples require him to examine the legitimacy of such an extrapolation, to measure the whole extension of our mind, and to discover its limits *(limites ingenii definire).* The analogy between the design of the *Rules* and the design of the *Critique* (such as it is stated particularly in the second edition) is striking.

Of course, neither Kant nor Husserl places reason in doubt. Metaphysical doubt does not appear for them. And this difference must be considered. But nothing requires us to push this difference to the extreme in order to make it into a radical opposition. In fact, metaphysical doubt is a light, feigned, and provisional artifice, in Descartes, while the trust accorded to reason in Kant must remain in abeyance as long as the critical process is not learned and does not put an end to the internal struggle of the antithetical, which strikes *reason itself* with suspicion.

Of course, the reflective Cartesian *ego* is not the intentional Husserlian *ego*. The relation of the self to the world is not the same. But the Cartesian *ego* does not make the world disappear definitively; the Cogito is there only to rediscover the world, by revealing it according to its essence, according to its true authenticity, and in the differentiation of its regions. Moreover, intentionality does not define all transcendentalism. Transcendentalism is concerned with knowing if the *ego* fills a constitutive function, if it is affirmed necessarily only to the extent that it turns out to be a necessary condition of the possibility of all knowledge of objects. The Cogito, the Cartesian thinking self, echoes exactly this definition. If I can posit its necessary existence, that is because I have perceived that without it any kind of thought would be impossible. If I know the soul before the body, it is because the innate ideas of my understanding render a priori possible and constitute the representations I have of material things. No doubt, the fact of constituting or of rendering possible these representations does not suffice for Descartes to give me the certainty that through them I know the thing. But that is precisely because I cannot affirm without proof, for Descartes, that *being for us* (the representation of the thing constituted by my idea) is true being (that this *being for us* is *realitas phenomenon,* in the manner of Kant, or that it is the accurate image of something in itself, in the manner of Descartes). We can therefore say that in this way Descartes transcends a transcendentalism satisfied with identifying without proof *being* and *being for us.* The doubt with respect to this postulate is metaphysical doubt. Thévenaz has noted that it was absent in Husserl. But how does the presence of such a doubt belie the spirit of transcendentalism, if it is responding to the need to examine the latter's postulate, that *being for us is being,*[5] and if it also involves the suspension of the thesis of the world? Fichte, without the benefit of the hypothesis of the evil genius, posed the same problem for himself when he gave himself the task to prove that being can be nothing other than being for us. Is Fichte a transcendental philosopher or not? And yet, if he invokes the Kantian *I think,* he also invokes by preference the Cartesian Cogito. Does Kant's self cease to be transcendental because it is not intentional, but is pure form? And does the pure self of Fichte, which is both centripetal and centrifugal, intentionality and reflectivity, cease being transcendental because it is not just centrifugal?

The assertion that "attention constitutes the essential structure of the self" cannot be supported by any text and seems even to be excluded by the very theory of attention. The intellect can be without attention, but attention cannot be without intellect. Attention is one of the ways my will makes use of the intellect. To say that attention is the essence of my thought is to say that the essence of an instrument is the manner in which one uses it. My intellect is limited. Within its limits, I always dispose of the *same quantity of thought* or light. Will can allow this light to be diluted over several objects or to be concentrated over one alone, by being turned away from the others. These various states of my intellect are accidental to it, and the intellect remains identical to itself, conserving its same quantity in all cases.[6] That is why the method aims, not to increase the forces of the mind, which is a pretension outside man's power, but to regulate them. It is the same for corporeal substances: the substance wax is always a *same quantity of extension* and this invariable quantity defines it with respect to other substances whose invariant is different—whether it loses in depth in order to gain in length or width, whether, on the other hand, it contracts, so as to lose in length and width and gain in depth, it remains wax, that is, the same immutable quantity of extension, and these different forms are its accidents.[7] The concentration of light that my will operates on an object is attention; the fact that other objects cease being illuminated then is abstraction. That is what happens at each instant in mathematics, when my will concentrates all my intelligence on a particular segment or a particular property of a figure, and leaves the rest in darkness. That is what happens in the Cogito, when my will condenses all my light on the thinking self by keeping in darkness all the contents of my thought. Thus attention is to my intelligence what accommodation is to vision. Certainly, any vision incapable of accommodation would be almost unusable, as would the intellect be without attention; from this arises the extreme importance of accommodation and attention. But accommodation is no more the essence of vision than attention is the essence of my intelligence, for vision can be without accommodation, but accommodation cannot be without vision.

Moreover, it is impossible to admit that the Cogito (obtained by the "elaborate mechanism" that we know, the fruit of a painful effort, since it is both the first uprooting from the sensible world and the result of a process of analysis) is not a new object. What is more new than this first truth of science, which is so disconcerting to common sense? Instead of being "quite frankly" the attentive consciousness of self which is not ordinarily noticed and which accompanies the consciousness of all objects, it is the knowledge that 1) this self is the necessary condition of all thoughts— which explains that it *must* always accompany them; that 2) the essence of this self is pure intelligence;[8] that 3) I exist indubitably for myself only to the extent that I am pure intelligence; and that 4) the existence I affirm necessarily is, in this case, only an essence that I posit as actual—which prepares for this other knowledge that existence is everywhere identical to essence, existence being only the actuality of essence. There are so many new truths that were hidden to common consciousness, which has as much difficulty in conceiving that the whole reality of my soul consists in pure understanding as it has difficulty in conceiving that the whole reality of matter consists in pure extension.

The Cogito is not this "fiat," this "creation *ex nihilo.*" It does not arise in the void; it does not stem from a sudden decree of a reflection that is satisfied by it, stemming from nothing, leading to nothing—to nothing that is this world. It is neither absolute beginning, nor final end. It is a stage in the analytic linkage of reasons, which, starting from the current vision of the sensible world, rises to the discovery of the essence of the soul and the essence of God, in order to go from there to the discovery of natures that constitute the world. It supposes, before it, a process of breaking up the complex into simples, which goes successively over the plane of sensible representation (common sense, "as it is called"), and the plane of mathematical notions (the plane of the *Rules*). This process is completed on the latter plane, and another begins, starting from it. The Cogito cannot be understood if we isolate it from what precedes it and from what follows it, from the apparatus that conditions its being instituted, as from the constitutive function it assumes. It is isolated only because we isolate it.

It seems therefore that when sketching, with great phlosophical talent, his parallels between Descartes and Husserl, Thévenaz has not succeeded in exorcising the classical fiction of a linear Descartes, the inventor-maker of a fictional world, who has been able to forget the real because of mathematics, and who goes straight forward as a maker of abstract theorems. This fiction is as dangerous as the fiction of Descartes reduced to a psychologist of attention, relating day by day his intellectual autobiography, his personal experience, according to chronological order. On the contrary, we have seen Descartes as rigorously rational as he is strictly positive, solidly rooted to the earth, given to discovering in their authenticity, behind the double falsification due to the abuses of reason and of the senses, the authentic reality of the various regions or natures that constitute our being, true understanding, and true sensation, as well as the true essence of mind and the true essence of matter.

If we needed to seek why "transcendentalism did not take hold in France," we would perhaps find one of the reasons for this in the misunderstanding, and less in the influence, of Descartes' real thought.

5. On the Equality of Human Intelligences

(Cf. vol. II, appendix 4.) G. Lewis (University of Rennes) has written to us "concerning note 175 of vol. I, chap. iii . . . because of the number of texts about the inequality of intelligences or understandings *(intellectus,* says the dedicational letter of the *Principles)*—and about the unity that is also a character of individuation," as testified by the "express affirmations in the correspondence with Mesland on the role of form."

Let us discuss this objection, since it refers to incontestable texts.

At first sight, there is no inconsistency for the coherence of the system to admit inequalities between pure intellects and to admit, consequently, an inequality in the capacity to think, imparted once and for all to different souls. The problem of the individuation of souls would be thus simplified, while perhaps complicating other questions. For, if the capacity of various understandings is different, could we still admit, as Descartes wishes it, that all of them have equally an indefinite number of simple innate ideas, or *semina scientiae?*

But the text of the beginning of the *Discourse* is categorical in its rejection. The note referred to above merely registers this refusal and leans toward it. This text is fundamental: it is an important text that founds the relations between method and man's intelligence. It confirms the *Rules,* in which Descartes declares that any man, as long as he follows some easy rules, "will remain fully convinced that if he does not know something, it is not through lack of mind or capacity, and that someone else cannot know something he is incapable of knowing, as long as he applies his intelligence to it" (Rule 8, X, p. 399).

Can we abolish this in favor of texts that appear to state the opposite? Obviously not. Can this abolish them? No, again. Therefore we must admit, either that Descartes grossly contradicted himself (which is what we must reject), or that the two statements are reconcilable (which is what it seems we must accept).

This reconciliation appears more probable to the extent that, without it, Descartes would be contradicting himself in the same texts. Thus, in the *Rules,* in which he states that any man has sufficient capacity for intelligence in order to attain any science or any degree of science, he does not cease to oppose "lesser minds" (Rule 8, X, p. 399, l. 26; cf. *Search after Truth,* p. 498, l. 25) to "superior minds" (Rule 4, p. 373, l. 14), and "greater minds" (Rule 4, p. 377, l. 3; Rule 13, p. 433, l. 14). He affirms that "all minds are not equally capable of discovering the truth only with their own strength" (Rule 10, p. 404, l. 5). But this difference of aptitude, this mediocrity on the one hand, and this superiority, on the other, does not entail that these minds have a pure understanding of different capacities, since "whoever would be penetrated by this method, whatever is the *mediocrity of their mind,* sees that no study is prohibited to him more than to others, and that if he does not know something, it is not because he lacks *mind or capacity*" (Rule 8, p. 399, l. 24; cf. *Search after Truth,* p. 498, l. 26).

We must therefore believe that in these texts, as in the dedicational epistle of the *Principles,* in which Descartes notes that will is equal for all of us, but that "the understanding of some is not as good as that of others," Descartes is appealing to current experience: there are "good minds," "good brains," let us say, and others that are less good. But these differences, however, do not concern pure intellects considered in themselves, detached from bodies; they concern the brains to which these intelligences, all equal and identical, are joined. From this arises quick or slow, superior or mediocre minds.

In fact, the auxiliaries of the understanding (imagination, memory) depend on the nature of our brain, but more importantly, the greater and lesser power of the senses to blind our intelligence also depend on it. In his *Letter to Arnauld* of 29 July 1648 (sec. 1)[9] Descartes explains that, depending upon whether the soul is or is not "joined" to an "excessively humid or soft brain" or "to a brain whose temperament is otherwise badly affected, as with lethargics, apoplectics, and frenetics, etc.," it is more or less able to detach itself from the senses, and consequently to be elevated to pure intellectual thought, and attain the true. Thus, mind can be said, in accordance with what men say, to be more or less good, and one's "aptitude for the true" may be said to be greater or lesser in each, without the *capacity* for understanding or *quantity of thought* being any different.

At birth no man can do mathematics; as an adult he can excel at it. Descartes will say, as everyone does, that his intelligence has developed. However, his soul, according to him, was *completely* there from the beginning, and it has not gradually enlarged its capacity to think. Still, the brain to which it is joined, ceasing with age to be "humid and soft," allows intelligence (which has remained the same) to be exercised fully. If all of a sudden a man becomes mad and loses his intellectual faculties, he does not stop being man, in order to become animal-machine; he preserves his soul, and therefore he preserves his whole intelligence, since intelligence is the essence of the soul. His capacity to think has therefore neither vanished nor shrunk, but his body, his brain, has become such that it can no longer be used.

Of course, it is not as if the operations of pure intelligence are conditioned to any extent by the play of cerebral mechanisms. By hypothesis, the latter concern only the composite substance and condition the exercise of the imagination, the corporeal memory, and the senses—in brief, the faculties foreign to the pure nature of the soul, which accrue to it only because of the fact of its union with body. The purely intellectual operations (intuition, deduction insofar as the latter has recourse only to intellectual memory) depend on the understanding alone, without any recourse to the brain. That is why intelligence remains basically the same in each man, and for all men, no matter what are the different dispositions of their brains. The body and the brain to which the soul is joined are always only an obstacle for pure intelligence; they are never a positive condition— indeed, even an instrument. If intelligence seems to vary with brains, that is because the obstacles they bring to it are more or less considerable.

With respect to the soul as form *(Letter to Mesland,* cf. above, vol. II, chap. xvii, sec. 5) the function of unity it assumes with respect to the human body does not at all entail the individuality of each man, but the unity of *every man:* "Intelligence or thinking principle" is like "a first act" or "principal form *of man* . . . to which the name *soul* refers, etc." *(Replies V,* VII, p. 356, ll. 12-22). There is nothing in these texts that destroys the assertion of the *Discourse,* according to which "more and less exist only between *accidents,* and not between *forms* or natures of individuals of the same species."

Of course, Descartes considers each soul, independently from body, as an individual substance. That is what founds for each of them their immortality (cf. *Summary of the Meditations).* But Descartes does not tell us what constitutes their principle of individuation, that is, their *difference.* The individuality of each is therefore simply affirmed without being founded; it is, as Leibniz will say, only *solo numero.* Thought or reason, as intelligence constituting the form of every man, such as the Cogito posits it, excludes from it the accidents that individualize.

6. [A Difficulty with the First Proof from Effects]

(Cf. vol. I, chap. iv, sec. 14.) The first Cartesian proof from effects, so remarkable because of its novelty, its rigor, and the analysis of the contents of knowledge that introduces it, appears to run against a difficulty that appeared insurmountable, but that now seems able to be resolved easily.

I recall briefly the background: since there must be at least as much perfection in the efficient and total cause as in its effect, the cause of the idea of God must involve at least as much formal reality as there is objective reality in this idea. Since this objective reality is infinite, its cause must be a formal infinite reality, that is, God himself. Thus necessarily God exists, given that I have his idea in me. But Descartes accepts without discussion, as "taught by natural light" the opinion according to which the objective reality of an idea "is deficient"[10] with respect to the thing or formal reality of which it is the image, and that it admits of less perfection than the formal reality, because of this. Thus the idea of God has less perfection than God himself. This is a current opinion, which is not specifically Cartesian—the contrary is true—since it transposes to Cartesian use the popular adage that the shadow is less than reality, so that the image is said to be less perfect than its model—the idea of the sun in my understanding is less perfect (*loinge imperfectior*) than the formal being of the sun in heaven—in brief, the *res in repraesentando* is less perfect than the *res in essendo.*[11]

From this arises the following objection: on the one hand, God's formal reality admits of, in itself, by hypothesis, much more perfection than the objective reality of the idea that represents it; on the other hand, the only thing *necessarily* required as cause of this objective reality is a formal reality containing *at least as much* perfection as does the objective reality. Consequently, we cannot require *necessarily* of this cause that it contain *more,* meaning that it be the formal reality of God. Thus, the *extra,* meaning God himself, is not proven: it remains merely possible.

The reply would be as follows:

1) The objective reality of an idea representing something finite is less perfect than the formal reality of that thing.

2) The objective reality of an idea representing something infinite is less perfect than the formal reality of that thing.

3) No matter how weak is the perfection of the objective reality of the idea of the infinite with respect to the formal reality of the infinite, it is always infinitely greater than that of the formal reality of any finite thing; for the disproportion between the finite and the infinite is absolute. In brief, everywhere there is infinity (even only *in repraesentando*), the perfection of the finite (even *in essendo*) appears almost null.

4) No formal finite reality can therefore produce the objective reality of the idea of the infinite; and my self, a finite formal reality, cannot be its cause.

Having recalled these four principles, we can ask what could be the formal reality other than myself that would enclose enough perfection (and nothing more) in order to cause in me the objective reality of the idea of the infinite. Since it would not be God, who contains more of it, it would be a formal reality less perfect than God's formal reality. But, lacking the perfection that belongs to God, it would be imperfect, therefore finite. From this fact, it could not cause in me the objective reality of the idea of the infinite, since no finite formal reality can cause infinite objective reality (cf. 4). Consequently, a formal reality outside of me could not enclose the *minimum* of perfection required to produce in me the objective reality of the infinite, unless it is the *maximum*—meaning God. Therefore, I must *necessarily* conclude that God exists, since God himself, and nothing other, is the cause of my idea.

The core of this reply is that we cannot posit the *minimum* required without positing the *maximum,* for, since there is no other formal infinite reality other than God, nor any other alternative except between a formal infinite reality and a formal finite reality, the exclusion of the latter imposes necessarily the positing of the former, meaning God.

Notes

Notes

Unless otherwise indicated, all references to Descartes' works are to Charles Adam and Paul Tannery's edition, *Oeuvres de Descartes* (Paris: Cerf, 1897-1913; new revised ed. Vrin, 1964-74), in 11 vols. Cross-references within this text are designated with "see above" or "see below" (e.g., "see below, vol. II, chap. x, sec. 3").

Chapter IX. Concerning The Existence of Material Things. The *Nexus rationem* of *Meditation VI*

1. *Meditation VI*, VII, p. 71, ll. 12-13; IX, p. 57.
2. Ibid., VII, p. 73, l. 24; IX, p. 58.
3. Ibid., VII, p. 74, l. 9; IX, p. 59.
4. Ibid., IX, pp. 78 seq.; IX, p. 62; *Replies to Objections II, Geometrical Summary,* prop. IV; VII, p. 169; IX, p. 131.
5. *Letter to Elizabeth,* 21 May 1643, III, p. 664, l. 23, p. 665, ll. 1-4.
6. *Replies to Objections VI,* IX, pp. 239 seq; *Principles,* II, art. 3-4, etc.
7. *Replies to Objections IV,* VII, p. 227, l. 25, p. 228, ll. 1-5; IX, p. 177; *Summary of Meditations,* IX, pp. 11-12.
8. *Letter to Elizabeth,* 21 May 1643, III, pp. 664-65.
9. *Replies to Objections IV,* VII, p. 228, ll. 27 seq.; IX, p. 177.
10. *Replies to Objections VI,* VII, p. 440, ll. 1 seq.; IX, p. 239.
11. *To Elizabeth,* 28 June 1643, III, p. 693, ll. 21-26; *Replies to Objections IV,* VII, p. 228, l. 27, p. 229, ll. 1-2; IX, p. 175.
12. *Meditation III,* VII, p. 34, ll. 12-13; IX, p. 27.
13. *To Elizabeth,* pp. 693-94.
14. *Summary of the Meditations,* VII, p. 16; IX, p. 12.
15. "Since God is supremely good and the source of all truth, since he has created us, it is certain that the power or faculty he has given us to distinguish the true from the false is not deceived when we use it well, and that it shows us evidently that something is true. Thus this certainty extends to everything that is demonstrated in mathematics. . . . It also extends to the knowledge we have that there are bodies in the world. . . . Then it extends to all the things that can be demonstrated with respect to these bodies by the principles of mathematics or by other principles as evident and certain." *Principles,* IV, art. 205. Moreover, let us note that this absolute certainty attributed to physics by the *Principles* does not square with the conception of the equivalence of hypotheses, which, if it agrees with the purely relative definition of movement *(Principles,* III, art. 15) can allow one to achieve only a moral certainty. In fact, what, in the case of equivalent hypotheses, allows one to opt for one hypothesis rather than another, is that one leads to a better explanation of a greater number of phenomena than the other one. Certainty is then entirely of the same order as in the case of the decoder who does not doubt the truth of his whole system when he can, because of it, give a coherent meaning to a long cryptogram. And Descartes specifies (IV, art. 205) that the certainty of the decoder, as high as it may be, is only a moral certainty,

for its explanation is based on principles "assumed haphazardly" (namely the decoding hypothesis that is suddenly inspired by good luck after numerous attempts and unfruitful gropings), while the certainty of the physicist is absolute, for it concerns causes that were not assumed haphazardly, but deduced rigorously and "satisfied by reason" (ibid.). That is why Descartes opposes, in the fourth part of the *Discourse,* the method of *Dioptrics* and of *Metereology,* a method that demonstrates causes by means of the explanation they bring to effects, which are certain, to the true method (which will be the method of the *Principles),* in which causes are deduced from first truths. That is why, in spite of the demonstration by effects, causes are still only called "suppositions," for they do not attain in this way the absolute certainty of the mathematician (VI, p. 76, ll. 6-28). Cf. above, vol. I, chap. v, sec. 22.

16. *Entretien avec Burman,* V, p. 160.

17. *Discourse on Method,* 6th pt., VI, p. 64, l. 26, p. 65, ll. 1-25; *Principles,* II, art. 4.

18. "And certainly, from the fact that I perceive different kinds of colors, odors, tastes, heat, hardness, and so forth, I readily conclude that in the bodies from which these sense perceptions proceed there are some corresponding variations, although these variations are not really similar to the perceptions." *Meditation VI,* VII, p. 81, ll. 15 seq.

19. Ibid., p. 80, ll. 4-19; *Replies to Objections VI,* VII, p. 440, ll. 6-29; IX, p. 239.

20. *Meditation VI,* VII, p. 89, ll. 4 seq.; IX, p. 63.

21. Gilson, *Etudes sur le rôle de la pensée médievale dans la formation du système cartésien* (Paris: [Vrin], 1930), p. 301; cf. also pp. 245, 300.

22. *Meditation VI,* VII, p. 78, ll. 28 seq.; IX, p. 63.

23. VII, p. 80, ll. 11 seq.; IX, pp. 63-64.

24. "Ordinem naturae pervertere," VII, p. 83, l. 15; "Pervertir et confondre," IX, Pt. 1, p. 66; *Replies to Objections VI,* VII, pp. 436-38; IX, pp. 236-37.

25. "Sed nova hic occurrit difficultas," VII, p. 83, l. 25; IX, Pt. 1, p. 66.

26. We are referring to the whole thing (the second perspective) with the letter *y.* Let us recall that we referred to the first perspective with the letter *x.* See above, this chapter, sec. 1.

27. VII, p. 73; IX, p. 57.

28. VII, p. 74; IX, p. 59.

29. VII, p. 73; IX, p. 58.

30. VII, p. 78, ll. 2 seq.; IX, p. 62.

31. VII, p. 79, ll. 6 seq.; IX, p. 63.

32. VII, p. 80, l. 26; IX, p. 64. The problem of the union of soul and body (psychophysics) is partly centered (that is, with respect to what concerns the more particular union of the soul with a part of the body) on the solution of the problem of the intrinsic falsity of the senses. The theory of the conditions of the more particular union of the soul with a part of the body plays, with respect to the doctrine of intrinsic falsity, exactly the same role that the theory of the union of the infinite will and the finite understanding plays in the doctrine of formal error: the union of the indivisible and the divisible account for the material falsity of the senses, in *Meditation VI.* In the end, psychology and psychophysics are equally dependent on the problem of exculpating God.

Chapter X. The Realm of the Understanding: The Possibility of the Existence of Material Things. The General Theory of Possibility

1. VII, p. 71, ll. 13-20.

2. *Meditation IV,* VII, p. 62, ll. 11-20; IX, pp. 50-51; *Meditation V,* VII, p. 65, ll. 2-4; IX, p. 51; VII, p. 69, l. 16, p. 70, l. 10; IX, pp. 55-56.

3. "Existence is contained in the idea or concept of everything, because we can conceive nothing except as existent; but with the difference that only possible or contingent existence is contained in the concept of a limited thing, and necessary and perfect existence is included in the concept of a Supremely Perfect Being." *Geometrical Summary, Replies to Objections II*, axiom 10; cf. *Replies to Objections I*, IX, pp. 88-89, 94; *Replies to Objections IV*, IX, p. 183.

4. *Meditation V*, VII, p. 71, ll. 17-20; IX, p. 57.

5. *Geometrical Summary, Replies to Objections II*, axiom 10.

6. *Replies to Objections IV*, VII, p. 249, ll. 12-13. "I know that my intelligence is finite and God's power is infinite, and so I do not claim to set any bounds to it, but I examine only what I can conceive and what I cannot conceive. That is why I boldly assert that God can do everything that I conceive to be possible, but I am not bold enough to assert that he cannot do whatever is repugnant to my manner of conceiving—I merely say that it involves a contradiction. . . ." *Letter to Morus*, 5 February 1649, V, p. 272, ll. 21-25. "I do not think that we should ever say of anything that it is impossible for God, for, since everything true and good depends on his omnipotence, I do not even dare say that God cannot make a mountain without a valley, or that one and two does not add up to three. I only say that he has given me a mind of such nature that I cannot conceive a mountain without a valley, or that one and two should not add up to three, etc. I only say that such things involve a contradiction in my conception." *To Arnauld*, 29 July 1648, V, p. 223; cf. also *To Mersenne*, 15 April 1630, I, p. 146.

7. *Replies to Objections IV*, ibid.

8. Saint Augustine, *Contra Faustum*, XXVI, chap. 5, p. 274.

9. "It would be an imperfection in God to be able to deprive himself of his own existence; that is why, in order to obviate the evil talk of slanderers, I would advise you to use the following words: 'It is repugnant that God could deprive himself of his own existence, or that he could lose it in any other way. . . .'" V, pp. 545-46. God's fundamental freedom can be reconciled with the impossibility to limit his omnipotence; but it still remains that this impossibility requires that God could not will himself not to exist. It is impossible to conceive, along with A. Koyré *(Essai sur l'idée* de Dieu chez Descartes [Paris: Leroux, 1922], p. 197), that if God exists necessarily, it is not because he could not have done otherwise, but because he willed it to be thus. As we have just seen, the necessity of God's existence does not belong to the sphere of eternal truths that were freely instituted by his will. Moreover, the necessity to exist is not imposed on God by his understanding, but by the nature of his will: it flows from his omnipotence, and consequently it cannot limit it.

10. *Meditation I*, VII, p. 21, ll. 22-24; IX, pp. 16-17.

11. *Meditation III*, VII, ll. 7-9; IX, p. 52; *Meditation IV*, VII, p. 53, ll. 25-29; IX, p. 43; *Principles*, I, art. 29.

12. "We conceive clearly that this is impossible—that it is possible that what has been not be—and that thus there is no defect of power in God that he does not do it." *To Morus*, 5 February 1649, V, p. 273, ll. 22-26.

13. *Meditation II*, VII, p. 40, l. 21; IX, p. 32; *Meditation VI*, VII, p. 79, ll. 14-18; IX, p. 63; *Replies II*, VII, p. 135, ll. 11-19; IX, p. 106; VII, p. 165, l. 7; IX, p. 128.

14. "It is not the case that God would be showing the immensity of his power if he made things that could exist without him; on the contrary, he would thus be showing that his power is finite, since the thing he had once created would no longer depend upon him in order *to be*." *To Hyperaspistes*, August 1641, III, p. 429; *To Elizabeth*, 6 November 1643, IV, p. 332. Cf. the *Letter to Mesland* of 2 May 1644: "I agree that there are contradictions that are so evident that we cannot represent them to our mind without judging them entirely impossible, like the one you suggest: *that God might have made creatures independent of*

him. But in order to know the immensity of his power, we should not put these thoughts before our minds, nor should we conceive any preference or priority between his understanding and his will; for the idea we have of God teaches us that there is only one activity in him, entirely simple and pure." IV, p. 119. Descartes does not indicate by this that the impossibility for God to create beings independent of him is a truth at the same level of freely created eternal truths, for this impossibility is absolute, meaning valid in itself even for God, in virtue of his omnipotence. But he warns us not to attribute this impossibility to a rule imposed by God's understanding on his will. In fact, not only is God's act simple and does not assume a distinction between the understanding and will, this impossibility cannot be due to his understanding since it emanates from the infinite omnipotence of his will considered intrinsically. Moreover, Descartes indicates that the proposition, *God cannot create independent beings,* because of its negative and limiting characteristics, is not well suited to represent the positive immensity of God's power, which is not limited by anything, even though the impossibility in question results necessarily from it. Gouhier, in some penetrating remarks ("Les Exigences de l'existence [de la métaphysique de Descartes," in *Revue Internationale de Philosophie* (April 1950)], p. 29), notes that "with respect to the good defined by God's hatred, and especially with respect to God creating beings independent of him, Descartes no longer affirms anything," that he "hesitates" to affirm. However, Descartes *does not hesitate to affirm* with respect to the first point concerning not good in itself, but good such that God ordered his creatures to represent it to themselves: "Why couldn't have God been able to prescribe such a commandment to his creatures?" *Entretien avec Burman,* V, p. 160. In fact, although God in himself cannot be evil, insofar as malice implies nothingness, nothing proves that goodness in itself is such that we represent it to ourselves, or at least that it is so only in virtue of divine veracity which wills that God does not deceive us with respect to what he teaches us. But God could have taught us otherwise, since the aims of God are impenetrable, and the order to hate him could have been a relative good in the general framework of a work ordered according to the principle of the best, in the same way that error enters into it in fact, even though we judge it to be an evil. Gouhier specifies with respect to the second point that "Descartes does not state that God could have created beings not dependent upon him; but we do not have the right to think that he could not have created beings not dependent upon him." But Descartes does state that we do not have the right to think that he could have created beings independent of him, for we would be conceiving of an absurdity by conceiving that God, by means of his very omnipotence, would deny his omnipotence by limiting it. Descartes simply warns us that the terminology we use— "cannot"—contradicts the content that it affirms, namely the omnipotence that nothing can limit, and he advises us, consequently, to avoid using this terminology in order to represent omnipotence.

15. *To Arnauld,* 29 July 1648, V, p. 223.

16. *Principles,* II, art. 20. "We cannot conceive that he [God—M. G.] could have deprived himself of the power of dividing them [atoms—M. G.], for we do not take it as a mark of impotence when someone cannot do something we do not comprehend to be possible, but only when he cannot do something that we distinctly conceive to be possible. And we conceive the division of an atom to be possible, since we conceive it as extended." *To Morus,* 5 February 1649, V, p. 273; *To Gibieuf,* 19 January 1646, III, p. 477. We ought to note that the two primary Cartesian dogmas of physics, the rejection of atoms and the denial of void, are presented as necessities for God, and not as the result of a divine free choice. This impossibility to limit God's power poses, moreover, a problem relative to the created world, of which it is difficult to conceive that it is itself limited, since God would have thus limited his creative omnipotence in this way—a problem whose difficulty will be conceived fully by Malebranche, and for whose solving he will use the full resources of his system.

Descartes has two arguments for positing the world as merely indefinite instead of absolutely infinite. The first is based on God's perfection, which must be necessarily greater than the perfection of the world: "It is repugnant to my ideas to assign boundaries to the world, because I do not recognize any boundaries for it. . . . That is why I say that it is indeterminate or indefinite . . . ; but I would not dare to say that it is infinite, because I conceive that God is greater than the world, not by reason of his extension, since I do not conceive any extension in God, as I have said several times, but by reason of his perfection." *To Morus,* 15 April 1649; *Reply to the Penultimate Instances,* V, p. 344, ll. 5-14, p. 345, ll. 9-16. What this argument does not explain is how God could have, by means of his great perfection, limited his omnipotence to the creation of a less perfect world. The second argument is based on divine incomprehensibility: God may have reasons that are incomprehensible to us for making the world finite *(To Chanut,* 6 June 1647, V, p. 52, ll. 21-25; cf. also *Principles,* III, art. 1 and 2). But God is incomprehensible because he is perfect; he cannot make something imperfect except by limiting his will by nothingness and by contradicting his incomprehensible omnipotence. Therefore it seems that we ought to have, on the contrary, a sufficient reason derived from the very nature of God to conclude positively the perfection and infinity of his work. Cf. above, vol. I, chap. vii, sec. 6. Finally, we should note that all the arguments that demonstrate the impossibility of the atom can be turned against the noninfinity of the world. In fact, i) we conceive this infinity clearly and distinctly as possible—it would be a mark of impotency if God were not able to create the world infinite; and ii) we conceive it as a mark of impotency for a will to limit its omnipotence, and to wish to be limited to the finite, which would entail some nothingness—God, in virtue of his infinite omnipotence, could not therefore have reasons in him, that are incomprehensible for us, to create a merely finite world. We have seen, when dealing with error, that Descartes adopted the hypothesis that God has created an extremely perfect world (cf. above, vol. I, chap. vii, sec. 6), and we will see that all of *Meditation VI* attempts to show that God has created at least the best possible world. The conception of the world as imperfect and not infinite truly seems a doctrine imposed by Catholic dogma. That is what arises from a comparison between articles 1 and 2 of part III of the *Principles.*

17. Saint Anselm, *Proslogion,* chap. 7.

18. *To Arnauld,* 19 July 1648, p. 223. Cf. above, vol. I, chap. iii, n. 3, articles by Gouhier and Dreyfus that have already been cited.

19. *Principles,* II, art. 36 seq.

20. *Replies to Objections VI,* VII, pp. 444-45; IX, p. 242.

21. *Letter to Clerselier,* June 1646, IV, p. 447; *Principles,* I, art. 49. [In the *Principles*] Descartes enumerates on the same plane, as eternal truths, the following "common notions" or "maxims": the principle of contradiction, what has been done cannot be undone, he who thinks cannot fail to be or exist while he is thinking, etc., all propositions necessarily derived from the idea of the infinite being (cf. *Principles,* art. 7 and 10); cf. also art. 75: "We shall know first of all that we exist, insofar as our nature is to think, and that there is a God upon whom we depend; and after having considered his attributes, we shall be in a position to inquire into the truth of all other things, since God is their cause. In addition to the notions we have of God and of our thoughts, we shall likewise find in us a knowledge of many propositions that are eternally true, for example, that nothingness cannot be the cause of anything whatsoever." In this way the first notions that are above doubt—Cogito, God, cause, being, exclusion of nothingness—are linked to one another. Cf. *Geometrical Summary, Replies to Objections II,* postulate 3.

22. This is a problem that we have examined in the work we are preparing on the metaphysics of Malebranche. According to Malebranche, the Cogito is based on the principle, "nothingness has no properties," or nothingness is indivisible (*Entretiens sur la métaphysique et la religion*

[available as *Dialogues on Metaphysics* (New York: Abaris Books, 1980)], I, sec. 1). The final edition of the *Recherche de la Vérité* specifies that this principle is "the first principle of our knowledge," from which the following principle of the Cartesians is deduced: "one can certify that something conceived clearly and distinctly is contained in the idea that represents it." *Recherche de la Vérité* [available as *The Search after Truth* (Columbus: The Ohio State University Press, 1980)], IV, chap. 6, sec. 3; ed. Lewis [2d ed. (Paris: Vrin, 1962)], II, p. 58.

23. *Replies to Objections II*, IX, p. 119; *Entretien avec Burman*, V, p. 161.

24. *Replies to Objections IV*, VII, p. 249, ll. 8-13; IX, p. 192; *To Morus*, 5 February 1649, V, p. 272, ll. 21-26; *To Mersenne*, 15 April 1630, I, p. 146; *To Arnauld*, 29 April 1648, V, p. 224.

25. Cf. Boutroux, *De veritatibus aeternis apud Cartesium* [trans. G. Canguilhem (Paris: Alcan, 1927)], pp. 23 seq., 84: "God does not admit anything repugnant to his perfection, meaning that excludes *absolute contradiction*. As for the things that proceed from him, they can be contradictory among themselves, meaning *relatively*." Cf. also Laporte *[Le Rationalisme de Descartes* (Paris: Presses Universitaires de France, 1945)], p. 171, who cites this text, ibid., n. 6; Gouhier ["Les Exigences de l'existence," see above, n. 14], pp. 29-30.

26. "As for the difficulty in conceiving how God could have been free and indifferent toward making it not be true that the three angles of a triangle were equal to two right angles, or in general that contradictories could not be true together, we can easily dispel this difficulty by considering that the power of God cannot have any limits, and that our mind is finite and so created as to be able to conceive as possible things that God has wished truly to be possible, but not to be able to conceive as possible things which God could have made possible, but which he has, in fact, wished to make impossible. The first consideration shows us that God could not have been determined to make it true that contradictories cannot be true together, and therefore that he could have done the opposite. The second consideration shows us that even if this were true, we should not try to understand it because our nature is incapable of doing so." *To Mesland*, May 1644, IV, p. 118, ll. 6-25.

27. "Certainly our ideas depend on things, insofar as they represent them, but nonetheless, there is no contradiction in things, but only in ideas, because it is only our ideas that we judge repugnant among themselves. And things are not repugnant among themselves, because they can all exist, so one thing is not repugnant to another. It is the opposite for ideas, because in them we judge of different *(diversas)* things that are not contradictory separately, but we judge them in such a way as to make a unity of them. This is the origin of contradiction." *Entretien avec Burman*, V, p. 161. The contradiction in our understanding would therefore be the sign that God has given us in order to recognize truly different beings—meaning separate beings. That is exactly the role that we see contradiction play with respect to body and soul. But God can, if he wishes it, unite substances that we judge separate or separate modes from their substances, which we judge inseparable. *Replies to Objections IV*, VII, p. 249; IX, p. 192.

28. *To Arnauld*, 29 June 1648, V, p. 223. The example of a mountain without a valley is Descartes' traditional example of contradiction. In the ontological proof, since the necessity for existence to be included in God's essence is assimilated to the necessity that makes it impossible for a mountain to be without a valley, we can be tempted to believe that this necessity is like mathematical or logical necessity, and not absolute necessity, but relative to God's decree giving rise to the eternal truths. But Descartes simply wished to establish that all necessity perceived in my understanding, whether absolute and immanent in God, or relative to me and decreed by God, must prove its objective validity. Consequently, the ontological proof does not escape this requirement any more than mathematical or logical proofs do.

29. "But we have to recall the rule already stated, that we cannot have knowledge of things except by the idea we conceive of them, and consequently, that we must not judge of them except in accordance with these ideas, and we must even think that everything repugnant to these ideas is absolutely impossible and entails a contradiction. Thus we have no reason to assert that there can be no mountain without a valley, unless we see that their ideas cannot be complete when we consider the one without the other, even though we can, by abstraction, obtain the idea of a mountain as an upward slope without considering that the same slope can be traveled downhill." *To Gibieuf,* 19 January 1642, III, p. 478. It is the same case for the notions of action and passion, which are, like those of mountain and valley, only two names for one and the same thing. Cf. *To Hyperaspistes,* August 1641: "But I have always thought that it was one and the same thing that is called an action in relation to a *terminus ad quo* and a passion in relation to a terminus ad quem: if that is so, it is repugnant that there should be a passion without an action." III, p. 428; *Treatise on Passions* [I], art. 1.

30. *Letter to Mesland,* 9 February 1645, IV, pp. 161 seq.; *Replies IV,* IX, pp. 191 seq. The substantial union constitutes *an exception* with respect to the general laws of possibility that are valid for our understanding. Descartes explains this exception to the law in the same way as Malebranche, by means of the principle of the best.

31. "That they are inseparable implies a contradiction." *To Gibieuf,* 19 January 1642, III, p. 478.

32. *To Chanut,* 6 June 1647, V, pp. 51-52.

33. *To Morus,* 5 February 1649, V, p. 273; *Principles,* I, art. 26; *Replies to Objections I,* IX, pp. 89-91; *To Mersenne,* 28 January 1641, III, p. 294.

34. Not the problem of the antinomy between the continuous and discontinuous, the simple and the complex, but that of the antinomy between infinitely continuous divisibility and infinite effectively realized divisibility, a difficulty which is referred in Leibnizian philosophy, to the conflict between the ideal and the actual, and that is resolved, by Leibniz, by means of the distinction between these two points of view and his positing the monad.

35. *To Morus,* 5 February 1649, V, p. 273; *Principles,* II, art. 34.

Chapter XI. The Realm of the Imagination: The Probability of the Existence of Material Things

1. "Et quidem jam ad minimum scio." VII, p. 71, l. 14; IX, p. 57.

2. *Rules,* Rule 12, X, pp. 412-17.

3. *Studium Bonae Mentis,* X, pp. 200-201.

4. "When imagining [the mind] turns toward the body and considers in it something conformable to the idea that it has either formed by itself or received through the senses." VII, p. 73, ll. 18-20; IX, p. 58.

5. The *Rules* specifically apply the term "imagination" to the faculty of creating new shapes: "If it applies itself in order to create new ideas, it is said to imagine or to conceive." Rule 12, X, p. 416. The mental force applying to shapes preserved in corporeal imagination is called the faculty of remembrance, ibid. If we understand by imagination that part of the body (the brain) in which common sense etches the shapes that are impressed in it by the action of the senses, imagination is confused with corporeal memory. *Rules,* Rule 12, X, p. 414: "This, then, is what is called memory."

6. *Meditation VI,* VII, p. 72; IX, p. 57. Imaginative clearness and distinctness therefore consist in transforming the idea by giving it a definite contour, by making it like "something one can touch and see," *Rules,* Rule 12, X, p. 413, ll. 6-7, thus rendering it "more lively and expressive." That is how imagination helps the intellect: "If the intellect proposes to

examine something that can be related to body, it should produce in the imagination the most distinct idea of it possible." Ibid., pp. 416-17. "The body—meaning extension, shape, and movement—can also be known by the understanding alone, but it can be known much better by the understanding helped by imagination. *To Elizabeth,* 28 June 1643, III, p. 691, l. 22. "This distinct idea of corporeal nature that I have in my imagination," *Meditation VI,* VII, p. 73, l. 25; IX, p. 58. But since imagination cannot allow one to know clearly and distinctly these ideas except through the real vision of their details, it does not allow one to recognize and distinguish them except externally, and within extremely tight limits, meaning, as long as we are concerned with a notion that offers few details. However, the understanding, by allowing us to know the internal reason of notions, allows us to distinguish them immediately without risk of error and regardless of their degree of complication. That is why imaginative representation, in spite of its sensible clearness and distinctness, is obscure and confused with respect to the understanding.

7. *To Mersenne,* July 1641, III, p. 395, ll. 14-16.

8. *Meditation VI,* VII, p. 73; IX, p. 58; *Rules,* Rule 12, X, pp. 416 seq. The most illuminating text is the *Entretien avec Burman:* "When external objects act on our senses, they trace on them an idea, or rather an image of themselves; and when the mind turns toward images thus traced on a small gland, it is said to have a sensation. And when these images are traced on the small gland, not by external bodies, but by the mind itself, which, in the absence of external objects, represents them to itself and shapes them in the brain, it is then said to *imagine. . . .* The difference between *sensation* and *imagination* consists in this alone: in the former, images are traced by external objects, with these objects present, while in the latter they are traced by the soul without external objects, and as if with windows closed. This makes it clear why I can imagine a triangle, a pentagon, and similar shapes, but not, for example, a chiliagon. For, since my mind can easily trace three lines in the brain and construct a figure from it, it can easily have knowledge of them and thus imagine a triangle, a pentagon, etc. But it cannot, however, trace and form a thousand little lines in the brain without confusion; and this is why it cannot imagine a chiliagon distinctly, but only in a confused manner. This limitation is so great that we have difficulty in imagining even a heptagon or an octagon. The author, who is a fairly imaginative man, and who has trained his mind in this for a long time, can imagine these figures reasonably distinctly; but others lack this ability. From this we see in what way these little lines are present with respect to the mind, and the extent to which the mind needs a particular concentration in order to imagine and consequently to have knowledge of the body." V, p. 162. Omitted from this text is the imaginative faculty of sensible ideas, in which images, having been traced by external objects, are perceived again by the soul turning toward them when the objects that caused them have become absent, and the mental effort is directed to the trace present on the brain; the soul then does not attempt to modify the brain in order to impress a trace upon it.

9. *Meditation VI,* VII, p. 73, ll. 20 seq.; IX, p. 58.

10. *Discourse,* 6th pt., VI, p. 76, ll. 6-28; *Principles,* IV, art. 205; *Rules,* Rule 12, p. 411, l. 17, to p. 412, l. 13. See above, vol. I, chap. v, sec. 22, and vol. II, chap. ix, n. 5.

11. *Meditation III,* IX, p. 31.

12. "Tanquam clausis fenestris," V, p. 162.

13. "One can generally call passion all the thoughts that are aroused in the soul by impressions on the brain alone, without the concurrence of will, and consequently, without any action of the soul; for whatever is not action is passion. . . . When the soul, on the other hand, uses the will to determine itself to something that is not just intelligible, but imaginable, this thought makes a new impression on the brain; this is not a passion in it, but an action that is properly called imagination." *To Elizabeth,* 6 October 1646, IV, p. 310, ll. 16-21, p. 311, ll. 8-13. The involuntary revival of traces in dreams or in spontaneous memory is

a passion. Ibid. It is completely the effect of a corporeal mechanism. Imagination, as a mode of the understanding in us, is an action, since the understanding is "the force [vis—M. G.] by which we know." *Rules,* Rule 12, X, p. 415. In addition, the understanding can "act on the imagination." Ibid., p. 416. Then how could Descartes have affirmed that my understanding was passive, and have drawn from the passivity of the understanding in the knowledge of the idea of God the thought of the correlative existence of an active being as external cause of his idea (namely God)? That is because we must distinguish two orders of activity and passivity. Insofar as it does not depend upon the intervention of some external cause for me to conceive or imagine an idea, and insofar as I draw everything from myself, I am active. But I am passive insofar as what I draw from myself has been placed by God in me and has a nature such that I cannot change it in any way. However, this passivity of the understanding has no relation with the passivity of sensation, for it is not sensed, but perceived by the intellect. And if it is stripped of all affectivity, that is because in this passion my nature has not experienced any action of a thing opposed to its nature. That is why an external, purely spiritual correlative (namely God) can be concluded from this purely spiritual passivity. On the other hand, that I sense this or that, depends on an external cause, and the action exercised here stems from a thing whose nature is opposed to mine; that is why this passivity is affective. And that is why I conclude from this affectivity a correlate that is a cause foreign to the *nature* of my soul—the body. With respect to this affective passivity, my understanding appears always as active and spontaneous; and from this activity proceeds the imaginative *action* or *effort.* But given the evidence, we would never be able to derive from this spiritual action an external cause, whether spiritual or not, because we always need a passion in order to arrive at an active cause. Cf. below, vol. II, chap. xiv, n. 5.

14. *Meditation VI,* VII, p. 73, ll. 20-21; IX, p. 58.

15. VII, p. 74, ll. 1 seq.; IX, p. 58.

16. VII, p. 74, ll. 3-4.

17. Ibid., ll. 4-6.

18. VII, p. 75, ll. 16-18.

19. VII, p. 74, ll. 6-10.

Chapter XII. The Realm of the Senses: The Certainty of the Existence of Material Things

1. *Replies to Objections VI,* VII, pp. 436 seq.; IX, p. 236. The first element is still "unknown" here.

2. *Meditation II,* IX, p. 25. Descartes rediscovers here the sensible element, the unbreakable constituent of representation, which the preliminary steps of the analysis had isolated as such in *Meditation I* (at the same time as the mathematical elements) and which he had, until now, excluded from the circle of science. Cf. above, vol. I, chap. ii, n. 7.

3. This will also be, in other respects, Dilthey's preoccupation (to discover the unified life above the fragmentation of constructed concepts) and Husserl's (to return to the authentic transcendental subjectivity, the source of perfect objectivity, by setting aside the various layers of interpretation that habit has rendered unconscious), etc. Because it recognizes different regions, that is, a plurality of immediate givens, Husserlian phenomenology is closer to the Cartesian point of view than is Bergsonian psychology. However, the term "immediate given" ought to be used with reservation with respect to Husserl, who is mostly interested in the manner in which the immediate given is given originally to consciousness; there are not only several orders, but several meanings of immediate given in Husserl's philosophy. Similarly,

in Fichte's philosophy, the Pure Self as transcendental *ego* is immediately given by intellectual intuition, without however being a given, since it is *Tathandlung* and not *Tatsache,* and sensation is an immediate given, without however being immediate as is intuition, since it is given only through the cooperation of the original *Tathandlung.*

4. We ought not lose sight that, in Descartes' philosophy, among the immediate givens is free will, which is also a "primitive notion" (the term that replaces *immediate given* in Descartes' philosophy; cf. III, p. 259, and *Principles,* I, art. 39). But free will belongs to the founding act upon which the construction of the edifice of science belongs, and not to the foundation upon which the edifice is supported. We have seen above [vol. I, chap. iii] that the first part of the *Principles* took free will as the foundation of the Cogito, precisely because it is situated first from the point of view of the founding act. It is notable, but also natural, that Bergson contrasts this immediate given to others in Descartes' philosophy, that he sees in it and in what it implies (the indeterminism of human actions, true succession, and continuously creating God) a general anticipation of the true philosophy, which is his own, that is, the philosophy of pure duration. The path of universal mechanism, as Descartes understands it, implies on the contrary, that *everything is given,* and leads to the negation of the point of view of true freedom, meaning, it leads to the death of philosophy, which thus becomes the study of old errors. *Evolution créatrice* [1st. ed. (Paris, 1907)], pp. 373-74. Brunschvicg's interpretation is exactly opposite to this. Brunschvicg sees in the theory of the creative freedom of eternal truths the remains of a primitive mentality in contrast to the new spirit of modern mathematics; cf. *L'Esprit européen,* [Neuchâtel: La Baconnière, 1947], p. 97. The statement of the theory of the free creation of eternal truths cannot be read by a Cartesian without experiencing "a feeling of scandal." Ibid. That is because, for Brunschvicg, the only immediate given is mathematical intelligence, not as a static and passive faculty, but as an active spiritual activity in perpetual progress with respect to itself, and indefinitely creative of new concepts. The judgments of these noted authors with respect to Descartes are most valuable as a function of their own doctrine. However, we have seen, in chap. vi [above, vol. I], in the section on the discontinuity of time, that Bergson's thesis contains a large measure of truth.

5. *Meditation VI,* VII, p. 74, ll. 11-16; IX, p. 59.

6. VII, p. 74, ll. 17-28, p. 75, ll. 1-15; IX, p. 59.

7. VII, p. 75, ll. 8-14; IX, p. 59.

8. *Principles,* II, art. 2.

9. *Meditation III,* VII, p. 38, ll. 15 seq.; IX, p. 30.

10. *Meditation VI,* p. 75, ll. 14-20; IX, p. 60.

11. VII, p. 75, ll. 20-23; IX, p. 60.

12. *Meditation III,* VII, p. 38, ll. 20-23; IX, p. 30.

13. *Meditation VI,* VII, p. 75, ll. 23-29; IX, p. 60.

14. Ibid., VII, p. 76, ll. 2-3; IX, p. 60.

15. VII, p. 76, ll. 3-4; IX, p. 60.

16. VII, p. 76, ll. 4-6; IX, p. 60.

17. VII, p. 76, ll. 6-20; IX, p. 60.

18. *Meditation III,* VII, p. 38, ll. 11 seq.; IX, p. 30: "The first of these reasons is that it seems to me that this is taught to me by nature."

19. Ibid., VII, p. 38, ll. 22 seq., p. 39, ll. 1-5; IX, p. 30.

20. Ibid.

21. VII, p. 39, ll. 6 seq.; IX, p. 31.

22. *Principles,* II, art. 1; *To Hyperaspistes,* III, pp. 428-29.

23. *Meditation VI,* VII, p. 76, ll. 21; IX, p. 61.

24. Ibid., VII, pp. 76-77; IX, p. 61.

25. VII, p. 76, l. 7; IX, p. 61.

26. VII, p. 77, ll. 18-27; IX, p. 61.

27. This argument recurs five times during the *Meditations: II,* VII, p. 24, ll. 23-24; IX, p. 19; *III,* VII, p. 39, ll. 8 seq.; IX, p. 31; VII, p. 46, ll. 29 seq.; IX, p. 37; VII, p. 49, ll. 12-20; IX, p. 39; *VI,* VII, p. 77, ll. 23-28; IX, p. 61.

28. *Meditation III,* VII, p. 39, ll. 8 scq.; IX, p. 31.

29. VII, p. 39, ll. 15-29; IX, p. 31.

30. *Meditation VI,* VII, p. 77, l. 28, p. 78, l. 1; IX, p. 61 (our emphasis).

31. VII, p. 80, ll. 11-26; IX, pp. 63-64.

Chapter XIII. Proof of the Real Distinction between Soul and Body

1. *Meditation VI,* VII, p. 78, ll. 2-20; IX, p. 62.

2. Ibid., VII, p. 78, ll. 21 seq., p. 79, l. 16; IX, p. 62.

3. "Generally, what constitutes the nature of a thing is always there while it exists." *To Gibieuf,* 19 January 1642, III, p. 478, ll. 18-20.

4. "Because they can be posited separately, at least by means of God's omnipotence, and it does not matter by what power this separation can be accomplished in order to require me to judge them different." *Meditation VI,* VII, p. 79, ll. 6-8; IX, p. 62; *To Regius,* June 1642, III, p. 567, ll. 10-26.

5. *To Elizabeth,* 28 June 1642, III, p. 694.

6. "It implies a contradiction that they [these substances—M. G.] are inseparable." *To Gibieuf,* 19 January 1642, III, p. 478.

7. "And we must note that I used God's omnipotence to derive my proof, not because there is a need for some extraordinary power to separate the mind from the body, but because, treating only God in the preceding propositions, there was nothing else from which to derive this. But our knowledge of the real distinction of the two things is unaffected by any question as to the power that separates them." *Replies to Objections II, Geometrical Summary,* prop. IV, VII, p. 170; IX, p. 132. "And even if God had united a body to a soul so closely that it was impossible to unite them further, and had made a single composite thing out of two, we also conceive that they would remain *really distinct* from one another, notwithstanding the union; because, however closely God connected them, *he could not set aside the power that he possessed of separating them, or keeping them apart one from the other,* and those things that God *can* separate or keep one without the other are *really* distinct." *Principles,* I, art. 60 (our emphasis). "Whatever can exist separately is substance, not accident. And it makes no difference if it is said that real accidents cannot naturally be separated from their subjects, but only by divine power; for coming to pass naturally is nothing other than coming to pass by God's ordinary power, which does not differ from his extraordinary power, and which does not place anything new in things, and thus does not change their nature; so that, since everything that can be naturally without subject is a substance, everything that can be without subject by the power of God, as extraordinary as that power can be, must also be called substance." *Replies to Objections VI,* VII, p. 434, l. 25, p. 435, ll. 1-8; IX, p. 235. The same reasoning is valid with respect to the possibility that God can separate the accidents of substance by his omnipotence, accidents that my understanding conceives as necessarily inseparable; cf. *Replies to Objections IV,* VII, p. 249, ll. 9-13; IX, p. 192.

8. *Meditation VI,* VII, p. 78, ll. 13 seq.; IX, p. 62.

9. *To Morus,* V, p. 273, ll. 13-17.

10. "From the fact that we often see two thing conjoined, we cannot draw from that that they are one and the same thing; but from the fact that we sometimes notice one of them

apart from the other, one can rightly conclude that they are diverse. And God's omnipotence should not prevent us from drawing this conclusion; for it is not less repugnant to think that things we conceive clearly and distinctly as two diverse things are made into one thing in essence without any composition than to think that we can separate what is not distinct." *Replies to Objections VI,* VII, p. 444, ll. 21 seq.; IX, p. 242.

11. Cf. the *Letter to Mesland,* 9 February 1645, IV, pp. 167 seq., in which transubstantiation is explained by the Cartesian conception of the substantial union of soul and body, and the *Replies to Objections IV,* in which Descartes applies, with respect to the possibility that omnipotence can separate the accidents of substance, what he has stated about the possibility that this omnipotence can unite substances among themselves: "And we ought not infer, from what I said about modes not being conceived without some substance in which they reside, that I have denied that they can be separated by God's omnipotence, because I firmly hold that God can make an infinity of things that we are not capable of understanding or conceiving." *Replies to Objections IV,* VII, p. 249, ll. 9-13; IX, p. 192; *Replies to Objections VI,* VII, pp. 434-35; IX, p. 235.

12. Merleau-Ponty, in *La Structure du comportement* [Paris: Presses Universitaires de France, 1952], rightly notes: "Descartes has not sought to integrate the knowledge of truth and the experience of reality, intellection and sensation. [For Descartes] they are not tied together in the soul, but in God. But after him, this integration will appear as the solution of the philosophical problems posed by realism" (pp. 267-68). Spinoza specifically criticizes the Cartesian conception of the substantial union of soul and body in the name of this integration; and that is what weakens the legitimacy of his critique, for this integration is precisely what is in question.

13. "Descartes' *Metaphysical Meditations* are entirely constructed so as to demonstrate the real distinction of soul and body, which is the foundation of the physical geometry of extension and movement. In order for soul to be really distinct from body, body must exist really; that is why Descartes' metaphysics cannot be completed without a demonstration of the real existence of the external world." Gilson, *Etudes sur le rôle de la pensée médievale dans la formation du système cartésien* (Paris: [Vrin], 1930), p. 300. "Descartes needs a real external world in order to prove the real distinction of soul and body." Ibid., p. 301. "Constructed "Constructed with an absolute logical rigor, the metaphysics of the *Meditations,* however, end up with what one can call the *Cartesian paradox.* The conclusion toward which it leads as a whole is the real distinction of soul and body. This distinction first supposes that we have distinct ideas of soul and body, then that souls really exist, and finally that bodies really exist. And since we cannot prove the real existence of bodies except by relying on what is confused and involuntary in sensible knowledge, we must suppose a kind of violence inflicted on thought from the outside, a kind of confusion of natures that explains the confusion of knowledge. As a result, the Cartesian proof for the existence of an external world seems to imply as an essential element the union of soul and body. But since the proof of existence has no other end than to establish the real distinction between soul and body, we must go so far as to assert that the proof of their distinction relies on the fact of their union." Ibid., p. 225. Gilson sees in this paradox one of the basic defects of Descartes' thought, one that is at the heart of all idealism: "The difficulty resides in Descartes' very thought, and no person in the world, no one who is inside Descartes' thought could cover one end of the difficulty without uncovering the other end." Ibid., p. 310.

14. In his *Commentaire au Discours de la Méthode* [Paris: Vrin, 1925], Gilson identifies real and existing: "A real distinction implies the *reality* of things distinguished. Therefore, if we placed in doubt the *existence* of body, it is no longer sufficient to have proven the existence of thought, nor even its complete independence of body, in order to have proven the *real* distinction of soul and body; we must also lift the doubt with respect to the *existence* of body by proving the *reality* of the external world. It is because these two theses are unable

to be dissociated that *Meditation VI* is entitled: *De rerum materialum existentia et reali mentis a corpore distinctione*" (p. 309). There is an obvious misreading here: *Realis* does not have the sense of *existens* in Descartes' philosophy. That can be supported fully by the texts, the following in particular: "Thus all the demonstrations of mathematics deal with real entities and objects; and thus the object of mathematics . . . is a *true and real entity (ens verum et reale)* that has a *true and real nature* just as much as the object of physics itself. The only difference is that physics considers its object not just as *a true and real entity,* but also as something *actual and existing as such (qua tale existens)* while mathematics considers its own as something possible. . ." *Entretien avec Burman, Meditation V,* V, p. 160 (our emphasis).

Moreover, Gilson has partially corrected himself in his *Etudes sur le rôle de la pensée médiévale dans la formation du système cartésien* (Paris, 1930). There he opposes a *real* distinction of things as substances as a rule (which establishes a merely *possible* distinction as a fact) and a real distinction as a fact (supported by the *demonstrated existence* of bodies, which would be truly real). *Etudes,* p. 304. However, we can find no trace of a real distinction as rule and a real distinction as a fact in Descartes' writings. And we will see later that if we do not find them, that is because we *should not find them.*

15. *Geometrical Summary, Replies to Objections II,* prop. IV, VII, pp. 168-69; IX, p. 131; *Principles,* I, art. 60: "We can conclude that two substances are really distinct from one another from the sole fact that we can conceive one clearly and distinctly without thinking of the other; for, in accordance with the knowledge we have of God, we are certain that he can make everything of which we have a clear and distinct idea."

16. *To Mersenne,* 24 December 1640, III, p. 266, l. 9. Cf. *Replies to Objections IV,* VII, p. 219, ll. 10-16; p. 226, ll. 8-9; IX, pp. 171, 175. Descartes does not indicate there that the proof of the distinction of soul and body can only be achieved in *Meditation VI* because the existence of body would be necessary for this.

17. Therefore it is not the doubt that weighs on the existence of external things, as Gilson thinks *(Commentaire),* but the doubt that weighs on divine veracity that does not allow the proof of the distinction of substances to be possible until the end of *Meditation II.* The two texts quoted by Gilson—*Replies VI,* VII, p. 224, ll. 8-26, and *Replies V,* VII, p. 357, ll. 7-10—do not contain even the least reference to the necessity of proving the existence of bodies in order to establish that they are really distinct from mind.

18. Gilson *[Commentaire],* p. 304.

19. Ibid., p. 306.

20. At least with respect to *finite* essences.

21. "Everything in these ideas is *necessarily* in things." *To Gibieuf,* 19 January 1642, p. 474, ll. 18-20 (our emphasis).

22. *Principles,* I, art. 60 (our emphasis).

23. Gilson *[Commentaire],* p. 244.

24. Ibid., p. 304.

25. *Replies to Objections VI,* VII, p. 440, ll. 1 seq.; IX, p. 239; *To Elizabeth,* III, 28 June 1643, p. 693, ll. 21-26; *Replies to Objections VI,* VII, p. 228, l. 27, p. 229, ll. 1-2; IX, p. 175.

26. *Meditation VI,* VII, p. 78, l. 21, to p. 79, l. 6; IX, p. 62.

27. *Meditation VI,* VII, p. 79, ll. 6 seq.; IX, p. 63.

Chapter XIV. Proof of the Existence of Material Things

1. *Meditation VI,* VII, p. 78, ll. 21-30, p. 79, l. 1-6; IX, pp. 62-63.

2. Ibid., VII, ll. 6-14; IX, p. 63.

3. Ibid., VII, ll. 14-21. Let us recall that there are two different meanings of the word *formal:* formal cause, which is a cause not greater than its effect, and formal reality, the reality of a thing outside its idea, an idea whose representative content constitutes its *objective reality.* (In addition, we know that formal cause can be contrasted with efficient cause, insofar as it designates the cause as reason or as essence. In God, formal and efficient causes are not distinguishable, cf. *Replies to Objections IV.)*

4. Ibid., VII, ll. 14-28, p. 80, l. 1-4.

5. Passion is the character of all knowledge, whether it is intellectual or sensible. Even the knowledge of our activity is a passion. "We can generally call . . . passions [of the soul—M. G.] all kinds of perceptions or items of knowledge that are in us, because often it is not our soul that makes them as they are, and because it always receives them from things that are represented by them." *Passions of the Soul,* I, art. 17. "It is certain that we would not be able to will anything without perceiving by the same means that we will it; and although with respect to our soul it is an action to will something, we can say that it is also a passion in it to perceive that it wills. However, because this perception and this will are really one and the same thing, the more noble always supplies the denomination, and thus we are not in the habit of calling it a passion, but only an action." Ibid., art. 19. "Just as it is not properly speaking an action but a passion of wax to take on various shapes, so it seems to me that it is also a passion of the soul to receive this or that idea." *To Mesland,* 2 May 1644, IV, p. 113, l. 24 seq. "Intellection and volition differ only as the action and passion of a single substance. Intellection properly speaking is the passion of the soul, and will is its action; but since we do not will anything without at the same time knowing by the understanding what we will, and we scarcely ever understand something without having at the same time some volition, it is not easy to distinguish action from passion in this matter." *To Regius,* May 1641, III, p. 372.

6. There are three senses of the word *passion* in Descartes: 1) an extremely general sense that concerns all knowledge; 2) a more restricted sense that concerns all thoughts received in the soul in virtue of impressions in the brain; 3) an even more restricted sense that concerns what we ordinarily understand by passions, that is, what concerns the thoughts arising from a particular agitation of the mind. Cf. *Letter to Elizabeth* of October 1645, IV, p. 310, ll. 16-27, p. 311, ll. 1-23.

7. *Meditation III,* IX, p. 29.

8. Ibid., p. 30.

9. Malebranche, *Recherche de la Vérité* [available as *The Search for Truth* (Columbus: Ohio State University Press, 1980)], I, chap. 1; *Réponses à Arnauld* [Paris, 1709], Recueuil I, pp. 365-68; [Recueuil], IV, pp. 40-41, p. 93; *Entretien sur la Métaphysique* [available as *Dialogues on Metaphysics* (New York: Abaris Books, 1980)], II, sec. 11; *Entretien sur la mort* [Paris], 1703, II, pp. 362-64; *Réponses à Régis* [1693-94], II, sec. 14.

10. *Principles,* I, art. 10. We ought to note that Descartes does not posit the correlative action of passion solely in virtue of the intrinsic necessity of the relation action-passion, but in virtue of a psychological consideration: there is in us a passive faculty that effectively enters into the game, but it would not enter into the game and would remain useless if there were not an active faculty that gave it the occasion to be exercised: "But I could in no way use it if there were not in me . . . another active faculty capable of forming and producing these ideas." *Meditation VI,* VII, p. 79, l. 9.

11. *To Hyperaspistes,* 27 July 1641, III, p. 428; *Treatise on Passions,* [pt. I], art. 1, [IX]. With respect to the necessary bond between mountain and valley, cf. *To Gibieuf,* 19 January 1642, III, p. 478. What is said there about action and passion must also be valid for cause and effect, as is proved by the reduction of everything worthy of the name to a formal cause or *ratio* and the instantaneousness of the cause, or the simultaneity of cause and effect, VII, pp. 108, 165, 236, 240-41.

12. *Meditation VI,* VII, p. 79, ll. 13-14; IX, p. 63. The specification "As long as I am only a thing that thinks," does not occur in the Latin text.

13. In his *Reply to Arnauld,* Descartes has given the best formulation of this doctrine: "We ought to note that we have an actual knowledge of acts or operations of our mind, but not always of its faculties or powers, except potentially. So that when we are about to use some faculty, as soon as the faculty is in our mind, we acquire an actual knowledge of it; that is why we can assuredly deny that it is in the mind, if we cannot acquire this actual knowledge of it." VII, p. 246, ll. 21 seq., p. 247, ll. 1-2; IX, p. 190.

14. "The whole difficulty they contain [the questions about the way the soul moves the body, and the way in which it can receive the kinds of corporeal objects—M. G.] arises entirely from a false supposition, that cannot in any way be proven, namely, that if the soul and body are two substances diverse in their nature, that prevents them from being capable of acting on each other." *To Clerselier, On Objections V,* VII, p. 213, ll. 18-23. The fact of substantial union suppresses the problem of the incommensurability of the two substances.

15. "Without my contributing to them in any way, and even against my will." VII, p. 79, l. 13.

16. *Objection of Gassendi,* VII, p. 293, l. 11; *Letter of Hyperaspistes,* III, p. 404, l. 19.

17. *Replies to Objections VI,* VII, pp. 436-39; IX, pp. 236-39.

18. It is true that for Fichte, according to the standard of reflection, this nonself can appear in turn as God himself or as a sensible thing.

19. *To Elizabeth,* 28 June 1643, IV, pp. 691-92.

20. *Replies to Objections II,* VII, p. 135, ll. 19-26 (IX, p. 127), p. 165, ll. 13-27; texts quoted by Gilson in *Etudes sur le role de la pensée medievale dans la formation du système cartésien* (Paris: Vrin, 1930), p. 301.

21. *Meditation III,* VII, p. 43, ll. 10-13; IX, p. 34. Gilson writes, "If we wish to summarize the contents of the *Meditations* in a saying that is as simple as possible, we could say that it can be reduced exclusively to an exhaustive explanation of the contents of the Cogito by means of the principle of causality. Within the thought that grasps itself are located: the idea of the soul that is explained by the existence of the thinking substance, the idea of the extended body that is also explained by the existence of the thinking substance capable of forming it, and the idea of God that is explained only by an eminent cause, God himself." *Etudes,* pp. 300-301. This reflection requires some cautions. The principle of causality cannot alone suffice to advance the explanation of the idea except with respect to the idea of God, but not with respect to ideas of finite things (and in particular the idea of an extended thing whose objective reality is not explained by the existence of the thinking thing, but by God who has placed it in me). Gilson adds in a note: "there is, in fact, more formal reality in the soul than objective reality in the idea of body, and consequently, the soul *is sufficient* for forming the clear and distinct idea of extended body with three dimensions." Descartes says only "and consequently, the soul *could* suffice to form. . . ." ("Quantum autem ad ideas rerum corporalium, nihil in illis occurit quod sit tantum ut non videatur a me ipso *potuisse* proficisci.") The consideration of the quantity of objective reality in addition to the definition given by Descartes about the causal relation therefore allows only the indication of a minima and sine qua non condition, but not a sufficient condition, of the cause to be discovered: consequently, it allows only the consideration of the multitude of causes that can fulfill this minimal condition. The condition becomes sufficient only for the idea of God in which the required *minimum* is precisely the *maximum*. And since there is only one absolute *maximum,* the cause is at the same time determined necessarily in a precise manner.

22. See n. 5 of this chapter.

23. Let us recall that in the *Meditations* Descartes distinguishes ideas from other facts

of consciousness and that they add something by "the action of the mind." *Meditation III,* IX, p. 5. Passion, taken in itself, is never deceptive; all errors depend on action, that is, on free will. Descartes' assertion, "all passions are good" (*Treatise on Passions,* art. 211) has therefore an extremely general validity and concerns sensitivity as well as affectivity. Moreover, since passion refers our understanding to action (or to the agent, with respect to the patient), as necessarily as the mountain refers to the valley, it is necessary for our understanding that the intellectual constraint of pure idea and the affective constraint of sensation both refer to an active thing that is the cause of these passions. In one case that will be God, and in the other case, body. From this we see that it is impossible to prove God's existence, at least a posteriori, except by means of a passion in us. This is another reason for condemning all the interpretations that make will, which is action, a path allowing us to go out from ourselves and to posit God as agent of the idea we have of him. Clear and distinct ideas other than those of God refer, however, to essence-things that God has implanted in us—these ideas being completely merged with the essence-things, once they have been invested with their objective validity. The difference between the objective reality of ideas and the intelligible formal reality of essences that they reflect is practically unassignable. It is only a difference of reason that vanishes once the objective validity of the ideas is manifest for science. Cf. on this topic, the text on idea as picture and idea as essence, above, vol. I, chap. iv, sec. 15, and chap. viii, sec. 14, 16.

24. *Meditation V,* VII, p. 67, ll. 5 seq.; IX, p. 53. "They are not figments of my imagination, even though it is in my power to think them or not to think them"; they have their own true and immutable nature, "a nature, form or essence, . . . which is immutable and eternal, which I have not invented, and which does not in any way depend on my mind." *Meditation V,* VII, p. 64, ll. 9 seq.; IX, p. 51. "Whether I wish it or not, I recognize that the properties of such a triangle are in it." Ibid., VII, p. 64, ll. 21-22; IX, p. 51.

25. *Meditation III,* VII, p. 43, l. 31, p. 44, ll. 1-8.

26. "The nature of soul . . . is more noble than it [body—M. G.]." *To Elizabeth,* 15 September 1645, IV, p. 292, ll. 6-8.

27. Cf. the comparison with the blind man: "When he touches bodies with his stick . . . [these bodies — M. G.] making the stick move variously according to the various qualities in them, move the nerves of his hand by the same means, and then [they move] the places in the brain from which these nerves come; this gives his soul an opportunity to sense as many various qualities in these bodies as there are variations in the movements caused by them in his brain." *Dioptrics,* 4th Discourse, VI, p. 114.

28. Cf. above, sec. 3 of this chapter.

29. Malebranche, *Recherche de la Verité,* Eclaircissement VI: "Even though it is evident that God is not a deceiver, and that we can say that he would be deceiving us effectively if we deceived ourselves by making the use that we ought to of our mind and the *other faculties of which he is the author* . . ." (ed. Lewis [2d ed. (Paris: Vrin, 1962)], III, p. 29; our emphasis). What Malebranche contests is the invincible character of the inclination that leads us to believe that bodies are the cause of our sensations; and if the inclination is not invincible, God could not guarantee it (ibid., p. 30).

30. Cf. O. Hamelin, *Système de Descartes* [Paris: Alcan, 1911], p. 253, and especially Gilson: "The divine guarantee for the evidence can cover, in Cartesianism, the whole proof of the evof sensations by geometrical extension is itself a clear and distinct idea." *Etudes,* p. 311. "Spinoza modifies the form of the divine guarantee of evidence in order not to force its meaning at the decisive moment when it will have to guarantee an inclination that is not a clear idea." Ibid., p. 308. "The evidence of a truthful God can indeed guarantee, in Cartesianism, the truth of clear and distinct ideas . . . but what clear and distinct idea will it guarantee with respect to the existence of bodies? . . . An inclination to conclude is not a clear idea and therefore does not have any guarantee from God." Ibid., p. 307.

31. "Saltem," VII, p. 80, ll. 7-8; IX, p. 63.

32. Ibid., p. 80, ll. 4-10; IX, p. 63 (our emphasis).

33. VII, p. 80, ll. 11-14; IX, p. 63. *Less clearly and distinctly,* because these are secondary qualities, which, in their very representation, do not involve anything with respect to the essence of body, while the particular magnitudes of sensible things such that they appear to me (so that they are subjective to the extent that they are the obscure and confused expression in my soul of cerebral traces determined by these things in me and not the authentic image of these things themselves) involve a determination of magnitude and shape that is referred to extension, the real essence of bodies, to a geometrical idea that belongs to pure understanding. Light and sound, etc., correspond to the geometrical variations of bodies without representing in themselves anything geometrical to the mind.

34. VII, p. 80, l. 14.

35. VII, p. 80, ll. 15-19; IX, pp. 63-64.

36. Cf. above, vol. II, chap. xiv, sec. 3 and 5.

37. VII, p. 81, ll. 17-22; IX, p. 64. "For, as long as we merely believe that there is something I know not what in objects (that is, in things such as they are) that causes these confused thoughts in us which we call sensations, we do not go wrong; on the contrary we guard against error in advance." *Principles,* I, art. 70. "And although when approaching the fire I sense heat, and even though in approaching it a little too close I feel pain, there is still no reason that can convince me that there is something in the flame similar to the heat, any more than to this pain; I only have reason to believe that there is something in it, whatever it may be, which arouses in me these sensations of heat and pain." VII, p. 83, ll. 6-12. The notions of sign and of occasional, nonexemplary cause are linked indissolubly, since the sign perceived by me has no resemblance to its cause, given that it draws its whole physionomy from myself and not from the cause.

38. The true innate ideas are, as we see, clear and distinct ideas, for they are in the soul in virtue of its intellectual nature, that is, they are in the understanding alone. Consequently they are immortal, as is the soul. On the contrary, the innate ideas of my composite nature, since they are contingent with respect to my soul, whose nature is only pure understanding, must disappear from my mind once body is destroyed and survive in it only from the moment when my mind is substantially united to my body. Since they are perishable like body, they are innate only in the second degree, and we ought to call them congenital, rather than innate.

39. *To Mersenne,* 22 July 1641, III, p. 418, ll. 5-8; *Notes against a Program,* VIII, pt. 2, p. 358, ll. 20-30, p. 359, ll. 1-5; *Dioptrics,* 6th Discourse, VI, pp. 134-37.

40. Cf. above, vol. I, chap. v, sec. 3; vol. II, sec. 3 of this chapter.

41. *Meditation III,* IX, p. 30.

42. Objective reality can be counted as a fourth element; but we discover it in all ideas and not just in sensation.

43. With respect to the use of figurative processes in order to express geometrically the difference of the qualitative *varietas,* cf. *Rules,* Rule 12, X, p. 413.

44. VII, p. 80, ll. 11-26; IX, p. 63, from "However, they perhaps are not," to p. 64: "I have in me the means to know them with certainty."

45. On one hand, God's veracity is invoked to assure me that I can correct my opinion relative to particular things revealed by the senses, that is, I can elevate myself to a real physics, which is amenable to extension alone, and not to the composite of mind and body. On the other hand, the definition of nature referred to the veracious God concerns the set of teachings of the senses relative to my composite nature. The correlative association and disassociation of the two aspects is particularly manifest in VII, p. 81: "Moreover," l. 15, to "are not similar to them," l. 22; and p. 82, l. 25, from "And this nature," to "But I have already," p. 83, l. 23.

46. E. Gilson, *Etudes,* pp. 312-13.

47. *Rules,* Rule 6, X, p. 383.

48. Ibid., Rule 12, p. 418.

49. E. Gilson, *Etudes,* p. 313.

50. *Letter to Clerselier on Objections V,* IX, pp. 210-11.

51. *Rules,* Rule 12, X, p. 418.

52. *Replies to Objections II,* IX, p. 121.

53. *Principles,* II, art. 64; IX, pt. 2, p. 102. The use of the "geometrical" method in the *Meditations* implies the absolute generalization of this method relative to the precepts of the *Discourse,* for there is no question of measure or shape in this case. This generalization supposes that we have penetrated the *spirit of geometry.* Moreover, it is this penetration that allows the algebratization from which analytic geometry has arisen. That is how Descartes' assertion that there is not even one out of a hundred Scholastic philosophers who understands the *Elements* of Euclid must be understood, for he wrote to Elizabeth (November 1643, IV, p. 42, l. 6) that "experience has allowed me to know that most of the minds that can easily understand the reasoning of metaphysics cannot conceive those of algebra, and reciprocally that those who easily understand the latter are incapable of conceiving the former." He adds that those who are incapable of generalizing Euclid's geometry through algebra are novice geometers: "To look for construction and demonstration by means of Euclid's propositions while hiding the processes of algebra is only an amusement for novice geometers, an amusement that does not require much thought or science." Ibid., p. 47, ll. 2 seq. Finally, this algebratization of geometry is needed in order to follow a perfectly analytic method in mathematics, and if "the ancient geometers followed only synthesis in their writings," it is not because "they were unaware of analysis entirely, but, in my opinion, because they reserved it for themselves alone, as a secret of some importance." *Replies II,* IX, p. 122. This is clearly a debatable opinion, and more so since algebra was an Assyrian science foreign to Greek science in antiquity. But the exactness of the historical assertion does not matter here. The whole difficulty of the *Meditations* arises from 1) its application of the geometrical method to metaphysical matters, a disconcerting application for the Scholastic metaphysician who is a stranger to the true spirit of geometry, meaning to algebraism, which requires the *maxima* generalization of this method (which must procede here through the understanding alone, without any help from imagination); from 2) the fact that they procede on the analytic path alone—which excludes the statement of "definitions, postulates, axioms, theorems, and problems," statements reserved for the synthetic method (*Replies II,* ibid.); from 3) the fact that metaphysical notions that are incompatible with the imagination and the senses, cannot be acquired and kept save by a constant battle against sensation and passions; from this arises a psychological tension and a process of elevation and initiation with affinities to religion (cf. vol. I, chap. i, sec. 3; vol. II, chap. xxi, sec. 5). That is how the mathematical process, which, as Descartes emphasizes, is the frame of the work, remains at first quasi-invisible.

54. Gilson, *Etudes,* pp. 305-15.

55. Spinoza, *Ethics,* V, Preface.

56. Ibid., I, iii, prop. 2, Scholium.

57. *To Elizabeth,* 28 June 1643, V, pp. 692 seq.

58. Spinoza, *Ethics,* I, i, prop. 12.

59. *Meditation V,* IX, p. 55.

60. *Meditation V,* VII, pp. 68-69; IX, p. 54.

61. In Fichte's second philosophy.

62. Fichte, *Grundlage der Gesamten Wissenschaftslehre (Sämtlische Werke* [1794]), I, p. 301, etc.

63. *Summary of the Meditations,* VII, p. 15, l. 26, p. 16, ll. 1-8; IX, p. 12.

64. *Meditation IV,* VII, p. 59, l. 2; IX, p. 47.

65. *Meditation V,* VII, p. 68, ll. 21-23; IX, p. 54.

66. Cf. above, vol. II, chap. ix, sec. 1.

67. Malebranche, *Recherche de la Vérité,* Eclaircissement VI, III, ed. Lewis [2d ed. (Paris: Vrin, 1962)], pp. 31-32.

68. Malebranche, *Recherche de la Vérité,* I, chap. 1, sec. 2, [ed. Lewis] p. 8.

69. *To Mesland,* 9 February 1645, IV, p. 173.

70. IX, p. 12.

71. Malebranche, ibid.

Chapter XV. Proof of the Union of Soul and Body

1. *Letter to Elizabeth,* 21 May 1643, III, pp. 666-67, and *Replies to Objections VI:* "Examining first the notions or ideas of each thing that I discovered in me, then carefully distinguishing them from one another in order that my judgments can have a complete relation with them." VII, pp. 440, ll. 14-17, p. 445, ll. 19-22; IX, pp. 239, 243.

2. "I call false [the idea of cold—M. G.] because, since it is obscure and confused, I cannot discern whether it represents something that is positive or not, outside my understanding. . . . I do not say that it is materially false because of some positive being, but only by obscurity, which nevertheless has as subject and foundation some positive being, namely sensation itself. And truly this positive being is in me to the extent that I am a true thing; but the obscurity, which gives me occasion to judge that the idea of this sensation represents something outside of me that I call cold, arises only from the fact that my nature is not completely perfect." *Replies to Objections IV,* VII, p. 233; IX, p. 161. From all evidence, in order to know clearly and distinctly an idea whose objective reality is infinitely small, requires an infinite understanding that we do not possess. This doctrine could entail that God has a merely intellectual knowledge of sensation. Thus, in Malebranche's philosophy, God knows our pain, not insofar as he senses it, but insofar as he has an idea of it; and for Leibniz, the infinite understanding unfolds the confusion, and perceives clearly and distinctly the most intimate details within it. Moreover, as we shall see later on, this imperfection of my nature entails more elements than the simple finiteness of my understanding. But Descartes does not explain further the question of how God can know in himself the pain in us. Moreover, the composite substance is *in itself* obscure and confused.

3. *Meditation VI,* VII, p. 81, ll. 20-22; IX, p. 64. "Like something I know not what." *Principles,* I, art. 70.

4. *Replies to Objections VI,* VII, pp. 438-39; IX, pp. 237-38.

5. *Letter to Elizabeth,* 21 May 1643, III, pp. 665-68.

6. *To Elizabeth,* 28 June 1643, III, pp. 692-95.

7. "When we assert that the certainty of the understanding is greater than the certainty of the senses, our words mean no more than that the judgments we form when we are older . . . are more certain than those we formed in our childhood without reflection; this cannot be doubted, for it is clear that here there is no question of the first and second degree of sensation, *since there can be no falsity in them." Replies to Objections VI,* VII, pp. 438-39; IX, pp. 237-38. "Those who make judgments about things by impulse are led to a belief without being convinced by reason, but reach it either by some superior force, or by their own free will, or by the state of their imagination. *The first type of impulse never deceives,* the second rarely, and the third almost always." *Rules* Rule 12, X, p. 424. The assertion that material things exist as causes of my sensations, the localization of my sensations at the place where the body is affected and not elsewhere, enters into the case of the first type, which is the result of a law instituted by God.

8. See below, vol. II, chap. xviii, sec. 6.

9. *Meditation VI*, VII, p. 80, ll. 20 seq.; IX, p. 64.

10. VII, pp. 80-81; IX, pp. 64-65.

11. VII, p. 83, ll. 16-19; IX, p. 66.

12. "Satis clarae et distinctae." VII, p. 83, l. 19.

13. *Meditation VI*, VII, p. 81, ll. 11-14; IX, p. 64.

14. *To Regius*, January 1642, III, p. 493, ll. 14-17; *Meditation IV*, VII, p. 81, ll. 6-11.

15. *Replies to Objections II*, VII, p. 147, ll. 9-11; IX, p. 115.

16. *Rules*, X, p. 420.

17. *To Elizabeth*, 21 May 1643, III, p. 667; *Principles*, I, art. 48.

18. *Replies to Objections II*, VII, p. 147; IX, p. 115.

19. "The sense perceptions were given to me only to indicate to my mind which objects are useful or harmful to the composite body of which it is a part, and are, for that purpose, sufficiently clear and distinct." VII, p. 83, ll. 16-19.

20. *Principles*, I, art. 66, 68.

21. *Rules*, Rule 12, X, p. 420. Perhaps Laporte expresses himself in too sharp a manner when he writes: "Like all primitive notions, it [the notion of the union of soul and body— M. G.] is simple; since it is simple, it is known absolutely and completely once it is touched by the mind in the least fashion, . . . it does not contain anything that can remain hidden when our attention is brought toward it." *Le Rationalisme de Descartes* [Paris: Presses Universitaires de France, 1945], pp. 250-51. It is true that Laporte specifies that the content of the knowledge *(permixtio)* is extremely confused. However, he adds that the notion of the union of soul and body "does not teach us less evidently, therefore clearly, that this *permixtio* exists. Thus it is a primitive notion." But can we identify the clear and distinct knowledge of the existence of something with the knowledge of a simple nature "known absolutely and completely once it is touched, and containing nothing in it that is hidden from one's notice"? Of course it is evident that, when sensation has been stripped bare and everything that the understanding adds to it has been removed, there remains nothing, *in this respect*, that is hidden from one's notice. But the authentic and indubitable result obtained is no less something opaque in itself, which has some unknown and unknowable substrata, since it involves something "I know not what." *Principles*, I, art. 70. And no effort of attention could make the mind penetrate it. This opacity, which contains some mystery, arises from the fact that the soul no longer deals only with itself or only with extension, but with this sui generis mixture, which in itself is completely disconcerting for our understanding. Moreover, let us note that the text of the *Rules*, invoked by Laporte on this occasion, concerns only the three simple intellectual natures—pure understanding, extension alone, and common notions. The text does not mention the fourth simple notion mentioned in the *Letter to Elizabeth* of May 1643, which is the simple, nonintellectual notion of the composite substance. Malebranche, who makes sensation into a mode of the soul considered alone, will make of it, on the other hand, something which, although obscure and confused, does not involve anything unknown, does not have anything hidden, and reveals itself immediately as it is. *Recherche de la Vérité* [available as *The Search after Truth* (Columbus: Ohio State University Press, 1980)], I, chap. 8, sec. 2-4. That is a natural consequence of the rejection of composite substance, which leads to a very different interpretation of article 68 of *Principles*, I.

22. Cf. above, vol. I, chap. iii, sec. 9.

23. *Principles*, I, art. 70.

24. *Meditation VI*, VII, p. 76, ll. 6 seq.; IX, p. 60.

25. *Replies to Objections IV*, VII, p. 233; IX, p. 161.

26. *Meditation VI*, VII, p. 83; IX, p. 66.

27. "Naturam strictius sumo," VII, p. 82, l. 15.

28. VII, p. 82, ll. 25 seq.; IX, p. 65.

29. "Ordinem naturae pervertere," VII, p. 83, ll. 12-22; IX, p. 66.

30. VII, pp. 436-39; IX, pp. 236-39.

31. We use the word *nature* in the sense of sensation, composite substance, nature in the narrow sense: "Compositum ex mente et corpore," VII, p. 82, l. 24.

32. See above, this chapter, sec. 1.

33. *Meditation VI*, VII, p. 80, ll. 20-26; IX, p. 64.

34. Descartes will explain why this teaching is not *absolutely true*, but only *as true as possible* (the maximum possible), cf. below, vol. II chap. xviii, sec. 3.

35. "It is the almost common vice of all imperfect knowledge to assemble several things into one and to take them all for one and the same thing; that is why it is necessary to take the trouble to separate them and distinguish them from one another by means of a more precise examination." *Replies to Objections VI*, VII, p. 445, ll. 19-22.

36. *Meditation VI*, VII, p. 80, ll. 15-19; IX, p. 63.

37. *Meditation VI*, VII, p. 79, l. 27, to p. 80, ll. 1-4; IX, p. 63.

38. Ibid., VII, p. 83, ll. 15-19; IX, p. 66. The French text specifies, "these sensations or perceptions"; *eatenus* is rendered by "until now."

39. VII, p. 82, ll. 25-26; IX, p. 65.

40. Similarly, the relation of cause to effect tends toward a minimum, since cause is no more than an occasion.

41. Cf. above, vol. II, chap. xiv, sec. 11.

42. Except in the sense of psychological presence in me, cf. above, this chapter, sec. 1.

43. The sensation of substantial union is for Malebranche an illusion due to original sin. Cf. *Recherche de la Vérité,* Preface (ed. Lewis [2d ed. (Paris: Vrin, 1962)], I, p. viii).

44. We ought to note that Descartes accounts for the relativity of quality for my composite nature by appealing solely to the constitution of our body. Qualities or sensations "which truly represent nothing to us that exists outside our thought" are "varied according to the diversities that are encountered in movements that go from all places of our body to the place in the brain to which the soul is closely joined and linked." *Principles*, I, art. 71. This explanation is imposed by the nature of things such as Descartes perceives them; since the soul is indivisible, the relativity of qualities can only be explained by the variety of the portion of divisible extension to which the soul is linked as with a receptor organ.

45. VII, p. 80, ll. 20-26; IX, p. 64 (our emphasis).

46. Moreover we have seen that, in conformity with the medieval theory of transcendental predicates, Descartes identifies *ens, verum,* and *bonum*. This does not prevent him from distinguishing them also.

47. From which arises the thesis that "all passions are good." Of course, sensation is not for Descartes the same thing as the sensation of nature is generally for the authors at the end of the eighteenth century. The only common trait is that for both it is considered as infallible, guardian, like the voice of God itself. But, for Descartes, nature as the world of sensation is strictly limited to the sphere of man, since the sphere of the universe, of minds as well as bodies, is foreign to him—the former is only pure intelligence, and the latter pure extension and movement. And sensation cannot enable us to communicate with pure minds or with external nature, that is, with the universe of inert or living bodies (animals), which cannot be considered as a whole more or less penetrated with life, in the psychical sense of the word. Since sensation exists for us alone and concerns only us, it encloses us rigorously within the limits of our composite nature.

48. Cf. above, vol. I, chap. vii, sec. 9.

49. Cf. the perceptive article of Jean Laporte, "La Finalité chez Descartes," in *Revue d'Histoire de la Philosophie,* October-December 1928.

50. *Principles*, I, art. 28; III, art. 1 to 3.

51. Ibid., III, art. 1. This text is difficult to reconcile with the affirmation of a finite and imperfect work. Cf. above, vol. I, chap. vii, sec. 6, and vol. II, chap. x, sec. 3.

52. Ibid., art. 2. This article reestablishes the agreement with the thesis of the finiteness of the world. Cf. above, ibid.

Chapter XVI. Of the True and of the False in the Realm of the Senses, First Problem: Formal Error of Judgment—the Analysis of the Concept of Nature

1. *Meditation VI,* VII, pp. 82-83; IX, pp. 65-66; *Replies to Objections VI,* VII, pp. 438-39; IX, pp. 237-38.

2. *Principles,* I, art. 70-71; *Replies to Objections VI,* ibid.

3. *Meditation VI,* VII, p. 82, ll. 15-31, p. 83, ll. 1-2; IX, p. 65.

4. "In order that there should be nothing in this that I do not conceive *sufficiently distinctly,* I should define precisely what I mean when I say that nature teaches me something. For here I am using nature in a stricter sense than when I use it to mean an assemblage of everything God has given me, seeing that this assemblage includes many things which pertain to the mind alone, to which I do not intend to refer here when speaking of nature—as, for example, my knowledge that what has been done can never not have been done, and other similar truths known to me by the light of nature. Such an assemblage also includes many other things that belong to body alone and are not included here under nature, such as its quality of being heavy and many other similar ones; for I am not concerned with these either, but only with those things that God has presented to me as being composed of mind and body." *Meditation VI,* VII, p. 82, ll. 12-26.

5. *Meditation VI,* VII, p. 83, ll. 14-23; IX, p. 66.

6. "Thus I see that both here and in many other cases. . ." (ibid., ll. 14 seq.); the statement refers to previously given examples—belief that heat exists in fire, that the void exists in spaces in which I find nothing that excites and moves my senses, etc.

7. "Because . . ." ibid., ll. 15 seq.

8. That will be the hypothesis, examined later on by Descartes, concerning the example of the clock. VII, p. 84, ll. 17 seq.; IX, pp. 67-68.

9. *Meditation VI,* VII, p. 75, ll. 23 seq.

10. Descartes, *Dioptrics,* 6th Discourse: "It is the soul and not the eye that sees." VI, p. 141, ll. 7-8.

11. "It [the soul—M. G.] sees immediately only through the intermediary of the brain." Ibid., ll. 8-9. "It is the soul that sees, even though it is through the intermediary of the eyes." *To Christina,* 20 November 1647.

12. Descartes renders his thought more specific in the *Letter To Elizabeth* of 25 May 1643, using his well-known distinction about the three primitive notions—extension or body, thought or soul alone, and soul united to a body, a union that is "my nature." "The notion that the force the soul has to move the body and the body to act on the soul by causing its sensations and passions" depends on the notion of union. And he adds, "I consider also that *all human science consists only in clearly distinguishing these notions, and in attributing each of them only to the things to which they belong.*" Thus we are mistaken each time that we try to explain one of these notions by means of another or explain a difficulty by a notion that is not the one it entails. For example, when we try to explain the nature of the soul by geometrical and physical notions, we are mistaken in confusing the notion of the soul almoved by another by the way the soul moves the body, or the way the soul moves the body by the way a body moves another, we are mistaken in confusing the primitive notion of body alone with the primitive notion of the composite substance of soul and body. The false notion of weight is the mixture of elements derived from the experience of our power to move bodies with properly physical elements—in brief, it arises from the confusion

of the composite substance soul-body and the substance body alone, although weight as movement of body toward the center of the earth is explained entirely by body alone, that is, by extension and movement, etc. *To Elizabeth,* III, pp. 665 seq. See also the letter of 28 June 1643, pp. 690-95, and the end of the *Replies to Objections VI.* What we commonly call "man's nature" by reference to his nature in the broad sense, is most often only the confusion of the three notions, which are absolutely distinct from one another; concerning weight, see *To Elizabeth,* 25 May 1643, p. 667; *Principles,* IV, art. 20-27; *To Arnauld,* 29 July 1648, V, pp. 222-23.

13. Kant, *Prolegomena to Any Future Metaphysics,* Introduction, Academy ed., IV, p. 263: ". . . either all or nothing."

14. Descartes, *Discourse,* 3d pt.: "It suffices to judge well in order to act well." VI, p. 28, ll. 9-10. "All sins are ignorance." *To Mersenne,* 27 April 1637, I, p. 366, ll. 10-11.

15. Malebranche will add a third category, that of the "splendid men" *(Méditations chrétiennes* [1683], sec. 19), which includes Descartes and the Cartesians. The latter believe that the transformation of man, the passage from disorder to order, from the rule of obscurity and confusion to that of clarity and distinctness is accomplished naturally and depends only on man. Reason for them is only a natural light proper to man instead of being the light of God himself, enlightening man from above. Moreover, for them the knowledge of the truth is sufficient to engender good conduct, although, with respect to the judgment of love, the adherence of will to the true good supposes, in addition, the intervention of the grace of sensation, which is necessary in order to neutralize the attraction of the senses. The latter, which is capable of deferring the assent of will, gives to the clear vision of the good the time to be obscured and to the senses the opportunity to carry it off. The dependence of man with respect to body (obscuring by the senses, rebellion of the senses, enslavement by the passions), which for Descartes derives from purely natural causes (habits, inattention, weakness of our mind) and must be fought against by purely natural means (effort of attention, effort to detach oneself from the senses, perspicacity, sagacity, etc.), for Malebranche derives from an ethico-religious cause (original sin) and a supernatural cause (God's will to put an end, after the fall, to Adam's privilege of being respectfully warned by the senses, and of never being subject to their independent or rebellious action). Hence there results, in order to reestablish man's independence, the necessary intervention of a historical ethico-religious event (the advent of the Christian mind, from the supernatural fact of redemption, of incarnation, and the actual intervention of an effect of which Jesus Christ is the occasional cause: medicinal grace). We understand, under these conditions, that the passions cannot be said to be "all good," as Descartes affirms on the naturalist plane. They were originally all good, *in man in the state of nature,* meaning in Adam before sin. They are actually perverted because man has fallen. Malebranchian psychology therefore unfolds on the plane of a fallen nature, and not on the plane of a normal nature, since nature is no longer normal. Thus is introduced within the science of sensibility and passions a supernatural ethico-religious factor, which profoundly modifies the whole internal economy of Cartesianism. From this arises in Malebranche's philosophy an extremely complicated and varied theory of disorders and perversions in the different regions of God's work. We describe these theories in a work in progress on *The Metaphysics of Malebranche.* For Descartes, nature is *actually* basically good, and the cause of its depravation is not an ethico-religious event situated at the basis of the history of man, but a purely human and natural fact. It is in that sense that the philosophers of the eighteenth century will be closer to Descartes—for example, for Rousseau, socialization, the principle of the degradation of the state of nature, will hold the place that sin holds for Malebranche. Cf. Burgelin, *La Philosophie et l'existence chez J. J. Rousseau* (Paris: [Presses Universitaires de France], 1952), p. 77.

16. Cf. below, chap. xx, sec. 3.

17. See above, vol. I, chap. vii, sec. 12.

18. *Replies to Objections VI,* IX, pp. 234-40; *Principles,* I, art. 71.

19. Cf. above, vol. I, chap. ii, sec. 4.

20. This delimitation of faculties and their competence, of the constitutive realities of human beings and of their boundaries is implied in the definition that Descartes gives to human science. *To Elizabeth,* III, p. 665; *Replies to Objections V,* VII, p. 440, ll. 10-29; IX, p. 239. However, the distinction of the various faculties must not allow the unity of the soul to be lost from sight: "He claims that there are as many faculties in us as there are different things to know. But such a way of speaking seems to me quite useless. . . . That is why I prefer to conceive . . . that the soul acquires all its knowledge by the reflection that it makes, either on itself, for intellectual things, or on the various dispositions of the brain to which it is joined, for corporeal things. . . . But it is very useful not to accept any belief without considering in what name and for what cause one accepts it   which comes to the same as what he has stated, that one must always consider what faculty one is using, etc." *To Mersenne,* 16 October 1639, II, p. 598, ll. 10 seq.

21. "In the previous discussion I have already sufficiently explained how it happens, despite God's goodness, that falsity occurs in my judgments." VII, p. 83, ll. 24-25.

Chapter XVII. Of the True and of the False in the Realm of the Senses, Second Problem: The Intrinsic Falsity of the Senses—Internal Conditions of the Psychophysical Substance. The Union of the Soul with Every Part of the Body

1. As Descartes understands that word. Today we would say *practically.*

2. VII, p. 83, ll. 26-29; IX, p. 66.

3. "Nova hic occurrit difficultas." VII, p. 83, l. 26.

4. VII, p. 84, ll. 1-7; IX, pp. 65-67.

5. VII, p. 84, ll. 8-10.

6. Ibid., ll. 10-15.

7. That is why, in the same way that animals must be reduced to machines, since everything in them are only modes of extension governed by the laws of mechanics, reciprocally, machines made by men must be considered as natural things, for they function only in virtue of the laws of mechanics that govern physical nature: "I do not recognize any difference between the machines made by artisans and the various bodies that nature alone composes, except that the effects of machines depend only on the use of certain tubes, or springs, or other instruments, which, needing to have some relation with the hands of those who make them, are always so large that their shapes and movements can be seen, whereas the tubes and springs that cause the effects of natural bodies are normally too small to be perceived by our senses. And it is certain that all the things that are artificial are natural in this way. Thus, for example, when a clock marks the hours by means of the gears by which it is made, it is not less natural for it to do so as it is for a tree to bear fruits." *Principles,* IV, art. 203.

8. On the comparison of the corporeal machine with a clock, cf. *Discourse,* 5th pt., VI, p. 59; *Treatise on the Description of the Human Body,* XI, p. 226.

9. VII, p. 84, l. 15, to p. 85, l. 17; IX, pp. 66-67.

10. Expression from *Meditation IV,* VII, p. 55, ll. 1-13; IX, pp. 43-44.

11. *Meditation IV,* VII, p. 55, l. 3; and above all *To Mersenne,* May 1630 (?): "And then you ask me about the perfection of dumb animals and what becomes of their souls after death. That question is not outside my competence, and I reply that God leads everything

to its perfection—everything taken *collectively* and not each thing in particular. The very fact that some particular things perish and other are born in their place is one of the principal perfections of the universe." I, p. 153.

12. *To Mesland,* 9 February 1645, IV, pp. 166-67; *To Mesland* (1645-46?), p. 346; *The World,* IX, p. 15.

13. *Letter to Plempius,* 3 October 1637, I, p. 413, l. 12. Cf. Epicurus, *Letter to Herodotus,* sec. 65; Lucretius, *De Natura Rerum,* pt. III, ll. 125 to 580; Gassendi, *Objections V,* VII, pp. 269-71.

14. Neither can the substantiality of a clock be proven by means of its finality: "All the reasons to prove substantial forms could be applied to the form of the clock, which nobody says is a substantial form." *To Regius,* January 1642, III, p. 505, ll. 4-6.

15. *To Mesland,* 9 February 1645, IV, p. 167.

16. *To Mesland* (1645-46?), IV, p. 346. Cf. also *Rules,* Rule 12, X, p. 441, l. 17.

17. *Replies to Objections V,* VII, p. 374, ll. 20-23.

18. Ibid., and *To Regius,* January 1642, III, p. 504.

19. Cf. Leibniz, *Leibniz Philosophischen Schriften* (ed. Gerhardt [Berlin, 1885]), VI, pp. 132-33.

20. *To Morus,* 5 February 1649, V, pp. 276-77. We are concerned there with *equivalent hypotheses,* of which one triumphs over the other because of its greater capacity for explaining the phenomena. We know that in this case we can attain only a moral certainty (that of the decoder), not an absolute certainty. Although physical hypotheses can be transformed into absolutely certain truths by their deduction from an evident principle, the hypothesis of animal-machines cannot be; it is only a "cipher" allowing one to interpret their behavior from the outside. See above, vol. II, chap. x, sec. 3. This hypothesis is not an invention of Descartes, but an idea current at the time, cf. R. Lenoble, "L'évolution de l'idée de nature, etc." *Revue Métaphysique* (1953): 121.

21. Descartes allows the words *sensation* and *life* for animals, but under the condition that we understand purely phenomenal materials by them. Thus an animal's sensation would be analogous to nothing other than, for example, the "sensibility" of a litmus solution to acid and ammonia solutions: "I do not deny life to animals, since I regard it as consisting simply of the heat of the heart; and I do not deny them sensation, insofar as it depends on organs of the body." *To Morus,* 5 February 1649, V, p. 278. Cf. also *to Plempius,* October 1637, I, pp. 414-16.

22. *Letter to X***,* May 1638, II, pp. 39-41; *To Morus,* 5 February 1649, V, pp. 275-79; *Discourse,* 5th pt., VI, p. 57; *To the Marquis of Newcastle,* 23 November 1646, IV, pp. 573-76, etc. The argument is directed against Aristotle (*History of Animals,* IX, chap. 47); Lucretius, *De Natura Rerum,* V, ll. 1056-90; Montaigne (*Essais,* II, chap. 12 [ed. Strowsky (Bordeaux: Pech, 1906-33)]), II, p. 177); Charron (*De la Sagesse* [1601], I, chap. 8).

23. *To Newcastle,* 23 November 1646, IV, p. 573; *Replies to Objections IV,* VII, p. 229, ll. 10 seq.

24. *To Mesland,* IV, p. 167 (our emphasis).

25. "I judge that the soul's first passion was joy, because it is not believable that it was put in the body at a time when the body was not well disposed for it; and the body being well disposed naturally gives us joy. I say also that love followed because the matter of our body flows endlessly like the water in a stream, and there is always need for new matter to take its place, so that it is scarcely likely that the body would have been well disposed unless there were nearby some matter suitable for food. The soul, uniting itself willingly to this new matter felt love for it; and later, if the food happened to be lacking, the soul would have felt sadness. And if its place was taken by some other matter unfit to nourish the body, it felt hatred for it. Those are the four passions that I think we felt first, and

the only ones we felt before our birth." *To Chanut,* 1 February 1647, IV, p. 604, l. 30, to p. 605, l. 16. We see that passions have exactly the same kind of innateness as sensations properly speaking—it is the innateness of composite nature. Joy is not simply a *truthful testimony* of the suitability of the soul for the dispositions of the body to which it is united, but also an *attraction* that excites in it the desire to do everything in order to maintain these dispositions (love). The passions therefore are at the same time *useful for maintaining life,* "so useful . . . that our soul would not want to remain joined to its body for a single moment, if it did not feel them." *To Chanut,* 1 November 1646, IV, pp. 538, ll. 9 seq. Finality is always, in this realm of composite substance, the mark of all the psychical elements that figure in it. We rediscover in passion the two characteristics proper to these elements, which we had already discovered in sensation: it is something experienced whose validity, restricted to the biological, is in part *information* on the state of the body, and in part *instrument* for the conservation of the body. Moreover, the information in this case is completely subordinate to the utilitarian end (knowledge is subordinate to action). Thus, here again is a perfect contrast with the realm of the understanding alone, in which idea is, on the contrary, completely defined and justified by the knowledge of truth, and action is completely at the service of speculation. Since man is constituted by a pure understanding and a composite substance, we see that the conception of a morality founded on pure science (realm of the understanding alone) but entirely governed by the primacy of happiness in the *present life* (realm of the composite substance) must pose for Descartes some singularly difficult problems.

26. *To Mesland,* IV, p. 166.

27. Ibid., p. 167.

28. "Death never happens through the fault of the soul." *Treatise on Passions,* [pt. I], art. 6, [IX]. Cf. also the *Description of the Human Body,* XI, pp. 224-25. Therefore we could conceive that body continues to function, if the machine were in a good state, after the soul has left: it would function as the body of an animal. But we must conceive that as long as the human body is in good state, meaning disposed in such a way that its union with soul is possible, the soul would not leave it, for there is no sufficient reason for it, in fact, to separate itself from body, God having created the human body in order that it be united with a soul.

29. The materialist argument, based on the example of the clock, is completely valid for animals, as for all automata.

30. III, p. 694; *To Arnauld,* 29 June 1648, V, p. 223; *To Hyperaspistes,* August 1641, III, p. 424; *Replies to Objections V* (Against *Meditation VI*), sec. 4.

31. Gassendi, *Objections V,* VII, pp. 343-44 (our emphasis).

32. *Replies V,* VII, pp. 389-90; *Letter to Clerselier,* VII, p. 213. Cf. *To Arnauld,* 29 July 1648, V, p. 227: "That the mind, which is incorporeal, can move the body, is something shown by no reasoning and no comparison derived from other things that allow us to apprehend it; but nevertheless we cannot doubt it since experiences that are too certain and too evident allow us to know it manifestly every day. And we have to be careful because that is one of those things that are self-evident and that we obscure every time we try to explain it by others."

33. *To Elizabeth,* 28 June 1643, III, p. 694, l. 1. "That is extremely difficult to explain, but experience suffices; it is so clear here that we would not be able to deny it." Cf. *Entretien avec Burman,* V, p. 163.

34. *Meditation VI,* IX, p. 64.

35. *To Morus,* IV, p. 167.

36. *To Arnauld:* "The mind can be called corporeal, since it is united to the body." 29 July 1648, V, p. 223. "Without at the same time denying the substantial union by which the mind is joined with the body, nor the natural aptitude that every part has for this union." *To Dinet,* 1642, VII, p. 585.

37. *To Mesland,* end of 1645, beginning 1646, IV, p. 547.

38. *Treatise on Passions,* XI, p. 351 (our emphasis).

39. *To Mesland,* IV, p. 166.

40. Moreover, the theory of animal-machines assures the perfect functioning and conservation of the machine without any intervention of a soul; we do not see why it is necessary that a soul be introduced in the body (for man) for the proper functioning and preservation of the machine: "I know that animals do many things better than we do, but this does not surprise me. For that can even be used to prove that they act naturally and mechanically, like the clock that marks the hour better than our judgment does." *To the Marquis of Newcastle,* 23 November 1646, IV, p. 575, ll. 21 seq. Here again we should resign ourself to noting the fact. We will find this difficulty considerably worse in Malebranche. However, Malebranche does not give to the union of soul and body the unique reason of the advantages the soul can derive from it for its preservation (moreover he draws several inconsistencies from this); he adds to it a reason of religious order—body is given to the soul as a kind of instrument of pain that allows it, through mortifications, to affirm its spirituality, and to acquire ethico-religious credits. But, because of this double function (biological and ethico-religious) there result several series of inextricable complications. We will develop them in the work we are preparing on the metaphysics of Malebranche.

Chapter XVIII. Of the True and of the False in the Realm of the Senses: Internal Conditions of the Psychophysical Substance—More Particular Union of the Soul with a Part of the Body

1. *Meditation VI,* VII, p. 85, ll. 25-27; IX, p. 68.

2. *Treatise on Passions,* pt. I, art. 30, XI, p. 351.

3. Ibid., art. 31, XI, pp. 351-52.

4. The first corollary is that there can be no error when God has not given us the means to recognize it or redress it, cf. above, vol. II, chap. xvii, sec. 7.

5. II, p. 598, ll. 26-30.

6. VII, p. 85, ll. 27-30, p. 86, l. 1; IX, p. 68.

7. VII, p. 86, ll. 1-13.

8. VII, p. 86, ll. 7-10; IX, p. 68; *Treatise on Passions,* art. 47; *To Plempius,* 15 February 1638, I, p. 523.

9. The argument for the immortality of the soul based on its indivisibility, meaning its immateriality, can only be a subsidiary argument for Descartes, as long as the substantiality of the soul and the real distinction of substances are not established. In the seventeenth century, the demonstration generally in use consisted in proving the immortality of the soul simply by its immateriality; and, since all forms are immaterial, the soul of animals can seem immortal also. Symmetrically, the empiricists, using the continuity between man and animals, between the intellect and the senses, concluded for the destructibility of the human soul in the same fashion as for the soul of animals. Descartes, through his theory of the substantiality of the soul as really distinct from extended substance, and through the reduction of animals to extended machines, destroys the Scholastic and empiricist theses at their foundation; he can believe that, by means of this refutation, he has established the natural immortality of the soul rationally and sufficiently. Cf. with respect to this subject the unpublished thesis of J. Russier, *Le Problème de l'immortalité de l'âme chez Descartes.*

10. VII, p. 86, l. 15; IX, p. 68.

11. Cf. *Replies VI* (Objection VI), IX, p. 240.

12. *Objections V*, VII, pp. 313-14.

13. *To Clerselier*, ibid., p. 213, ll. 16-17. "Of which he has not yet treated" (that will be the object of the *Treatise on Passions*).

14. *Meditation VI*, VII, pp. 86-87.

15. VII, pp. 86-87; IX, p. 65.

16. VII, p. 87, ll. 19-28, p. 88, ll. 15-18; IX, pp. 69, 70.

17. VII, p. 89, ll. 5-8; IX, p. 71.

18. "Physics teaches me that . . ." VII, p. 87, l. 5; IX, p. 69. "As an infinity of experiences testify . . . " VII, p. 68, l. 18; IX, p. 69. "Experience allows me to know that all the sensations that nature has given us are such as I have just stated . . ." VII, p. 87, ll. 25-26; IX, p. 72. On these experiences: *Principles*, IV, art. 196.

19. *Gassendi's Objection*, VII, p. 344.

20. It is a movement without a transfer; we are concerned with a traction—from this results the absolute instantaneousness of movement. Cf. also *Dioptrics*, 4th Discourse: Of the Senses in General, and 6th Discourse: Of Vision; *To Newcastle*, October 1645, IV, p. 326, ll. 15 seq.

21. J. Laporte, *Le Rationalisme de Descartes* [Paris: Presses Universitaires de France, 1945], p. 236.

22. Ibid., n. 1.

23. *Treatise on Passions*, art. 30.

24. We have seen above (vol. II, chap. xvii, sec. 5) that although finality penetrates the human body completely, it does not intervene as genetic and explicative factor of its organization.

25. *To Chanut*, 1 February 1647, IV, p. 604.

26. *Meditation VI*, VII, p. 81; IX, p. 64.

27. *Treatise on Passions*, art. 31-44. Malebranche denied completely the first aspect of union: "The soul is not scattered through all the parts of body." *Recherche de la Vérité* [available as *The Search after Truth* (Columbus: Ohio State University Press, 1980)], II, pt. 1, chap. 5, sec. 1. He retains only the second: The union of the soul "with a part of the brain that responds to all the parts of the body." Moreover, this union is only a correspondence established externally by God between the modalities of mind and the modalities of this part of the brain, the two substances remaining foreign to one another. Ibid. and *Entretien sur la Métaphysique* [available as *Dialogues on Metaphysics* (New York: Abaris Books, 1980)], IV, sec. 11; VII, sec. 13, etc. Considered in itself, the human body is in no way different from the animal-machine: it is not penetrated by soul.

28. *Meditation VI*, VII, p. 68, ll. 1-13; *Rules*, Rule 12, X, p. 415.

29. VII, p. 87, ll. 19-28; IX, p. 69.

30. VII, p. 89, ll. 8-17; IX, p. 71.

31. *Entretien avec Burman*, V, pp. 163-64; *Principles*, II, art. 37, 42.

32. "We cannot *desire* or imagine anything better." *Meditation VI*, IX, p. 69. Cf. Leibniz, *Discourse on Metaphysics* [1686], I, sec. 1: "That God does everything in the most desirable way."

33. VII, p. 89, ll. 20-28, p. 90, ll. 1-6; IX, p. 71.

34. VII, p. 89, ll. 17-18; IX, p. 71.

35. Ibid., ll. 19-20.

36. "And I should not *in any way* doubt the truth of those things." VII, p. 90, l. 7.

37. VII, p. 90, ll. 12-17; IX, p. 72.

38. *To Elizabeth*, 21 May 1643, III, p. 665, ll. 25-28.

39. *Entretien avec Burman*, V, pp. 178-79.

40. Ibid., V, p. 166.

41. In the same way that he subscribes to the adage: "Good comes from the whole cause, while evil comes from any defect." *To Elizabeth,* January 1646, IV, p. 354, l. 26. Cf. *To Clerselier,* 23 April 1649, V, p. 354; also IV, p. 308.

42. *Principles,* I, art. 60.

Chapter XIX. Some Consequences Concerning Medicine and Morality: Medicine and Morality as Techniques of the Good for the Present Life

1. *To Elizabeth,* 1 September 1645, IV, p. 282, l. 7. It is the start of the *De Vita Beata* of Seneca: "Gallio frater, omnes colunt vivere beate: sed caligant ad pervidendum quid efficiat vitam beatam." Seneca, *De Vita Beata,* chap. 1.

2. *To Elizabeth,* 4 August 1645, IV, p. 264, ll. 7-9, 11-12.

3. *To Elizabeth,* 18 August 1645, IV, p. 277, ll. 17-20; *To Christina of Sweden,* 20 November 1647, V, p. 84.

4. *Discourse,* 6th pt., VI, p. 62.

5. *To Elizabeth,* May 1646, IV, p. 411, ll. 10 seq.

6. *To Elizabeth,* 1 September 1645, IV, pp. 283-87; *To Christina of Sweden,* 20 November 1647, V, p. 85.

7. Descartes sometimes designates the excesses of passion as "illnesses," *Treatise on Passions,* [pt. II], art. 78 [IX]. This word, like the word "remedy," does not have its specific meaning here. Descartes merely uses the traditional terminology of the ancient moralists—for example, Cicero: "Brutus, why has man, composed of body and soul, always searched for the art of healing and preserving the body, which he has attributed to the immortal Gods because of its utility? Why, on the contrary, has the medicine of the soul *(animi medicina)* been so little desired, before being discovered, and so little cultivated afterwards? Why have so few praised it and thanked it, while so many have suspected it and hated it? Is it not because the soul is the judge of the oppression and pain of the body, while the body cannot feel the illness of the soul *(animi morbus)?* Thus the soul brings forth a judgment on itself, while it, who is the principle of this judgment, is ill." *Tusculanes,* III, chap. 1. Compare this with Descartes, *Private Thoughts,* X, p. 215, ll. 11-13.

8. *Discourse,* pt. I, VI, p. 3, ll. 23-24.

9. "It suffices for a philosopher to consider man only in his natural state, insofar as he issues only from it; as for me, I have written my philosophy in such a way as not to shock anyone, and so that it can be received everywhere, even by the Turks." *Entretien avec Burman,* V, p. 159.

10. *To Elizabeth,* 6 October 1645, I, p. 314, ll. 9 seq.; *To Elizabeth,* 4 August 1645, IV, p. 267, l. 24.

11. *To Christina of Sweden,* 20 November 1647, V, p. 82, ll. 15 seq. It is true that Christina had herself requested Descartes to detail his opinion on the supreme good, "in the way that the ancient philosophers had spoken of it"; but it happens that the point of view of the ancients is that of natural light, meaning precisely, as Descartes tells us, the only point of view in which he wishes to be placed.

12. That is how Descartes is distinguished from Aristotle, "who considers the supreme good of human nature in general, meaning the one that the most accomplished of men can have; he was right to constitute it of all the perfections of which human nature is capable, but that does not suit our own usage." *To Elizabeth,* 18 August 1645, IV, p. 276, ll. 3-8. *To Christina,* 20 November 1647, V, p. 82, ll. 24-31.

13. *To Christina of Sweden,* 20 November 1647, V, p. 85, ll. 12-17.

14. *To Chanut*, 1 February 1647: "He does not refuse evils and afflictions because they come to him from divine providence; still less does he refuse the permissible goods or pleasures he may enjoy in this life since they too come from God. He accepts them with joy, without having any fear of evils, and his love makes him perfectly happy." IV, p. 609, ll. 23-29.

15. *To Elizabeth*, 1 September 1645, IV, p. 284, ll. 14-17, 24-30; pp. 286-87.

16. Plotinus, *The Enneads*, I, vi, 8. Cf. Malebranche: "our home is heaven." *Entretiens sur la Mort*, I, ed. Cuvillier [Paris: Vrin, 1961], pp. 199-200.

17. *Treatise on the Passions*, art. 211, 212.

18. *To Chanut*, 1 November 1646, IV, p. 538.

19. *To Elizabeth*, 6 October 1645: "The knowledge of the immortality of the soul, and of the felicity of which it will be capable after this life, might give occasion to those who are tired of this life to leave it, if they were certain that they would afterward enjoy this felicity. But no reason assures them of this." IV, p. 315. "As for the state of the soul after this life . . . setting aside what faith tells us, I agree that by reason alone we can make favorable conjectures and have fine hopes, but we cannot have any assurance. But since natural reason teaches us also that we have always more good than evil in this life, and that we should never leave what is certain for what is uncertain, it seems to teach us that although we should not truly fear death, we should equally never seek it." *To Elizabeth*, 3 November 1645, IV, p. 333, ll. 8 seq.

20. Malebranche, *Méditations chrétiennes* [1683], V, sec. 12.

21. *To Elizabeth*, 15 September 1645, IV, p. 290, ll. 5-7.

22. *To Huyghens*, 13 October 1647, III, p. 580.

23. He follows, in this case, the counsel of Cleanthes on the duties of the consoler: "Sunt qui unum officium consolantis putent illud malum omnino non esse, ut Cleanthi placet." Cicero, *Tusculanes*, III, chap. 31. This advice agrees well with the Cartesian technique that prescribes changing the representation of the thing joined to the passion in order to modify the passion; thus by considering a danger as small, we dispel our fear. *Treatise on Passions*, art. 45. We rediscover here Chrysippus' thesis on the link between passion and judgment.

24. On the defense of "God's cause," cf. *To Gibieuf*, III, p. 238.

25. *Treatise on Passions*, art. 211.

26. *To Chanut*, 1 November 646, IV, p. 538, ll. 9-11.

27. *To Chanut*, 1 February 1647, IV, pp. 607-9. In this way Descartes rejoined to some extent the methods of Ignacius of Loyola. The detachment from the sensible, with respect to spiritual things, seemed to render the Cartesian *Meditations* the antagonist of the "meditations" of Ignacius of Loyola, meaning the opposite of the *Spiritual Exercises* that Descartes had known at La Flèche. Ignacius proposed, in order to engender the force of religious sensation, [that we set out to] have concrete images arise in us—for example, to represent to ourselves the sufferings of Jesus in a vivid manner. *Exercise spirituels*, 1541, third week, first day (p. 226 of the French translation by Jennesseaux, Paris, 1879); fifth day (p. 228). He always wanted one to have a *distinct impression*. Inversely, Descartes states: "If the understanding is concerned with those things in which there is nothing corporeal or similar to the body, it cannot be assisted by these faculties. On the contrary, in order to avoid being hindered by them, it must maintain its independence from the senses, and as far as possible, it must divest the imagination of every distinct impression." *Rules*, Rule 12, X, p. 416. But we are concerned there solely with engendering the clarity of conception. When, on the other hand, we are concerned with engendering a vivid and true religious *sensation*—a passion—love of God, for example—Descartes, like Ignacius, recommends imaginative representation, meaning the concrete representation (by distinct impression) of our union with the infinite being. Cf. *Exercises spirituels*, "Contemplation in Order to Obtain Divine Love," p. 244. Descartes himself notes the divergence of the two paths, the one leading to the representation of truth, the other to the (passionate) love arising from this truth: "It

is true that the soul must be very detached from the traffic of the senses if it is to represent to itself the truths that arouse such a love; that is why it appears that it cannot communicate this love to the imaginative faculty so as to make it a passion. But nevertheless, I do not doubt that it does communicate it." *To Chanut.* Thus the religious life requires, as does the practice of mathematics, but for completely different reasons, and in another way, the simultaneous exercise of pure understanding and imagination. Metaphysics is the only discipline that requires the exercise of understanding alone.

28. Plato, *Phaedo,* 62; Epictetus, *Diatribes,* I, 26, 28, 29; II, 17, 33; Plotinus, *Enneads,* I, 9.

29. *Discourse,* 3d pt., VI, p. 27, ll. 12-21; 6th pt., p. 61, l. 28 seq., p. 62, ll. 1-20; *To Elizabeth,* 6 October 1645, IV, p. 305.

30. *Rules,* Rule 1, X, p. 361, ll. 20-21.

31. Ibid., p. 361, ll. 3-7. The unity of science overlaps the unity of virtue and vice versa. Virtue resides wholly in only one thing: the firmness of a will enlightened by solid judgments. When man aims at this single virtue and wishes above all to increase his natural light, he cultivates science according to its necessary unity, which is the unity of *humana sapientia,* and then his progress becomes considerable. When, on the contrary, he cultivates science by pursuing the satisfaction of this or that particular interest, he gives himself to this or that particular science and breaks the unity of knowledge. Progress is then very meager (*Rules,* Rule 1). Moreover, the diversity of science only manifests the diversity of objects to which it is applied: "All the sciences are nothing more than human wisdom, which always remains one and the same, no matter how different are the objects to which it is applied." (Ibid., p. 360, ll. 3-10.) And, in the same way, the diversity of virtues only manifests the diversity of objects over which virtue extends: "It is the firmness of this resolution that I believe must be taken for virtue . . . but we have divided it into several kinds, for which we have given various names, because of the various objects to which it extends." *To Elizabeth,* 4 August 1645, IV, p. 265.

32. Seneca, *De Vita Beata,* chap. 12 and 13.

33. *To Elizabeth,* 18 August 1645, IV, pp. 275-76. Cf. Seneca, whom Descartes discusses— *De Vita Beata,* in particular, chap. 1 to 5; *To Christina of Sweden,* 20 November 1647, V, p. 83, ll. 20 seq.

34. *To Elizabeth,* September 1646, IV, p. 492; *To Christina,* V, pp. 82-84.

35. *To Elizabeth,* 1 September 1645, IV, pp. 283-86.

36. *To Elizabeth,* 18 March 1645, IV, p. 203; *To Christina,* "From this alone results the greatest contentment of life," p. 82.

37. *To Elizabeth,* 18 May 1645, IV, p. 203; 18 August 1645, IV, p. 286.

38. This is an allusion to a Stoic comparison: in the sphere of morality, the last object of the marksman would be to do everything in order to aim well, not to strike the mark. Descartes is here in agreement with Plutarch (De communibus notiis adversus stoices, 26) against that assertion. Cf. Cicero, *De Finibus,* III, 6, sec. 22, ll. 33 seq.; Alexander of Aphrodisias, *Aporias kai ludeis;* [Arnim], *Stoic. vet. frag.* [Leipzig, 1903-24], II, 16, 61; III, 19. However, elsewhere he often agrees with the properly Stoic thesis—see below.

39. *To Elizabeth,* 4 August 1645, IV, pp. 264-65.

40. Diogenes Laertius, VII, p. 127; Cicero, *Paradoxa,* 2; *Tusculanes,* V; Seneca, *De Vita Beata;* Arnim, *Stoic. vet. frag.,* III, pp. 49-50.

41. Cicero, *De Finibus,* III, sec. 24; Stobeus, *Eclogae (Stoic. vet. frag.,* 208). Cf. also the conception of Antipater, Plutarch, *De communibus notiis,* 27.

42. *To Elizabeth,* 6 October 1645, IV, p. 317, ll. 7-10.

43. *To Elizabeth,* 1 September 1645, IV, p. 283, ll. 23 seq.

44. Ibid., p. 284.

45. Ibid., p. 287; *To Christina of Sweden,* 20 November 1647, V, p. 85.

46. *To Christina of Sweden*, 20 November 1647, V, p. 84.

47. "The soul can have its pleasures apart; but those that are common with the body depend completely on the passions; whoever can most be moved by them is capable of tasting most the sweetness of this life." *Treatise on Passions*, art. 212.

48. *To Elizabeth*, May-June 1645, IV, p. 220, ll. 18-19; *Discourse*, pt. VI, VI, p. 62.

49. Cicero, *De Finibus*, III, sec. 60-61; Diogenes Laertius, VII, 130; Seneca, *De Providentia*, chap. 6, p. 7; *Letters*, 12, 10, 104, 21; Arnim, *Stoic. vet. frag.*, III, 757-68.

50. *To Elizabeth*, 6 October 1645, IV, pp. 315-17; 3 November 1645, p. 333.

51. *Treatise on Passions*, art. 211. Concerning the bad passions, and the necessity for apathy in Stoicism, cf. Arnim, *Stoic. vet. frag.*, III, 443-55. By recommending making a "moderate usage" of the passions, instead of extirpating them, Descartes appears to be closer to the Peripatetics than the Stoics, since the Peripatetics consider even the violent passions as advantageous gifts of nature, as the seeds of all our good actions (Cicero, *Tusculanes*, IV, chap. 19), and wish to curtail them, not to uproot them. Ibid., chap. 20, and Seneca, *Epistles*, 116, 1: "Utrum satius sit modicos habere affectus an nullos saepe quaesitum est: nostri illos expellunt, Peripatetici temperant." The foundations of the Cartesian conception are altogether different, however, for to moderate the passions signifies only regulating them by reason through proportioning their force to the real magnitude of the goods to which they are applied; the excess of a passion applied to a higher perfection is desirable in the eyes of reason. *To Elizabeth*, 18 August 1645, IV, p. 287, ll. 8-11. That is something which differs from the Peripatetic conception of the golden means, for which Descartes has, however, a certain sympathy. Cf. *Discourse*, pt. III, VI, p. 23, ll. 24-31.

52. "We must hold ourselves distant from the empire of Fortune, such that, although *we must not lose occasions to retain the advantages that Fortune offers*, we must not think ourselves unhappy when it refuses them to us" (our emphasis). *To Elizabeth*, September 1646, IV, p. 492, and 1 September 1645, IV, p. 286, ll. 24-31.

53. "Sola sapientia in se tota conversa est." Cicero, *De Finibus*, III, sec. 24, sub finem.

54. "Free will is the most noble thing we can have because it makes us in some way equal to God and seems to exempt us from being his subjects. Consequently, its good use is the greatest of all our goods; it is also the one that is most properly ours and the one that matters most." *To Christina*, 20 November 1647, V, p. 85, ll. 12-19.

55. *To Elizabeth*, 6 October 1645, IV, p. 307, ll. 13 seq. Because of this last trait, Descartes would be opposed to Cleanthes' and Zeno's philosophy, and be nearer to Antipater's, whose formulation is as follows: "Facere omnia ut adipiscamur quae secundum naturam, etiamsi ea non assequamur." Cicero, *De Finibus*, V, chap. 7, sec. 20, sub finem; cf. Plutarch's discussion in the *De Communibus notiis adversus Stoices*, 27; Arnim, *Stoic. vet. frag.* (Antipater), 57-59.

56. In fact, we cannot call Chrysippus' theory technique: it is a theory in which the passions, defined completely as excesses, result from faulty judgments and can be extirpated by rectifying these judgments through reason. No doubt Descartes retains something of that thesis when he considers the false judgments of the respective value of different goods as one of the causes of the excess of passion, and not of passions. But other than the fact that he does not reduce passion to an excess (which defines only their bad usage, and it does not even do this always, for the excess of certain passions is authorized by reason), the technique consists precisely in teaching us how we can acquire good judgments and how we can give will the power to follow them, in order to avoid the impotency that the poet's verse expresses: "Video meliora, proboque, deteriora sequor." One of Spinoza's principal critiques will bear on the insufficiency of technique in Descartes, in this respect, and on its absence in Stoicism. On the defect of technique in Seneca, cf. *To Elizabeth*, 4 August 1645, IV, p. 275, ll. 20-25.

57. "We do not think that wisdom is similar to the art of navigation or medicine, but rather to the acting of the actor about which I am speaking to you, and to the dance: in fact, it has its end in itself, and it does not seek it outside, since this end is the realization of the art." Cicero, *De Finibus*, III, chap. 6, sec. 24. Nevertheless, it is a trait of Stoicism to compare the passions to illnesses, and philosophy to a medicine that heals them. Cicero, *Tusculanes*, IV, chap. 37-38. However, this characteristic of moral philosophy does not constitute for them its essential definition, since the end of virtue is always in itself.

58. Not that we are concerned with contesting the religious sincerity of Descartes in any way. His pilgrimage to Notre-Dame de Lorette would be sufficient to attest to this religious sincerity. But Descartes' enterprise is foreign to religious preoccupation. The fact that he has called upon the benediction of the Virgin on his work is not sufficient to give his enterprise a religious intention and signification. It proves only the importance that this work had for him. The merchant of Nantes who solicited the protection of the Holy Virgin for his ships did not thereby transform his business into an apostolic mission. At the most, we can say that the "enthusiasm" that Descartes feels at the moment he delivers himself to his great scientific enterprise is accompanied with a certain religious exaltation.

59. *To Elizabeth,* 26 June 1643, III, pp. 692-93.

60. *Entretien avec Burman,* V, p. 155; *To Elizabeth,* 28 June 1643, III, pp. 692-93.

61. *To Elizabeth,* p. 695.

62. *Principles,* Preface, VIII, p. 5, ll. 8 seq.

63. E. Gilson, *Discourse, Commentaire [au Discours de la Méthode* (Paris: Vrin, 1925)], p. 93.

64. Kant, *Critique of Practical Reason* [1788], I, 1, sec. 7, scholium 2 of theorem IV.

65. Ibid., sec. 3, scholium 2 of theorem II.

Chapter XX. Some Consequences Concerning Medicine and Morality: Three Ideas of Medicine and Morality

1. Cf. above, vol. II, chap. xix, sec. 2.

2. *Discourse,* 1st pt., VI, p. 10, ll. 9-11.

3. "Since I expected to obtain all the knowledge of which I was capable, I thought, by the same means, that I would obtain all the true goods that would ever be in my power." *Discourse,* 3d pt., VI, p. 28, l. 5. "It suffices to judge well in order to act well." Ibid., p. 28, l. 9; *Replies to Objections II,* VII, p. 166, ll. 3-7; IX, p. 128, art. 7.

4. *Discourse,* 3d pt., VI, p. 22, ll. 23-25; *Replies to Objections II,* VII, p. 149, ll. 3 seq.; *To Buitendjick,* IV, p. 62, l. 5, p. 63, l. 17.

5. *Discourse,* 3d pt., VI, p. 22, l. 24, l. 26-27, p. 25, l. 15; *Treatise on Passions,* art. 60, 63, 170, [IX]; *To Elizabeth,* 10 September 1645, IV, p. 284, ll. 17 to 24; 15 September 1645, IV, p. 284, ll. 20-21.

6. Our emphasis.

7. Discourse, p. 25, ll. 6 seq.; *To Elizabeth,* 4 August 1645, IV, p. 265; 15 September 1645, p. 295, ll. 11-21; *Treatise on Passions,* art. 48, 49; *To Hyperaspistes,* II, p. 34, l. 16, p. 35, l. 8; *Principles,* Preface, IX, 2, p. 13, ll. 17 seq. That is why virtue will combine a double effort, one toward the force of the soul, the other toward the force of the truth. *Treatise on Passions,* art. 48, 49, 50. However, we shall see that there can be no firmness without enlightened reason. Ibid., art. 49.

8. *Discourse,* 6th pt., VI, p. 62, ll. 17-20.

9. *Principles,* Preface, IX, p. 14, ll. 2 seq.

10. Ibid., p. 17.

11. *Discourse,* 3d pt., VI, p. 28, ll. 9-10; *To Mersenne,* 27 April 1637, I, p. 366, ll. 6-11.

12. "Often passion leads us to believe that some things are much better and more desirable than they truly are . . . that is why the true function of reason is to examine the right value of all goods whose acquisition seems to depend in some way on our conduct." *To Elizabeth,* 1 September 1645, IV, p. 284, ll. 17-19, 24-25.

13. *Treatise on Passions,* art. 211, XI, p. 485, l. 25.

14. *Discourse,* VI, p. 28, l. 8; *Letter of March 1638,* II, p. 35, ll. 4-5; *To Elizabeth,* 18 August 1645, IV, p. 277, ll. 16 seq.

15. *Principles,* IX, p. 14, l. 17.

16. *Description of the Human body,* IX, pp. 224-25.

17. *Anatomica* (Partes similares et excrementa et morbi), XI, p. 606, l. 9, p. 607, l. 2; *Remedia et vires medicamentorum,* XI, pp. 641-44.

18. Cf. above, vol. II, chap. xvii, sec. 4.

19. Cf. ibid.

20. "There is a great difference between the general notion of sun and earth, which I give in my *Principles,* and the particular notion of the nature of man." IV, p. 441.

21. "I am emboldened (but only for the past eight or ten days) to add to it an explanation of the manner in which animals are formed, from the beginning of their origin; I say animals, for I would not dare to undertake man in particular, for want of experiments adequate to the task." *To Elizabeth,* 31 January 1648, V, p. 112, ll. 12-25. "The preservation of health has always been the principal aim of my studies, and I do not doubt that there are means of acquiring much knowledge about medicine that have hitherto been unknown. But the *Treatise on Animals* . . . is only a beginning to the acquisition of this knowledge. I am careful not to boast that I possess the knowledge already." *To the Marquis of Newcastle,* October 1645, IV, p. 329.

22. "But for all that, I do not yet know enough to be able to cure a fever. For I claim only to know animals in general, which are not subject to fevers, and not yet man in particular, who is." *To Mersenne,* 20 February 1639, II, pp. 525-26.

23. Cf. Dreyfus le Foyer, "Les Conceptions médicales de Descartes," *Revue de Métaphysique et de Morale* (1937): 239 seq.

24. *To Chanut,* 15 June 1646, V, p. 441, l. 28, p. 442, ll. 1-3.

25. Cf. Dreyfus le Foyer ["Les Conceptions"].

26. *To Mersenne,* January 1630, I, p. 106.

27. *Principles,* Preface, IX, pt. 2, p. 17, l. 8.

28. *Treatise on Passions,* art. 40; *To Chanut,* 1 February 1647, IV, p. 603, ll. 22-25.

29. *Treatise on Passions,* art. 211, XI, p. 485, l. 25. "Almost all good." *To Chanut,* 1 February 1647, IV, p. 538, l. 8.

30. *To Chanut,* 1 February 1647, p. 538.

31. "As the health of the body and the presence of pleasant objects very much aid the mind to rid itself of all the passions that are involved in sadness, and to let enter those that participate in joy, so too, reciprocally, when the mind is full of joy, that serves very much to make the body bear up better and to make present objects seem more agreeable." *To Elizabeth,* November 1646, IV, p. 529.

32. "It seems even that nature plunges us into illnesses so that we can emerge all the stronger, and in a state to make light of what is contrary to health and compromises it. But in order to do that, we must obey it. . . . Nature works to effect its own recovery; it has perfect internal awareness of its own state of health and it knows it better than any doctor who is sees it only from the outside." *Entretien avec Burman,* V, p. 179.

33. Cf. the examples cited by Dreyfus le Foyer, ["Les Conceptions"], p. 275.

34. *To Newcastle,* October 1645, IV, p. 329, l. 16, p. 330, l. 5.

35. *Meditation VI,* VII, p. 84, ll. 9-10, p. 85, ll. 18-21; IX, pp. 67-68.

36. *Entretien avec Burman,* V, p. 179.

37. *To Chanut,* 15 June 1646, V, p. 441, l. 28, p. 442, ll. 1-3.

38. *Principles,* Preface, IX, 2, p. 17, ll. 6-7.

39. *Discourse,* 6th pt., VI, p. 62, ll. 17 seq.; *Principles,* Preface, IX, p. 14, ll. 27 seq.

40. Ibid., p. 4, l. 19, p. 2, l. 8.

41. Ibid., pp. 5-6; p. 9, ll. 12 seq.

42. *Treatise on Passions,* art. 60, 170; *To Elizabeth,* 1 September 1645, IV, p. 284, ll. 17-24; 15 September 1645, p. 295, ll. 11-21. Since irresolution is the worst evil, the best good would be, on the contrary, the state of resolution, or firmness of will. The remedy against irresolution is, in fact, "to accustom ourselves to believing that we always do our duty when we do what we judge to be best, even though we may possibly judge very badly." *Treatise on Passions,* art. 170. The second rule of morality is "to have a firm and constant resolution to execute everything that reason recommends. . . . It is the firmness of this resolution that I take to be virtue, even though I know that no one has ever described it in this way; instead they have divided it into different types to which they have given various names, because of the various objects to which it applies." *To Elizabeth,* 4 August 1645, IV, p. 265, ll. 12-26. Thus generosity is itself essentially defined by this firm resolution accompanied with the sensation of freedom and responsibility. Cf. *Treatise on Passions,* art. 153 and also art. 148. Descartes professes, with the Stoics, the unity of virtue. We have seen above (vol. II, chap. xix, sec. 5) that the unity of virtue responds to the unity of science.

43. *Discourse,* 3d pt., VI, p. 22, ll. 27-28; cf. the *Commentaire [au Discours de la Methode* (Paris: Vrin, 1925)] of Gilson, pp. 230-31. "A man who as yet has merely common and imperfect knowledge . . . should above all try to form for himself a morality that is sufficient to regulate the actions of his life, because this cannot stand any delay, and we ought to endeavor to live well." *Principles,* Preface, IX, pt. 2, p. 13, ll. 17 seq. "An imperfect morality that we can follow provisionally while we do not have knowledge of any better one." Ibid., p. 15, ll. 9-15.

44. *Discourse,* p. 27, l. 22; Latin text, VI, p. 555. Cf. Gilson *[Commentaire],* p. 256.

45. Ibid., p. 231.

46. C. Adams, *Vie de Descartes,* XII, p. 58.

47. *Principles,* Preface, IX, pt. 2, p. 17, ll. 13-22.

48. "In order to understand these things more perfectly, we need to know that the soul is truly joined to the whole body." *Treatise on Passions,* art. 30.

49. *Treatise on Passions,* art. 28.

50. Ibid., p. 326.

51. That is M. Mesnard's thesis, in *Essai sur la morale de Descartes* [Paris: Boivin, 1936], pp. 97-98. This reading depends on article 52, in which Descartes, according to the interpreter, is classifying passions exclusively according to the corporeal phenomena that accompany them. In reality, they are classified, not simply according to the different ways our senses can be moved by their objects, but according to "their importance to us," thus referring to a double aspect of the passions, psychological and physiological: movement of the soul toward the things that nature teaches us and disposition of the body toward the movements that serve its execution. In order to maintain his interpretation, Mesnard must accuse Descartes of having failed at his program (ibid, p. 100) as early as the study of the first passion (admiration), considering this passion solely from the psychological point of view. But it remains for us to find out whether the program attributed to Descartes is truly his. In addition, like all other passions, admiration is considered from two points of view, psychological and physiological, for if it is not tied to the movements of the heart and the blood, it is tied to the movement of the animal spirits. *Treatise on Passions,* art. 70-73; *To Elizabeth,* May

1646, IV, p. 409, l. 20. Cf. on this topic the pertinent remarks of L. Teixeira, professor of history of philosophy of the University of Sao Paulo, in chap. 10 of a work to appear in 1953-54: *Ensayo sobre a Morale de Descartes.*

52. *Treatise on Passions,* art. 147-48; To Chanut, 1 February 1648, IV, p. 602.

53. Ibid., art. 7-15.

54. Ibid., art. 17-20, 91, 146, 148. "All these movements of will that constitute love, joy, sadness, and desire, insofar as they are rational thoughts and not passions, could exist in our soul, even if it had no body. . . . There is nothing in all these movements of its will which would be obscure to it, or of which it would not have a perfect knowledge, if it reflected on its own passions." *To Chanut,* 1 February 1647, IV, p. 602, ll. 3-8. The "emotions" correspond to the Stoics' reasonable dispositions of the soul. But the Stoics, in agreement with Spinoza, against Descartes, exclude sadness from these (cf. Diogenes Laertius, VII; Cicero, *Tusculanes;* Arnim, *Stoic. vet. frag.* [Leipzig, 1903-24], I, 205-15, 570-75; III, 377, 490).

55. *Treatise on Passions,* art. 3 and 40.

56. *To Chanut,* 26 February 1649, V, p. 290, l. 27, p. 291, l. 1.

57. *To Chanut,* 15 June 1646, IV, p. 441, ll. 25-28.

58. *To Elizabeth,* 15 September 1645, IV, p. 292, ll. 13 seq.; *To Chanut,* 1 February 1647, IV, pp. 608-9; *Treatise on Passions,* art. 145-46, 148.

59. "What I have written [in my *Principles*] is only distantly connected with the morality that you have chosen to make your principal study. Of course, I entirely agree with you, in that you judge that the most assured way, in order to know how we should live, is to recognize first what we are, what kind of world we live in, and who is the Creator of this world—or the Master of the house in which we live. But . . . there is a great distance between the general notion of heaven and earth, which I have attempted to give in my *Principles,* and the particular knowledge of the nature of man, which I have not yet treated." *To Chanut,* 15 June 1646, IV, ll. 8-23.

60. *To Elizabeth,* 15 September 1645, IV, pp. 291-93.

61. Ibid., 4 August 1645, IV, pp. 263-67; 1 September 1645, IV, pp. 283-87.

62. *To Chanut,* 15 June 1646, IV, p. 441, l. 27, p. 442, l. 3.

63. Therefore one cannot consider the *Treatise on Passions* an application of medicine to morality, which was written when Descartes understood that medicine can be constituted only on the plane of the substantial union, or a sample of this new medicine whose secret he is delivering here (the definition of a series of morbid entities through the anarchical isolation of an idea, a thesis defended by Dreyfus le Foyer ["Les Conceptions"—see n. 23 above], pp. 275 and 278). In the *Letter to Chanut* of 15 June 1646, in which Descartes announces his small *Treatise on the Nature of the Passions of the Soul,* in his letter of 20 November 1647, in which he states to Chanut that the treatise will allow the supreme good to be obtained, Descartes establishes a contrast between medicine, in which he has failed, and morality, in which he has succeeded; therefore the *Treatise on Passions* is not related to medicine. But it goes without saying that the new medicine and the morality of the *Treatise,* both situated on the plane of the union of soul and body, profess similar theories with respect to the influence of the psychical on the somatic: if it is possible to modify the disposition of the body in the passion by changing the course of ideas, it is even possible to conceive the curing of a fever or cough by changes in the representations of the person who is ill. Cf. IV, pp. 201, 208, and texts cited by Dreyfus le Foyer ["Les Conceptions"], p. 275: "But since the health of the body and the presence of pleasant objects very much aid the mind to rid itself of all the passions that participate in sadness, and to let enter those that participate in joy, thus, reciprocally, when the body is full of joy, it serves very much to make the body bear up better, and to make present objects seem more agreeable." *To Elizabeth,* November 1646, IV, p. 531. Still less is the *Treatise on Passions* the commentary

on the passage of the *Discourse* (pt. VI, cf. above, vol. II, chap. xx, sec. 2) in which Descartes considers that medicine is the key to morality, as Gilson thinks *(Commentaire au Discours* [see n. 43, above], p. 447), for the medicine of the *Discourse* was mechanistic medicine, and Descartes also notes to Chanut that morality is radically distinct from medicine. Even if the *Treatise on Passions* can impart some suggestions on what medicine based on the substantial union would be, it does not involve any pathology, therapeutics, or medication of the body for the soul. It deals only with the *normal* interactions that produce the passions, which are all useful for man's equilibrium, and which are natural phenomena of the complex of body and soul. The excesses or the defects of the passions are not pathological. They result normally from union: if soul were not united to body, love and joy would never have any excess (art. 141). The remedies for the passions (art. 50, 211) are conceived with respect to the normal conditions of man united with his body, not with respect to pathological circumstances; and the word "remedy" does not have its specific medical sense. Nowhere in the *Treatise* can the idea of rendering men wiser by acting on the physiology of their bodies, or even on their temperament, be found. Cf. on this subject the remarks of Livio Teixeira *[Ensayo Sobre—*see n. 51 above], chap. 9.

64. "It seems to me that every man can make himself contented without any other aid, provided that he observes three things, which are related to the three rules of morality that I have discussed in the *Discourse on Method.*" *To Elizabeth,* 4 August 1645, IV, p. 265, ll. 7-11. The first maxim of the *Discourse,* which prescribes a provisional conformity ("to obey the laws and customs of my country, adhering constantly to the religion in which by God's grace I had been instructed since my childhood, and in all other things, directing my conduct by following the most moderate opinions, and the ones farthest from excess, in all those that are commonly received and practiced by the most judicious of the people with which I will live") and the first maxim formulated in the letter ("to use his mind as best as possible in order to know what he should or should not do in all the circumstances of life") appear however very different. That is because the first maxim of the *Discourse,* instead of formulating the precept explicitly, presents it in its application in a particular circumstance: how to best use one's mind while waiting for science to be constituted. The *Discourse* recommends also "to choose between the best opinions and to perfect our judgments more and more." The common element is this effort to use reason as best as possible in each circumstance. Cf. Livio Teixeira, ibid.

65. *Treatise on Passions,* art. 91, 141, 147, 148, etc.; *To Elizabeth,* 18 August 1645, 1 September 1645, 15 September 1645; *To Chanut,* 1 February 1647.

66. Elizabeth noted: "But in order thus to evaluate the goods [according to whether they can contribute to contentment—M. G.] we must know them perfectly; and to know all those goods about which one is compelled to make a choice in an active life, we must possess an infinite science." *To Descartes,* 13 September 1645, IV, p. 289, ll. 3-6. To which Descartes replies: "Although we do not possess an infinite science to know perfectly all the goods about which we have to make a choice, in the different contingencies of life, we must, it seems to me, be content with having a moderate number of the things that are more necessary, such as those I have shown in my last letter (of 15 September 1645)." *To Elizabeth,* 6 October 1645, IV, p. 308, ll. 3-9.

67. "And although we cannot have certain demonstrations about everything, we nevertheless ought to take a position and embrace the opinions that seem most likely to us, with respect to the things in common use, so that whenever we must act, we may never be irresolute." *To Elizabeth,* 15 September 1645, IV, p. 295, ll. 14 seq. "[The goods of the soul—M. G.] can be reduced to two principal goods, the one being to know, and the other to will, what is good. But knowledge is often beyond our powers, and so there remains only our will that we can dispose of absolutely. I do not see that it is possible to dispose of it better

than by a firm and constant resolution to do exactly all things we judge to be the best things, and to use all the power of one's mind to know them well. In this alone consists all the virtues. . . . Thus I consider that this is where the supreme good lies." *To Christina of Sweden,* 20 November 1647, V, p. 83, ll. 4 seq.; cf. also *Treatise on Passions,* art. 148. "I am surprised," declares Hyperaspistes, "that you have dared to affirm that in the conduct of life we must not seek the same truth as that which we pursue in speculation. Must not life be led as best as possible?" III, p. 398. To which Descartes replies (ibid., pp. 422-29): "It is easy to demonstrate that we must wish for a degree of certainty equal to the one we desire when we seek to acquire science, in things that concern the conduct of life, but that we must not seek or hope for it. This can be demonstrated a priori from the fact that the human composite is by nature corruptible, while the mind is incorruptible and immortal; but this can be demonstrated more easily a posteriori." Cf. also the *Treatise on Passions,* art. 148; *Principles,* Preface, IX, pt. 2, p. 13, ll. 17 seq. From this results the fundamental importance of generosity, which resides essentially in the good use of free will, meaning, "in the firm and constant resolution never to lack will to undertake and execute all the things that we judge the best—which is to follow virtue perfectly." *Treatise on Passions,* art. 153. Concerning the best, cf. *To Elizabeth,* dedication of the *Principles,* VIII, p. 2, l. 25; *To Christina of Sweden,* 20 November 1647, V, p. 83, ll. 4 seq.; *Treatise on Passions,* art. 148.

68. "Of the two things that are required for the wisdom thus described, namely, that the understanding knows everything good, and that right will is always disposed to follow it, only the one that consists in will is such that all men can have it equally, since the understanding of some is not as good as that of others." Dedication of the *Principles,* VIII, p. 5, ll. 8 seq.

69. "In order that our soul may thus have something with which to be content, it has no need but to follow exactly after virtue. For whoever has lived in such a way that his conscience cannot reproach him for ever having failed to perform those things that he has judged to be the best (which is what I here call following after virtue) receives from this a satisfaction so powerful in rendering him happy that the most violent efforts of the passions never have sufficient power to disturb the tranquillity of his soul." *Treatise on Passions,* art. 148; cf. *To Christina of Sweden,* 20 November 1647, V, pp. 82-83. "Moral error occurs when we believe, with reason, something false because a good man has told it to us . . . it contains no privation, when we assure it only to regulate our life, insofar as we could not morally know better; and thus it is not properly an error. But it would be an error if we assured it as a truth of physics, since the testimony of a good man is not sufficient for that." *To Mesland,* 2 May 1641, IV, p. 115. "Generous people . . . do not esteem themselves much above those they surpass, because all these things (material goods, honors, wit, knowledge, beauty, etc.) appear to them as having little worth in comparison with good will, for which alone they esteem themselves, and which they also suppose to exist, or at least to be able to exist, in each man." *Treatise on Passions,* art. 154. The effort toward virtue consists in "accustoming ourself to believing that we have done our duty when we do what we judge to be best, even though perhaps we judge very badly." Ibid., art. 170. "It is not also necessary [in order to enjoy natural beatitude—M. G.] that reason is not mistaken; it is sufficient that our consciousness testifies to us that we have never lacked resolution or virtue." *To Elizabeth,* 15 August 1645, IV, p. 260, ll. 24-27. "Virtue consists only in the resolution and vigor with which we are inclined to do the things that we think good, as long as this vigor does not stem from stubbornness, but from our knowledge of having examined the things as well as we morally can. And even though what we have done might turn out to be bad, we are then assured of having done our duty." *To Christina of Sweden,* 20 November 1647, V, pp. 83-84. That is a pure Stoic doctrine, cf. Seneca, *Letters to Lucilius,* 57, 95 (Arnim, *Stoic. vet. frag.* [see n. 54, above], III, p. 517).

70. *Replies to Objections II,* VII, p. 149, ll. 3-13. Text cited by Gilson, *Commentaire au Discours* [see n. 43, above], p. 232.

71. E. Gilson, ibid., p. 232.

72. *To Buitendijck,* 1645, IV, p. 62, l. 5, p. 63, ll. 1-17. Text cited by Gilson, ibid., p. 233.

73. Gilson, ibid., pp. 233-34.

74. "Virtue alone is sufficient to render us content in this life. But virtue unenlightened by the understanding can be false," and "the contentment that we feel is not solid. . . . The right use of reason, on the other hand, by imparting true knowledge of the good, prevents virtue from being false even by accommodating it to licit pleasures, makes it easy to practice, and by making us realize the condition of our nature, sets bounds to our desires. Hence, we must confess that the greatest felicity of man depends on the right use of reason, and consequently, the study that leads to its acquisition is the most useful occupation one can have, as it is the most agreeable and the sweetest." *To Elizabeth,* 4 August 1645, IV, p. 260, l. 22, p. 267, l. 19. "But although those who are inferior in mind may be as wise as their nature permits and may render themselves acceptable to God by their virtue, if they only form a firm and constant resolution to do what they judge to be right, and spare no effort in learning what they do not know, yet those who, while possessing a constant desire to do well and taking very special care in reference to their instruction, are endowed with an excellent mind, will doubtless attain a higher degree of wisdom than the others." *To Elizabeth,* Dedication to the *Principles* (Latin text, VIII, p. 5). This degree of wisdom is the fifth degree, that of the Cartesian philosopher who has assimilated the *Principles of Philosophy.* Cf. Preface to the *Principles,* VIII, p. 5, ll. 18 seq. "Yet there is a great difference between the resolutions that proceed from a false opinion and those that are founded only on the knowledge of the truth, inasmuch as if we follow the latter we are assured that we shall never regret or repent them, whereas we do so always when we have followed the former." *Treatise on Passions,* art. 49. This text is inconsistent with art. 148 of the same *Treatise* and the *Letter to Christina* of 20 November 1647. We can attempt to reconcile these two texts by conceiving that this regret would not be able to disturb the tranquillity of the man who has consciousness of having acted as he thought best, meaning virtuously. In reality, Descartes oscillates between these two completely different positions, without opting definitively for either one of them. This text is also inconsistent with the following texts: "There is nothing other than desire and regret or repentance that can prevent us from being content; but if we always did what our reason told us to do, we would have no cause to repent, even though events might make us see afterward that we have been mistaken, even though we are not at fault." *To Elizabeth,* 4 August 1645, IV, p. 266, ll. 2-8. "It seems to me that we have no subject for repentance when we have done what we judged best at the time we had a decision to make, even though in rethinking the matter afterward, when we have more leisure, we judge ourselves to have failed. Rather we should be repentant if we have done something against our conscience, even though we recognized afterward that we have done better than we had thought: for we are responsible only for our thoughts; nor it is man's nature to know everything, or always to judge as well on the spot as when he has much time to deliberate." *To Elizabeth,* 6 October 1645, IV, p. 307, ll. 13-24. The progress in wisdom through the progress in science is not external to virtue for Descartes, but a "preferable," "indifferent" thing, as it is with the Stoics. Cf. Arnim, *Stoic. vet. frag.,* III, pp. 127-39. Moral progress presents two aspects: 1) an increase of the power of my will to exert the effort that defines virtue; 2) an increase of my science and the perfection of my judgments, which enables the matter of my actions to become more appropriate with respect to the end to be realized. *Treatise on Passions,* art. 50. Since virtue exists once this effort exists, moral progress is internal to virtue: the notion of progress cannot be dissociated from the notion of the effort that defines the virtue (analogy with Kant).

75. "Whoever has a firm and constant will to use his reason to the best of his power, and to do what he judges to be best in all his actions, is truly wise, so far as his nature allows him to be." *To Elizabeth,* Dedication of the *Principles,* VIII, p. 2, ll. 25 seq. Cf. "Beatitude consists only in the contentment of the mind, that is, in contentment in general . . . but in order to have a contentment that is solid, we need to heed virtue, meaning, we need to have a firm and constant will to execute everything that we judge best and to use the whole strength of our understanding to judge well." *To Elizabeth* 18 August 1645, IV, p. 277, ll. 16 seq.

76. "It is certain that with respect to the conduct of our life, we are required to follow opinions that are merely probable, because the opportunities to act in our affairs would almost always pass before we could deliver ourselves from all our doubts. And when several courses of action meet on the same subject, we do not perceive any likely advantage of one over the other; if action suffers no delay, *reason* [our emphasis—M. G.] requires that we choose one over the other, and that, after having chosen it, we follow it constantly, as if we had judged it most certain." *Principles,* I, art. 3, IX, pt. 2, p. 26. "But because I recognized that nothing in the world was unchanging, and that in my own case I was proposing to perfect my judgments more and more, and not to render them worse, I would have thought that I was committing a great fault against good sense, if I required myself to continue to accept a thing I formerly approved when it ceased to merit approval or after I ceased to deem it as such." *Discourse,* pt. III, VI, p. 24, ll. 8 seq.; *Descartes to X.,* March 1638, II, p. 35, ll. 16-19.

77. *To Mersenne,* December 1640, III, p. 259, ll. 5-8; *Notes against a Program,* VIII, p. 353, l. 27, p. 354, l. 1.

78. *Letter to Clerselier on Objections V,* IX, p. 208, ll. 13-30.

79. "But although we say that faith has obscure things for object, however the grounds on which we embrace them is not obscure; it is clearer than any natural light. This is more so given that we must distinguish between the matter or the thing to which we give our credence and the formal reason that moves our will to give it. For it is in this formal reason alone that we require clearness and evidence. . . . Further it should be noted that the clearness and evidence by which our will can be led to believe is of two kinds: the one proceeding from natural light, and the other from divine grace. But although we ordinarily say that faith is about obscure things, this is understood only concerning its matter and not concerning the formal reason for which we believe; for on the contrary, this formal reason consists in a certain internal light, and it is when God fills us up supernaturally with this illumination that we are confident that what is proposed for our belief has been revealed by him, and that it is impossible that he should lie and deceive us—a fact more certain than any natural light and often more evident than it, on account of the light of grace." *Replies to Objections II,* VII, p. 147, ll. 15 seq.; IX, pp. 115-16. This conception is opposed to that of Malebranche, for whom there is no grace other than that of sensation, a sensation that neutralizes the adverse sensation of concupiscence. The grace of the light (or of the Creator) is, in fact, no more than the divine reason in which all men participate and which Descartes wrongly calls "natural," given that all human reason is nothing more than supernatural reason itself.

80. *Principles,* II, art. 40. The fragment of the *Treatise on Man* (which has remained incomplete and was published ten years after the death of Descartes) concerns only the mechanics of body, and does not raise metaphysical and moral problems.

Chapter XXI. Conclusions

1. *Meditation II,* VII, p. 32, ll. 18-19; IX, p. 25.
2. *Meditation I,* VII, p. 18, ll. 10-18; IX, p. 14. Cf. *Entretien avec Burman,* V, p. 146.

3. X, p. 203.

4. *Rules,* Rule 1, X, p. 361.

5. *To Elizabeth,* 28 June 1643, III, p. 693.

6. Cf. above, vol. II, chap. xix, n. 26, the *Letter to Chanut.*

7. Cf. above, ibid., and the reconciliation with Saint Ignacius.

8. Ignacius of Loyola, *Exercises* (trans. Jeunesseaux), pp. 159-67.

9. "Fieri non posse ut cogitet, nisi existat." VII, p. 149, ll. 27-28.

10. IX, p. 21.

11. *Meditation III,* VII, pp. 36-37, 40, l. 6.

12. *To Clerselier, On Objections V,* IX, pt. 1, pp. 210-11.

13. *Principles,* II, art. 64, IX, pt. 2, p. 102.

14. Cf. vol. I, chap. i, sec. 4; vol. II, chap. xxi, sec. 2. The use of the first person, the monologue of the soul, the recital of an experience of spiritual transformation, the constant temptation by old habits (cf. the end of *Meditation I*), the effort to confirm the mind in its new path (cf. the end of *Meditation II*), etc., all these traits are specific to the religious genre: prayers, confessions, soliloquies, considerations, meditations, elevations, and spiritual exercises.

15. *Entretien avec Burman,* V, p. 160.

16. See, for example, *Les Quinze Livres* (with the addition of a sixteenth) of the *Elements* of Euclid, edited in 1607 at Frankfurt, by R. P. Clavius, which relates the original demonstrations that Descartes had on hand since his days at La Flèche. Clavius, the author of an *Algebra* (Rome, 1607-8) was one of these Cossists on whom Descartes meditated much during the course of his efforts to reform algebra. Leibniz also practiced this meditation. Malebranche, however, has only an extremely mitigated admiration for Euclid and his commentators. Cf. *Recherche de la Vérité,* II, pt. 2, chap. vi

17. *Rules,* Rule 12, X, p. 418.

18. *Replies to Objections VI,* VII, p. 444, l. 19.

19. *To Mersenne,* 16 October 1639, II, p. 598, ll. 10 seq.

20. Ibid., ll. 27-28.

21. Souriau, *L'Instauration philosophique* [Paris: Felix Alcan, 1939], chap. 4, sec. 3, p. 304. Cf. besides the section from the chapter cited, sec. 3 from chap. 2 of the same work, which contains some extremely pointed remarks against Descartes.

22. *Replies to Objections II,* IX, pp. 115-16 (text cited above, vol. II, chap. xx, n. 79). The reflection of natural light on the constitutive realities of human nature in the broad sense has allowed Descartes to emphasize the irreducibility of sensible perception and mathematical knowledge, without ceasing to perceive the role of the understanding in the operation of perception. We can see thus that the Cartesian conception of composite substance can appear as a distant prefiguration of some contemporary points of view: "Returning to perception as a kind of original experience, in which the real world is constituted in its specificity, is an inversion of the natural movement of consciousness that we impose upon ourselves. We are defining here the "phenomenological reduction," in the sense given to it by Husserl; moreover, this does not suppress all questions: we are concerned with understanding, without confusing it with a logical relation, the relation of *experience* [our emphasis—M. G.] for the "things" presented, and for the perspectives on the ideal significations that are seen through them." Merleau-Ponty, *La structure du comportement* [Paris: Presses Universitaires de France, 1952], pp. 298-99.

23. Cf. above, vol. II, Appendix 3.

24. *To Mersenne,* 16 October 1639, II, p. 599.

25. "It is an evident thing that the idea we have of infinity does not represent only one of its parts, but infinity as a whole (in the fashion that it must be represented to human ideas, even though it is certain that God, or some other intellectual nature, can have another,

more perfect idea of it, that is, a much more exact and distinct idea than the one men have. This is parallel to the case of someone who is [not] well versed in geometry; no doubt he has the idea of a whole triangle when he conceives it as a figure composed of three lines, although geometers can know several other properties of the triangle and can note a quantity of things in his idea that he does not see in it." *Replies to Objections V,* VII, p. 368, ll. 5 seq.

26. *Replies to Objections II,* IX, pp. 115-16; *Replies to Objections V (Letter to Clerselier),* IX, p. 208, ll. 19 seq.

27. We have seen in the preceding chapter that Descartes, in some of his letters (*To Huyghens,* 13 October 1642, III, p. 580; *To Elizabeth,* 18 May 1645, IV, p. 202) affirmed that reason assures us, in all evidence, that the soul would enjoy, after death, greater felicities than in this life—the body constituting an obstacle to joy—but that he modified this statement in part, by specifying to Elizabeth that reason cannot give us any certainty, but rather hopes, with respect to this subject. Moreover, this joy felt by the soul delivered from the body would not be a passion at all; it would be a simple emotion of the soul deriving its origin from this soul alone, entirely intellectual and active (*To Chanut,* 1 February 1647). It is true that Descartes admits that the soul, after death, has a "remembrance of the past," because there exists an intellectual memory that is independent of the body (*To Huyghens,* ibid., ll. 15-19). But we do not see how this memory can preserve the memory of the past as such, since for Descartes, intellectual memory, in the absence of cerebral activity, is not the memory of particular things: "Intellectual memory is rather the memory of general ideas than of particular ideas; and thus we cannot remember all the things we did, in particular, with it." *Entretien avec Burman,* V, p. 150.

28. The doctrine of the impenetrability of ends does not seem to be, as thought Gilson, the attenuated expression of a conception that, in reality, would banish God from every kind of finality. It only excludes anthropomorphism from him, as Jean Laporte has established ("La Finalité chez Descartes, *Revue d'histoire de la philosophie,* 1928, pp. 366-96; *Le Rationalisme de Descartes,* pp. 351-52). Moreover, the mystery of divine ends does not risk weakening our certainty relative to the exclusive empire of mechanism over the material world. No doubt, Victor Delbos was able to observe that to extirpate God's finality itself was to destroy at its root the objection that Descartes never ceased to reject; "Who knows whether in themselves things are not other than what our understanding conceives them to be?" But by creating the world all at once in its completed form, to which physical laws would have carried it infallibly by degrees, God has acted teleologically without compromising the rigor of the mechanism by which he preserves it. Moreover, divine teleology can found mechanism without needing necessarily to weaken it, or to render it relative to ourselves, for the essence of extension guarantees, whatever is our ignorance of the multitude of properties or possible forms of that substance, that there is never anything in it that is not reducible to mathematical properties and relations. To found the mechanism of material nature on a divine teleology does not necessarily lead to introducing a hidden teleology in matter. With Malebranche, for example, a complete system of divine teleology, which is exempt of anthropomorphism, founds the absolute validity of mechanism in the world of bodies on the doctrine of nature and grace.

29. *Entretien avec Burman,* V, p. 157. About the impossibility of knowing angels through natural light. Cf. *To Morus,* August 1649, V, p. 402, ll. 1-12.

30. It is barely worth the bother to note that the Kantian refutation of the "problematic" Cartesian idealism does not succeed. Descartes has merely upheld that we can conceive the pure self and affirm its existence, having abstracted away the body; and does not Kant affirm that "experience" and everything that refers to it is "something completely contingent with respect to the understanding"? Of course, Descartes does not demonstrate, as does Kant,

that the empirical knowledge of my self in time is conditioned by the intuition of a spatial permanent; but, since all empirical knowledge is, for Descartes, enclosed within the realm of sensation, and since this realm is conditioned by the passion exercised by the body on the soul to which it is united, we see that the disagreement on the principle is not very deep. Finally, neither in *Meditation II* nor in *Meditation VI* does Descartes claim that empirical knowledge of my self in time is the condition of the empirical knowledge of real things in space. He has only demonstrated in *Meditation II* that (using Kantian terminology) pure a priori consciousness of self and of the concepts of my pure understanding (in this case the idea of extension) are conditions of possibility of my empirical representation of external things. Here again there is a coincidence of principle with Kantian doctrine, except, of course, that for Kant, extension is not a concept of the understanding, nor is the pure self a reality knowable through intuition, nor are empirical representations anything other than *realitas phenomenon.* What Kant aimed at, in his *Refutation,* was to do justice to the accusations of idealism that Feder and Garve had thrown at him, and consequently, to refute the type of doctrine that affirms that the immediate given is the universe of images in the subjects, and that consciousness of the perception of real things is merely added to it secondarily, through the consideration of the regularity of the linkage of representations—for example, before him, Berkeley, and the Leibnizian doctrine of well-linked dreams, and, after him, the true hallucination of Taine. For him, on the contrary, the perception of the external thing in space is a first given: dream must be explained beginning with perception, not perception beginning with dream. But on this point Descartes is closer to Kant than all the other Cartesians, since sensation, or the perception of external things, is a primitive notion for him, an irreducible sui generis given, that reveals to me immediately by itself the existence of the external thing. The regular linkage that differentiates perception from dream plays for him only an extremely secondary role, as it does for Kant *(Antinomy III,* Antithesis, sub finem). In both, we are concerned to establish the validity, the legitimacy, and the limit of the various functions of knowledge, which are irreducible among themselves. The singular analogies that we can discover between some aspects of Cartesian doctrine and Fichtean doctrine confirm the affinity of the two points of view.

31. Fink, "Die Phänomenologische Philosophie E. Husserl in der gegenwartigen Kritik," *Kantstudien* 38 (1933): 339. "There is a radical difference in the way that the *Phenomenology* and the *Critique* establish the positive sciences. In the *Critique* we are concerned with a relation of the foundation to what is founded, what is immanent to the world, [a relation] to be established between philosophy, as a construction of the sphere of the senses that establishes all that "is" *(Seiend),* and the positive sciences, naively referred to "being." In phenomenology, we are concerned with the relation of the foundation to what is being founded, to be established between a philosophy that knows the origin of the world and all worldly knowledge in general. Thus, phenomenology can claim to assume the function of foundation with respect to the knowledge of this sphere of problem to which criticism refers." Fink, ibid., p. 341.

32. Cf. above, vol. II, Appendix 4, the discussion of Thévenaz's thesis.

33. Fink, "L'Analyse intentionelle et le problème de la pensée spéculative," *Problèmes actuels de la phénoménologie* (Brussels, 1951), pp. 70-79.

34. The transcendental philosophy of Fichte is a perpetually renewed effort to allow into the circle of the phenomenon the act and the moment when the inside and the outside are separated and united. It constrains thus the phenomenality of the phenomenon to be given to us as phenomenon. To this task, which it expressly defines as we have just done, it reserves the name, *phenomenology (Wissenschaftslehre,* S.W. [1804], X, pp. 272-73). From 1801, Fichte captured origin as first beginning, which is the end *(Ende),* in the oscillation between being and nothingness, freedom being the annihilation of being, which is the annihilation of freedom or consciousness. From this arises the passage to a positive beyond, which annihilates this

oscillation that is still tainted with consciousness, freedom, and nothingness: "Pure knowledge is considered as origin *(Ursprung)* for itself, and its contrary as nothingness of knowledge, for otherwise it could not spring up *(entspringen);* it is pure being." *(Wissenshaftslehre,* S. W. [1801], II, sec. 26, p. 63). Many conceptions that we believe contemporary had already been (as have been many others) expressed fifty years ago by Fichte, in another climate, but with an unequaled force and depth.

Appendixes

1. Communication to the International Congress of Philosophy of 1937.

2. Or, for example: "a body that is alive, or a man who is clothed." *Rules,* Rule 12, X, p. 421, ll. 26-27.

3. This difficulty, which came to mind when correcting the final proofs for this book, was also conveyed to us in a letter by Jean Wahl.

4. IX, p. 21.

5. Cf. Fink, "L'Analyse intentionelle et le problème de la pensée spéculative," in *Problèmes actuels de la phénoménologie* (Brussels, 1951), p. 71.

6. Cf. above, vol. 1, chap. iii, sec. 10; this is an identical quantity in all men, in opposition to Fontenelle (cf. *Le Troisième Faux Démétrius*), for whom the genius thinks more than others in the same amount of time. Cf. above, vol. II, Appendix 5.

7. See above, vol. I, chap. iii, sec. 11.

8. "I am surprised," states Descartes to Gassendi, "that you accept that all the things I consider prove that I distinctly know that I am, but not what I am or what is my nature, given that the one cannot be demonstrated without the other." VII, p. 359.

9. Cf. also the *Letter of August 1641*, III, pp. 423 seq.

10. "Deficere a perfectione rerum a quibus sunt desumptae."

11. Cf. *Meditation III,* VII, p. 41, ll. 26-29, p. 42, ll. 11-15; *Replies I,* VII, p. 102, ll. 24-28, p. 103, ll. 1-4.

Name Index

Name Index

Volumes I and II

Martial Gueroult (1891-1976) was a professor at the Collège de France. His work centered on seventeenth-century European philosophy and included major studies of Leibniz and Spinoza. Translator *Roger Ariew* is assistant professor of philosophy and humanities at Virginia Polytechnic Institute and State University. *Alan Donagan,* who reviewed the philosophical aspects of the translation, is professor of philosophy at the California Institute of Technology. *Robert Ariew,* associate professor of French at Pennsylvania State University, checked the translation for linguistic accuracy.